All the
APOSTLES
of the Bible

THE "ALL" SERIES BY HERBERT LOCKYER

All the Apostles of the Bible

All the Divine Names and Titles of the Bible

All the Doctrines of the Bible

All the Kings and Queens of the Bible

All the Men of the Bible

All the Messianic Prophecies of the Bible

All the Miracles of the Bible

All the Parables of the Bible

All the Prayers of the Bible

All the Promises of the Bible

All the Trades and Occupations of the Bible

All the Women of the Bible

Studies in the Characters
of the Apostles—The Men
Jesus Chose and the
Message They Proclaimed

All the
APOSTLES
of the Bible

. . . . .

Herbert Lockyer

**Lamplighter
Books** Grand Rapids,
Michigan
Zondervan Publishing House

*Dedicated
to
Edgar and Adelaide Petty,
Who,
As Devoted Disciples
of Their Lord,
Are in True Apostolic Succession*

Contents

Introduction

Introduction

Some time ago, *The Readers' Digest* carried a most illuminating article by Ernest Hauser on *The Miracle of the Twelve,* which bore the subtitle, "Hand-picked by Jesus, they were the missionaries of a message that changed the world." Who were these men whom Jesus chose, in whose honor cathedrals have been built, around whom legend has spun golden webs, and whose names have been used in naming multitudes since? How was it that principally through their evangelistic efforts within three and a half centuries, proud, imperial Rome succumbed to the glad tidings of the Redeemer from the East?

A fact we cannot deny is that no body of men, few or many, has ever exercised so vast an influence on the world as the small circle of ordinary men Jesus called, trained, commissioned and empowered to further His cause. Surveyed from the human angle, the twelve had meager equipment for the great tasks before them. They are referred to as being "unlettered and ignorant men," which means they were unprofessional men absolutely outside the current schools of philosophical, political and religious thought.

To all appearances, no mission seemed more hopeless than theirs. Were they not facing an enterprise doomed to failure, seeing they had no social status, no organization behind them, no wealth of their own or wealthy backers? How could they then expect success in the world-wide campaign awaiting them? They became companions of a Man who was born in poverty, spent most of His years in obscurity, never had any position in life, never wrote a book, was gibbeted as a felon between two thieves, and who lived for only 33 years. How could they expect to bring the impact of their witness to bear upon the world as followers of One who was despised and rejected of men? Yet forward they went to summon the world to His feet, and the world came — and is still coming, for in spite of the godlessness of our age, there are millions today in the world who love this Man of Galilee.

In a series of articles written for *The Christian,* London, England more than 45 years ago, Allan Poole in dealing with *The Men of the Upper Room,* said of them:

> To plant a new organization in the earth, which was to defy time, death, and all the powers of the underworld, working now through human, and now through demonic agency; to create a society which should gather within its compass the most enlightened minds, the loftiest ideals, and the saintliest souls! That they — through moral and spiritual impact on their own age and succeeding ages — purified and so saved society, created a high state of civilization, and changed history for nearly two millenniums, is a fact beyond dispute.

We believe that the study we have undertaken will make an immediate appeal to all who love the entrancing story of Jesus and the men whom He called into the circle of His friendship. To walk anew with these men in quiet thought and keen observation, to see with their eyes, think with their minds, dream with their fancy, glow with their ardor, burn with their passion for the Master — is a privilege and a pleasure to be desired and cherished. From such a fascinating meditation we should arise more determined to be as devoted to Christ, as the apostles were in their day and generation.

In his militant hymn, "The Son of God Goes Forth to War," Bishop Heber faces us with the daring of these early saints who hazarded their lives for Christ's sake:

A glorious band, the chosen few
  On whom the Spirit came,
  Twelve valiant saints, their hope they
    knew,
  And mocked the cross and flame.
They met the tyrant's brandished steel,
  The lion's gory mane,
They bowed their necks, the death to
    feel:
  Who follows in their train?

Further, because the Bible is the Biography of Humanity, the apostles are well worth studying for their own sakes. It was Thomas Carlyle who said that, "Great men taken up in any way are profitable company. We cannot look, however imperfectly, upon a great man without gaining something by him." When we company with the apostles — all of them — we company not simply with men who became great in their way, but we are in fellowship with some of the world's *greatest* men, in spite of their earlier obscurity. Dr. J. D. Jones affirms that among those born of women none are greater than, "the holy and blessed Twelve. When we are in the society of the apostles we are in the *best* society, and it is simply impossible for us to make friends of Peter and James and John and

Andrew and the rest without gaining something by them, without catching from them something of that zeal and devotion and sacrificial love which have graven their names on the foundations of the New Jerusalem and have set them on twelve thrones judging the twelve tribes of Israel."

Preachers and teachers of the Word have proved how the presentation of Bible characters can hold the interest of an audience. Dr. F. B. Meyer, one of the most outstanding British expositors to use the effectiveness of Bible biography, would have us know that, "To recruit a dwindling congregation, to sustain interest in a crowded one; to awaken new devotion to the Bible, and to touch the chords of human life, there is nothing to be compared to the retelling of the stories of Bible heroes and saints." Preachers and hearers alike are encouraged as the apostles are summoned into the pulpit to speak, for they were men with like passions as ourselves. With all their noble qualities, they had their imperfections and limitations, as we shall discover in our delineation of their characters. They mirror our own hearts and lives and so we are drawn to them in sympathy. If Christ could use the best of men, who were *only men* at the best, then He can use us.

As, of old, Apostles heard Him
  By the Galilean Lake,
Turned from home and toil and
    kindred,
  Leaving all for His dear sake.
Jesus calls us; o'er the tumult
  Of our life's wild, restless sea,
Day by day His sweet voice soundeth,
  Saying, "Christian, follow Me!"

All the
APOSTLES
of the Bible

. . . . .

I

The Prayerful, Purposeful, and Particular
Choice of the Twelve

Jesus is calling in accents of tender-
ness,
Jesus is calling, my brother, to thee,
Just as of old, by the waters of Galilee,
  Fell from His lips the command,
    Follow Me!

Approaching the fact and features of our Lord's choice of the twelve apostles, an evident truth that must be emphasized is that He called them to follow Him, not because of what they were in themselves when He met them for the first time, but because of what, under His tuition, and by His power they would become. Like Michelangelo, the famous sculptor, Jesus saw the angel in the rough, uncut marble. Such a vision and decision is found in His declaration to Peter, "*Thou art* Simon the son of Jona: *thou shalt be* called Cephas . . . A stone" (John 1:42).

To the outward eye it seemed as if the Divine Potter had chosen very common clay indeed out of which to fashion His witnesses and mighty workmen. If there was anything extraordinary about them, it was visible to His omniscient eyes for He alone "knew what was in man." And so, "because he knew all men" (John 2: 24, 25), He chose peasants from the village, provincial townsmen, and toilers of the sea as His first disciples. While most of them earned their livelihood by ordinary handicrafts, and were evidently respectable men from the moral point of view, with a religious bent in their character, there was nothing about them to give one the slightest indication of exceptional qualities or fitness for the remark-

able service they were to render. But the whole world came to know what the example and equipment of Christ made them — twelve of the strongest, noblest, and most fearless and service-able men(except for Judas Iscariot) who have appeared in human history. The transformation of the twelve was not the least, it was almost the greatest of Christ's miracles.

The Master, then, chose twelve obscure men to be His apostles for His mind was not upon their immediate ministry, but upon the mighty things they were to accomplish after His ascension to heaven. They were to certify the facts of their Lord's life, death, and resurrection (see Luke 1:1-24; John 15:27; Acts 1:1-3; II Pet. 1:16; I John 1:1-3). As there are no facts of history more irrefutable than those relating to Christ, and the establishment and expansion of His Church, it was necesssary to have eye-witnesses whose testimony would be overwhelmingly convincing. To them had been granted "many infallible proofs" of their Leader's resurrection from the dead, and it was for the purpose of certainty and certitude of such a dynamic Gospel that He chose the twelve, and prepared them in every way for their gigantic task (Luke 24:48, 49; Acts 1:8; 2:1-5, 32, 33).

The application for our hearts in all this is that it is not what we are, in ourselves, when we hear and respond to Christ's call, but what by His grace and power He can make us as we company with Him. When Jesus called those first disciples, He said,

"Follow me, and *I will make you*" — and there are no *self-made* Christians in His service; they are all *Christ-made*. Self-made men are usually not made up of good material, and they can be wrapped up in a very small parcel. But those whom the Lord wants and wins, are those He is able to fashion into human books to tell the story of His love and grace. As did those He gathered around Him in the days of His flesh, disciples today begin their apprenticeship by following Christ, daily learning of, and from, Him (Matt. 11:29). Then, as they grow in grace and knowledge, they become more fitted to represent the Savior in a world of sin and need.

There are several aspects, noteworthy and profitable to ponder, arresting our attention in respect to the Lord's choice and appointment of the twelve. Notice that their first meetings in life contained the elements of future destiny. The decision made at such points of experience colored and controlled the course of after-years. They are the mysterious birth-times in personal history, and often in world history. It was thus with those who rose up and followed Christ.

1. The Choice Was of His Sovereign Will and Plan

We read that Christ "calleth unto him whom he would" (Mark 3:13). Those called were not consulted beforehand, nor did He seek anyone's advice upon the qualifications of those He was to call. The choice was of His own sovereign will and purpose. As He foresaw the whole path stretched before Him, so He instinctively knew the kind of men He needed as trustworthy witnesses of the entire sacred drama of His life, death, resurrection, and ascension. It is this distinctive feature that makes the story of the twelve so memorable.

Their appointment was carefully foreordained, deliberate, and momentous and far-reaching in results. In connection with our Lord's foreknowledge, the problem of the inclusion of Judas Iscariot in the apostolate is fully dealt with in our cameo about the betrayer.

2. The Choice Was Made After a Night of Prayer

It is Luke who informs us that "[Jesus] went out into a mountain to pray, and continued all night in prayer to God. And when it was day, he called unto him his disciples: and of them he chose twelve, whom also he named apostles" (Luke 6:12, 13).

The number of the disciples from whom a selection of the twelve was ultimately made, we are not told, nor are we given any hint of the method of choice. We do know that for some eighteen months Jesus made, taught, and watched those who followed Him, as only He could, with that perfect intuition of His. Faced with the necessity of laborers to help Him gather in the harvest, few prayers left His holy lips more frequently or fervently than the one for heaven's guidance in regard to the selection of the apostles from among His disciples. Thereafter, His intercession focused on the twelve whom He chose, that they might be separated from the world and unto Him, and bring forth fruit (John 15:16-19).

Even in His great intercessory prayer in the upper room, when the treachery of Judas was unmasked, Christ's conviction was unwavering and unruffled. Listen to His tone of assurance, "Thine they were, and thou gavest them me.... none of them is lost, but the son of perdition; that the scripture might be fulfilled" (John 17:6, 12).

In the light of this assertion, it is

clearly seen that the defection of Judas — so far from showing an error of judgment on Christ's part in His choice of Judas — is but the unfolding of events which were comprehended in the divine will, and the endorsement of an age-long prophecy (Zech. 11:12, 13). The most remarkable prayer ever prayed in the upper room was but an echo of that night with God spent on the mountain, before Christ's choice of the twelve was made. Can we say that all our decisions in life are preceded by intense and prolonged prayer for guidance?

3. *The Choice Was Limited to* TWELVE

Why did Jesus select exactly twelve, no more, no less? This was a considerable retinue for a teacher to have. *Three* men would have been a respectable following; *six* men would attract notice; *twelve* men are remarkable. Every village must have turned out to see what it meant to band *twelve* young men of character and purpose under one head. Dr. J. Elder Cumming suggests that the selection of *twelve* was extraordinary because, for a time, there seemed to be nothing for them to do.

> Now they have no occupation. They have given up the pursuits in which they were engaged: their fishing, their tax-gathering, their agriculture. They carry on no business. They simply walk on around and behind their leader, talking to each other, or to Him; and when He speaks to the people who begin to gather, they listen just like others. The only thing they do is to go with Him from place to place. They are idle! And it begins to be a question whether it is not doing harm, and giving rise to reproach, that *twelve* men are being kept idle for no apparent purpose, and neglecting obvious duties in order to be so. This was at the begin-

ning of the movement, after the disciples had been chosen.

For a time they were *disciples,* or "learners," and they had to *learn* before they could *teach;* hence their observation of Christ as they began to follow Him. But what is the significance behind the exact number chosen, as well as behind the men Christ chose? *Twelve* is the number suggesting *governmental perfection,* so it was no accident that He selected such a number. Dr. Samuel Chadwick says that the fact that "Jesus appointed twelve is clear illustration to the tribes of a new people, another peculiar people." He came as the Messsiah and was cut off that He might bring a spiritual nation into being (Isa. 11:6-10). Before Him, no other rabbi had dared to assert such a claim.

In dealing with the symbolic reasons of the *number* of the apostolic company in his monumental work, *The Training of the Twelve,* A. B. Bruce says that —

> It happily expressed in figures what Jesus claimed to be, and what He had come to do, and thus furnished a support to the faith and a stimulus to the devotion of His followers. It significantly hinted that Jesus was the Divine Messianic King of Israel, come to set up the kingdom whose advent was foretold by prophets in glowing language, suggested by the balmy days of Israel's history, when the theocratic consisted in its integrity, and all the twelve tribes were united under the royal house of David. That the *number twelve* was designed to be such a mystic meaning, we know from Christ's own words to the Apostles on a later occasion, when, describing to them the rewards awaiting them in the kingdom for past services and sacrifices, He said, "Verily I say unto you, that ye which have followed me, in the regeneration when the

Son of man shall sit in the throne of his glory, ye also shall sit upon twelve thrones, judging the twelve tribes of Israel" (Matt. 19:28).

The religious leaders of the time eagerly scanned the prophecies and prophets with minds alert to the latest signs of their times (John 1:19), and it would seem as if Christ was making a direct appeal to their imagination and faith, which the twelve shared. So by this number, thoughts were directed, not only to the patriarchs, but also to the "sure word of prophecy," the bond of One with whom it was impossible to lie. This was to be the anchor of the twelve enabling them to outride those storms which, later, were to break on them with hurricane force.

There are four records given in the New Testament of the names of the twelve apostles: three are found in the gospels, and one in the book of Acts. The following reveals the varying order of mention.

Matthew	*Mark*
Simon Peter,	Simon Peter,
Andrew,	James,
James, son of Zebedee,	John,
John,	Andrew,
Philip,	Philip,
Bartholomew,	Bartholomew,
Thomas,	Matthew,
Matthew,	Thomas,
James, son of Alphaeus,	James,
Lebbaeus, or Thaddaeus,	Thaddaeus,
Simon the Canaanite,	Simon the Canaanite,
Judas Iscariot, (10:2-4)	Judas Iscariot, (3:16-19)

Luke	*Acts*
Simon Peter,	Peter,
Andrew,	James,

James,	John,
John,	Andrew,
Philip,	Philip,
Bartholomew,	Thomas,
Matthew,	Bartholomew,
Thomas,	Matthew,
James,	James,
Simon,	Simon,
Judas,	Judas,
Judas Iscariot, (6:14-16)	Matthias (1:13-26)

A characteristic feature of the gospel lists is that Peter, the most prominent character among the twelve is always at the head, while Judas Iscariot ends the first three lists with the infamous title branded on his brow, "who also betrayed him." Several theologians take the names on the apostolic role and divide them into groups, or pair them off. A. B. Bruce, borrowing distinctive epithets from the gospel history at large, gives us the following divisions —

First Group

Simon Peter	The man of rock
Andrew	Peter's brother
James	Sons of Zebedee and
John	Sons of thunder

Second Group

Philip	The earnest inquirer
Bartholomew, or Nathaniel	The guileless Israelite
Thomas	The melancholy
Matthew	The publican (as he called himself)

Third Group

James, son of Alphaeus,	James the less? (Mark 15:40)
Lebbaeus, or Thaddaeus, or Judas of James	The three-named disciple
Simon	The zealot
Judas, of Kerioth	The traitor

Daniel McLean observes that it is remarkable that the grouping of the names is almost the same in all the lists. "The classification evidently rests on an order of merit or eminence in service in the kingdom of light and truth. Promotion was found in the line of character, ability and duty; favoritism had no place; the family of Christ are least distinguished in the history; and four simple fishermen attain the first rank of distinction. The standard of Christ is character more than condition, and even the man that carried the bag was forced to recognize this." Cash, rather than character, puts many at the top of some lists in our human society, but in the choice of the twelve, Christ reversed the world's estimate of importance and influence, by offering a way of promotion on moral and spiritual principles.

4. The Choice Reveals Twelve Typical Men

Christ's calling of the twelve was certainly not based on prudential reasons, otherwise the band would not have included a publican, much less an Iscariot. In this strange disregard of worldly wisdom there is manifested in opposite directions the influence of Divine wisdom in developing faith and detecting hypocrisy. Suppose the Master had made up His first church out of cultured, rich, rare and elevated nature — those who never would have doubted what He said, or flinched from peril, or acted on the lower motive when a higher was possible. How much we should have lost! To us, the apostles were not exceptional men, strangers to our weaknesses, temptations and difficulties. Jesus chose twelve typical representative men, and as we study their personalities we instinctively know them as bone of our bone.

The Apostle Paul left it on record that, "Not many wise, not many mighty, not many noble are called." Bless God, some are called, and Paul was one of them; but in the main, the wise and noble do not feel their need of the Savior, as more ordinary folk do. Thus the list of the twelve does not contain the name of a nobleman, or a rabbi, or a man of great wealth. If the rich young ruler had been willing to follow Christ, he might have become an apostle. Lowly men like fishermen — humble and obscure—were chosen because they were the best that could be had. Yet, perhaps, in spite of their lowly station, better men could not have been found. Because the Lord hides from the wise and prudent what He reveals to babes, He chose those who were poor and teachable as the clay out of which to fashion spiritual geniuses, just as, in after history, He chose a Moody, a Spurgeon, a Bunyan — men of immense spiritual power who were innocent of college training (which one does not deprecate). How apt are the lines of J. P. S. Strickland at this point —

Unlearnt, though wise in things
    that mattered most,
  Those men of God were valiant
    'midst a host,
And proved that they had been
    with Him who died,
  And for the sinful world was
    crucified,
And by that nearness had a wisdom vast,
  That proved sufficient for their
    hardsome task.

For they had been with Jesus,
    heard Him speak,
  Knew of His worth and of His
    manner meek;
But knew beneath it all He was of
    God,
  And following where their risen
    Master trod

> Were versed in knowledge, not of
>   earth-taught men,
> Nor written yet by men's God-
>   guided pen.

The twelve Christ chose, then, were twelve *men*, distinguished by marked degrees of difference and varieties of temper and disposition. They were not twelve copies, twelve imitative machines, twelve plaster figures taken out of the same mold. Not one of the group reminds us of another. Each stands out with his own distinctive character. For instance, Peter is forward and self-assertive, but Andrew, his brother, keeps in the background and is never obtrusive. James is like a volcano, but Nathanael is like a quiet summer pool. Philip always looked before he leaped, but Peter leaped before he looked. Some of the band were born to lead, others were content to be led.

These twelve types were selected as a representation of a narrow circle of the whole human race, in which there is a great variety of types. What a monotonous world it would be if we were all exactly alike in all things! That God loves variety is seen throughout nature, as well as among humans. It has been suggested that in the choice of the twelve, Christ was experimenting on the entire human race. If He could bring these twelve under His power and subdue them to His qualities, it would be proof that all men might be made to yield to His sway. It was a prophetic demonstration that His salvation was adapted to all classes with varieties of disposition and qualities. The selection was also a proof that Jesus was both willing and able to employ all manner of gifts and all manner of natures in His service. Doubtless if the choice had been ours we should have left several of the twelve out, and chosen others. Not all leaders

would have included a modest Andrew, a melancholy Thomas, and a hesitating Philip in their ranks. But Jesus, who came as the Son of Man and knew what was in man, had room for all kinds in His fellowship and service. All personalities, whether conspicuous or obscure, can be molded by the Potter and made mighty to the pulling down of strongholds.

Jesus said, "Whosoever cometh I will in no wise cast out," and the list given of the twelve, suffices to prove His all-embracing love; that He has no favorites; that men of varying temperament and diverse gifts are equally welcome to Him. More than one writer has indicated the infinite variety and difference among the apostles.

For difference in *temperament,* we have it in Peter and John.

Peter — the man of action — of bold, impulsive, eager spirit.

John — the man of prayer — of a quiet, contemplative, loving heart.

For difference in *spiritual gifts* we have an example in Bartholomew and Thomas.

Bartholomew, or Nathaniel — was a believing soul and ever ready to confess.

Thomas, was of a skeptical spirit and slow to accept the witness of others.

For difference in *political opinion,* we have it in the most extreme and violent form in the contrast between Matthew and Simon the Canaanite.

Matthew, was a publican or tax-gatherer, the servant of the Roman governor, and wore the livery of Rome.

Simon was a Zealot, a rebel against Rome, whose sword was drawn against it and who hated its taxes.

All down the ages Christ has drawn

to Him men of all colors — white, black, red and yellow; men as diverse as Augustine and Bunyan; men from all religions as well as the non-religious. There is room for all, and in His service there is variety in unity.

The names of the twelve appear on the foundation stones of the New Jerusalem which their devotion and dedication helped to build. Surely the apparent lesson in the variety of men whom Jesus chose is that we should despise no man's gifts, and have no man despise our own. Also, is there any significance that the twelve are called Galileans? Peter was identified as a Galilean by his accent (Mark 14:70), Multitudes followed Jesus from Galilee (Matt. 4: 25). Jesus was looked upon as the Prophet of Galilee (Matt. 21:11; John 7:41). The disciples were looked upon as "men of Galilee" — "Behold, are not all . . . which speak Galileans?" (Acts 1:11; 2:7). As a province, Galilee was looked upon by the people of Jerusalem and Judaea as "old-fashioned, narrowly provincial, and unpolished."

Judaeans felt themselves somewhat superior to the Galileans, with advanced refinement and educational equipment. They were certainly more rigidly conservative in religious matters, and wedded to rabbinical traditions and the priestly system than the Galileans. Those of the South were more obstinately proud with hearts and minds closed to new ideas than the men of the North, and so Jesus turned to the latter because they were better fitted for His training — less wise in their own conceits, and therefore more teachable. Although the Galileans may have lacked the superficial culture, upon which the southern Jews prided themselves, they were still intelligent and mentally alert, and in close contact with the Gentile world. Theirs was a rougher but more practical education which adapted them in larger measure for the purpose and training they were to receive from the Man of Galilee.

What must never be forgotten is that His choice was made in true wisdom! Righteous and just, He could not be guided by feelings of antagonism toward those having cultural and social advantages, or manifest partiality for men of His own humble class. Provincial prejudice did not lead Jesus to choose rude, unlearned and humble men, nor was He animated by any petty jealousy of knowledge, culture or good birth. Had any of the Judaeans shown any willingness to yield themselves to His call and claims, He would have chosen them, even as later He chose the cultured Hebrew of Tarsus. Those who are too proud to become His disciples cannot become princes in His kingdom, and this is why He turns to humble men out of which He can make apostles. As the great apostle himself expresses it, "God hath chosen the foolish things of the world to confound the wise; and God hath chosen the weak things of the world to confound the things which are mighty, and base things of the world, and things which are despised, hath God chosen, yea, and things which are not, to bring to nought things that are: that no flesh should glory in his presence" (I Cor. 1:27-31, See Matt. 21:31).

It was the Galileans, then, who received their privileges, orders, and instructions in their collective capacity rather than in their personal positions, as the following expressions indicate —

"He called unto him his twelve disciples" (Matt. 10:1; Mark 6:7). "The names of the twelve apostles are these" (Matt. 10:2).

"These twelve Jesus sent forth" (Matt. 10:5).

"Commanding his twelve disciples" (Matt. 11:1).

"[He] took the twelve disciples apart" (Matt. 20:17).

"One of the twelve" (Matt. 26:14, 47; Mark 14:20, 43).

"He sat down with the twelve" (Matt. 26:20).

"He ordained twelve" (Mark 3:14).

"He . . . called the twelve" (Mark 9:35; Luke 9:1).

"He went out unto Bethany with the twelve" (Mark 11:11).

"In the evening he cometh with the twelve" (Mark 14:17).

"He chose twelve" (Luke 6:13).

"The twelve were with him" (Luke 8:1).

"Then came the twelve" (Luke 9:12).

"He took unto him the twelve" (Luke 18:31).

"He sat down, and the twelve apostles with him" (Luke 22:14).

"Then said Jesus unto the twelve" (John 6:67).

"Have I not chosen you twelve?" (John 6:70).

"Thomas, one of the twelve" (John 20:24).

"The twelve called the multitude" (Acts 6:2).

"Then of the twelve" (I Cor. 15:5).

"The names of the twelve apostles" (Rev. 21:14).

As we think of the named disciples, and the even more numerous unnamed disciples whom Jesus gathered around Him, it would seem as if they fall into distinct groups. There were the *seventy* He chose and sent forth and who formed, we might say, "the outer fringe," all of whom were truly His, but who did not have the same intimate contact with Him as others. Then we have the *twelve*, whom Jesus selected and depended so much

upon, those who were His "cabinet." But among the twelve, there were *three*, who are linked together on several occasions. These three were eye-witnesses of their Lord's majesty at His transfiguration. As we have noted, Paul calls Peter, James and John, *pillars* of the church, and we might look upon them as the Master's "inner" cabinet. Further, among the three there was *one* who seemed to have the place of pre-eminence, namely, John who is also spoken of as "the disciple Jesus loved." He it was who leaned upon the bosom of his Master, and who had a more spiritual understanding of His mind than any other. This may be one reason why John was chosen to give us the sublime "Revelation of Jesus Christ," contained in the last book of the Bible.

Later on we shall deal with the twelve separately; in the foregoing, we look at them unitedly, and can gather from the phrases selected, their commission as a whole, as well as an intimation of Christ's purpose in their choice. They formed a close-knit brotherhood. Unalike as they were, individually, collectively, there was one center of attraction to them all, namely, the Man Christ Jesus, in whom we all have a heritage. He is the Vine, we are the branches.

5. *The Choice Resulted in the Twelve Becoming* APOSTLES

An understanding of the term *apostle* prepares us for a consideration of the function of one known as such. The word is from the Greek, "apo-stolos," meaning a messenger and is derived from the Greek "apostello," *stellein* implying to send. *Stello* means to dispatch on an expedition, to set out on a journey. *Apo* means "away from," so that *apo-stello* means to send forth, or away, usually on some mission; and the *apostolos* is the one sent. Both verb and noun occur frequently in the New Testament, the verb usually being translated *send,* and the noun, *apostle.* The verb occurs 97 times, and the noun 9 times in the Gospels. Maclean observes that — "In classical Greek the word was almost entirely restricted to the meaning of a 'naval expedition,' a fleet dispatched on foreign service" (I Kings 14:6; Heb. 3:1).

The title *apostoloi,* then, was given in a special sense to *the twelve,* although not confined to them as we shall presently see. The Christian religion began in Palestine as a *way* within Judaism. "If he found any of this *way*" (Acts 9:2; 16:17). "No small stir about that *way*" (Acts 19:23; 22:4; 24:14; Heb. 10:20). Jesus spoke of Himself as *the Way* (John 14:6). The earliest leaders, or missionaries of this way, or sect, were the apostles, "those who were sent," or spiritual envoys. Later on, in Judaism, *apostoloi* were envoys sent out by the patriarchate in Jerusalem to collect the sacred tribute from the Jews of the Dispersion.

The Hebrew word signified not merely a *messenger* but a *delegate,* bearing a commission, and, so far as his commission extended, wielding his commissioner's authority. The Talmud puts it, "The apostle of any one is even as the man himself by whom he is deputed." It was in this sense that the apostles were the authorized representatives of Christ who commissioned them. "Even as thou didst *commission* me unto the world, I also *commissioned* them unto the world" (John 17:18). Here the verb, *commission,* is cognate to apostle. When Jesus said, "All power is given unto me, Go ye," He implied that He was bestowing upon the apostles all necessary power and authority to act as His representatives. So they went forth "in his name." But as Dr. J. C. Lambert expresses it in *The International Standard Bible Encyclopedia:*

> The *authority* of the apostolate was of a spiritual, ethical and personal kind. It was not official, and in the nature of the case could not be transmitted to others. Paul claimed for himself complete independence of the opinion of the whole body of the earlier apostles (Gal. 2:6, 11), and in seeking to influence his own converts endeavored by manifestation of the truth to commend himself to every man's conscience in the sight of God (2 Cor. 4:2). There is no sign that the apostles collectively exercised a separate and autocratic authority.

It was because of this entrusted authority that the apostles went forth to the uttermost parts, with credentials as potent and convincing as those the Lord Himself had possessed, if not more so (Matt. 28:18-20; Mark 16:19, 20; John 14:12). The marvelous establishment and expansion of the Church in all parts as described in the Acts, proves how the commissioned ones perpetuated the work of the Master.

Further, the *call* to the task of an apostle came in a variety of ways. At the commencement of His earthly ministry Jesus found His prospective disciples where they were laboring for their daily bread and called them to follow Him (Matt. 10:1). After His resurrection this call was repeated, made permanent, and given a universal scope (Matt. 28:19, 20; Acts 1:8).

Matthias was called first by the voice of the general body of the brethren and thereafter by the decision of the lot (Acts 1:15-26).

Paul received his call in a heavenly vision (Acts 26:17-19), which was subsequently ratified by the church at Antioch, and by the Holy Spirit

(Acts 13:1). Paul firmly maintained that his apostleship was received directly from heaven (Gal. 1:1).

Barnabas was sent forth by the churches at Jerusalem and Antioch (Acts 11:22; 13:1). The mission of Paul and Barnabas explains the title given them (Acts 14:4). They were apostles not only of the Church, but of Christ and of the Holy Spirit (14: 27).

What, actually, constitutes a *call?* Is it not made up of a need and the ability to meet that need? Paul was *called* to be an apostle. He lived in a world that needed Christ and He endowed the rebel He met on that Damascus road, transformed his life and mantled Paul with all necessary ability and authority to challenge the need. The apostles then, were *called* to be *sent.* Luke says of the twelve that they were "chosen to be apostles." Called to, and chosen for — what? They were called and chosen not to have a life of ease and quietness, but to a fellowship of His sufferings. As Dr. J. D. Jones puts it:

They were called that they might be sent — sent to preach —
> To the barbarians of Lycaonia,
> To the Celts of Salatra,
> To the Diana worshippers of Ephesus,
> To the philosophers of Athens,
> To the legionaries of Rome.
> Called —
> To be stoned at Lystra,
> To be scourged at Philippi,
> To be imprisoned at Caesarea,
> To die without the gate.

Were they chosen just to be with Christ, and enjoy His sweet and blessed fellowship? No, chosen —
> That they might be sent;
> Saved that they might save others;
> Blessed that they might become a blessing;
> Redeemed that they might preach the Gospel of Redemption,
> Chosen that they might hear Christ's name before governors and kings and before the children of Israel, and suffer many things for that Name's sake.

What we are so slow to learn is that the *calling* and *sending* are the two sides of the one coin. When Christ saved us it was not that we might spend all our time in fellowship with Him, although such fellowship is our primary necessity. The end of His call is that we might do His work, proclaim His name, run His errands, further His cause. Is it not sadly possible to rejoice in the *calling,* and, folding our arms, bless God because we are *saved,* and forget all about the *sending?* Discipleship must end in apostleship. Saved, we must be prepared to be sent wherever the Master will.

> "If Jesus has found you,
> Tell others the story."

With the apostles of old it would seem as if there were three successive stages in their training in the School of Christ, as the various terms used of them imply. Did He not say that if those He called would follow Him that He would *make* them? It has been said that unlike some teachers, Christ wrote no book to perpetuate His work and influence. There was no need. He made *men,* not manuscripts; and He makes them still. What were the three aspects of the preparation of the men of Galilee for the service of the Galilean Himself?

The first step of discipleship

Associated with the Master's opening invitation, "Follow me," there was the crisis of a personal decision — a definite, personal commitment to Christ. Unless we are truly *forgiven* we cannot follow, and when those He called immediately responded, they became Christ's. Had they known the hymn of assurance which Philip Doddridge gave us, they would have sung —

'Tis done, the great transaction's done,
I am my Lord's and He is mine;
He drew me, and I followed on,
Charmed to confess the voice Divine.

Several times over the apostle Paul emphasizes the primacy of salvation. "Who hath *saved* us, and *called* us with an holy calling" (II Tim. 1:9). Conversion precedes the call. *Service* is not acceptable to God unless there is first of all salvation. Many are active in religious work who seek to serve in order to be saved — which is putting the cart before the horse. We serve because we have been saved. There must come committal to the claims of Christ before He will commit to us the Spirit's power for service (II Tim. 1:12, 14). Paul magnified Christ Jesus his Lord for putting him into the ministry — but it was only after he, the chief of sinners, had been brought to understand that Christ came into the world to save him (I Tim. 1:12-17).

Responding to the Master's initial invitation to follow, the twelve embarked upon their discipleship and entered what might be called the receptive stage when, as they moved around with Him they saw His mighty works, listened to His marvelous words, and felt the touch of His holy, dedicated life upon their own. They were to *learn* of Christ, before teaching others about Him. *Disciple* means "a learner," and the first disciples were as pupils in the primary department. Thus, their first contact with Christ was as their "Teacher-Master." They could not function as apostles until they had studied with Christ.

Because the great Founder of the faith wanted His kingdom founded on the rock of deep and indestructible convictions in the minds of the few, rather than scatter His truth "on the shifting sands of superficial evanescent impressions on the minds of many," Jesus was careful and painstaking in the spiritual education of His discipless, insuring, thereby, the permanency of His influence. They were to become as finely polished mirrors designed to reflect the image of their Lord. Often, although loyalty attached them to His person, they were surprised at His teaching, sometimes pleased, often vexed and perplexed, yet all the while they grew larger in faith and feeling, and rose above the fetters of tradition to a liberty of living truth. Following in a state of awe, they were often unable to reconcile their expectation of the Messiah with their experience. "Art thou he that should come, or look we for another?"

The discipline of the school, or as A. B. Bruce puts it, *The Training of the Twelve,* bore fruit. The apprenticeship for future work, or the school-time of Christ's coming witnesses, was not in vain even though the Teacher often sighed over the slow progress of His scholars. After the first year spent in listening and learning, in "hearing and seeing" (I John 1:1, 2), the disciples passed from the discipline of the school more or less prepared for practical service.

The second stage of ambassadorship

After their direct instructions the disciples entered upon a course of practical training as apostles, and became ambassadors or messengers of Christ, who said, "Go, preach, saying, the kingdom of heaven is at hand." Their mission was limited to the lost sheep of the house of Israel, and was also restricted in its range to the advent of Christ as King. Their varied experiences as they went forth in His name, tested their fitness for the larger sphere of heroic service and confirmed their faith through signs of divine favor.

In this further development of the disciples an important stage was reached in that the students were now trained agents for the propagation of the truth. Now as pupil-teachers in the kingdom, they learn the deeper secrets as they seek to impart them to others. Again and again, the Master warned His emissaries against imprudence and sought to adjust their inexperience to their new relation. During this period of evangelism, He stood over them as the mother eagle training her fledglings to flight. Such practical training was designed to discipline and instruct, and the tuition was fruitful. Describing this period of ministry, Daniel McLean says that:

> This first attempt at evangelising among the towns of Galilee was an educational experiment, but it was also an urgent effort to meet the spiritual destitution everywhere evident. The evangelists were thus to gain sympathy and the experience of the mighty power of God on their behalf, that with deepening conviction they might be able to stand as witnesses for Christ when His personal presence was removed. Compassion for the perishing inspired the mission of the Twelve, and contact with the perishing was meant to evoke sympathy, so that both results were reached by sending them forth to proclaim the Gospel of Peace.

The third stage of apostleship

This final stage received its confirmation on the eve of Christ's departure from the earth. Knowing that His wise counsel would no longer be at the service of His own, He promised them the Holy Spirit as an abiding source of wisdom, comfort, and strength (Acts 1:8). Chosen, ordained and sent forth as heralds of the King and His kingdom, discipleship passed to apostleship with their office as apostles having a relation to their tremendous tasks. Such an apostleship brought with it a deeper bond. No longer were they sent as slaves on the errands of their owner but *friends* of the Lord, sharers of His thought, partners in His world-wide redemptive purpose. As the result of Pentecost such a relationship became more vital and intense as the apostles bore much fruit to His glory (John 15:1-6). As brethren we have an indication of their attitude one to another, their equality in a great confederacy, their unity as "a little band of brothers against the world."

As *disciples* the twelve came to understand the mind and message of their Master, and went forth to proclaim the apostolic Gospel of Christ as the Lord and Lover of man. As *friends* they shared the thoughts of Jesus, and the purposes concerning His elect, and captured His vision of coming triumph (Isa. 42:4; Matt. 13:43). As *brethren,* they were a united body and manifested the characteristic marks of the apostolic church: unity, prayer, boldness, power, grace and triumph (Acts 1:14; 2:1, 4; 4:13, 31, 33; 5:14). As apostles, they were the living link between their ascended, reigning Lord and His mission to emancipate the souls of men from sin's guilt and thraldom.

The fifth book of the New Testament should not be called *The Acts of the Apostles,* but *The Acts of the Holy Spirit Through the Apostles,* for He was the One bequeathed to them by the Redeemer ere the Lord breathed His last tender farewell. What a mighty change the Spirit wrought in the hearts and lives of the men who had felt that the death of this Master had blasted their Messianic hopes. "We trusted that it had been he who should have redeemed Israel!" (Luke 24:21). But the resurrection and Pentecost transformed these dejected followers into dynamic witnesses, and Acts is the evidence of their fidelity to the divine commission, and a thorough vindication of the Master's choice and cultivation of them as His apostles.

What a dramatic story of heroism is unfolded as the poor, somewhat illiterate men of Galilee emerge into "the glorious company of the apostles!" Freed from the fetters of prejudice and doubt, and rising above the dreams of political ambition, full of the Spirit of Power, undismayed by all the powers of earth and hell, they remained strong in the strength of God, steadfast in their witness to their risen Lord until cruel martyrdom closed their lips. Is there a more thrilling record than this, or a miracle in the history of the church more significant? It is impossible to have any evidence of the truth of the Gospel of Christ more touchingly convincing than Acts portrays.

Concluding this section of our study it must be pointed out that although "the twelve" were the apostles *par excellence,* there was a wider circle included in the apostolic calling. The twelve had been with Jesus, and their peculiar mission was to testify of Him, especially of His resurrection (Acts 1:8-21; Luke 24:48); however, they were not the only witnesses known as *apostles.*

Paul, who belonged neither to the twelve nor to the seventy, was commissioned directly by the Lord Himself whom he saw on that Damascus road. He was called to be an apostle (I Cor. 9:1; 15:8).

Barnabas also received the honored title (Acts 14:14; I Cor. 9:5, 6).

Andronicus and *Junia,* who perhaps were of the seventy, are likewise named apostles (Rom. 16:7).

Epaphroditus is referred to as "your apostle" (Phil. 2:25, R.V. margin).

Silas and *Timothy,* who were men of apostolic character, are included with Paul as apostles (I Thess. 1:1, 6; See II Cor. 6:1; Col. 1:1).

Apollos. It seems as if Paul included Apollos among the apostles who were made a spectacle to the world, angels, and men (I Cor. 4:6, 9).

The Lord Jesus is spoken of as "the Apostle" in respect to His relationship to God (Heb. 3:1; see John 17:3).

Among the apostles of the primitive church, there were differences due to natural talents, to personal requirements and experience, and to spiritual gifts. Peter was greater than Thaddaeus, and John than Simon the Canaanite; and Paul was greater than either Barnabas or Silvanus; but no one was more truly an apostle than another. Each contributed in his own way to the furtherance of the Gospel, and each served the Lord to the limit of his own personal capacity. Paul denounced certain workers as "false apostles" (II Cor. 11:13). The term *apostleship* (Acts 1:25; Rom. 1:5; I Cor. 9:2; Gal. 2:8), implies "a sending, a mission."

The apostolate, then, was not a limited circle of officials holding a well-defined position of authority in the church, but a large body of consecrated men exercising the highest function of the prophetic ministry (I Cor. 12:28; Eph. 4:11). They were all envoys of the Gospel to an unbelieving world (Gal. 2:7, 9). In the course of time the name apostles came to be applied to a whole class of nameless missionaries who, after the boundary line of New Testament history, settled in no church, but moved from place to place as messengers of the Gospel, and who, in the exercise of their missionary functions braved the hardships of those heralds before them.

6. The Choice Had Ideal Objectives

While a passing reference or two has been made as to why Jesus chose the twelve, we now come to examine more specifically the object and end in the choice made. Hand-picked by Him, these men were to be set aside to witness His life, serve at His bidding, receive His teaching, participate in His miraculous ministry, share His hardship, drink of His bitter cup, and become the pillars of a spiritual and eternal temple. What were these followers supposed to do? Mark, who is not named among "the twelve," but who gave us the earliest gospel, describes their three-fold function: they were to be *with* Jesus; to be "sent forth" to proclaim the message of the Gospel; to possess "power (or authority) to cast out demons." Luke (who is another not included among the apostles) informs us that it was Jesus who named the twelve. He chose *apostles,* and decreed also that "healing" was to be one of their responsibilities. The office and commission of apostleship associated with following Christ were remarkable in these particulars.

They followed that they might be with Jesus

Mark tells us that the twelve were ordained "that they should be with him [Jesus]" (3:14). They not only formed a traveling college, with the Lord as their Teacher, but they were a circle of friends in which He could find love, fellowship, partnership and

sympathy. Surely there is nothing more touching in the record of His earthly life than His desire for companionship. Often we find Him alone. When He came to die, the very men He chose as companions forsook Him and fled. In the Garden, they failed in the sympathetic fellowship for which He sought. Finding them sleeping, He gave that sorrowful reproach reechoing the cry of a heart aching for human sympathy, "Could ye not watch *with me* one hour?" Christ ever appreciated loving and trustworthy friends, hence His retreat to that Bethany home where Mary, Martha and Lazarus, all of whom He loved, were living. With loving gratitude in the upper room the night before He died, He required the companionship of His own in the words, "Ye are they which have continued *with me* in my temptations" (Luke 22:28).

Thus, while the majority of all those who believed in Him could only be occasional followers, the twelve were selected to be with Him at all times and in all places, "His travelling companions in all His wanderings, witnessing all His work, and ministering to His daily needs." They were more than His menial servants, however, for in the privacy of an intimate daily fellowship with Him they were being fashioned to become His ambassadors to a lost world. They were to become apostles whose main business would be that of witnessing to the reality and power of Christian truth.

Picture the disciples moving from place to place somewhat poor and with no visible occupation. But Jesus was in the midst of the little band as their "neverfailing Treasury, filled with boundless stores of grace." Evidently there was a common purse for their support, and when it was empty and the payment of an unexpected tribute or tax was demanded, the Master knew where to find the necessary money (Matt. 17:27). Is it not profitable to link the requirements, "That they should be with him," to His promise, "I am *with you* alway, even unto the end of the world"? We sing that —

"The fellowship of kindred minds, Is like to that above" —

and such a bond is more than an instinct of human nature, it is a necessity. In the days of His flesh, Jesus could question His companions as He could not others without being misunderstood (Matt. 16:13-15); He could unburden His mind to them as to no other (John 15:15; 17:8); He could expect from them what others could not supply (Matt. 26: 38-40). Ever grateful for the friendship given, Jesus showed His appreciation of what others did for Him by their contact, confidence, and comradeship. Is He not the same today as yesterday?

They followed that they might preach

Christ called the twelve that "he might send them forth to preach" (Mark 3:14), and what fearless, dynamic preachers they became, as with their Master, they went everywhere preaching the Gospel! Fellowship with the greatest Preacher of all time gave them a unique training in the art and craft of preaching. "Unlearned men" they might have been, but they were not ignorant men. From their course on *Homiletics* they went forth to discourse on the sublimest themes, persuading the inhabitants of Roman and Grecian cities to cast away their idols, to renounce the religion of their fathers, to reject the instructions of their fancied philosophy, and to receive instead, a Teacher

sent from heaven, a Jew of humble station who had been put to a shameful death. And such was the impact of their convincing and courageous preaching that multitudes were saved (Acts 2:41; 4:4 etc.). What a mighty spiritual upheaval would be experienced if only all who preach could "preach the preaching," inspired by the Pentecostal power that apostolic preaching reveals (Jonah 3:2).

Conspicuous as a Preacher, after His baptism by John, Jesus needed others to reach out after others. At the outset, He worked alone, and His preaching created great excitement for "no man spake like this man." People crowded to hear Him, but of necessity His labors were confined to a small area. Only a few towns could enjoy the privilege of hearing Him preach, but wherever He looked He saw a plenteous harvest and few laborers to gather it. Now, with twelve fellow-preachers, He could cope with the growing demands for the hearing of the Gospel, He was anointed by the Spirit to preach. Jesus sent His disciples, two by two, to different places, chiefly to announce that He was about to visit there, and to tell what they could about Him and His object and purpose. As the demand for preaching became more widespread, the band of mission preachers became larger till another seventy disciples were sent forth to evangelize. Thus the gracious activities of Christ took on an ever-widening range.

The instructions Jesus gave the young evangelists as He commissioned them to preach and teach all they had received from Him, are full of spiritual import for all ministers of the Word in any age. Inexperienced as they were yet they went forth at His bidding. He warned them, not only of the dangers they would face, but of the necessity of developing certain qualities so necessary for an effective witness. It was thus that, at the outset of their missionary enterprise, Jesus dwelt upon the duties, perils and rewards of their apostolic vocation. As they listened to His remarkable Sermon on the Mount, the twelve heard of the virtues they must manifest now that they had put their hands to the task unto which they had been called. A. B. Bruce reminds us that there were two phrases which appear to summarize Christ's instructions to the twelve — *Care not; Fear not.* "These are all the soul and marrow of all that He said by way of prelude to the first missionary enterprise. . . . For here Jesus speaks to all ages and to all times, telling the Church in what spirit all her missionary enterprises must be undertaken and carried on, that they may have His blessing."

CARE NOT

Having "turned from home and toil and kindred," leaving all for His dear sake, it would have been only natural on the part of the apostles to wonder where their support and that of their homes was coming from. But they found out that their decision to forsake all and follow the Stranger from Galilee was no leap in the dark. Having selected them, He would support them. They had made His concern theirs; and their concern would be His. Thus He urged them to go forth and labor without carefulness, relying on Him for the necessities of life. In strong and lively terms Jesus impressed upon them the danger of the cares of this life. They had to go forth without provisions for their journeys, leaning upon the promise that "As thy days, so shall thy strength be," and praying the petition the Master had taught them, "Give us *this* day our daily bread."

The spirit, and not the letter, of His injunctions about providing nothing for their itinerary can be expressed thus: "Go and learn to seek the kingdom of God with a single heart unconcerned about food and raiment; for till ye can do that ye are not fit to be my apostles." Is not this direction as to temporalities, an indication that Christ expected those He commissioned to live by faith? Furthermore, because *He* had spoken thus, was there not the assurance that He would not send them forth altogether at their own risk but that they would prove that "the workman is worthy of his hire" (Matt. 10:10)? When Abraham left his father's house and became a pilgrim in an unknown country, he received the promise that God would be his Guide, his Shield, and his Provider. It was a similar situation with the disciples to whom Jesus said in effect, "Go at once, and go as you are, and trouble not yourselves about food and raiment, or any bodily want; trust in God for these." These instructions "proceeded on the principle of the division of labor, assigning to the servants of the kingdom military duty, and to God the commissariat department." And all down the ages there have been those who, sent forth by God to labor for the salvation of lost souls, at home and abroad, dared to trust Him, as Hudson Taylor did, to meet their every need.

But Jesus did not exhort His disciples to walk by faith without giving such faith something to rest upon. They were encouraged to hope that what they did not provide for themselves God would provide for them through the instrumentality of those to whom they were sent to minister. Wherever the preachers went they would find someone with a warm and hospitable heart who would welcome them to his home and table. "In whatsoever city or town ye shall enter, inquire who in it is worthy, and there abide till ye go thence" (Matt. 10:11). Those, then, who because the love of God abounded in them, received the evangelists and treated them kindly had their reward in knowing that in entertaining the messengers they had actually entertained the Master who had sent them (Matt. 10:40-42). There were times, however, when they would be poorly received. Hospitality would be refused them, but they were not to be discouraged, even though both their presence and preaching were unwanted. They would be free from the blood of the guilty (Ezek. 3:17-21; Matt. 10:13-15).

At this point there are three observations to be emphasized, namely —

1. Equipment

"He charged them that they should take nothing for their journey, save a staff only." The chief point about their equipment was that there was to be so little of it. In Matthew's account (Matt. 10:10), they are forbidden even to procure a staff. There is no necessary conflict in the two statements. "If you have a staff, take it, if you have none, don't trouble to acquire one." Such a statement harmonizes the two commands. The list of exclusions is fairly complete: "no bread, no wallet, no money in the girdle." The simplest kind of shoewear, sandals, is prescribed, and the gospelers are specially warned against wearing two tunics, which was the badge of the well-to-do. Everything was to be of the simplest kind. They were to travel light.

These special injunctions are not permanent. Our Lord Himself withdrew them when He said in effect, "When I sent you without purse, and scrip [wallet], and shoes, lacked ye any thing? And they said, Nothing. And He said unto them, But now, he that hath a purse, let him take it, and likewise his scrip" (Luke 22:35, 36). But on this first occasion, they were to live entirely by trustfulness. That was part of their training. The temporary arrangement is in keeping with our Lord's usual plan. He taught the disciples that God could fulfill His purposes without ordinary means. To make them sure of this, He sometimes forbade the use of means; but, as a rule, God works through ordinary channels, and if they are there, they are to be used.

There is here, obviously, no emphasis on asceticism, no glorification of austerity. But there is laid down an abiding principle that Christ's gospelers are to keep themselves as free as possible from worldly entanglements and encumbrances. The missionary to China who made the experiment of cutting himself off from all home supplies soon found that he was mistaken. On the other hand, the minister who made money by a literary success but refused to undertake his own investments or to interest himself in the rise and fall of prices on the stock exchange, was exemplifying the principle here laid down. The compulsion of the simple life is not a limitation according to Jesus. It is an assistance for a preacher, if only he learns to live the carefree life through faith in a providing God.

2. Disposition

"In what place soever ye enter into an house, there abide till ye depart from that place" (Mark 6:10). There was to be no picking and choosing as to shelter and food. These were necessities. So long as they were provided, that was sufficient. Discomfort was not to be an excuse for looking round for fresh quarters. The messengers were to be too busy with their message to spend time on planning for their own ease.

There is something practical in this injunction. It illustrates our Lord's close contact with life. On the one hand, He does not take for granted that His disciples will be so taken up with their exalted task that they will be incapable of yielding to self-indulgence. He marks a particular temptation to which they will be open. On the other hand, He recognizes the needs of the body. He does not advocate an asceticism which will neglect shelter and food and be content with any kind of bivouac. This is always His attitude. Do not make too much of the earthly side of your life, is His advice. Take these things in your stride. Make the best arrangements you can without spending time over them and then be content. Keep your mind centered on the big things and on your task.

3. The Sacrament of Failure

This is Dr. Oman's striking title for the observance our Lord prescribes — "Whosoever shall not receive you, nor hear you, when ye depart thence, shake off the dust under your feet for a testimony against them" (Mark 6: 11).

The significant thing is that the messengers are to be prepared for rejection of their message and are not to be disheartened by it. There is a limit to their responsibility. They are to recognize that do what they will, there will be some one who will present a stone wall of indifference and hostility to their appeal. The correct way to meet impenetrable prejudice is to make the warning as solemn as possible. By action as well as by word, they are to give expression to it. It meant, "We have done our best for you." It also meant, "Your blood be on your own head."

This is a prescription to be used only with extreme caution. Our Lord presented the other side when He said, "How often would I have gathered you . . . but ye would not." Not one but repeated efforts are to be made to win the indifferent. Yet there is instruction here for the modern witness for Christ. We too often fumble with our failures. We have not a clear conscience about them. We are not sure whether the fault is our own or that of our hearers. We must try and clear up the situation, and give warning as well as make appeal. The one word which may awaken some people is to say, "I give you up."

FEAR NOT

Like the refrain of a song, this exhortation is repeated again and again (Matt. 10:26, 28, 31). Going forth, the disciples would find themselves hated for the Master's sake, and in the future ministry they would be brought face to face with death because of their allegiance to Him. But they were not to fear those who could only kill the body. They would be as sheep in the midst of wolves, but their perils were not to create fear. With them would be the One who had said that He would never leave them. As their Provider, He said, *Care* not — and as their Protector, *Fear not* (Matt. 10: 16-18; Heb. 13:6). Amid all dangers encountered, two virtues would be specially needful, namely, *caution* and *fidelity*. They must be "wise as serpents and harmless as doves" (Matt. 10:16). No two creatures are more unlike — the serpent is the symbol of cunning, and the dove represents simplicity. At once the disciples must be as serpents in cautiousness, and as doves in simplicity of aim and purity of heart. They would find themselves among wolves in civil and ecclesiastical tribunals, where craft was met with craft, but they were to meet all malicious charges with the simplicity of doves. They were not to manifest any rebellious spirit, but believe that God was working out His purpose even in their tribulations. Even if they died for the faith, there was the crown of life beyond (Matt. 10:32, 33; Rev. 2:10).

In his most fascinating volume, *My History of Warfare*, Field Marshall Montgomery describes Lord Nelson of Trafalgar. He says that the famous admiral's amazing influence over his fellow man was perhaps as much responsible for his unique record of success in battle as were his brilliant actions:

> The moment he stepped on board ship some magnetic power radiated from him, a motley collection of men with no common purpose became a band of brothers, and this power radiated far beyond his own ship — being felt in every ship in the fleets he commanded.

Was it not something like this that bound a motley company of men to Christ and to each other? The impact of His personality upon the apostles during the time they traveled together, and more so after His resurrection, made them all that they were. "Having loved his own, he loved them unto the end"; and with a united voice they could say, "Thou knowest all things, thou knowest that we love thee." Theirs was not a blind allegiance. In Him, they had found their Messiah, and they had become His slaves through love. His demands were explicit and exacting, but devotion to Him constrained the disciples to follow Him even to martyrdom for His dear sake. Bearded and sandal-shod, and dressed in coarsely woven robes and flowing headdresses as seen among men in the Galilean hills today, those men of Galilee looked no different from other men. These were ordinary mortals who

shared the intimacy of our Lord's daily life; and it was their warm, intensely human presence that often consoled His heart and led Him to call them, not "servants" but *friends*.

Countless thousands have climbed the steep ascent to heaven through peril, toil and pain, but the first place of honor in the church must surely be assigned to those chosen companions of Jesus whom He sent forth to preach. And does not their faithful devotion to, and dependence upon, the Lord seem to say to our hearts —

CARE NOT

Cast care aside, lean on thy Guide;
His boundless mercy will provide;
Trust, and thy trusting soul shall prove
Christ is its life, and Christ its love.

FEAR NOT

Faint not nor fear, His arms are near,
He changeth not, and thou art dear;
Only believe, and thou shalt see
That Christ is all in all to thee.

They followed that they might share Christ's miraculous ministry

Mark goes on to tell us that Jesus chose the twelve not only to preach but to have "power to heal sickness" and "to cast out devils." They had no power of their own to perform miracles (Mark 6:7). "All power is mine," said Jesus, yet when He added, "Go ye," they went with delegated power. In the commission was their enablement. "Faithful is he that calleth you, who also will do it." Those who performed miracles in Christ's name disclaimed any inherent power of their own to heal and exorcise. Faith in His power was most necessary to perform what was impossible from the human standpoint (Matt. 17:20; 21:21; Mark 6:7; John 14:21; Acts 3:12, 16; 6:8). They received a new endowment of power. The expulsion of "unclean spirits" is the typical miracle with Mark, and is specified here. This communicableness of our Lord's own power may be termed His greatest miracle. "That He could, by His mere will, endow a dozen men with such power, is more, if degree come into view at all, than that He Himself should exercise it."

The day of such special endowment is past. But the principle remains. It is useless for a preacher to go forth in his own strength. Unless he depends upon special succor, which the ordinary lecturer or political agent cannot claim, he will fail. It is on the magnetism of Christ, somehow mediated through him though only a weak disciple, that he must depend.

Confirmation of the commission to relieve the physically and mentally distressed was given by Christ before His ascension (Mark 16:17, 18). Paul includes the gift of healing among divine gifts to the church. As the miracles of Christ witnessed to, and established His deity, so the miraculous ministry of the first disciples confirmed their apostleship. For a thorough treatment of apostolic miracles the reader is referred to *All the Miracles of the Bible*.* A fact that must not be lost sight of is that no human agent can act of himself. Power to perform acts of healing can only be delegated by God. Agents He uses are but channels of divine operation (Acts 2:43; II Cor. 12:12). After the ascension, the Holy Spirit was to be the source of their power (John 16:13; Acts 1:8).

"They went out and preached that men should repent. And they cast out many demons and anointed with oil many that were sick, and healed them" (Mark 6:12, 13). Preaching and healing went hand-in-hand as they do in the most effective missionary work today. The burden of their

* Published by Zondervan in 1961.

message was the necessity of repentance if their hearers were to partake in the new era. There is no estimate of the results of this part of their work. But it is well to remember the subject of their preaching when we, too, are looking forward to a new era. Reconstruction is useless without repentance. A new attitude to life is needed, as well as a reshaping of the fabric of society, if there is to be true progress.

It is interesting to discover the apostles' use of a customary medical method of that day in the form of anointing with oil, when they performed their miracles of healing. The only other reference to this method is in James 5:14. It has been stereotyped by some as a ritual enjoined by our Lord in the treatment of the sick. But there is no trace of this in the New Testament. Both references are interpreted better by looking on it simply as an approval of any means at hand to give bodily relief. This does not invalidate the prayer of faith. Rather, it should make us free to pray more confidently. The rule is always the same, "Exhaust the human possibilities of a situation and then trust God for what is humanly impossible."

The upshot of this experience was a great encouragement of the apostles and the extension of the message over a still wider area. The first lesson in the arduous career of the apostolate had been taught and learned. The first step toward independent action had been taken without stumbling. The disciples were on the way to becoming apostles.

They followed that they might perpetuate His cause

Christ chose the twelve not only that they might be His companions as He tarried on the earth, but also to continue His work and influence after His ascension. Requiring their help in His public ministry, Jesus yet had His mind set on their future ministry after His own voice was silent. He had forethought for the continuance of His plan after He was gone. Christ knew from His earliest years that He was born to die as the Redeemer, and the shadow of the cross was ever over Him. Thus, ever conscious of the bitter end awaiting Him, He took measures to perpetuate and expand the task He came into the world to accomplish. "Most men seek to perpetuate their influence by putting truth they have to teach into writing," says J. D. Jones. And so —

Plato wrote his *Republic,*
Aristotle his *Philosophy,*
Dante his great poem on *Purgatory, Hell, Paradise,*
Shakespeare his *King Lear* and *Hamlet,*
Milton his *Paradise Lost.*

But He who inspired the greatest literary masterpieces of the world, never wrote a line, except the unknown word He wrote in the sand, which was easily erased. What books He could have written! They would have had a marvellous power over the minds and lives of men all down the ages, and they would have remained as a perpetual evidence of His philosophy!

Men, and not *manuscripts,* however, were His chosen avenues of a ceaseless ministry. This is why, although He died, He yet speaks through the lives and literature of the apostles. Christ's greatest gift to the world was not only what He said, but what He was and did. Christianity is *Christ* — not a religion but a Redeemer, not a precept but a Person. It was thus that He brought to bear all that He was in Himself upon the twelve He chose, and through them

He saw the fruit of His selection of them and was satisfied. The propagation of His Gospel depended upon them, and they became the beginnings of the Christian Church, which still continues to develop.

The apostles had heard Jesus say, "I will build my church"; and Paul affirmed that James, Peter and John were pillars of this spiritual edifice (Gal. 2:9); and also that all the apostles were the foundation of this household of God of which Christ was the chief cornerstone (Eph. 2:19-22). The summary of A. B. Bruce is most apt at this point:

> Among the noblest in the supernal commonwealth will be the twelve men who cast in their lot with the Son of Man, and were His companions in His wanderings and temptations. There will probably be many in Heaven greater than they in intellect and otherwise; but the greatest will most readily concede to them the place of honour as the first believers in Jesus, the personal friends of the Man of Sorrows, and the chosen vessels who carried His name to the nations, and in a sense opened the kingdom of heaven to all who believe.

The Apostle John recognized the superior rank of the twelve in the eternal kingdom when, in describing the Holy City of God, he said that "the walls of the city had twelve foundations, and in them the names of the twelve apostles of the Lamb" (Rev. 21:14). Dr. S. D. Gordon in *Quiet Talks on Service* has a most vivid description of Jesus walking down the golden street one day, arm in arm with the Archangel Gabriel, talking intently, earnestly. Gabriel is saying:

> "Master, you died for the whole world down there, did you not?"
> "Yes."
> "You must have suffered much," with an earnest look into that great

face with its unremovable marks.

"Yes," again comes the answer in a wondrous voice, very quiet, but strangely full of deepest feeling.

"And do they all know about it?"

"Oh, no! Only a few in Palestine know about it so far."

"Well, Master, what's your plan? What have you done about telling the world that you died for, that you *have* died for them? What's your plan?"

"Well," the Master is supposed to answer, "I asked Peter, and James and John, and little Scotch Andrew, and some more of them down there, just to make it the business of their lives to tell others, and the others others, and yet others, and still others, until the last man in the farthest circle has heard the story and has felt the thrilling and thralling power of it."

Gordon goes on to say that Gabriel knows us folk down here pretty well. He has had more than one contact with earth. He knows the kind of stuff in us. And he is supposed to answer, with a sort of hesitating reluctance, as though he could see difficulties in the working of the plan.

"Yes — but suppose Peter fails. Suppose after a while John simply *does not* tell others. Suppose their descendants, their successors away off in the first edge of the twentieth get *so busy about things* — some of them proper enough, some may be not quite so proper — that *they do not* tell others — *what then?*"

And Gabriel's eyes are big with the intenseness of his thought, for he is thinking of — the *suffering,* and he is thinking too of the difference to the man who hasn't been told — "what then." Back comes that quiet wondrous voice of Jesus —

"Gabriel, *I haven't made any other plans — I'm counting on them.*"

True, this is a bit of Gordon's graphic dialogue for which he was noted, but the idea expressed is correct. Jesus chose the twelve to tell others. He had no other plan, and counted upon them to carry out the purpose for which He selected them. The genius of such a plan could not, and did not fail. As the Master had won the disciples, out they went to win others with the same exquisite tact in winning them as He had. Succeeding generations of disciples, inspired by the apostolic soul-winning as found in the Acts, were unfailing in their part of the divine plan of reaching others. The question is, "Are we — you and I — in our age, in fellowship with His plan, or are we failing Him?"

II

The Privileged Preparation of the Twelve

Of all men of any age trained for the ministry of the Word, none have been so privileged in their preparation for the highest vocation on earth as the apostolic twelve who graduated from the school of Christ. For their future career, the most important part of their education consisted in the simple fact that they had spent three years with such a one as Jesus, the Teacher sent from God (John 3:2). We may deem the instruction communicated by Him to His disciples as being somewhat unsystematic and occasional, therein differing utterly from the ordered and close teaching given in theological schools. But, as we are to see, in the course of the time during which He and they were together, tuition in a variety of subjects of cardinal importance and of priceless worth was given by the Divine Teacher to His pupils.

1. The Teacher Who Taught Them

In school and college days, the formative minds of students are greatly influenced, one way or the other, by the caliber of their instructors. There are teachers who, because of their unique personality and profound knowledge and unusual form of instruction, not only cast a spell over those they teach, but shape their lives for all time. It was thus with the small group of young men from Galilee who had gathered around Him who had said to them, *Learn of Me!* And in His Academy of Love, He prepared His chosen ones for their life's mission by the way He lived, by the works He did, and by the words He spoke. If they were to go out and "teach all nations," (Matt. 28:19), then how necessary it was for them to have an Instructor beyond compare.

The record of the apostolic labors of the twelve proves how effective the education of their hearts and minds had been. Looking back upon their days in school with Christ their united acclaim was, "Who teacheth like him?" (Job 36:22). They had been taken from different ranks, and had followed different occupations. No two of the twelve were alike. Each differed from the other in tastes, prejudices, mentality, personality, and outlook. Yet the Teacher drew each of the twelve into fellowship with Himself, and when, after some three years He left them, they kept together. While they were with Him each received the individual tuition and training fitting him for his work.

Of course, each of them must undergo training and discipline, but the Teacher, knowing the abilities and peculiarities of each scholar, adapted His instruction accordingly. Each had his own weakness and infirmity, and the gospels reveal how Jesus varied His method of approach to aid the individual. To outsiders it might have appeared impossible for Him to teach the kind of men He chose about the spiritual nature of His kingdom and then to fashion them as preachers of that kingdom, but how wonderfully they developed through sitting at His feet!

It was no easy task to equip the twelve. The most perceptive among them failed to grasp the significance of His mission until after His resurrection. They were slow of heart to believe all the prophets had spoken of Him. It was with the feeling of disappointment any good teacher feels when his scholars fail to grasp the lessons taught, that Jesus said to those He had sought to equip, "What I do thou knowest not now; but thou shalt know hereafter." Christ had to upbraid His own for their unbelief and hardness of heart (Mark 16:14). "Are ye also yet without understanding?" (Matt. 15:16). A phrase like "they understood none of these things" implies that their prejudices had obscured from their view the great fundamental doctrine of the atonement (Luke 8:24, 25; 18:34; 24:11).

In secular biography the best is generally magnified and delinquencies either omitted or swiftly passed over, but with its biographies, the Bible is careful to tell the whole story. Thus the defects of the apostles — although they were *apostles* — are not glossed over. Their faults and petty weaknesses are recorded, and Jesus who could read them like a book, knew them incomparably better than they knew themselves. "He saw their hidden weaknesses and the incipient elements of strength," wrote J. G. Greenhough. "There was abundance of chaff with the scanty grains of wheat which would need much winnowing; but He was equal to the task. The germs of promise were there, and in time would yield the perfect fruit. He believed in the men He had chosen, and, what was more, He had absolute confidence in His own power to make them what He wished."

Although they had declared their willingness to die for their sublime Teacher they were guilty of cowardice, as Eaton Stannard Barrett implies in the lines:

"She, while apostles shrank, could dangers brave,

Last at His cross and earliest at His grave."

They had been told that they were of more value than many sparrows, and that as they had trusted their lives to His care, they were to go forth without fear, but they were guilty of doubt. Vanity and jealousy lie very near to each other, so idle disputes as to who should have the largest share in Christ's kingdom were rebuked in the discourse He gave His disciples on humility (Matt. 18:1-14). To become great in His kingdom, it was necessary to become like a little child.

Although it may seem an ungrateful task to search the records for the faults and failings of the twelve, and frankly acknowledge some of the defects of their character and conduct, yet such a painful exercise is needful even as a safeguard for ourselves. When we come to consider the apostles, individually, we hope to draw attention to the shortcomings each had. Considering them as a whole, there are at least five great defects in them as a body.

Lack of spiritual understanding

How saddened and disappointed Christ was when those whom He had chosen failed to understand the import of His parables and precepts! How unable they were to grasp the significance of Christ Himself, or His purpose, or His way of working! Think of how He tried to explain the fact of His coming suffering and death, even going into the fullest details of His betrayal, His seizure by soldiers, His trial, His judge and enemies, His death and resurrection and ascension, but His closest friends could not conceive the reality of what He said. Their own Jewish prejudices and expectations closed their eyes so that they could not see.

Defect of mutual jealousy

This vice, as cruel as the grave, frequently made its appearance. When two of the number sought future honor, the other ten were filled with indignation. Even as the bitter death of Jesus drew near, "they disputed among themselves which of them should be the greatest." How this spirit of division and sectarianism, which showed itself early in the association with Jesus, and appeared in its worst light in the fight for position, must have grieved the heart of Him who came, not to be served, but to serve, and to die as a felon on a wooden gibbet.

Lamentable lack of faith

It would seem as if this was their most conspicuous and painful lack, for often they were charged with it.
"How is it that ye have no faith?" (Mark 4:40).
"O thou of little faith!" (Matt. 14: 31).
"I spake to thy disciples, that they should cast him out and they could not" (Mark 9:18).
"O faithless generation! . . . how long shall I suffer you? Bring him unto me" (Mark 9:19).

Desertion in the hour of need

There are two opposite phrases, which, when brought together, throw light upon the defect of the apostles' desertion in the terrible hour when Christ needed their companionship most. At the beginning of their discipleship we read that they "forsook all, and followed him" (Luke 5:11). When a noble sacrifice that was! But now as He emerges from the agony of Gethsemane He is taken captive, and "they *all* forsook Him, and fled" (Mark 14:50) — the same men in both cases! Remember these were His close friends, on whom He had relied, and with whom His cause was bound up. Two of them on the way to Emmaus said, "We trusted that it had been he" — but trust fled when they saw the swords and staves drawn against Him. Faith vanished at the prospect of death.

Helplessness in the face of challenge

The weakness and helplessness they showed in view of the glorious, future task of making Christ known, and for which He had striven so hard to prepare them, are also apparent. As Dr. Elder Cumming expresses it —

Take them as they were up till the day of the Crucifixion; take them even farther on, up till the meeting at the Lake of Galilee, when Jesus appeared on the shore at early morning; and say, "What hope of the world was there from these twelve men? Hope of making Christ known as the Saviour of all nations? Hope of overcoming the enemies which opposed; such as the heathen Empire of Rome, with all its force?" These men knew so little, who could not understand, who were so much concerned as to their own advancement and place; the fearful men who could not face a difficulty; the men who fled from twenty soldiers; the men who could hardly speak a word in public: in a word, the Apostles as we know, from Peter to Judas — what hope is there for a blessed and world-wide Gospel?

But, as we shall presently see, the miracle happened, and the poor material in the hand of the Divine Builder Himself became a powerful weapon for the pulling down of strongholds. By His Spirit, He took the things which are not, to bring to nought the things which are.

But from the crude and rude stage of their formation as Christ called the twelve to follow and learn of

Him, He persevered with His disciples and the tuition of them until, as if touched by a sculptor's chisel, He brought the angel out of the marble. He had set Himself to transform and re-create these men, and, apart from Judas, His purpose did not fail (John 17:12). Being the Teacher He was, He set out to reproduce Himself in their minds and lives, and triumph over their unfitness in spite of themselves. Such a determination was pursued without wavering or doubt, and He won through, saying to them, "Ye are the salt of the earth; ye are the light of the world."

Having yielded fully to His fashioning Spirit and passed through His school, His elect scholars went out to preach and teach His Gospel in great power. One of the marvelous miracles of Jesus was the way He transformed the son of thunder into the apostle of love. He did not make one prodigy, but raised the intellectual, moral, and spiritual tone of the apostles, and all this made for the uniqueness and originality of His selection and schooling of the twelve.

2. *The Lessons They Learned*

To understand the particular tuition the twelve were to receive, it is essential to examine their background. The rulers, elders, and people of Jerusalem spoke of Peter and John as being "unlearned and ignorant men," or, as Phillips' translation has it "who were obviously uneducated and untrained men" (Acts 4:13). We must not adduce from this observation that they were *ignoramuses.* "Unlearned," seems to imply that they were unacquainted with the rabbinical school of thought. "Ignorant" meant, primarily, a private person in contrast with a state official, hence, a person without professional knowledge, unskilled, uneducated — a lay-man in contrast to a skilled religious official. Thus, for the most part, the twelve were simple, rough, untutored fishermen with little knowledge of life beyond the limits of a small province in Palestine, under the heel of Rome.

Yet, as Jews, these men were not without general knowledge, for from what we read of Jewish life at their time, there was spread over the land a good system of local schools to which they would go. Almost every synagogue became a school for children, with the rabbi of the synagogue as its teacher. Every Jewish child was taught first at home, like Timothy, who from his very early childhood knew the Scriptures (II Tim. 3:15). Then, at the age of six every child went to school. Josephus, the great Jewish historian, tells us that such a thing as a child untaught was almost unknown. The Scriptures were the chief subject taught, which was why the disciples could understand the Master's allusions to Old Testament history. They had no New Testament — theirs was to be the privilege of writing it. So, although unlearned in other directions, they were *not* ignorant as we understand the term. At the call of Christ they made a great sacrifice and left home, family, friends, business, and income to be educated in the great Teacher's traveling college and five words tell us what made their training the best the world could give: "*They had been with Jesus*" (Acts 4:13).

How important were the lessons they learned from the life, example, and teaching of Jesus! How His matchless wisdom strengthened their belief in Him as the Messiah they had read about in their ancient Scriptures! How their faith was confirmed by the miracles He performed! Following Him day by day; listening to His marvelous discourses and parables;

seeing Him manifest His power as the Son of God as He healed the sick, cast out demons, raised the dead; living with Him as a family and able to ask what questions they pleased, all added to their spiritual and moral equipment for the great services they were to render.

Think of how the character of Jesus contributed to the formation of their own character! They discovered that all His words were wise and truthful; that He was never angry except when He was righteously indignant over wrong and fraud; that He never secured the pleasant things of the world for Himself; that He never spared Himself fatigue and trouble when the needy sought His help; that He never saved Himself but went about continually doing good; that He never sinned; that He was indeed "the Christ, the Son of the living God." How could they be with a Man like Him without learning in some degree to be like Him? This was indeed the most important part of their training. It was their peculiar privilege, to hear His words and to see His works during the period of their discipleship.

As the result of the Master's personal and patient instruction, and the power, enlightenment and sanctification of the Holy Spirit, the apostles became "enlightened in mind, endowed with a charity wide enough to embrace all mankind, having their consciences tremulously sensitive to all claims of duty. Yet delivered from the superstitious scruples, emancipated from the fetters of custom, tradition, and the commandments of men, and possessing tempers purged from pride, self-will, impatience, angry passions, vindictiveness, and implacability." They were slow to learn of Him, but learn they did, and became under Him the founders of a new society, the Church of the Living God.

Among some of the areas of truth in which they received lessons from their Teacher are the following:

The nature of the divine kingdom

The privilege and power of prayer

The influence of religious liberty

The force of His own Person and claims

The doctrine of His death and resurrection

The truth of His ascension and exaltation

The mission of the divine Comforter

The second advent and millennial reign of Christ

The future tragedy and triumph of the Jewish nation

The necessity and virtue of self-sacrifice

The importance of rectitude in their private and religious life

The attractiveness of humility, and kindred virtues.

A study of the Acts, the Epistles, and the book of Revelation reveals how the above lessons were not lost on the apostles, for the Holy Spirit took of these sublime truths and opened to their minds the inner significance of the things of Christ, and inspired them to record the unfoldings of the Spirit for our enlightenment, edification and encouragement.

3. *The Enduement They Experienced*

What happened at Pentecost constituted a dynamic crisis in the lives of the apostles! They were never the same after it. Through the effusion of the Holy Spirit they were transformed from a group of timid, discouraged and frightened men into a band of fearless and daring men of faith and power. With Christ no longer *with* them in person, they had to have His working *in* them (Phil. 2:13). Thus they waited for the "promise of the Father." The essence of Pentecost was the perpetual presence of God the Holy Spirit as the Worker, in and through them, as they gave evidence of all they had seen and heard of Christ. For the needful testimony to Him they must experience the fullness of His Spirit, and He came upon them (John 16:8). The test was to be, not their wisdom, eloquence, or courage, but whether they were infilled with the Spirit. That they were is evidenced by the fact that the Acts is heavy with the records of the early triumphs of Christianity — of the triumphs of that dispensation which is distinguished as the ministration of the Spirit (II Cor. 3:8).

After the descent of the Spirit on that historic day, the apostles were no longer deluded by the hope of a temporal kingdom (Luke 24:51-53; Acts 1:6). Out they went to establish the spiritual kingdom receiving its birth on the day of Pentecost, and thereafter bear the fruit of the Spirit. Such fruit is seen in —

Their liberty from the fear of man, Acts 2:14.

Their unity in the Spirit, Acts 4:32.

Their diligence in spreading the Gospel, Acts 8:5.

Their Christian liberality, Acts 2: 45; 4:34.

Their spirit of prayer and intercession, Acts 2:42.

Their love for God's ordinances, Acts 3:1.

Their joy amid severest sufferings, Acts 7:55; 16:25.

In Volume 2 of my set on *The Man Who Changed the World,* I emphasize the rich legacies Christ left His own. A full exposition of these legacies, which the saints of succeeding ages have shared, are given as —

The legacy of His presence,

The legacy of His precepts,

The legacy of His power,

The legacy of His peace,

The legacy of His predominance.

Luke, the writer who gave us The Acts, tells us of a former treatise he had sent to his friend, Theophilus, about "all that Jesus *began* to do and teach" (Luke 1:3; Acts 1:1); and the thrilling story he goes on to tell in The Acts is a continuation of all Jesus began to do and teach, which ministry, beginning at Jerusalem, then going on to Judaea and Samaria, reached out to the uttermost parts of the earth — and still does! Two aspects of the enduement for the apostolic ministry of furthering the cause of Christ can be noted:

Theirs was a promised empowerment

After an intense forty-day Bible course conducted by the risen Master Himself on the kind of Gospel the apostles were to preach (Luke 24:27, 44; Acts 1:2, 3), the promise was given them that after the ascension they would be endued with power from on high (Luke 24:49; Acts 1:4, 5, 8). Accordingly they waited at Jerusalem for the promised Holy Spirit, spending the time in prayer and supplication, thereby creating a spiritual atmosphere within their hearts for the reception of the Coming One. There are at least two features to be distinguished here:

1. The coming of the Spirit was not dependent upon the tarrying and praying of the 120 gathered in the upper chamber. Both the Father and the Son had promised the effusion of the Spirit, and at the precise moment He came to those who were of one accord in one place (2:1). And He has remained in the world since He was sent.

He *has* come! We often pray most earnestly, "O Lord, send Thy Spirit!" and the Lord understands our yearning for spiritual quickening. But the Spirit was sent to the world over 1900 years ago, and longs to manifest His power again in and through those who have been regenerated by Him. All saints have the Spirit: "If any man have not the Spirit of Christ, he is none of his." We possess the Spirit then. The question is, does He possess us? Within our hearts is the promised Spirit as a well of living water, but is He welling up within us and then flowing out of us to refresh the arid wilderness around? (John 7:37-39). As the result of Pentecost the apostles became channels of blessing to Jew and Gentile alike.

2. The further thought is that we must never divorce the promised power from the Promiser Himself. The power the apostles were to receive was not *something* but SOMEONE. "Ye shall receive *power . . . the Holy Spirit* coming upon you." Power, then, is the Person, or the manifestation of His Presence. The cry for "power," as if it is some kind of energy we can possess in varying quantities, is to be deprecated. Any miraculous ministry is but the Spirit of God revealing Himself through the channels He can use. "I . . . by the Spirit of God" (Matt. 12:28; Acts 3:12). The mere shadow of Peter had no power to heal. The apostle's hands and presence were the media of the Spirit's demonstration of power over sickness and demon-possession (Acts 5:12-16).

Theirs was a pentecost experience.

The day selected for the fulfillment of the divine promise was one of the yearly feasts prescribed by the Mosaic Law (Lev. 23:15, 16). *Pentecost,* as a word, means, "Fiftieth," that is, the feast of the fiftieth day after the 16th of Nisan. This Feast of Weeks (Ex. 34:22; Deut. 16:10), celebrated at the end of the Seven Weeks, occurred at the completion of the harvest, and was therefore sometimes called "The Feast of Harvest" (Ex. 23:16). *The Day of the First Fruits* (Num. 28:26), was associated with the distinctive rite of the two loaves (Lev. 23:17). Jewish tradition affirms that Pentecost was the very day the Law was given to Moses on Mount Sinai. If the *Passover Feast* finds its completion in the death and resurrection of Jesus, *Pentecost* symbolizes the beginning of His harvest of souls. From that memorable day, He was to see of the travail of His soul and be satisfied.

Suddenly, from heaven, the Spirit came accompianied by sounds and signs which the ears and eyes of those assembled immediately understood. This mighty effusion that came upon the apostles and the rest of the disciples is spoken of as a "baptism" (Acts 1:5) — not a baptism *of* the Holy Spirit, a phrase the Bible never uses, but a baptism *with* the Spirit. Christ is the Baptizer with the Spirit (John 1:33). The Spirit, then, is not the Baptizer, but the element in which the disciples were baptized or immersed (just as the Israelites were all baptized unto Moses *in* the cloud and in the sea) (I Cor. 10:2).

What a mighty change Pentecost wrought! What wonderful scenes were witnessed on that historic day! Cowardice disappeared, and the holy audacity of the apostles caused those around to marvel at their boldness. From Pentecost on, the presence and presidency of the Spirit are conspicuous throughout The Acts. Unceasingly vitalized by the Spirit, the apostles became supremely successful in the divine call to witness (11:12). The Spirit made them fruitful branches of the Vine.

4. *The Magnificence of Their Ministry*.

Impelled and compelled by the Spirit, the apostles sowed the seed of the Word beside all waters. They became instant in season and out of season. They never faltered or halted in their courageous witness. They warned the enemies of the cross day and night with tears, and multitudes were saved. The dramatic story of The Acts can be told in three related lines —

The Lord Jesus going up,

The Holy Spirit coming down,

The Apostles going out — and as they went out in the name of their Risen Lord and empowered by the Spirit, great and mighty things were accomplished. They were effective because —

Theirs was a perennial evidence

At all times and in all places they were active, planting and extending the Church which Jesus had bought with His own blood, both among Jews and Gentiles. Beginning at Jerusalem, the apostles multiplied centers of Christian worship and witness until pagan Rome itself was reached and made to feel the impact of their Spirit-empowered ministry.

While this Book of Witness falls into two parts grouped around a central figure —

Peter, the Apostle to the Jews, 1-12

Paul, the Apostle to the Gentiles, 13-28 — yet there were others like Luke, James, Philip, Barnabas, Mark, and Timothy who played a vital part in the unending expansion of the Church. The diffusion of the Christian faith, characteristic of the first century, can hardly be explained except by the labors of many fiery heralds of the cross. Whether before kings, rulers, governors, or in public places or deserts, it made no differ-ence to the apostles who were bold in their witness even at the peril of courting death. Although in bonds, Paul was still an ambassador. Christianity spread like a prairie fire simply because every Christian was a witness, testifying to the grace of God (Acts 20:17-24). Consequences never concerned them. For the sake of Him who died for them they were willing to hazard their lives (15:26). Tradition has it, as we shall later see, that all the apostles suffered martyrdom. Alas! ours is a day of good news, but we hold our peace. Multitudes are rushing headlong into hell, yet we are guilty of a sinful silence.

Go through the Acts and weave together the references to the price those first disciples paid for their unashamed witness. They were effective because they scorned a persecuted existence. The fury of persecution did not cease with Paul's conversion on that Damascus road. The apostle himself had been the chief instigator of the early persecution of the church. Acting on behalf of the Sanhedrin, Paul set out to suppress the new cause even to the point of slaughter, but the Lord made the rebel a priest and a king (Acts 9). Then Paul's remarkable conversion and following mighty witness added fuel to the fire of persecution. This is why prisons and martyrdoms crowd the book of Acts. But all who suffered manifested a patient endurance in the fiery baptism the Master had promised them (Matt. 20:22-23).

Theirs was a positive evangel

The promise and appropriation of the divine enduement was for the proclamation of a divine evangel. The Spirit's power is never manifested unless the Word He inspired is preached. He always rides triumphant in His own chariot. Preachers who doubt their beliefs and believe their doubts are not those with power to turn the world upside down. With the apostles, there were no *maybes* or *perhapses,* but an authoritative declaration, a "Thus saith the Lord." They could preach the Word of God with all boldness and secure results because they believed it to be the Word of God, divinely inspired.

The leading truths they preached were the life, death and resurrection of Jesus Christ — truths the Holy Spirit ever blesses (Acts 2:23, 24, 30, 31, 36; 8:5, 32 etc.). Having witnessed Christ's death and resurrection (Acts 3:15), they could preach these realities with conviction (Acts 4:20, 33; 10:39), even though such a message was rejected by the religious leaders (Acts 4:1, 2). Wherever they went, the apostles preached this Word (Acts 8:4; 13:49). Hundreds of present-day preachers never click simply because theirs is not the blood-red message of the early church. They have reservations about the purpose of Christ's death and entertain doubts as to the fact of His physical resurrection. They cannot subscribe to the only Gospel Paul loves to preach, "Christ died for our sins according to the scriptures: and that he was buried, and that he rose again the third day according to the scriptures" (I Cor. 15:3, 4). The preaching of the cross is still the power of God unto salvation in the experience of those who believe. The apostles not only preached a crucified Christ — they lived a crucified life, hence their potent ministry. Alive to Christ, they were dead to the world: (Gal. 2:20; 6:14). When a crucified man is behind a crucified message, there are always fresh victories for the crucified, risen, and glorified Lord.

Theirs was a prayerful exercise

What a remarkable handbook on the study of *prayer* is the book of Acts! The church was born in a prayer meeting, and lived in the same atmosphere. As the disciples gave themselves to the holy exercise of intercession, marvelous things were accomplished. Gather out the references to prayer, noting divine manifestations in response to such, and you will discover how the church lived on her knees and became as terrible as an army with banners (1:14; 6:4).

Is the place where we meet for prayer ever shaken, and the presence of the Spirit experienced (4:31)? Prison cells can never hold those who prevail in intercession (12:5). A prayerless church or Christian cannot expect great things or do them. There can only be divine success in human performance when saints "pray without ceasing." Queen Mary — *Bloody Mary* they called her — is said to have feared the prayers of John Knox, the Scottish Reformer, more than an army of soldiers. Do our prayers strike terror in the caverns of hell? Content with *saying* prayers, we have forgotten how to pray in the Holy Ghost. If our sin-ridden world is to experience a gracious revival it will only be as the saints of God experience the agony of Gethsemane. It is only as Zion travails that she is able to bring forth children. We have plenty of preachers — we sadly need more pleaders, exercising the ministry of intercession as Abraham did for Sodom (Gen. 18: 23-33).

Theirs was a purifying expectancy

Those men of Galilee were present that day in the upper room when Jesus promised that He would come again, and after His ascension, they heard the two men from heaven confirm the Master's promise to return (John 14:1-3; Acts 1:10, 11). From Pentecost on, they rested on this repeated advent declaration, preached it, and labored in the light of such a blessed event (Acts 3:20, 21). Combining the Epistles, which are so full with the truth of "the blessed hope," with the Acts, we know that apostles like Peter, Paul, James, John and Jude gave prominence to the glorious appearing of Christ in their instruction of converts (I Thess. 1:9, 10). Letters to the churches they founded are heavy with "the more sure word of prophecy."

Loving the very thought of Christ's return, the apostles labored incessantly to gather in the lost. To them, the second advent was not a mere doctrine but a dynamic, compelling them to live holy lives, and also to rescue the perishing around. As with their Master before them, courage and loneliness went hand in hand as they witnessed for Him, but amid all their tears and trials there was the assuring and comforting hope of His descent to the air for their translation.

"Upheld by hope," in darkest days,
    Faith can the light descry;
The deepening glory in the East
    Proclaims deliverance nigh.

Theirs is a permanent entity.

Some men are soon forgotten. They vanish into oblivion. Like the snowflake which Robert Burns describes, they are one "moment white, then melt forever." But with others their names remain, and their continuing influence is an inspiration. Dead — yet they speak! The most ordinary of mortals, they succeeded in filling the world with their fame. Is this not so with many of the apostles? They had heard their Master say, "Because I live, ye shall live also" (John 14:19), and like Him they live on in their witness and teaching. Such was their consecrated enthusiasm that before the destruction of Jerusalem in the year A.D. 70, and within thirty years

of the death of their Lord, the apostles had preached the Gospel in Macedonia and Syria. In many regions, churches were formed almost at the same time. Rapidly the seed of the kingdom sprang up and seemed to fill the earth (Mark 16:15-20). When we come to consider the personalities of the apostles, separately, we shall indicate the records of the widespread activities as cited by tradition and legend.

Without doubt, they exerted a tremendous sovereign influence in their lifetime, but this did not end with their death. They continue to exercise an extensive sway over the lives of multitudes. "Their word not only was, *but still is, law;* their example has ever been regarded as binding on all ages." From their gospels and epistles, the inspired expositions of their Master's rich sayings, the Church derived the system of doctrine she embodied in her creed. As further expressed by A. B. Bruce, "The fishermen of Galilee did become fishers of men on a most extensive scale, and, by the help of God, gathered many souls into the Church of such as should be saved. In a sense they are casting their nets into the sea of the world still, and, by their testimony to Jesus in Gospel and Epistle, are bringing multitudes to become disciples of Him among whose first followers they had the happiness to be numbered."

They were obscure and average persons until Jesus called and commissioned them. He it was who breathed on the apostles and made many of them illustrious for all time. As Whittier expressed it —

They touched His garment's fold, and
    soon
The Heavenly Alchemist transformed
    their very dust to gold.

Since they lived their dynamic life, posterity has given several of the apostles abiding renown. Colleges and cities have been named after them. Cathedrals and churches have borne their names. Ships, hospitals, orphanages, and children have been called after them. Think of how we still use their names in family life! In 1950 Elsdon C. Smith wrote a fascinating book bearing the title, *The Story of Our Names,* in which he gives carefully compiled lists of the most common names of males and females in America *only,* at that time. Among those early Christians who still live on in their names others bear, we have the following —

Name	Estimated Number
John	5,837,000
James	2,998,000
Thomas	1,910,000
Paul	361,000
Andrew	342,000
Peter	334,000
Philip	298,000
Stephen	273,000
Nathaniel	180,000
Matthew	105,000
Timothy	83,000

Multiply these apostolic names carried by Americans in one decade by those in all decades, not only in the United States, but the world over, then you have overwhelming evidence of the continuing influence of those disciples who bore and honored these names in the first century. Their sway and names remain. *Matthew* lives on, not only in his name, and in the gospel bearing it, but also in the heart-moving *Passion* which the composer dedicated to the memory of the apostle. Further, some of the greatest pieces of architecture such as St. Paul's Cathedral, London, have been dedicated to them, and some of the greatest masterpieces of painting, such as *The Last Supper,* by Leonardo da Vinci, have represented their faces. Millions of people in the Roman Catholic Church have prayed superstitiously to some of the apostles who became canonized as *Saints.* As for books about them and their labors, fictional and otherwise, the number is colossal. One thinks of the gripping novel on Peter, by Lloyd C. Douglas, *The Big Fisherman.* The crowns of immortality truly belong to those first missionaries, sent forth by Christ into all the world. We are indebted to John Boyle O'Reilly for the verse:

Great men grow greater by the lapse
    of time;
  We know those least whom we have
    seen the latest;
And they, 'mongst those whose names
    have grown sublime,
  Who worked for human liberty are
    greatest.

III

The Particular Personalities of All Named Apostles

I. THE ORIGINAL APOSTLES — THE TWELVE

Those whom the New Testament names *apostles* deserve the prayerful and particular attention of all lovers of the Word, seeing they have filled such a large place in Christian thought, and have had considerable space assigned to them in Christian literature. The great Greek poet wrote of his favorite hero *Achilles*, "He alone is the living Man, and all the rest are shades." Such adulation is blessedly true of the Christ of the gospel story. Yet though His is the Life of lives, He needed the "shades," hidden as they were in the majesty of His presence. Before the twelve became *apostles* there was nothing particularly attractive about them. They would be passed by in a crowd without bearing one distinguished feature. But after meeting Christ, they had more light than shade. As J. S. Greenhough so forcefully put it:

> There is now a charm about their honesty, simplicity, and emotional fervour; they are men in whom the child is not dead, and in whom the Divine was awakened. They have a great faculty or capacity for wonder, love, reverence, and awe. They are sweetly, pitiably, beautifully, and thoroughly human, appealing to us through every human chord in ourselves. Their plain, unexpressive faces begin to light up as we follow them into intelligence and eloquent meaning, and we learn that in calling them, as in everything else, Jesus had done the things well.

There is so much more that the New Testament does not tell us about the apostles. We would like to know: What about their wives and families? Peter is the only one referred to as having a wife, yet John must have had a home, otherwise Christ would not have urged him to care for His distressed mother. We would like to know more of their previous history and of their experiences after Pentecost. But all we have at the best are a few fragmentary details. A characteristic of the Bible is that it offers no complete biographies. There is a blank of almost thirty years in the life of Christ, except the one brief glimpse we see of Him when He was twelve years old. All we have of Him in the gospels is the beginning of His life and His ministry during the last three years of it.

Today a best-seller in biographical literature is a story written for a morbid or idly curious public who have an unhealthy interest in the vices, as well as the virtues of characters portrayed. But the writers of the gospels were not afflicted with "the biographic mania" as Bruce expresses it. There is no trace of this fond, idolatrous minuteness in the evangelic histories, for their writers did not set out to make the *apostles* their theme. Christ was their Hero, and their sole desire was to tell what they knew of Him. "They gazed stedfastly at the Sun of Righteousness, and in His effulgence they lost sight of the attendant stars. Whether they were stars of the first magnitude, or the second, or the third made little difference."

While it is true concerning the apostles, that the information we have

44

of them is somewhat meager, and, in some cases amounts to little more than nothing, yet from the few strokes we have we can build up the figures from inference and imagination. A few salient features, or incidents, or sayings give us an insight into their characters and dispositions. The Bible never lends itself to gratify a curiosity which serves no moral and spiritual purpose. Nearly all we are told about the men Jesus chose comes out incidentally in their more direct endeavor to present to us the One they loved. In the cameos that follow we hope to show that in the twelve He chose, we have a biography of humanity — mirrors of our own tragedies, tears, trials, temptations, and triumphs.

Before considering the twelve separately, and in *alphabetical* order, certain facts about them as a whole can be classified.

As to their relations

Simon Peter and Andrew were sons of Jonas, or John (John 1:42; 21:15, R.V.).

James and John were sons of Zebedee and Salome (Matt. 20:20; 27:56; Mark 15:40; 16:1).

Matthew, originally Levi, was the son of Alphaeus (Mark 2:14).

James the Less is also called the son of Alphaeus, so he and Matthew were probably brothers. From John 19:25 and Mark 15:40 it would seem that Mary, the wife of Clopas (not Cleopas, Luke 24:18), was the mother of James the Less, so that Clopas was Alphaeus.

Jude was not the brother of James, as the A.V. has it, but the son of another James (Luke 6:16, R.V.).

Judas was the son of Simon (John 6:71; 13:26). In these two references, the word *Iscariot* is attached to Simon and not to Judas, implying that father

and son had the same name because they came from Kerioth, in Judea.

As to their dwelling places

Peter, Andrew, James, John and Philip lived at Bethsaida (Mark 1:16-24; John 1:44; 12:21).

The first four of these later lived in Capernaum (Mark 1:21, 29).

John lived on in Jerusalem and then in Ephesus (Acts 3:1; 15:6; Gal. 2:1, 9).

Matthew belonged to Bethsaida Mark 2:1, 14).

Bartholomew, who is Nathanael, lived at Cana of Galilee (John 21:2).

Thomas, James the Less, Jude, and Simon the Zealot lived in Galilee.

Judas Iscariot was the only Judean among the apostles.

As to their trades

Peter, Andrew, James and John, were fishermen (Mark 1:16, 19).

Matthew had been a tax collector (Matt. 9:9).

We are not told the occupations of the other seven.

As to their connections

It would seem that many of the twelve were not only related to one another but to Christ, the Man of Galilee.

Simon and Andrew were brothers, and so were James and John, as well as James the Less and Matthew.

Philip and Bartholomew may have been brothers. As Andrew led his brother to Christ it is likely that Philip led his brother to Him (John 1:40-45).

James and John were cousins of Jesus, that is, if Salome the wife of Zebedee was the sister of Mary the Virgin (John 19:25).

As to their literature

Matthew wrote the gospel bearing his name.

Peter wrote two epistles and probably inspired Mark.

John wrote the fourth gospel, three epistles and Revelation.

Jude wrote a brief epistle.

Thus nine of the twenty-seven books of the New Testament or one third of the whole are the work of apostles. Out of the twenty-one epistles, Paul the apostle wrote fourteen, if we include Hebrews.

As legend and tradition have much to say about the lives and labors of the apostles, as well as of the way they died for Christ, we thought it might be better to gather such interesting material together into one section, as we have done in a following chapter. What we are presently attempting is a profile of each apostle from material found in the inspired New Testament. For added material, the reader is urged to consult the author's work, *All the Men of the Bible,* published by Zondervan.

ANDREW

THE APOSTLE WHO SHARED CHRIST PERSONALLY

Have you ever tried to imagine the gratitude of Andrew's heart and the glow on his face when, at Pentecost, he stood at his brother's side, and heard him charge the crowd before him with the crime of history, and then witnessed the mighty effect of such Holy Ghost preaching as thousands turned to Christ in penitence? I can hear Andrew say within himself as he gazed upon a sea of upturned faces listening to Peter's Pentecostal sermon with rapt attention: "Peter, my dear brother, how thrilled I am that I led you to Christ that day almost three years ago! Little did I realize then how wonderfully God was going to use you. Bless Him, for constraining me to urge you to accept the Messiah as I did!"

As the spiritual father of Peter, Andrew was the spiritual grandfather of the three thousand souls who, on the day of Pentecost, repented of their sins and turned to the Savior. Thus, as the founder of personal evangelism in the cause of Christ, Andrew will ever remain an inspiration to the saints as they seek to win the nearest around them for the Savior. Edward Kimball, that faithful soul-winner, little knew what great things would develop when he urged young Moody, the Boston shoe salesman, to accept Christ. How overwhelmed the Bible class teacher would have been had he known that the lad was destined to become Dwight L. Moody, the renowned evangelist who rocked two continents nearer God! It is so true in the realm of grace that mighty oaks from acorns grow. When we lead a child to Christ, we have no conception what a remarkable future that child may have.

With all the admiration Andrew had for his brother's prominence in the apostolic band, he had no aspiration whatever to become a second Peter. As with Joseph of old, he was content to ride in the second chariot, and he comes before us as the apostle happy with a second place. As a fisherman from a family of fishermen belonging to Bethsaida (John 1:14), Andrew, whose name means "manliness," was a manly man, as were the rough and hardy fishermen of his time. His brother Peter and he shared the same home until Peter married. The two worked together reaping a harvest from the sea (Matt. 4:18; Mark 1:16).

Although references to Andrew in the gospels are few indeed, what is recorded of him reveals him as a humble, unassuming, devoted and consistent disciple of Christ who enjoyed a special intimacy with the Master (Mark 13:3). In all likelihood the younger of the two, Andrew is known by the name, not of his father, but of his brother — "Andrew, Simon Peter's brother." Probably their father, John or Jonas, was dead at the time both Peter and his younger brother became disciples. John records a singular order in speaking of Bethsaida as "the city of Andrew and Peter" (John 1:44). The younger brother comes first, and the older and far more important last. Why? Because the verse speaks of the time when Jesus began His ministry — before the apostles were appointed and before Peter had come to see Him. At that time Andrew only was a disciple; the time of Peter had not yet come. But when it came to the choice of apostles, Peter heads the list, while his devoted brother comes second.

While Peter, as we shall see, figures most prominently in the gospels and the Acts, and became the leader of the apostles, we must not suffer the greater light to eclipse the lesser. In the providence of God, Andrew knew the Lord before Peter. Whom God thus honored, we must honor too. This was why, in the early church, he went by the name, "Andrew the first-called" — a reputation he shared with John to whom we are indebted for a fuller record of the circumstances under which Andrew came to know Jesus. It is also John who tells of the part Andrew took in bringing his brother, Simon, to Jesus; he also informs us that it was he who told Jesus about the lad with his loaves and fishes. John likewise is the one who tells us about the seeking Greeks, and of how Philip and Andrew introduced them to the Lord. It is from these references, as well as from further facts which Matthew and Mark give us about Andrew, that we can form our portrait of the man himself and from him learn some of the elements making for true discipleship.

1. *A Disciple of John the Baptist*

Although Andrew was one of the two first disciples of Jesus, he was a disciple of the Baptist before he became a disciple of Christ. We first meet Andrew not in Galilee, where he lived, but at Bethabara beyond Jordan, some fifty or sixty miles from his home. John the Baptist was preaching and baptizing there, and as a Jew, Andrew, with a mind immersed in Old Testament prophecies, was looking for daybreak through the gloom. Thus, with a soul awake in an age of indifference, he was deeply interested in what he had heard of a new movement down in the valley of the Jordan.

From this rugged preacher in the wilderness, Andrew, along with two other young fishermen, Simon and Philip, heard teaching far different from that of the scribes to which they were accustomed. Synagogue ministry was cold, formal and lifeless —

chiefly about the lesser things of religion. Such ceremonialism as Andrew had been taught touched no conscience, affected no heart, and left the deep need of the soul unsupplied. But here was a fearless preacher tearing to tatters the priestly marks. He was preaching the necessity of repentance with electric thrill to the religious leaders to whom holiness was an abstract term — resolvable into outward acts rather than a practical principle of conduct. Formalists and hypocrites were rebuked and as John the Baptist preached his severely searching doctrine, and told of One far greater than himself who was just about to come, young Andrew, as a seeker after truth, was aroused. "His sympathy was prophetic beyond his own knowledge, and the enthusiasm of hope possessed his soul as the *Voice* announced the good news of the coming of 'The Lamb of God'."

As John the Baptist preached repentance, he preached it with special reference to the coming of Christ, and as His forerunner he prepared His way. We can assume that after hearing John say, "I baptize with water," Andrew and his companions were baptized and became disciples of John, making his hope and expectation their own. If Andrew had not been zealous for God he would not have accepted the stern preaching of John, but as Herbert F. Stevenson expresses it in his *Galaxy of Saints,* "Andrew waited for the Messiah not vaguely and superstitiously, but actively and in living faith and was anxious to be found prepared to enter His service at His appearance." When, ultimately, Jesus came upon the scene and Andrew forsook all and followed Him, he was in no way disloyal to John the Baptist, for to this end alone he had become his disciple.

2. A Convert of the Lamb of God

The faith of instinct now opens out into the faith of experience as the memorable day comes for Andrew's first sight of the Messiah, the One of whom he had read in the ancient scroll and heard about from the Baptist's lips. Eager expectation was now to be fulfilled. "The next day John seeth Jesus coming unto him, and saith, Behold the Lamb of God, which taketh away the sin of the world. *This is he* of whom I said, After me cometh a man which is preferred before me: for he was before me." The Baptist's spiritual instinct constrained him to recognize the Man as the pre-existent One who had come as the Messiah, and the baptism with the Spirit at His immersion in Jordan was the sign to John that this was indeed the Son of God. We can safely assume that Andrew was among them who heard John's declaration of Jesus as the Lamb of God manifested to take away sin. The following day, "John stood, and two of his disciples; [one was Andrew; perhaps John, the brother of James was the other] and looking upon Jesus as he walked, he saith, Behold the Lamb of God!" (John 1: 36).

As He walked! There was a majesty about His stride, as well as His whole demeanor that singled Him out as the sacrificial Lamb the prophets of old had predicted would come. What a precious thought the phrase contains, "The two disciples heard John speak, and they followed Jesus." They had followed John, but now because of his testimony concerning the Messiah they turn from him and follow the Lamb of God. But John had no feeling of envy as he saw his disciples leave him for the One preferred before him. With true magnanimity of heart he could say, "He must increase — I must decrease." John had learned that the ascendancy of Christ meant the descendancy of self. Would that all who hear about Jesus and whose attention is drawn to Him would, like Andrew, forsake all and follow the Lamb whithersoever He goeth!

Andrew and his companion, seeing Jesus walk, followed Him, but they were not unnoticed. Jesus knew all about their expectation of His appearance, and conscious that they were following Him, He paused and said, "What seek ye?" How precious in His sight are these first steps, these first movements of the soul toward Him, the first beginning to love, trust and obey! As He never breaks the bruised reed (Isa. 42:3), Jesus dealt with those two young and weak beginners kindly, gently and encouragingly. Can we not imagine the kindness in His very look and voice as He asked, "What seek ye?", a question reminding us of that gracious encouragement which He afterwards gave to blind Bartimaeus "What wilt thou that I should do unto thee?"

The two young, enraptured hearts answered the Master's question with one of their own, "Rabbi, where dwellest thou?" Such a question was not asked out of idle curiosity, but from a desire to follow Him and learn of Him. Jesus did not turn from such a wish but immediately replied, "Come and see." They must go aside with Him and discover in secret all they sought to know. Thus they went with Him and "saw where he dwelt, and abode with him that day." What wonderful, unforgettable hours those first ones with Jesus must have been! What passed between them we are not told, but Andrew and John, who were to spend many days with Him afterward, ever remembered those first hours which marked a crisis in their spiritual history. What they learned from Jesus that first day of acquaint-

anceship convinced them that He was indeed the promised Lamb of God. From that secret, never-to-be-forgotten conversation Andrew believed, and returning home with a soul ablaze said to his friends, "We have found the Messiah!" Having found joy and peace in believing, Andrew immediately proceeded to tell others the story.

Thereafter, Andrew would date everything back to that first session with Jesus, for that was the time when his heart was strangely warmed. Andrew found the Savior, and He found His first disciple. Let it not be forgotten that Andrew had the honor of being "in Christ" before any of those who became his fellow-apostles, many of whom were to eclipse him in gifts and position. None, however, could rob Andrew of the glory of being the first to believe in Jesus.

3. *An Ardent Fisher of Souls*

If an evangelist is but a beggar telling another hungry beggar where to get bread, then without doubt, Andrew was a true evangelist, for, without delay, the first disciple became the first missionary, and the forerunner of personal evangelism. Having been won by Christ, Andrew immediately set out to win others for Him. The first recruit became the first witness. Bringing others to Jesus was characteristic of Andrew, as we are to discover. He brought his own brother to Him, then he brought the lad with his barley loaves and fishes to Jesus as He preached on the Gadarean shore, and, at the time of the Passover, he introduced the seeking Greeks to the Master. These references are sufficient to mark Andrew as a disciple absorbed in the task of sharing his great treasure with others. "Let the redeemed of the Lord say so." Having had his own load of sin taken away by the Lamb of God, Andrew felt he must declare such a Gospel to others. It was like a fire in his bones.

A further word is necessary on how this newly-made disciple became the first missionary of the faith. Burning with a desire to impart his secret to others, what better place could he find for such a purpose than his own home? Andrew could scarcely contain himself as he thought of others who looked for redemption in Israel, so he commenced his witness in the most difficult place of all. To the man out of whom Jesus had cast a legion of demons, and who wished to remain at his Deliverer's side all the time, Jesus commanded, "Go home to thy friends, and tell them what great things the Lord hath done for thee." Without being ordered, this is what Andrew did. "He findeth *first* his own brother Simon. And he brought him to Jesus." What a needy field of missionary labor the home affords if there are members of it who have never known the Savior!

Certainly Andrew's brother became a greater man, but there would have been no apostle to the Jews but for Andrew whose simple testimony at home gave Peter, the rock, the prince and primate of the twelve, to the primitive church. We never know what far-reaching results may issue from our willingness to tell a soul about Christ's redeeming love and grace. From the hour Andrew led Peter to the Savior, the two of them trod the higher path together, and entered upon a discipleship which became more precious with the passing days.

> Speak for the love of God,
> Speak for the love of man;
> The words of truth love sends abroad
> Can never be in vain.

After his discovery, Andrew did not rush into the office of a public preacher. His first testimony was to those nearest his home. Often in the warmth of a first love, and in the deep feeling that the discovery of Christ is more precious than rubies, converts feel as if they should shout the good news from the housetop for all to hear. Andrew loved his brother, Peter, and told him first, and thereafter he experienced the value of leading souls to Christ, one by one. Are you not happy because a brother, or sister, or parent told you about Jesus? Peter was to bring 3,000 to Jesus at once with that sort of gospel preaching responsible for the rapid extension of the early church. Yet notice the personal witness, as one finding Christ told his brother, friend and neighbor. Thus one illumined soul setting fire to another also helped further the cause of Christ.

4. *An Apostle of Christ*

The great day came when Jesus called Andrew from catching fish in the Sea of Galilee to be a fisher of men in the turbulent sea of the world. After his initial meeting with Christ, Andrew returned to his craft as a fisherman. About a year later as the Master was passing through Galilee, He found Andrew and Peter fishing but without much result. The miraculous draught of fishes convinced the fishermen of the deity and greatness of the Master, and there came the command to leave their nets, and no longer deal in fish, but men. Accordingly, the disciples left all and followed Him. Shortly after, Andrew, together with the rest, was called to the office and honor of the apostolate, and became one of Christ's immediate viceregents for establishing and extending the Christian church. Andrew came to learn that the service of the Master required from him the abandonment of his handicraft and home (Matt. 4:18-20; Luke 5:4-9).

Although Andrew left his calling to follow Christ in His itinerary labors, He does not call all to leave their trade and home. The majority abide in their vocation — if it is an honorable one — and their station in life furnishes them with opportunities of leading others to Christ. A fisherman can glorify God though he remains at his craft. A tradesman, receiving Christ into his life, becomes a better tradesman. If it is God's will for one to remain in an accustomed line of life, then true to Him, they find great opportunities of serving the One who saved them. There have been young men who left good positions to enter the ministry but who were misfits as pastors and were forced to return to their secular work.

Before we take up additional appearances and activities of Andrew, a further word is necessary regarding the change in the position of names as the Lord called the fishermen into His service. At the beginning Andrew's name came *first,* now Peter, his brother, comes first. "Simon Peter, and Andrew," and this is the order in which the brothers are afterward mentioned. Though Andrew knew the Lord first and told Peter of Him, it was Peter who was to have the ascendancy in apostolic lists. The one who was to become "The Apostle Extraordinary," was to write, "Love envieth not" (I Cor. 13:4), and Andrew exhibited such a virtue. Let us not feel sorry for Andrew for losing the first place. There was no pang of jealousy in his heart that from this time his more ardent and tempestuous brother was to take the lead, and on some occasions have the honor of acting as his Lord's companion when he himself was not there. A servant of Christ must never be envious because one who began the race later seems to outstrip him who started earlier. Position in His service is of His sovereign will.

The seeking Greeks

During his apostleship, Andrew does not appear as often as his more conspicuous brother, yet each time we do meet him, he is the same attractive character — approachable, kind, thoughtful, and sincere, ever bent on bringing others to the Lord of his life. When the Greeks came to Philip with the request, "Sir, we would see Jesus," it was to Andrew that Philip went for counsel (John 12:20-22). These Greeks were Gentile proselytes, that is, Jews by religion but not by birth. They were true seekers after God, and earnest inquirers, and being in Jerusalem for the Passover, they desired to see Jesus, not with the eye of the body merely, but, above all, with the eye of the spirit. They had heard that "the world had gone after Jesus," and they yearned to see and hear Him, and chose Philip as an intercessor. Philip took his brother-disciple into his counsels, and it was Andrew who went and told Jesus of the Greeks who sought Him. Partakers of the same hope in Christ, and found serving the same Master, Andrew and Philip brought to Him a request that fell on His ear like a strain of sweet music so that with abounding joy He exclaimed "Now is the hour come that the Son of Man should be glorified."

Andrew was a man who would imperil nothing by a mistake, and with a confidence in Christ perhaps stronger than Philip's and with sympathies evidently broader, Andrew immediately decided to make known the request of the Greeks, and so he introduced them to Jesus. How such an interview with the strangers enlarged the horizon of the kingdom of Christ, whose soul was stirred! Here were the firstfruits of the Gentiles, a foretaste and forerunner of the innumerable hosts of Gentiles who would constitute the fruit of His anguish. As for the apostle, he was an *embodied introduction* for he was apt at personal dealing and ever delighted at bringing others into contact with Christ.

The miraculous feeding

In connection with the miraculous feeding of the hungry crowds, Andrew again appears as a medium of blessing. The rest of the disciples were full of despair. To feed a multitude in the desert was impossible. There was no bread to be had and no money to pay for it, if it had been procurable. Shakespeare wrote of "the cleverest gods, who make them honours of men's impossibilities." Andrew's spiritual insight into his Master's ability to make possible the impossible to man, coupled with his practical mind, seized upon the little and knew that much was in it as God the Son handled it. So, seeing a lad with a few loaves and small fishes, Andrew brought him to Jesus. What the lad had would only provide a mouthful of food for a few, but what of the need of the great company?

Andrew was the personification of a committee of ways and means, and although as he looked at the scant supply of food and said of the loaves and fishes, "What are these among so many?" half in faith and half in fear, he led the lad with his small loaves to Jesus. He was rewarded as he witnessed what his Master could do with what the lad had. Andrew saw illustrated the great law of littles in the kingdom of God. Too often, the one talent is despised among men,

but Andrew had an eye that could see deeper into the possibilities of small capacity and means, and was taught the value of little things in the service of Christ. "The suggestion of Andrew in this emergency is a life lesson," says one expositor. "It lightens up obscurity, it sanctifies child-service, and encourages all to consecrate up to the measure of ability."

As for the *twelve* baskets of fragments gathered up after the crowd was satisfied, the same was a further proof to the *twelve* disciples for they saw in the miracle a parable of the beneficent spirit of their Master, and a call to each of them never to hesitate to bring his burden to His feet.

The times and seasons

The disciples were startled by the prophecy of Jesus about the utter destruction of the Temple and so Peter and James and John and Andrew asked Him privately what He actually meant by His prediction (Mark 13: 3, 4). The first three confidential apostles went with Andrew who possibly suggested that they go secretly to the Master. The solemn words of Jesus haunted their minds and they wanted to know more, and coming before Jesus, they asked Him three questions, namely:

When would Jerusalem be destroyed?

What should be the signs of His coming?

When could they expect the end of the age?

Then came that masterly, memorable Olivet discourse, which those two pairs of brothers, the four fishermen of Galilee never forgot. After that long quiet talk, Andrew and the rest had an actual, spiritual understanding of Christ's prediction. Andrew and John, from their natural bent of mind, probably saw further than Peter and

James into the answer to their questions. It does seem as if the first two lived nearer the spiritual center and grasped a wider range of thought than the last pair.

How enthralled that quartet of apostles must have been as they sat and listened to the Master's panorama of coming events! From the later writings of those who drank in that great exposition, Peter and John, we know that the impact of the exposition of prophetic truth which they heard that day on the Mount of Olives, shaped their thinking and molded their lives thereby, making them the advent heralds they became. As for Andrew, we can be confident that, as one whose ministry was personal and not public, his lips were not silent as to what he heard and learned during that wonderful teaching session.

The upper room

The next — and last — mention of Andrew in New Testament history comes after our Lord's ascension when, with the other apostles, he is found in the upper room at Jerusalem waiting "with one accord in prayer and supplication" (Acts 1:13, 14). When, on the day of Pentecost, the Holy Spirit came upon that group of waiting and praying men and women, Andrew shared in the unctions of the Holy One, and must have played his part in the remarkable expansion of the church, although we are told nothing of his apostolic labors. Strangely enough we hear no more of Andrew in the Acts, but from other sources, more or less authentic, as we shall find in our next chapter, we are given much interesting information about his ministry and death. But as he is not again referred to in Scripture, and it is with Scripture alone that we have to do

at this point, we leave Andrew where the Sacred Record does.

We take farewell of our charming, humble friend in the good company and under the happy circumstances which Luke the historian describes. There he was a faithful follower of the Lord even after He had vanished, one of the little, devoted band who believed and loved, waiting in prayer and faith for the fulfillment of the promise of the Holy Spirit which was so completely and wonderfully experienced on the historic day of Pentecost. The pleasing name of Andrew, however, will live forever. John tells us that the twelve foundations of the Eternal City bear the names of "the twelve apostles of the Lamb" (Rev. 21:14), and as Andrew was one of the most faithful of the twelve Jesus chose, his name is on one of those pillars and will be held in everlasting remembrance.

5. An Example to Emulate

Like "the Apostle and High Priest of our profession, Christ Jesus," Andrew has also left us an example that we should follow his steps. What are some of these steps we should make our own? What lesson does his life teach us? What inspiration can we gather from his witness?

The first grace Andrew manifested was that of *humility*. Later on, his esteemed brother in the flesh, and yet his spiritual son in Christ, Peter, could write about being clothed with humility, and Andrew is always seen wearing such a garment. In a special sense he is the "apostle of humble attainments," and he is a great encouragement to those of us who have but one talent. He is the example of a man who thought more of service than of reputation, more of *the work to be done* than of *the place given* to the

worker. There are far too many who
will not play in the band unless they
can have the big drum; who will not
work unless given a prominent position. James and John manifested
something of this spirit when they
wanted to be first in the kingdom. A
few of the disciples occasionally wran-
gled over who should be the greatest,
but Andrew was missing from these
angry debates; he had no craving for
a conspicuous place of honor. Andrew
anticipated the sentiment of the Christian poetess, Christina Rossetti, and
said to his Lord—

Give me the lowest place; not that I dare
Ask for that lowest place; but Thou hast
     died
That I might live and share Thy glory by
     Thy side.
Give me the lowest place; or if for me
That lowest place too high, make one
     more low
Where I may sit and see my God, and love
     Thee so.

It never concerned this man of humble mind and generous heart that men
talked more of Peter his brother, or of
James and John than they did of him.
All Andrew thought of was his *work*
for Him who had chosen him to be an
apostle. Ever concerned about his
character and devotion to Christ, he
was quite willing to leave his reputation to his Lord. Thus, Andrew will
ever remain the father and type of all
who labor quietly in humble places,
whether at home or abroad, not with
eye-service as men-pleasers, but as
servants of Christ, doing the will of
God from the heart.
     "Men heed thee, love thee, praise
          thee not.
     The Master praises—What are
          men?"

Another lesson we glean from the
record of Andrew is that of *the divine
observance of the obscure.* Jesus

taught that "the first shall be last,"
and although Andrew was His first
disciple, he never reached the first
place in prominence. He was not destined to play a conspicuous part in the
gospel drama. Somehow he was one
of the subordinate characters among
apostles, stepping on the stage here
and there to witness in a modest way,
and then vanishing into the background. The gospels do not present
Andrew as having any outstanding,
particular gifts. Evidently he was not
a preacher. Only a dozen or so words
he uttered have been preserved, and,
as far as we know he wrote no epistles
as some of his fellow-apostles did. He
seemed to have lacked the holy audacity of his brother, Peter, as well as
the literary ability of Matthew and the
inspired imagination of John. Described chiefly as the brother of Simon
Peter, he never displayed the trait of
leadership.

Peter, James, and John are referred
to as pillars of the church, but Andrew
was one of its humbler stones. He was
overshadowed by the superior energy
and skill of this apostolic triumvirate.
J. D. Jones suggests that Andrew's Old
Testament counterpart is Benaiah, one
of the heroes of the Old Dispensation.
This prototype and forerunner of Andrew was one of David's mighty men
of valor, and many of the exploits
which won for him his reputation for
daring courage have been preserved.
His chief feat and highest achievement, however, is not recorded, namely, his preservation of a sunny temper
and a generous heart in trying and
hazardous positions. "Behold, he was
more honourable than the thirty, but
he attained not unto the first three."
To Benaiah's credit let it be said
that he was never sullen or disappointed that a place in the front rank had
evaded him. In spite of his brave and

chivalrous deeds, David passed him over, but Benaiah accepted his subordinate position without a murmur. Now the place he occupied among the mighty men of valor, Andrew occupied among the twelve. While his name is always mentioned in the first group of apostles, he was certainly not on an equality with the great three, Peter and James and John. Andrew was not admitted into the intimacy of Christ as they were, or allowed to witness some of the great experiences of Christ as were they. Andrew was left behind when Christ took "the first three" to witness the raising of Jairus' daughter — His transfiguration glory on the Holy Mount — His sorrow in the garden.

We are not told why Andrew was not permitted to share the privileges of Peter, James, and John, or why he did not attain to the rank of the first three. Samuel Cox suggests that it may have been because Andrew was of a spirit less open and quick, less bold and adventurous than the other three. Well, this we do know, that it is his crowning grace and glory that he was content in being more obscure and self-effacing than some of the other apostles. He had no envy in his heart because "he attained not to the first three." He was content with his lesser place in the apostolate, and with sweetness and serenity of temper served his Master as He deemed best. Andrew was a stranger to that miserable "envy which turns pale, and sickens even if a friend prevail."

Although only a few things are recorded of Andrew, each occasion in which he appears is invested with a fadeless beauty, and to those of us who are most ordinary, he is a source of continuous encouragement. He may have been a man of slender powers, but his was a willing and devoted purpose and he used the best he had, sweetly and nobly. In *all* we have of his character and conduct, Andrew shows us the way we ought to go, and how we can serve the Lord to the limit of our limited ability. He will ever remain a *model disciple* in showing us that we are saved to save others. The greatest service we can render to those around is to confess with Andrew, "I have found the Christ."

How dependent the cause of Christ is upon those self-forgetting souls, content to occupy a small sphere, and free from self-seeking ambitions! Andrew attempted no great things, and never felt himself capable of them. Somehow he recognized the minor duties and humbler possibilities which superior minds are apt to forget. Can we say that like him we are faithful in that which is least? As we are to discover, ecclesiastical tradition has thrown a halo around the head of Andrew who represents those of simple faith, whose instincts are intuitions, and who ever remains the type of obscure yet earnest workers in Christ's vineyard. But, as Daniel McLean, in his summary of Andrew, so forcefully puts it —

Gathering together the traces of character found in Scripture we have neither the writer of an Epistle nor the founder of a Church, nor a leading figure in the Apostolic Age, but simply an earnest seeker after truth, an intimate disciple of Jesus Christ, ever anxious that others should know the spring of spiritual joy and share the blessing he so highly prized. A man of very moderate endowment, who scarcely redeemed his early promise, simple minded and sympathetic, without either dramatic power or heroic spirit, yet with that clinging confidence in Christ that brought him into that inner circle of the Twelve; a man of deep religious feeling with little power of expression, magnetic more than electric, better suited for the quiet walks of life than the stirring thoroughfares.

Andrew is the apostle of private life — the disciple of the hearth.

BARTHOLOMEW

THE APOSTLE CONSPICUOUS FOR HIS TRANSPARENCY

The familiar Latin phrase, *Multum in parvo,* means "much in little," and all we know from the Bible of Bartholomew's character is derived from seven verses John gives in the opening chapter of his gospel. Outside of these we have no further clue of the kind of man he was. Yet a great view may be seen through a window of seven panes, which is another way of saying that there can be much in little (John 1:45-51).

While the beginnings of Christianity may appear to be more or less obscure, and the first meeting of Jesus of Nazareth with five humble, obscure men, Andrew, Peter, Philip, Nathanael and another unnamed, an insignificant

event in the history of the church, yet they were to become constant attendants of Christ, and apostles of great influence. It will be noticed that mention of Nathanael is more detailed and more interesting than in the case of the other five in the first chapter of John, and it is somewhat surprising that we should be told so much in this chapter about one concerning whom we otherwise know almost nothing. Although he was a man of great moral excellence, Nathanael's biography is practically limited to this introductory chapter of John's gospel. Yet this is sufficient for a study of his character.

1. *A Man With a Double Name*

Actually, the full name of the apostle we are now considering is *Nathanael Bartholomew,* for the consensus among the best and most reliable commentators is that the *Nathanael* John mentions (1:45-51; 21:2), is the *Bartholomew* spoken of in the lists of the apostles in the Acts and the other three gospels (Matt. 10:3; Mark 3:18; Luke 6:14, and Acts 1:13). Perhaps we can try to gather the evidence for the identification of Nathanael with Bartholomew. It was common enough for a man to have more names than one — a fact the apostolic circle illustrates. Simon was surnamed Peter and Bar-jona; Matthew was called Levi; Lebbaeus, Thaddaeus, and Judas are names of one and the same person, as we shall presently discover. It is a general practice today for people to have several names. For instance, my full signature is *Herbert Henry John Lockyer.* Bar-Tolmai, then, corresponding to Bartholomew, was Nathanael's surname.

What is the significance of Tolmai or Talmai (II Sam. 13:37), or Tholmai? Among the Jews there was a sect known as *Tholmaens,* from Tholmai, a pupil of Heber, an ancient Hebrew master. It is possible that Nathanael, who was well-versed in Scripture, may have adhered to this school of thought in which much attention was given to ancient Scriptures. "The son of Tholmai" was a name not uncommon among Jews in Christ's time. *Bartholomew* is more of a patronymic than a name. Webster defines *patronymic* as "a name formed by the addition of a prefix or suffix indicating relationship to the name of one's father or paternal ancestor, as *Johnson* — son of John."

Evidence that Bartholomew and Nathanael are one and the same person may be adduced in this way. Nathanael is twice named by John, and on the first occasion John places him among the first disciples to respond to the call of Jesus. The somewhat lengthy account of his call would be altogether disproportionate unless he were afterward elevated to the apostolate. Then John mentions Nathanael as being among the seven disciples who went back to their fishing (21:2) and it is to be assumed that the word *disciples* here is equivalent to the word *apostles*, especially as Nathanael is chosen to be a personal witness of the Lord's resurrection — a great and glorious privilege!

Then through the process of elimination the cumulative evidence regarding the identification of Bartholomew with Nathanael becomes more convincing. Turning to John's account of Nathanael we find him linked with Peter, Andrew, and Philip (1:40-44), and later on with Thomas, John, James, and Peter (21:2). In these two instances six of the apostolic band are accounted for. Nathanael could not have been Matthew, who was named Levi; nor James the Less, a relative of Christ — Nathanael had not met Christ until Philip introduced him. This accounts for eight of the twelve. It was impossible for Nathanael to have been either Judas the traitor or the other Judas who asked Christ how He would appear to His friends and not to the world.

Thus we are left with Simon, the Zealot, and one other. Well, whatever Nathanael may have been, he certainly was not a revolutionist. His manifest guilelessness of character unfitted him for the forceful changes zealots set out to accomplish. One further bit of evidence remains by way of deduction. In Matthew, Mark, and Luke, where the apostles' names are given, Philip and Bartholomew are coupled together, which union is striking in the light of John's linking of Philip and Nathanael as companions. Evidently they were friends and who was more likely to become a disciple of Christ than a friend? It was the most natural thing in the world, therefore, for Philip to run to Nathanael with the startling and breath-taking news that he had found the Messiah. Who else could enter into his new-found joy as could his most intimate friend? The only conclusion, then, to be drawn from the above collation of different particulars is that Philip's companion apostle, Bartholomew, was that same Nathanael whom he had so successfully brought to Jesus on that memorable day.

As to the significance of both names, *Bartholomew,* as we have indicated, was the surname of Nathanael and means, "son of Talmai," or Tholmai. Shorter forms are in use, such as Barth, Bart, and Bat. Bartholomew was very popular in the Middle Ages when the cult of St. Bartholomew was at its height. A famous London hospital bearing this name was founded in the twelfth century, and an annual *Bartholomew Fair* was held in London to provide funds for the hospital. This *Fair*, which was the center of city life, continued for many centuries until it was suppressed in the nineteenth century. St. Bartholomew, as he became known, is said to have been martyred in Armenia, A.D. 44 (see next chapter). The Massacre of St. Bartholomew, representing the brutal slaughter of the French Huguenots in the reign of Charles IX, began on St. Bartholomew's Day, August 24, 1572, at the instigation of Catherine de Medici, the mother of the young king. It is recorded that some 30,000 brave men and women were killed in this dreadful persecution. The famous French name, *Barthélemy*, is another form of Bartholomew.

Nathanael, the abbreviated forms of which are Nathan (meaning, *a gift*) and Nat, is now spelt *Nathaniel,* and means "the gift of God." It was probably chosen by the parents of Nathanael to express the gratitude of parental piety at his birth. This Hebrew name is the same as the Greek *Theodore,* and is also preserved in *Dorothea.* (See Num. 1:8; I Chron. 2:14).

The name is found in the Old Testament in three forms —

Nathan, the prophet who stood by David so often;

El-Nathan, one of the princes in the time of Jeremiah;

Nethaneel, a prince in the days of Joshua, a brother of David, a son of Obed-edom.

2. A Man Who Learned of Christ's Omniscience

We take this aspect of the apostle next because before he came to see and know Jesus, He knew all about Nathanael. "When thou wast under the fig-tree, I saw thee" (John 1:48, 50). Doubtless it was the manifestation of that attribute that prompted John to go on to say, "He knew all

men, and needed not that any should testify of man: for he knew what was in man" (2:24, 25). The Psalmist confessed that the Lord knew all about him, and understood his thought afar off (Ps. 139:1-11). As the omniscient Lord, no one and nothing are hid from Him. As Ellicott expresses it in his comment on Nathanael —

Unseen as he thought by any eye, he was seen by Him to whose coming every true Israelite looked, and the answer to the true thought and prayer was then as ever close at hand; but at hand, in the human form in which men find it so hard to read the Divine, and in the ordinary events in which men find it hard to realise God. A travelling Rabbi! He is the Messiah. From Nazareth the All Good cometh! This meeting, then, was not the first. *There was an actual Messianic Presence in Nathanael's inmost thought.* He is now startled, and asks, "Whence knowest Thou me?" . . . But in the deepest sense, the Messiah was there; "When thou wast under the fig-tree, I saw thee."

Can we not appreciate why Nathanael asked in amazement, "Whence knowest thou me?" Up to that moment Jesus and he had not met, and had never spoken to each other until Philip brought them together. But as the result of their initial contact Nathanael was convinced that his secret thoughts and desires and acts were all open to this Man from Nazareth: that the inner region of inspiration was open to Him as a scroll. How sobering this truth of divine heart-knowledge and searching should be! We seldom pause to think that God knows us altogether, that His eye looks into the innermost recesses of our being; that He knows us through and through. Too often we pray for His presence, when our petition should be the knowledge and comfort that His presence is already ours. May we never forget His kind but searching glance in moments when sin, secret and otherwise, approaches! As Christ knew Nathanael and read him before Nathanael knew and read the Master, so, as did the father of the Prodigal, He sees the sinner "a great way off."

3. *A Man Who Was Introduced to Christ by a Friend*

What an impressive manual on personal soul-winning is the first chapter of John's gospel! John the Baptist meets the Lamb of God. Andrew and John follow Him, and Andrew leads his brother Peter to Him. Then Jesus found Philip and Philip finds Nathanael and brings him to the Lord. What a thrill would be ours if, when individuals cross our pathway, we could manifest the readiness to say as Philip did to Nathanael, *Come and see!* If only others would come and experience what the Lord is able to accomplish in their lives, there would be far fewer sceptics in the world.

Reading between the lines it would seem as if a bond of friendship or kinship had knit Philip and Nathanael together before they were united by the Lord in a higher fellowship. It may be that the former was tremendously influenced by the latter because of his culture and noble character. Both were sincere, orthodox Jews and had often spoken together of their God, their Nation, and of the sacred promises made of Redemption for their race. Thus, when Philip found the Messiah we can understand his great eagerness as he rushes to tell his bosom companion the good news, so that they might not be divided but be one in Christ. As the deeper thoughts and sympathy of both were in harmony, both embraced Him who had come as the Savior of the world.

Nathanael, then, owed his introduc-

tion to Jesus to his friend Philip. Had he refused to respond to the invitation, these two friends would have had a barrier between them. They would have been lost to each other, and Jesus would have lost a friend and companion throughout His ministry. But the miracle happened, for both came to value the friendship of Jesus. It was this that brought Philip and Nathanael together and that forged closer bonds than they had ever known before. Philip found in his friend one who was prepared to listen to what he had to say about the Messiah. Without fear, hesitation, or apology, Philip told of what he had seen and heard, and the interest of Nathanael was aroused and he, too, heard and believed. Surely, Philip's example is intensely encouraging to those of us who may hesitate to speak to our friends of the Savior we have found. For all we know they may be longing to share with us the realization of the divinest joy the soul can have — the joy of sin forgiven! Thus, "Philip consecrates companionship, and brings into the range of history one of those silent seekers after God who shrink from the gaze of the world." *Come and see.* Seeing is believing!

4. *A Man of Strong Prejudice*

When Philip broke upon the solitude of Nathanel with his stirring cry, "We have found him . . . Jesus of Nazareth," a strong prejudice led him to answer, "Can there any good thing come out of Nazareth?" As a village, Nazareth was not only remote, but it was of little or ill repute, and Nathanael was not interested in such a place or anyone living, or coming, from there. How could a man coming from this despised village evoke any enthusiasm! Bruce would have us know

Nathanael's prejudice against Nazareth, so unexpected in one so meek and amiable, sprung not from pride, as in the case of the people of Judaea, who despised the Galileans in general, but from humility. He was a Galilean himself, and as much an object of Jewish contempt as were the Nazarenes. His inward thought was, *Surely the Messiah can never come from among a poor despised people such as we are — from Nazareth, or any other Galilean town or village?*

While a feeling of incredulity awoke on Nathanael's first reception of the news of the Messiah, and the influence of popular opinion suggested his objection about Nazareth, and his prejudice had something, therefore, to go on, he was wrong to allow such prejudice to shut the door on inquiry and on evidence; to condemn Philip unheard; to say that, because the place had an evil name, "no good thing could come out of it." Nathanael's incredulous surprise, if based on ignorance, was not well-informed. As a student of the Old Testament, he should have known that there is no contradiction between prophecy and actual history. It is shown as being possible to be born in one place and be brought up in another, and also to live in low surroundings untainted by its vice. Jesus came from infamous Nazareth, and was called a Nazarene but was yet without sin.

Prejudices or preconceived ideas often prove the greatest obstacle in the way of the acceptance of the gospel message. John Bunyan, with incomparable insight, describes in his famous allegory, *The Holy War*, the terrible part Prejudice may play in the lives of men. You may recall how when Emmanuel's forces came to capture *Mansoul* they directed their attack first upon *Ear-Gate*. But *Diabolus* had taken his precautions to meet it, for he had stationed at *Ear-Gate* one whom Bunyan describes as: "Old Mr. Prejudice, an angry and ill-conditioned fellow, and put under his power sixty men, called deaf men — men advantageous for that service forasmuch as they muttered no words of the captains nor of the soldiers." Being interpreted Bunyan's parable means that men's ears are often closed against the gospel by *prejudice*. Was it not this that caused the Jewish nation as a whole to remain deaf to their Messiah's appeal? Prejudice blinded them to His beauty, divine majesty and power, and to the rejection of His claims.

Philip was wise and did not stay to argue with Nathanael. His own preconceived opinions had vanished at the sight of Jesus, and he knew the same would happen in the experience of the friend he was anxious to win. Prejudices are very rarely touched by arguments. They can only be put aside by facts. If Nathanael's objections had been intellectual or moral, the situation might have been different. But Philip knew that prejudice was the only obstacle, and he did not deepen his friend's prejudices by reasoning with him. He knew that if Nathanael came to Christ, his prejudice would vanish — as it quickly did. We are strongest in facts and experience, all of which are summed up in the wisdom and policy of Phillip's answer, "Come and see!"

There was honesty beneath all the prejudice of Nathanael. He was ready to listen to his companion. He had none of the unfortunate vice of supposing that already he had reached all the truth that he could ever know, and that there was nothing the future could bring. There was in his breast, the slumbering hope that his eyes would see Him of whom the Prophets spake, and when he saw Him, he was completely conquered. There are many Nathanaels around today who, with all their mental alertness, have their dangers also, the most perilous of which are superficial objections about the Nazarene Himself and about the claims of truth. These objections often block the way to faith, especially when they excite in the prejudiced one an admiration of his own cleverness. Their only cure, and our most effective approach to them, is that which Philip brought to Nathanael, *Come and see!* When their eyes see the King, the Lord of Hosts, doubts, arguments, prejudices quickly vanish as darkness does at the rising of the sun. Believing, they prove what wonderful good comes out of Nazareth.

5. *A Man With Deep Religious Sentiments*

Nathanael, or Bartholomew, was no dissipated prodigal who wasted his substance with riotous living. In his high moral fiber, he was akin to the rich young ruler. As soon as he came into Christ's presence, He said to him, "Now here is a true man of Israel; there is no deceit in him" (John 1:47, Phillips). Like Simeon, he waited for the consolation of Israel and was among the number of godly souls who looked for redemption in Jerusalem (Luke 2:25, 38). Meeting Nathanael, our Lord did not rebuke him for his prejudices but commended him for his virtues in a three-fold way:

His trust — "Here is a true Israelite"

How amazed Nathanael must have been that the Savior's first words to him were not those of condemnation for his pre-conceived notions and doubts of Philip's testimony as to the discovery of the Messiah, but of congratulation for all that he already was; that as a true Israelite — a Jew, not by chance or the accident of birth, but in character and disposition, and that, therefore, as a new disciple there was so little to unlearn! Profound astonishment must have overtaken Nathanael, as Jesus uttered His commendation for his trust in the God of Israel. Somehow he was a man to whom trust was instinctive, and he inspired in others that which he himself embodied.

What makes the divine appraisal more remarkable is the fact that it was spoken by Christ to the other disciples who were present, but Nathanael, who did not accept the compliment with unquestioning and elated satisfaction, also heard it. Living for higher purpose than the praise or blame of those around, this true Israelite was far removed above the level of self-conceit, and humbly asked the One who praised how He knew all about him. At His first approach, then, Jesus testified to Nathanael's honorable character. As "an Israelite," indeed, he was a man who feared God, a man of true simplicity and integrity. He had studied Old Testament Scriptures and given much thought to Messianic promises and the hope of Israel, and Jesus who had read his inmost heart gave him the singularly sincere testimony of being a pure Israelite because he was one who embodied in his thoughts and life the best qualities and traditions and trust of the Jewish people.

The Man of Nazareth knew the secret character of the man of Cana. Paul tells us that "they are not all Israel, which are *of* Israel" (Rom. 9:6), which statement implies that there was always a nation within the nation; an election within the election; an Isaac in Abraham's family; a Jacob in Isaac's family; a Joseph and a Benjamin in Jacob's family; Israelites indeed called and chosen, within the Israelites by name — and Nathanael was one of them! Jesus saw in him a genuine son of the Covenant, a child of Jacob purged of his ancestor's youthful deceit, without any religious mask, and the admiration of Christ for the ideal character of the man broke into honest praise.

His transparency — "In whom there is no guile"

Nathanael Bartholomew was the personification of sincerity. His eye was never "double." Guile never sent a shadow across his face, and Jesus, knowing that the outstanding quality of his character was transparency, extolled him as He did. Jesus hated marks of all kinds, especially the religious marks of the Scribes and Pharisees. "His searching, appreciative eyes, then, rested with pleasure upon the honest face of Philip's close friend as one finding an oasis in a wilderness of sand." *In whom there is no guile* was not a compliment of flattery, but the congratulation of truth.

The word for "guile" is the same word for *subtlety* in the LXX of Genesis 27:35. The thought then is, "Behold one who is true to the name of Israel, and in whom there is nothing of Jacob" (Gen. 27:36). Nathanael was like the patriarch Jacob in that he was a very prince of God in devotional life, but, unlike Jacob, he had not a trace of cunning or deceit in his nature. David describes the guileless man for us in Psalm 15:

Lord, who shall abide in thy tabernacle?
Who shall dwell in thy holy hill?
  He that walketh uprightly,
    and worketh righteousness,
    and speaketh the truth in his heart.
  He that backbiteth not with his tongue,
    nor doeth evil to his neighbour,

nor taketh up a reproach against his neighbour.
  In whose eyes a vile person is contemned;
But he honoureth them that fear the Lord.
  He that sweareth not to his own hurt, and changed not.
  He that putteth not out his money to usury, nor taketh reward against the innocent.
He that doeth these things shall never be moved.

Familiar with ancient Scriptures, Nathanael had often meditated upon this psalm and determined in his heart to be transparent, sincere, and a stranger to any duplicity. Guilelessness is as much a discredited virtue in this twentieth century as it was in the first. When we say, "So-and-so is a guileless sort of person," the phrase seems to breathe of a contemptuous pity. We by no means use it as a compliment. Many aspects of modern life are riddled with trickery, deceit and fraud. Honesty and simplicity of soul, however, are not to be scorned, for to be guileless, as Jesus meant it, is more precious than rubies. It was He who said that "the pure in heart shall see God."

Nathanael was clear as day and never lowered himself to deceitful contrivances. He was a man anyone could trust and so earned the warm salutation of Jesus. It was because he was guileless and possessed clear intelligence and fine spiritual sympathies that he instantly recognized in Jesus, the Messiah for whom he had longed.

His tryst — "under the fig-tree"

It would seem as if Nathanael was in his own house when Philip called to tell him the glad news of the Messiah, and that he found his intimate friend under the fig-tree in his own garden. Intimate friends usually know each other's habits. The "Fig-Tree," emblem of the Jewish nation (Matt. 24:32) was the favorite tree under which Jews would retire for prayer and meditation (I Kings 4:25; Micah 4:1-6; Zech. 3:10). Thus, it was under his own fig-tree Nathanael often went to commune with God, and not at the corners of streets to be seen of men as the Pharisees did. Under the shade of the tree, he thought he was unseen by any eye, but he was seen by the eye of Him from whom nothing is hid. "When thou wast under the fig-tree, I saw thee." Only One knew of that holy commerce with heaven, and that One now stands before the meditative soul. His eyes saw what the fig-leaves hid from all else, and His ears heard those prayers, too intimate for human ears.

That precious fig-tree, then, was the trysting place of Nathanael, the secret place where he mused upon the sacred Scriptures, and poured out his soul before the Lord. Although he was evidently a fisherman by trade, his main business was not on the sea, but under his fig-tree where his spirit was keyed up to God's pitch, and where he saw "the King in His beauty," and was rewarded by seeing Him in the flesh. If only we could grasp aright the privilege and power of prayer, as well as its nature and necessity, the soil beneath our own fig-tree would be wet with the tears of importunity. If Nathanael's fisher-companions did not see him in his boat, they knew they would be certain to find him underneath the leafy shade of the fig-tree in the garden of his humble home.

William Law in his *Serious Call* — a potent book unfortunately neglected today — has this advice to offer: "Pray always in the same place; reserve that place for devotion, and never allow yourself to do anything common in it."

Isaac had his special place — it was the green field at eventide.

Elijah had his special place — it was the mountain cave.

Jesus had His special place — it was the Garden of Gethsemane.

William Law goes on to say, "This would dispose you to be always in the spirit of religion when you were there, and fill you with wise and holy thought when you were there by yourself." The secret place Nathanael reserved for meditation and prayer made him the true and guileless Israelite whom Jesus declared him to be, because He knew that he had always been disposed in the spirit of religion. It is to be hoped, my friend, that *you* also have a special place set apart for devotion in your home corresponding to Nathanael's fig-tree. Did not Jesus mean that you should have some inner chamber, or little nook to which you can retire for meditation when He said, "Enter into thy closet and pray"? May the pathway leading to the fig-tree in the garden of your life never be neglected and overgrown with weeds! How appealing are the following anonymous lines as we think of all Nathanael's fig-tree suggests!

There is a place where thou canst touch
    the eyes
  Of blinded men to instant, perfect sight;
There is a place where thou canst say
    "Arise!"
  To dying captives, bound in chains of
    night.
There is a place where thou canst reach
    the store
  Of hoarded gold, and free it for the
    Lord;
There is a place whence, to some distant
    shore,
  Thou canst send forth the worker and
    the Word.
There is a place where Heaven's resistless
    power

Responsive moves to thine insistent
plea;
There is a place — a silent, holy hour,
Where God Himself descends and
works for thee.
Where is that secret place? Dost thou
ask where?
O soul! It is the secret place of prayer.

His testimony — "Thou art the Son
of God . . . the King of Israel"

Just and devout hearts in Israel,
eagerly anticipating the coming of the
Lord's Christ, instantly recognized
Him as such. When godly Simeon saw
the Holy Child, Jesus, he was ready to
die in peace for his eyes had seen the
One who had come as "a light to
lighten the Gentiles, and the glory of
thy people Israel" (Luke 2:25-35).
"Then, as Anna, the aged widow who
departed not from the temple, but
served God with fastings and prayers
night and day," gazed upon Him who
was born of Mary, she gave immediate
thanks unto the Lord, and went out
from the temple and "spake of him to
all them that looked for redemption
in Jerusalem" (Luke 2:36-38). Holiness of life and heart-longings to see
the Messiah, created a spiritual intuition, whereby they knew Him as the
sent One from God, as soon as they
saw Him.

This was so with righteous Nathanael who, as Jesus declared that He
knew all about him, believed, and exclaimed, "Master, you are the Son
of God, you are the King of Israel."
He had no doubt about this Man's
identity constraining him to ask, "Art
thou he that should come, Or must I
look for another?" With all readiness
His claims were recognized and admitted, and when Jesus said, "Because
thou hast seen thou hast believed,"
we have, not only the confirmation of
Nathanael's faith, but the expression
of the Savior's own surprise and joy

over the Israelite's immediate acceptance of Him. The reader of his heart,
who had entered into the secrets of
his life, was welcomed as the Master,
as the Son of God, and as the King of
Israel. Thus, another opening of the
avenues of his being to the One calling
him could confess, "I have found the
Messiah!" It will be recalled that the
woman of Samaria was similarly arrested by the thought-reading of the
Stranger at the well, and though her
character and condition were different
from those of Nathanael, yet her condition was the same, "Come, see a
man, which told me all things that
ever I did: is not this *the* Christ?"

As the faith of Nathanael leaped
in a lightning-like confession to his
lips, the revelation of deity and sovereignty were expressed, for he knew
that no one save the Son of God, the
Omniscient King, could have penetrated the thoughts of his mind, or interpreted the desires of his heart as he
prayed and pondered over the Scriptures under his fig-tree. The identity
of Jesus came to Nathanael with the
power of an irresistible conviction. He
needed no man to tell him who the
One before him was. Without hesitation, and in full assurance he assigned to Jesus two of His highest
Messianic titles which existed in the
Messianic expectation of that time
(Matt. 21:5; 26:63; John 11:27; 12:
13, 15). Thus, as Ellicott comments:

> The recognition begets recognition.
> That strange Presence he had felt as
> a spiritual power quickening hope
> and thought, making prophets' words
> living truths, filling with a true mean-
> ing the current beliefs about the
> Messiah; — yes, it goes through and
> through him again now. It is there
> before him —
>
> "Thou art the Son of God,
> Thou art the King of Israel."

6. The Man Who Was Graciously Rewarded

The reward of Nathanael's faith was commensurate with his sincerity, and the inrush of his Messiah's blessing as quick as his acceptance of Him. Because he believed that the Lord knew all about him while under the fig-tree, he received the promise, "Thou shalt see greater things than these." The reward of his faith was to be an enlarged capacity for trust; and the reward of his vision, still clearer sight. Receptivity was to be expanded so that he could follow on to know the Lord in fuller measure. From now on his faith was to grow, not from the root that he was known of God, but from the root that *he knew God.* "Heaven and earth should be to him united, and the Son of God whom he had received should be as the Son of Man leading him from the one to the other."

Nathanael, who possibly realized more of the glory of Christ than any of his fellow-disciples, was to behold with open face His greater glory. One writer suggests that we can rest the main proof for Nathanael's apostleship on the promise, "Verily, verily, thereafter ye shall see heaven open and the angels of God ascending and descending upon the Son of Man."

Let us examine the "greater things" in this declaration designed to strengthen the faith-faculty of Nathanael —

Verily, verily

This double seal upon the promise of the New Covenant meant that every child in the Israel of faith may claim its benefits and enjoy its blessings. It is interesting to note that this is the first use of this formula of doubled words, which is not found in the New Testament outside of John's gospel. Whenever used by our Lord — who alone employed the double *Verily* — it is always connected with some deeper truth, to which it directs attention. *Verily, verily* represents in a reduplicated form, the Hebrew AMEN, which is common in the Old Testament as an adverb, and twice occurs doubled (Num. 5:22; Neh. 8:6). John uses AMEN as a proper name of "The faithful and true witness" (Rev. 3:14).

Ye shall see

Earlier words were addressed personally to Nathanael but the truth Christ is now to express is for all disciples—to Andrew, John, Peter, James, and Philip, as well as to Nathanael who were present to hear such an utterance — and to the saints of succeeding ages. Would that the church today would give heed to the voice of the Master, "Ye shall see greater things than these!" The change of pronoun from the singular *thou* to the plural *ye* meant this promise of revelation was for all the apostles, and for all who follow Christ.

Heaven open

Past and present tense are implied in the original — made open and continuing open. At the Incarnation the heavens were rent and God in Christ came down, and now He stands before Nathanael as the answer to the longings of his soul. From now on the person, work, teaching, death and resurrection were all to illustrate in an ascending scale the mediatorial work of Christ. Having accepted the Messiahship of Jesus, more striking and heavenly revelations were to be given Nathanael to occupy and strengthen his faith in all the future might hold for him.

The angels of God ascending and descending

It would seem as if we have here a clear allusion to Jacob's ladder in the dream at Bethel (Gen. 28:12, 13). Can it be that when Jesus saw Nathanael reading the ancient scroll under his fig-tree, that as the Omniscient One He knew he was reading this wonderful chapter? If so? Then, about to go forth from his father's house at Cana to follow Jesus, Nathanael would be encouraged to know that the Lord would be to him all that He had been to the patriarch of old. Further, we must observe that it is *the angels* who go up and down the ladder, suggesting that they are ever with Jesus, at His disposal, to be used as He deemed best. These same angelic beings minister to the heirs of salvation (Heb. 1:13, 14). Thus we have a part in Nathanael's blessing since the services of the angels are given to us because we are heirs along with Christ.

Communication with heaven, fellowship with God, these Jesus made possible for all who believe. These are represented by *the ladder,* the mystery of which is unfolded in the cross, and the angels on the altar stairs of Bethel are winged with faith and prayer. The promise, then, of Jacob's blessing for Christ's new apostle is for all pilgrims. For Nathanael there is to be no minor privilege as a vision of a ladder, whose foot is beside the pillow of the weary sleeper, and whose other end is by the throne of God. No, the blessed reward of his guileless heart was to be an ever-enriching experience that his newly-found Messiah would walk with him all the way — Lord, Friend, Companion, Provider, and Protector, all in One.

The Son of man

Nathanael had just expressed his full assurance that Jesus was *the Son of God.* Now He intimates that He has another title, less lofty but not less needful, and almost more helpful to a man in Nathanael's state of mind — *the Son of Man!* As the Son of God, He is able to reveal what God is — good, gracious, and holy. As the Son of Man, He knows what man is — feeble, needy, and sorely tempted. As both, He is to be worshiped, trusted, followed and obeyed.

This ordinary title, *Son of Man,* employed by our Lord more than seventy times, is used here in the presence of His disciples for the first time. As *the* Son of Man, He is the true representative of the human race, the second Adam, in whom all are made alive. He is the Son of *Man,* that is, man as man. "Not Jew as holier than Greek; not free-man as nobler than bond-man; not man as distinct from woman; but humanity in all space and time and circumstance; in its weakness as in its strength; in its sorrows as in its joys; in its death as in its life." As the Son of Man, Jesus knows all about our human needs and problems, and as the Son of God He is able to meet every one of them. In a very real sense He is the ladder set up on earth, but reaching up to heaven. In the incarnation, deity took human form on earth: in the ascension, humanity was raised to heaven, where the center of glory is humanity's dust glorified, seated on a throne.

The last reference we have to Nathanael is when with six others, he returned to his old trade (John 21:15-17). Was this fishing expedition a relaxation for these men fatigued by sorrow, surprise, and watching, or was it a feeling that had overtaken them that it was better to be simple fishermen than to be apostles of Jesus?

Having left their nets to follow Him, did they expect better things? To change the figure of speech, having put their hands to the plough were they now beginning to look back? Well, a bad night on the sea awoke the seven fishermen out of their dream. "That night they caught nothing."

But the One who knew all about Nathanael's thoughts under the fig-tree was cognizant of all the failings of the disappointed fishermen and when morning dawned, "Jesus stood on the shore," with a cooked breakfast ready for them. That warm fire He had kindled, and the fish He had prepared for them, cured them of their earthly care, and then He gave them a sign or symbol to encourage them in their future apostolic work. The midnight fishing in the Sea of Galilee resulted in complete failure because the efforts of the apostles were self-directed. "I go a fishing," said Peter. The other six replied, "We also go with thee." No wonder the results were so barren that they could not catch even a few fish for breakfast after a night's hard toil. But when the fishermen went forth at Christ's bidding, how different the haul. The multitude of fishes was too great for them to handle. Was this a symbol of the harvest of souls they were to gather as directed by the Lord in their coming apostolic labors when they cast their nets on the right side of the ship? As He had fed their hungry mouths, so they were to go forth to feed multitudes with the Bread of Life — a gracious ministry in which Nathanael would share, although after the sea-shore experience he is not mentioned again.

When this guileless apostle first met Jesus, he was deeply impressed by His *omniscience* — now he must have been over-awed by his Lord's *omnipotence*.

It took a good lot of fish and bread to feed seven hungry men who had been out all night. They, themselves, had caught *nothing*, and they would have had to seek a meal somewhere else. But Jesus had a hearty breakfast ready for them. Where did He get the fish and bread, Nathanael must have wondered to himself? Well, the sea was His, He made it, and therefore, He had dominion over *all* the fish in it (Ps. 8:8). This the miracle of the silver piece in the mouth of a fish proved (Matt. 17:27).

As we take our farewell of this attractive apostle it is with the wish that we would have liked to have known more about him. We have only two glimpses of Nathanael, then he disappears, leaving us with nothing but conjecture of what the Master accomplished through him in the apostolic age, and of how the predictive beginnings were fulfilled. The elements of his character Christ cited contain the secret of his moral beauty. Living in the truth, after meeting Him who came as *the Truth*, his knowledge grew in all dimensions. The eulogium he received from Christ — higher by far than any other of the twelve received — revealed promising material the Lord had to work with. We cannot do anything else but believe that all the while he was with Him, this guileless man constantly, promptly and sympathetically, yielded to his Master's sway, and manifested an easy development in spiritual strength and beauty. After the inclusion of his name with the other apostles at the sea-side, and in the list of Acts 1:13, silence falls, and his subsequent life is hidden. We can, however, take this guileless Hebrew as our example, and Christ's eulogy of him for our encouragement.

JAMES, THE SON OF ALPHAEUS

THE APOSTLE WHO RENDERED
OBSCURE SERVICE

A modern hymn reminds us that we shall only be "remembered by what we have done." Here is an apostle who is remembered *only* by his name, for we do not have a single authentic word in the New Testament as to the life he lived or the service he rendered. To Jesus, this James was more than a name, for knowing all about his worth He included him in the twelve He chose to labor with Him, and then to go out into the world preaching and teaching the truth received from Him. The name *James,* which has its root in the name *Jacob,* was a common and favorite name in the time of Jesus, and therefore is one used several times in the New Testament. Thus it is necessary to distinguish the different men known as *James*:

1. James, the son of Zebedee, brother of the apostle John, who

was the second martyr of the faith, Stephen being the first one.

2. James, son of Mary, and brother of our Lord, who was not a member of the apostolic band, and not a disciple until a later date.

3. James, the father of that Judas who was neither the Iscariot nor the near relative of Jesus. He was Judas who kept his loyalty.

4. James, the son of Alphaeus. Tradition has it that he had been a tax-gatherer. He was a brother of Matthew who also is described as a son of Alphaeus. This family was highly honored in having two sons who became apostles. It is *this* James whom we are now discussing.

1. *His Genealogy*

Much discussion has raged over the controversy as to whether the James we are considering was a brother of our Lord and the writer of the epistle of James. Conservative opinion is that there is no basis of fact in such an identification. He could not have been one of the Lord's brothers, for Scripture states quite distinctly that "The brethren did not believe on him." Whenever Jesus' brothers are mentioned it is as a body quite distinct and separate from the apostles. We know absolutely nothing about James, the son of Alphaeus, but his name. He may have been a cousin of Jesus for his mother seems to be spoken of as the sister of our Lord's mother (John 19:25). But this passage can bear another interpretation. All we know about this man is his own name and his father's — Alphaeus. This comes down to us also as *Clopas.* He is probably the "James the Less," to whom Mark refers, which should be expressed as "James the Little," probably on account of his shortness of stature (a feature he shared with Zacchaeus) and to distinguish him from James, the son of Zebedee. He is numbered among the chosen twelve *before* the conversion of Jesus own kith and kin. We do not hold, therefore that James, the son of Alphaeus, was a brother of our Lord, nor the *James* whom Paul mentions, nor one who headed the Jerusalem Church at the time of the apostolic council there. He is not mentioned separately in Scripture, save in the lists of the apostles' names.

2. *His Apostleship*

Although no single incident is narrated of this son of Alphaeus, no word or single deed of his is recorded, yet his name is preserved for us as one chosen to be an apostle by our Lord after a night of prayer. There must have been something about James prompting Jesus to include him among the twelve, all of whom were sent forth to preach and teach the gospel, heal the sick and cast out demons. When, in His intercessory prayer, Jesus confessed to the Father, "Those Thou hast given me, I have kept," He had James in mind, as well as the rest whom He had selected to company with Him. Doubtless He knew that this disciple could be relied upon to render faithful yet unsung, unheralder service. The days James spent with Jesus until He died, came and went, as did the days after His ascension. James lived and died, and vanished from the scene of action past all tracing as far as the sacred record goes. We can imagine that what he lacked in stature as "James the Little," he made up for in service, that, although he was a background disciple he never caused his Master any anxiety by

backsliding, doubt, or misunderstanding.

Perhaps Jesus counted him as an apostle, or as representative of a long line of disciples of whom no record would be kept, and of whom the world would not be worthy, and whose names would not be remembered beyond their quiet, faithful, unknown ministry in His church. In that insight and wisdom and love that found a place for this James, we know that He who ordained the twelve has a place for the vast majority of us who have only one talent. Some of the greatest forces in nature are silent and unseen.

3. *His Obscurity*

The distinguishing feature of James, the son of Alphaeus, is the obscurity with which he was content. He sought no general recognition. Background discipleship was what the Lord willed for him, and he was happy to have it so. His merit consisted in that he went where he was sent by Jesus, fought the good fight, finished his course, and kept the faith, without any thought of applause. Only his name is graven on the pages of the gospel history, but his life and labors are hopelessly sunk in obscurity. The individuality of some men is striking, attracting attention, leaving a mark or indelible impression upon others. Most of us, however, are commonplace, having no exceptional gifts or powers. We are inconspicuous, simple, ordinary folk, models of mediocrity. Yet the commonplace character of our limitations should not make us indifferent about living to the full in our small corner. Much of the world's most needed and most blessed work is done by those about whom the world knows nothing.

The son of Alphaeus did nothing extraordinary, nothing the world thought needed any record. If he was not capable of anything great, nothing great was expected of him. But Jesus did expect James as an apostle to live at his best — which we feel he did. Peter stamped his personality and message upon the first Christian church. Paul left an indelible mark upon the church's theology. John, the apostle of love, left his own image upon the Christian life. James, however, left only his name. The silence about him is unbroken and the Master who elected him as one of His friends would have us remember that we must be faithful in that which is least. It may be hard and unpleasant to bury our seed and let it lie unseen, and for the reaper even not to know the name of the sower.

Faithful, patient, humble service may go unrecorded and unnoticed of men, but the faithfulness of brave and loyal hearts is not forgotten by Him whose eye is on the sparrow. Unknown to fame, they are among "the bravely dumb who did their deed and scorned to blot it with a name." The unrecognized saints and heroes of earth are a vast host. They do their best, even though others never notice them, and this is the triumph and final achievement of their fidelity.

J. B. Jones describes a visit he paid to Lincoln Cathedral in the company of the precentor of that time. With the utmost enthusiasm he described to Dr. Jones the two towers adorning the west front of that glorious edifice. He pointed out the beauties of the architecture and the extraordinary wealth and detail of the work, and then added quietly, "And no one knows who built them." So some of the most lovely work in that cathedral was done by an unknown tradesman who was faithful in his calling, and content that men should forget him; but his work lives on, a thing of beauty

and a joy forever. We think of missionaries in lonely spheres, Sunday school teachers, workers in the squalid corners of cities, visitors of the lonely, sick and needy, so content with humble yet hard spheres. They know their names will never figure in histories but they do their humble best for their Master and the world He loved enough to die for it. They trust someone will write the inscription upon their tombstone, "He hath done what he could" — an epitaph James truly earned!

4. *His Reward*

Unrecorded though the labors of James may be, they will not go unrewarded. The gospels may only give us his name, but his name lives forever engraven on one of the twelve pillars of the Eternal City, seeing he was one of "the twelve apostles of the Lamb" (Rev. 21:14). At the Judgment Seat, the Master's "Well done!" will be for the unknown as well as the well-known. Paul draws a sharp contrast between the condition of saints here and above. "As unknown (according to the records of earth) and yet well known" (on the books of heaven). Faithfulness is to be the basis of reward in eternity (Rev. 2: 10). The Judge will honor, not our fame but our fidelity. Unseen, loving, and devoted toil is never overlooked or forgotten in heaven. Obscure yet sweet and gracious lives may pass unnoticed of men, but are ever seen of Him from whom no one and nothing can be hid.

In respect to the silence of Scripture as to the life and labors of James and others, Alexander Maclaren suggests that after all the apostles were not the real workers in the church, but *Christ*. Had the apostles been all-important we should have had minute and detailed accounts of their careers.

But comparatively little is said even of some of the more outstanding disciples. Others are dismissed in absolute silence, the reason being the Bible's insistence upon the concentration of attention upon the all-important One, the Lord Jesus Christ.

Not I, but Christ, be honoured, loved, exalted,
  Not I, but Christ, be seen, be known and heard;
Not I, but Christ, in ev'ry look and action,
  Not I, but Christ, in ev'ry thought and word.
Christ, only Christ, ere long will fill my vision,
  Glory excelling soon, full soon I'll see;
Christ, only Christ, my every wish fulfilling,
  Christ, only Christ, my all in all.

We have all read of one of our great artists who painted a picture of the Last Supper, and when he was finished he invited his friends in to inspect it. After gazing at it for some time one of the company remarked, "How beautifully those cups upon the table are painted!" To the astonishment of the dumb-founded friend, the artist immediately took his brush and painted out the cups, saying, "I want men to look at the Christ." We cannot but feel that this was the undying passion of James, the son of Alphaeus. He wanted his Master to be all in all, and so all of self was lost in Him.

Live for self, you live in vain.
Live for Christ, you live again.

Since the hour James met Christ and became His apostle, he found himself harnessed to his Master's chariot, and as a slave to His love, lived only for His glory, and died without leaving any record. But in heaven, he lives again, and will shine as the stars forever. Full recognition and recompense are his in the realm where, "His servants serve Him, see His face, and wear His name in their foreheads."

There was a sense in which James found recompense in service itself although the service was done for its own sake. Conscious that his duties would be lowly and obscure, he yet faithfully and diligently discharged them. It was no mean reward to have the confidence of his Master, with the approbation of his own conscience, and without condemnation of his own heart. His master-motive was —

Dismiss me not Thy service, Lord,
  But train me for Thy will;
      * * * *
And I will ask for no reward,
  Except to serve Thee still.

Yet a full reward is now his where all unknown service here below has ample recognition. James' Master girded Himself to render obscure and lowly service, and His shunning of all the vulgarity of self-advertisement greatly influenced His humble follower, inspiring him to serve in the light of eternity where "every man shall receive his own reward according to his own labour."

JAMES, THE SON OF ZEBEDEE

THE APOSTLE WHO BECAME KNOWN AS GREAT

This particular *James* comes before the other apostle by the same name whom we have just considered. In all the four lists, James, the son of Zebedee, is always cited among the first three mentioned. Reference to him is fragmentary. "The materials for studying his character are scarce, and we must draw on our knowledge of humanity in general for the painting of the portrait of the first apostolic martyr of the Christian faith." Perhaps no other apostle suffers more from intervals of silence in his life than James. What a fascinating re-

who sealed the Gospel in his own heart's blood.

1. *His Name*

As already indicated in our cameo of his name-sake, *James* is a survival of the Hebrew ancestral name *Jacob,* and it is still a common name among Jews. In passing into Western lands it became *Jacobus* with variations — *Jago* of Spain, *Jacques* of France, and revives in English literature in Jacobite wars and songs. The name became established in Britain in the twelfth century, when pilgrims started to visit the shrine of St. James, the son of Zebedee, at Compostella in Spain. At that time the name was more common in Scotland. With the accession of James Stuart as first King of both England and Scotland, the name began to increase in popularity in England, in the seventeenth century. During the nineteenth century, however, it became unfashionable, when *James* was used as a general term for a manservant. Now it is more popular than ever.

2. *His Family*

James was the son of righteous parents, Zebedee and Salome, who lived on the shore of Galilee, consecrating their industry with piety and educating their children through honest toil to manly virtue. Zebedee is probably the same man whom the Jews mention in their *Talmud* as "Rabbi James, or Jacob, the son of Zebedee." His mother's name was Mary, surnamed Salome, who was most likely a relative of Mary, the mother of our Lord. According to Jewish custom near relations were called by the names of brothers and sisters. Thus James may have been a near relation to Jesus Himself (Matt. 27:56; Mark 15:40; John 19:25).

There are expositors who feel that

cord we would have of this "son of thunder," if only the gospels had given us an exhaustive account of his life! Although he was one of the intimate companions of Christ, it is only on rare occasions that James emerges with distinctness in the record until the gleam of the sword ended his career in a flash of eloquent silence.

"He passes before us in silhouette rather than in photograph," says Daniel McLean, "the outline clear enough to make identity in portraiture recognisable, but not with enough of detail to enable us to catch that subtle play of feature in which perfect character is expressed." John, the brother of James, in an appended note to his gospel, tells us that if all the acts of Jesus, and of those associated with Him, could be written in full, the world could not contain the books recording such facts and features (21:25). Let us try to gather together the hints we have of the history of this first disciple

Salome was a sister of Mary the Virgin. If this is so, we can understand her endeavor to secure for her two sons, positions of eminence in Christ's Kingdom. "Blood is thicker than water," the adage tells us, and because James and John were His cousins favors would be in order. Apart from this ambitious desire, however, Salome comes before us as an exemplary character. We are given many traces of her personal attachment to, and reverence for, the Master. She believed thoroughly in His coming Kingship (Matt. 20:20).

In the fondness for her sons, she revealed her deepest wish for them, but her faith in the Master's own future was firm, and likewise she had faith in His power to give and help. She was one of the women who ministered unto Him of her substance, and who followed Him on His last journey to Jerusalem. In the darkest hour of His trial, she was at the cross, as one of the sympathetic and sorrowing women who witnessed His final sufferings. She also came to anoint His body on the morning of the resurrection (Mark 15:40; 16:1). Altogether, Salome was a brave, true woman, willing, as were her sons, to give up all things for Christ, and we honor her as the worthy mother of two worthy sons, James and John, whose devotion she shared. As the gospels generally place the name of James before that of John, and allude to the latter as "the brother of James," it is inferred that James was the elder of the two brothers (Matt. 4:21; Mark 1:19; Luke 5:10).

As for Zebedee, the husband of Salome, and father of James and John, he appears only in the gospel narrative on the occasion when his sons left him to follow Jesus. Either he died shortly after they had entered on their discipleship, or, what is more probable, as an orthodox Jew, he did not share their faith in Jesus, nor approve of the discipleship they had chosen. One wonders whether Jesus had Zebedee and his opposition in mind when He spoke about forsaking father and mother for His sake (Matt. 10:37; 19:29). With Salome it was different. She was one of the first to believe in Jesus, and was one in the decision of her two sons to follow Him. As did her sons, she gave up all things for Christ.

3. *His Trade*

It was a Jewish custom that sons should follow the trade of the father, hence the reason Jesus became a carpenter as was His foster-father, Joseph. Zebedee was a fisherman on the Lake of Galilee and evidently a man of good social position as we gather from the fact that he had hired servants to assist him in the management of his fishing craft (Mark 1:20). Then there is the further fact that he had a house in Jerusalem and was known as a friend of the High Priest, Caiaphas, and his household. Evidently Zebedee was in the habit of frequently visiting the house (John 18:15-16).

James and John followed the occupation of their father who did not leave the entire management of his profession to his sons or servants. The glimpse we have of him mending his nets shows the secret of his success. He personally supervised his fishing material to keep it in good order, and the harvest of the sea was the reward of father and sons for their industrious care of boats and nets. Jona of Bethsaida, and his two sons, Andrew and Peter, were likewise fishermen of Galilee, and some sort of partnership seems to have existed between Jona and Zebedee in fishing operations. It is in assisting Peter with the miraculous catch that James first appears in the sacred record. What we are certain of is the fact that when the Master's invitation to become "fishers of men" was presented, these hardy toilers of the sea responded with alacrity. Both James and John, the sons of Zebedee, were among those to whom Jesus showed Himself again after His resurrection as they determined to go back to their fishing (John 21:2).

4. *His Discipleship*

Some seventy-five years ago, Frederick Edwards in his choice volume, *These Twelve*, gave us the following introduction to his chapter on "James, the Son of Zebedee":

> Seventeen years passed between the call which James received from the Master and the martyrdom he suffered for Him. The history we have of him is tolerably complete for three of those years, though it is silent, or nearly so, respecting the other fourteen. He is the first of those whose histories we have studied, about whose life we have not need to speculate, and to whom we can do ample justice by simply following the written record.

From the detached records we gather that the true story of the life of James commenced that day when Jesus, walking by the Sea of Galilee, saw James and John, along with their father, mending their nets, and addressing the hard-working brothers said, "Follow me!" And we read that *straightway*, or at once, without hesitation or questioning, they left their boat and their father and followed Him(Matt. 4:18-22).

We are not informed of the original event which led James to acknowledge and believe in the Lord, as we have in the first introduction of John, Andrew and Peter to Him. The call that came to him by the sea was not one

to the acceptance of Christ, but to follow Him in apostolic service. The gospels are silent as to his conversion. It may have occured when Peter, Andrew and John left their fishing to hear John the Baptist, and as the result of his preaching their contact with the Lamb of God came to a spiritual crisis. Perhaps, returning to Galilee they gave James an enthusiastic account of all they had seen and heard, and he, deeply moved by their testimony, inwardly dedicated his life to Jesus and awaited an opportunity to openly declare his allegiance to Him — which came as Jesus walked his way (Luke 5:1-11). The four fishers who obeyed the call to follow Jesus, continued as great personal friends. Because of their respective ages, they were at first classified in pairs — Andrew and John, the younger, and Peter and James, the elder pair.

As they journeyed around with Jesus, circles became apparent within the apostolic band. The outer circle was reserved for Judas Iscariot, the traitor. Seven apostles would seem to occupy the first circle, then there came the second circle of three, with Andrew just missing inclusion with the three. As for the innermost circle, Peter and James are excluded and John alone is enclosed with his Lord. In Matthew and Luke, Andrew ranks second to Peter, obviously because his chief distinction lay in being Simon Peter's brother. In Mark, James takes second place, and the order invariably is "Peter, James, and John." Mackintosh Mackay speaks of James as "The Man Who Took the Back Seat" — which description is true of what he became but certainly not of how he commenced.

5. *His Apostleship*

Companionship and partnership with his Master prepared James for apostleship, and he became one of an inner circle who shared some of Christ's most intimate experiences. The twelve, as a whole, were to be His witnesses in the world after His ascension, and "because it was to be their peculiar duty to give to the world a faithful account of their Master's words and deeds, a just image of His character, a true reflection of His spirit," He sought to make them as finely polished mirrors to reflect His image.

Christ was more concerned about qualification for the apostolic office than He was for the dignity of it. He knew that acquirement of qualification was the first consideration, and so for almost three years, He sought to prepare James and the rest by discipline and by learning. It was for no arbitrary reason that Christ allowed a year to elapse before He permitted James to pass from discipleship to apostleship. This "son of thunder" had to learn that the higher the calling the harder the discipline fitting one for it. Apostles were not born but made: "I will make you." Too frequently, men covet an office for which they are not prepared, simply because they skipped their apprenticeship. So as James followed and served, he learned, and became a workman who had no need to be ashamed.

Change of name

As James, and his brother John, graduated as apostles, Christ surnamed them, James and John Boanerges, or The sons of Thunder (Mark 3:17). In like manner, as we later see, He surnamed Simon, Peter. What is the significance of the epithet *Boanerges?* Scholars seem to differ as to its true meaning. Was such a strange name a record of their past lives? As fishermen had these brothers, being hot, impulsive men, given way perhaps to sudden outbursts of passion? Had they indulged in words that were too strong either for their own thoughts or the occasion which called them forth? Did such a new name, or nickname reveal that they had been men of a fiery, impetuous disposition? Well, because Jesus knew what was in man, He knew all about the natural disposition of James, and set about not its eradication but its sanctification. He harnessed the Niagara Falls in James to make him a driving force in His Kingdom.

Some writers have it that James and John were men of tempestuous eloquence; others say that they were men with strident voices, thunderers by means of the *vox humana*. Still others insist that *Boanerges* is an expression describing a fiery temperament, showing itself in an all-consuming zeal. William Cave, who, as long ago as 1840 wrote *The Lives of the Apostles*, says that:

> Probably the expression may denote no more, than that in general they were to be prime and eminent ministers in this new scene and state of things; the introducing of the Gospel, or evangelical dispensation, being called "a voice shaking the heavens and the earth" (Heb. 12:26); and so is exactly correspondent to the native importance of the word signifying an earthquake (Hag. 2:7), or a vehement commotion that makes a noise like thunder.

Thus we can gather that James had an all-consuming zeal, a passion for his Master that must have vibrated in his voice and glowed in his face. He could do nothing by halves, and so espoused his Lord's cause with an impetuosity which had but one rival among the apostles. We can look upon Jehu as the Old Testament counterpart of James, who said: "Come . . .

see my zeal for the Lord," and then uprooted the house of Ahab, and swept the worshipers of Baal from the land. In like manner, James may have used his thunderous voice as his weapon of reform; and Christ gradually transformed his passionate zeal into power so directed as to conserve it for the highest and most effective service. Yes, and the Master of whom it was said, "The zeal of thine house hath eaten me up" (John 2:17), fed the zeal of His disciple daily.

James' vigor of mind, ardor of spirit, and energy of body were all at the disposal of his Lord, and resulted in his coming to hold a prominent position in the Church at Jerusalem, and in bringing upon himself the wrath of a king resulting in his martyrdom. The abandonment of James to Jesus finds expression in the words of F.W. H. Myers:

He as He wills shall solder and shall
    sunder,
Slay in a day and quicken in an hour;
Tune Him in music from the Sons of
    Thunder,
Forge and transform my passion into
    power.

The apostle Paul would have us know that, "It is good to be zealously affected always in a good thing," and James was one who was zealously affected in the cause of Jesus Christ, although there were times when his passionate zeal was not according to knowledge. Zeal is indeed a noble and commendable virtue, but if ungoverned or misdirected, it becomes a vice. Some of the most terrible deeds in church history were perpetrated as the result of mistaken zeal. James, an earnest and zealous saint, had his faults — faults born almost out of his virtue. Alongside his strong points lay his weak ones — the defects of his quality.

Bigotry

Joseph Addison could write of "the honest prejudices which are naturally clear to the heart of a true *Englishman*," but we cannot say that the prejudice of the true Hebrew, James, was of an honest nature. A great lover, he could also be a great hater, and the very intensity of his affection made his wrath, intolerance, and bigotry more incandescent. The partiality and resolute disposition, not only of James, but also of his brother John, seem to have been of a more fiery and fierce temper than the rest of the apostles. This can be gathered from what happened when Jesus decided to journey to Jerusalem and sent some of His disciples as forerunners to prepare His way. Coming to Samaria, they were uncivilly rejected and refused entertainment. Doubtless the old and inveterate quarrel between the Samaritans and Jews, added to the apparent slight of Mount Gerizim (the recognized place of worship of the Samaritans) by Jesus who passed it by to worship at Jerusalem, constrained them to deny James and John the common courtesies and conveniences extended to all travelers.

Not only were the rights of hospitality refused, in all likelihood Jesus and His band were driven out with stones and curses, because the cleavage between the Jews and Samaritans was very wide (John 4:9). To the Jew, a Samaritan was but a *dog*. The somewhat cruel bigotry of James and John actually appears with sharp emphasis in two incidents recorded by Luke. First, they met some unknown person using the name of Christ to cast out devils. Evidently he was a believer in Christ, and bore witness in this apostolic fashion, but as he did not belong to the disciples' company, the apostles rebuked the exorcist with unnecessary sternness, on the ground that he was not one of the twelve.

But Jesus immediately chided their hasty intolerance and sectarian spirit, and laid down a principle applicable to the organized church at all times: "He that is not against us is for us." Everyone seeking to heal the sick and save souls in His name was to be regarded as a disciple and ally (Luke 9:49, 50). What bitterness a rigid sectarianism can cause! We must not forget that there are a good many vines growing over the outside wall of the vineyard.

Then the two brothers displayed their fiery intensity and pushy vehemence and lack of sweet reasonableness in their cruel demand that Jesus should call down fire from heaven to destroy the Samaritan village which was unwilling to receive Jesus and themselves. Such a spirit was repellent and could not be condoned. The words of James and John were hot as they sought a hotter judgment upon the people for their insult offered to their Lord.

Jesus, however, rebuked them in severe language, reminding them that the spirit of Elijah was not the spirit of the Evangel He came to proclaim, namely, that it was His mission not to destroy men's lives, but to save them. Evidently James had forgotten his Master's teaching about loving our enemies, doing good to those who hate us, and praying for those who despitefully use us. We need, of course, to guard ourselves against a false charity, and not to injure truth by becoming tolerant of evil. The remedy for error lies, not in the thunder of denunciation, nor in the fire of excommunication. Error is best overcome with truth, and even the truth needs to be spoken in love (Luke 9:51-56). While we cannot excuse the unchristian, hateful intolerance of James and his brother, there may be a touch of nobility in it. Was it not better to flame out in righteous wrath as they did, than witness insult done to their Lord without a quiver or a pang? May God save us in the church today from Laodicean indifference!

Ambition

Noble aspirations are to be cultivated. Lack of true ambition often results in mediocrity. The brand manifested by Salome for her sons was of the wrong kind. Shakespeare speaks of "Ill-weav'd ambition." The bard also wrote about "Vaulting ambition, which o'erleaps itself, And falls on the other."

On His last journey to Jerusalem, Jesus prepared the minds of His apostles for His death and departure from them. He fully explained that He would suffer and die, but yet after all would rise again. While many of the disciples had minds occupied with their Lord's future temporal power and monarchy, James and John, supposing the resurrection He spoke about would usher in His power and greatness, prompted their mother to present a petition on their behalf. Had He not promised that when He was come into His kingdom, they should "sit upon twelve thrones, judging the twelve tribes of Israel" (Matt. 19:28)?

Thus, emboldened by the action of Jesus in honoring her two sons with an intimate familiarity, she begged Him when He took possession of His kingdom to give James and John the principal places of honor and dignity next to His own person, one on His right hand, the other on His left. Jesus, replying to the request, directed His answer to James and John, for He knew that their mother had only voiced their ambition for them. The spirit of ambitious rivalry among the disciples reached an acute state when the two sons of Zebedee sought priority of position in the expected kingdom. Perhaps they were jealous of Peter's prominence, and wanted to be certain that they would not be left to play second fiddle. How this clamor for worldly dignities must have grieved the heart of Jesus who was within sight of His cross where He was to die as a felon! Here were "the persecutors of the Samaritans now ambitious place-hunters, making their zeal a stalking-horse to favor, and degrading their Lord into a despotic ruler who should dispense his patronage on a principle of favoritism, with no regard to merit."

Doubtless James and John as "sons of thunder," as Jesus Himself had named them, had passionate zeal to serve Him, but desired a reward equal to their merit, which in their own estimation, ranked high. Their self-estimation did not certainly err in the direction of modesty. Thinking of all they had left for His dear sake, second or third place in their Lord's coming kingdom would not be sufficient compensation; they wanted the best position. But such an irreverent, presumptuous request actually asked Him to become the tool of their own ambition and vanity. Such a solicitation was as ignorant as it was ignominious, because James and John thought only of the kingdom as being of this world. Among earthly rulers highest distinctions are often granted, not on merit or achievement, but by favor.

While the rest of the twelve were "moved with indignation" over the desire of James and John for the chief seats, it will be observed that Jesus did not rebuke these two for their selfish request. Knowing what was in man, He knew them better than they knew themselves, and so, cognizant of the higher, as well as the lower side of their character, He answered accordingly. The two brothers had not stopped to think of the disaster that would have resulted if their selfish petition had been granted. In His singularly mild reply, Jesus affirmed that rewards such as they sought were not at His disposal, but were in the hands of God who bestowed orders of divine merit only on certain conditions.

Exposing the ignorance behind the grave fault of their request Jesus said, more in compassion than in the way of blame, "Ye *know not* what ye ask!" Then came His heart-felt question, "Are ye able to drink of the cup that I am about to drink, and to be baptized with the baptism that I am baptized with?" In such a question, weighted more with sympathy than stricture, Jesus indicated that the only way to a throne was by the way of a cross, as He was about to exhibit in His coming death, resurrection and exaltation. James and his brother could only enter His kingdom through great tribulation. The price they must pay for the position desired was that of endurance under severe tests, fidelity under the utmost strain, loyalty even unto death.

Jesus asked the two suppliants if they were able to drink of His cup, share in His baptism of blood, and go to the uttermost of sacrifice. Their answer was instant: "They say unto him, *We are able!*" The question arises as to whether such a prompt reply indicated that the sacred fire of the martyr spirit had been kindled in their spirit or whether the two brothers were ready to promise anything so long as they could have the coveted prize. In the spirit of bravado, Peter said: "Though all men shall be offended because of thee, yet will I never be offended," but he went out to deny with an oath that he had ever known Jesus.

We like to think that, because of their love and zeal, these two aspirants for throne seats would be equal to all demands; that, if they were mean in their request, they were magnificent in their reply. Although Jesus alone knew all that was involved in the sharing of His cup, He accepted their declared willingness to descend with Him into the depths, at its face value. As far as James is concerned, as he saw his Master going out to His throne by the way of the tree, his spirit became enlightened, and as the result of Pentecost his bigotry vanished as did his ambitious grasp after power. For some fourteen years, his zeal for Christ became more intense, and with vehemence and unflagging devotion, he served the One he loved. James wanted a *crown* — Christ gave him a cup; he desired power and became a slave of Jesus Christ; he yearned to rule but found a martyr's grave. He came to prove the wise saying of Islam, "Heaven is found beneath the shadow of the sword."

When we take up the matter of James' martyrdom we shall discover how as the sword of Herod smote this noble "son of thunder," he passed through the pearly gate to perfect vision, likeness and rule (Rev. 22:3-5), and learned how true were the words of Him whose head was crowned with thorns before glory —
"To him that overcometh will I grant
to sit with me in my throne,
Even as I also overcame, and am set
down with my Father in his
throne"   (Rev. 3:21).

6. *His Prominence*

As the Apostle of Love, and the author of five New Testament books, John, it seems, would have been more prominent than his brother James in the first three gospels, and that the order should have read, "John the son of Zebedee and James his brother." But no! Whenever the two are named together it is always "James the son of Zebedee, and John his brother." A somewhat significant feature of the fourth gospel is that in it John never mentions his brother by name. The other apostle James is called by Mark "James the Less" to distinguish him from James, the son of Zebedee, who became known as "James the Great" — a term having no reference to bulk or eminence, only to age. The exact sense of the terms is probably *Junior* and *Senior*.

As the outset, let it be understood that the *James* we are considering was not the one who wrote the epistle of the same name, nor the one who became the president of the Council at Jerusalem. That James, the son of Zebedee, came to the front among his companions is proved by the fact that he became one of the trio of apostles invariably grouped together as "Peter, James and John." These three were selected by the Master for closer intimacy, nearer relationship, and more complete confidence. They shared some of the great experiences of His ministry, from which the rest of the apostolate seem to have been been excluded. What indelible impressions these events must have produced!

James and the other two were allowed to enter the chamber of death to witness Christ's first victory over death in the raising of Jairus' daughter. "He suffered no man to follow him save Peter, James, and John the brother of James" (Mark 5:37). The singular addition to John's name mentioned also by Matthew (17:1), may represent the feeling among the other apostles, as to the reason why the retiring, shy John should have been admitted at all. Yet he was a most reliable witness to vouch for the Master's resurrection-miracle. Then, the character and influence of Peter and James also qualified them as witnesses.

Then there was the awe-inspiring experience on the mount when Jesus was transfigured before Peter, James, and John. Writing of this remarkable event, Peter says that they were "eyewitnesses of his majesty" while on that holy mount. They were privileged to watch His essential deity gleam through the garment of His humanity. Borne along by the grandeur of the manifestation, the wish was expressed to stay there forever. But that vision was to prepare them for their vocation in the valley below.

The noticeable intimacy of James with his Master is also found in the record of Gethsemane, for he was one of three Jesus requested to accompany Him into the deepest shade of the olive trees, there to witness His deepest agony as the prelude of their entrance into the fellowship of His sufferings. "He taketh with him Peter and James and John" (Mark 14:33). Probably the others could not bear the burden of seeing His agony. As it was, the three chosen to see and listen, failed in their "watch," for "they all slumbered and slept" as Jesus confronted "the hour and power of darkness."

In each of these three events, James is named second, for the obvious reason that his more forceful personality overshadowed his brother John's. Comparing the two brothers it would seem that

James was resolute, vigorous, active, and forceful;

John was contemplative, intuitive and reflective.

The prominence of James is seen as an assured fact when, some fourteen years after our Lord's resurrection, Herod Agrippa "stretched forth his hands to vex certain of the church"

(Acts 12). But he did not arrest the least among the members — only the most conspicuous. He struck at two leaders, James and Peter, but first at James, for it is probable that by this time he had surpassed Peter in some respects. Here, again, comparison can be made —

The gifts of Peter were of the pioneer order; those of James were made for conservation of results.

Peter was conspicuous for oratory, for propaganda, for facing multitudes; James knew how to consolidate conquests, and had administrative and executive genius.

James, then, was one of those who lived near to Christ, and He still calls devout souls to enter into the innermost circle of His friends, and to receive from Him proofs of love and confidence unknown to others. They listen to His voice and think His thoughts after Him. The majority of His disciples seem content if they are allowed to touch the hem of His garment, or if this is too familiar an act of fellowship, then to follow Him at a distance. If James came nearer to Jesus than others, it was not favoritism which decided the nearness, but the Master's sovereign preference. It would seem as if the law of contrast made the son of thunder dear to Jesus who did not strive nor cry, and whose voice was not heard in the streets.

7. *His Martyrdom*

James was the first to feel the hostility of Herod, and the next to Stephen to win the honor of martyrdom in the early church (Acts 12:1-4). Because the cruel death of James pleased the Jews, Herod then seized Peter and cast him into prison, and so the two conspicuous *pillars* of the church became the victims of Herod's new-found zeal for Jewry. Why James was honored by martyrdom under

Herod, and Peter was spared from his cruelty, is one of the secrets of Him who . . .

Moves in a mysterious way
His wonders to perform.

After fourteen years of strenuous witness, the best testimony of which was the jealousy of Herod and the delight of the Jews over his death, there came James' obituary notice. The tyrant's sword ended a life laid on the altar, but James had no fear of those who could kill only the body. He was "girt by the grace of God on every hand" and death could not separate the apostle from "the love of God which is in Christ Jesus our Lord" (Rom. 8:37-39). James was the apostolic protomartyr, the first of that number to gain the crown, cheerfully taking that cup which they had told their Lord they were ready to drink.

The Acts of the apostles may not record one word James said, or any act he performed, but it does tell of of his readiness to be offered as a sacrifice for Christ's sake. His ambitious daring distinguished his career but hastened his gory but glorious consummation. His noble rage and fiery zeal thrust him into the forefront of danger and brought him his baptism of blood in the cause of truth which has ever defied the power of fire and sword. Further, as Daniel McLean so superbly expresses it —

> The blood of James consecrated the cause of Divine Truth, so that his death marks an epoch of increased energy over an enlarged area of operation.
> Herod I, resolved on "the slaughter of the innocents."
> Herod II, beheaded John the Baptist.
> Herod III, executed James, yet at every stage the attempt to crush the cause of God miserably failed; and the stain of blood upon the House of the Herods is prophetic of the ul-

timate issue of the conflict between brute force and earnest faith. The blood of the Cross sealed the covenant of Grace forever. The blood of the Martyrs has been the Seed of the Church.

Cultivating conscientious allegiance to God and to a Spirit-enlightened conscience, James rose above Herod and his sword bathed in blood to touch on bended knee the Royal Scepter of Heaven. Thus, he became greater in death than in life, for the sword of Herod was crossed by the Sword of the Spirit, and in the martyrdom of saints like Stephen and James, the immortal hope of the Gospel was liberated.

Oh, may Thy soldiers, faithful, true, and bold,
Fight as the Saints who nobly fought of old,
And win, with them, the victor's crown of gold, Alleluia!

8. *His Example*

James would have us follow him as he followed his Lord, and to gather spiritual learning from all the New Testament records of his life and witness. Does he not teach us that fellowship with Christ transforms violence into vigor, self-seeking into sacrifice, lightning into light? It was his intimacy with Christ, and faith in His power that made this "son of thunder" heroic, causing the halo of glory on his brow to become the crown of spiritual conquest. His character is well worthy of our most careful and prayerful meditation, for here was a strong man, able, ardent, and ambitious, intolerant of anything out of his own range of sympathy, who, once disillusioned of all his worldly dreams about the cause of Christ, rises into front rank by the same inherent qualities of nature, and leaves in duplicate a life from which to gain inspiration.

While we have indicated that we have no record of any message James uttered, there are those who suggest that possibly there is an exception in the prayer of thanksgiving offered when Peter and John were imprisoned for their bold witness and miraculous ministry (Acts 4:23-31). Who could have been the author and utterer of this remarkable prayer which Luke has preserved for us? Could it have been James, the son of Zebedee, who led the praises of the company? If so, then these solemn words are the only ones of his we have:

> Lord, thou art God, which hast made heaven, and earth, and the sea, and all that in them is: Who by the mouth of thy servant David hast said, Why did the heathen rage, and the people imagine vain things? The kings of the earth stood up, and the rulers were gathered together against the Lord, and against his Christ. For of a truth against thy holy child Jesus, whom thou hast anointed, both Herod, and Pontius Pilate, with the Gentiles, and the people of Israel, were gathered together, For to do whatsoever thy hand and thy counsel determined before to be done. And now, Lord, behold their threatenings: and grant unto thy servants, that with all boldness they may speak thy word. By stretching forth thine hand to heal; and that signs and wonders may be done by the name of thy holy child Jesus" (Acts 4:24-30.

Does not this remarkable prayer echo something of the defiant, zealous, and courageous spirit of James? Examining such a challenging petition we note these features —

It was full of reverence and yet of holy confidence and boldness.

It takes for granted that the threatenings of the Council will have no effect whatever in silencing the two prisoners of faith, Peter and John.

It sets forth so truly the power of God in their hearts, as that which alone can keep them firm and stedfast.

It uses Old Testament prophecy with such freedom as spoken of Christ and His enemies;

It sees God's working in all that they, the apostles, are to do and suffer;

It dwells so lovingly and trustfully on the twice-repeated name of "God's holy Child, Jesus."

If this was indeed a prayer coming from the lips of James then it is as a window through which we are privileged to catch a glimpse into the depth of strength and tenderness within the soul of this saint, who feared no one but God. Dr. J. Elder Cumming says that the following features can be stressed:

1. The deep love and true fellowship which passed between James and his Master, so often and so sweetly testified to by all the gospels. Here, too, was "a disciple whom Jesus loved." The presence of this man was a comfort, and his sympathy a boon, to the Man of Sorrows. And if for nothing else, we should love him for this and be grateful.

2. Here is a man who made a great sacrifice, willingly, for Jesus Christ. He, like all the apostles, left everything — father and mother, and house and friends — to follow Him. Perhaps James had more to leave than most — a happier home and easier post, a father of influence, and a mother's love. Nothing but the deepest crisis in his soul could have made him leave these; nothing but the truest faith. And the men who do not say much about themselves are not the least keen in feeling or in suffering.

3. Here, again, is a man whose character changed under the influence of Jesus Christ. At first the two broth-

ers are called *Boanerges* — noisy zeal-ots, who thundered against the evils of the day, and denounced the hypo-crites who were in high places. A simi-lar glimpse of the former man is given when he seeks to invoke curses and fire from heaven on those who reject his Master. But he is not always thus. He changes slowly into a man of peace and silence. Fellowship with Christ has done it. He has the command of his temper. He is able to bridle his tongue. Nay, his heart is calm within, and seeks no revenge. He has learned of Jesus Christ to be meek and lowly in heart. He has found rest. Can we testify to such a transformation?

4. Here, too, is a man of prayer, who takes hold of God, knowing His faithfulness, and rests assured of the love that He hath to us. Such rever-ence, such adoring nearness, such con-fidence, such intimate knowledge of the secret of the Lord, such boldness of access into the holiest of all! "The place was shaken where they were assembled together" (Acts 4:31), as the prayer of the apostles went up to heaven from this man's lips.

5. Here, once more, is a man who faced the prospect of martyrdom for some years, and did not turn away; and, when it came at last, he met it and went down without a word. Had there been a dying testimony, or fear, or cry, should it not have been writ-ten? There is not a word. He drinks the Master's cup, and follows Him, to be with Him where He is, on the other side.

6. And this, too, seems clear that there was no seeking for fame, or power; no love of a great name; no desire to be first in these later years. He was content to have been one of the disciples. And when his old friend Peter, and his young brother John, were both before him — more in evi-dence and honor — we find no remon-

strance and no envy. Not a murmur arises. To go after Jesus and be with Him, that is enough. Where did he learn it? Where you and I, and all poor sinful men, must learn the same lessons, if ever, and anywhere — at the feet of Jesus!

He climbed the steep ascent to Heaven,
  Through peril, toil, and pain,
Oh, God, to us, may grace be given,
  To follow in his train.

JOHN

THE APOSTLE WHO PERSONIFIED LOVE

As we proceed with our profiles of the apostles it becomes increasingly evident that few things are more in-teresting than the study of biography. How fascinating and profitable it is to trace a career from beginning to end, noting the various features, cir-cumstances, and crises, to discover the springs of character and the secret of power. It is often a rich experience to follow the course of a life from its opening to its close. This is why the Bible — The Biography of Humanity — is so appealing, dealing as it does with life, with personalities, with human problems, needs, weaknesses, trials and triumphs.

Further, our meditations prove that of all the lives recorded in the Bible there are none more truly valuable and inspiring than those of the apostles, because of their close association with Christ, which gave them exceptional opportunities of spiritual culture and service. Of all these apostolic lives perhaps the outstanding character is that of John because of his honored and intimate fellowship with his Master whom he served longer than any other apostle. Let us seek, then, to outline the salient features of one who entered into the inner secrets of His Lord as no other disciple had done. In many ways, John seems to occupy a niche all his own in the gallery of the apostles. Yet while more of his writings than those of any other apostle have been preserved, he scarcely makes mention of himself. There is little of an autobiographical nature in the books John wrote. It is different with the apostle Paul. His epistles, along with the Acts, give us many biographical sketches.

Yet even what John suppresses concerning himself is self-revealing. Of the twelve, the data concerning John is most complete. He is revealed to us, not only in the first three gospels, but by his own writings — *and by his reticence*. Our character study of John, as of all Bible characters coming under divine sway, confirms the striking saying of the English philosopher, John Locke, that, "God, when He makes a prophet, does not unmake the man." As all the men of the Upper Room pass before us in single file, we cannot escape their limitations, frailties, and humanness, all of which formed material for the divine Sculptor, who said, "I will make you." John and the rest of the band were as "rough diamonds to be polished on the wheel of service by the Master Lapidary." Each one whom Jesus selected, grew like Him in his own way. Individuality was not destroyed or suppressed, but developed and sanctified by the Maker of men.

1. *A Name of Honor*

When the apostle John came to write his gospel, it is interesting to observe that he referred to the forerunner of Jesus without the usual distinct *Baptist,* the one to whom the apostle stood in the relation of disciple to teacher. "A greater teacher had not then appeared, but when He did appear, former teacher and disciple alike bear witness to Him," comments Ellicott. "Great as was the forerunner, the least in the Kingdom of Heaven became greater than he was, and to the after ages the disciple became *the* John, and his earlier master is given the title *Baptist,* which distinguishes the man and commemorates his work." But the disciple we are now considering was also "a man sent from God, whose name was *John*" (John 1:6), and like his namesake he was raised up to bear witness to Him who came as the Light of the world.

While John mentioned John the Baptist distinctly and prominently, without giving any qualification, description, or parentage, as if he were the only John of the nation, of the time, and of the Gospel, his own name is never used by him in any of the twenty-one chapters of the gospel named after him. John is the only one of the four evangelists who does not give us a list of the twelve apostles, of which he was one. With true humility, John seldom alludes to his own existence — a fact upon which we shall elaborate later.

The name *John,* or Jonas — a common name of the time — corresponds in its Hebrew form, to the Old Testament *Jonah* whose name means "a dove," and who was the only man bearing that exact name as far as we know. It does not seem that such a significance had anything to do with Jonah's character which, to say the least, was not very dove-like. But with the apostle of love it is different. As our portrait of him will show, he exhibited many dove-like virtues. The name *John* implies, "The Lord is gracious," or "Grace of the Lord," and was a favorite name in the Eastern Church. It is said that the Crusaders brought it back to England, where it began to spread in the twelfth century. Its earliest form in Europe was the Latin *Johannes,* which was shortened to *Johan* and *Jon,* and hence *John.*

2. A Fisherman of Galilee

John was the younger son of Zebedee and Salome, and for this reason may be named after his brother, James. (The reader is asked to bear in mind that much of what we have said of James also applies to John.) John was likewise the youngest among the disciples of Christ and the longest-lived apostle of the church. Throughout the Master's sojourn on earth, the order "James and John," is given as indicating the order of their birth (Luke 9:28 is the only exception). John came from a more or less well-to-do family, for his father Zebedee owned a fleet of boats, and had hired servants to assist him in his lucrative fishing business (Mark 1:19, 20). John's position was probably somewhat better than that of an ordinary fisherman because of the servants his father employed.

Zebedee may have been influential (Matt. 27:56; John 18:15, 16; 19:27), and would be certainly well-known in his home town of Bethsaida (John 1:44). However, nothing is said of his reaction to the decision of his two sons to leave the family business and follow Christ. We are not told whether he was pleased or pained by their surrender of craft and home. As for John's mother, Salome, she was a disciple of Jesus, and her following Him suggests that after the boys left home, Zebedee died, and that the business was sold, allowing Salome to be one of the women who ministered unto Jesus of her substance. What an immense spiritual advantage it is to be children of a godly home!

As a boy, John, in following his father's calling must have been accustomed to danger and inured to hardship. Exposed to all kinds of weather, and to all sorts of risks associated with it, his manliness must have received early development, and stood him in good stead in trials of service for the Master. Probably because of his father's profitable business, John never knew poverty till he shared it with Jesus. Can you not picture John with hands hardened by toil, and having features bronzed by sea and storm? He was strong and daring, with a courage equal to any emergency, and never frightened by ordinary fear. Can it be that it was because of his strength, as well as his tenderness, that Jesus came to lean upon him for support and to trust in him? With all the advantages of youth, with all its strength and courage we are not surprised that the Savior's choice of John was justified by the greatness of the proportions which discipleship assumed in him.

Daniel McLean suggests that John's temperament suited his place in the household, and that he was allowed to indulge his tastes the more easily than James his senior. "He seems to have been the gifted son — the genius of the family, as we should say — and was evidently endowed with spiritual instincts of a high order, in short, the insight of the poet and the foresight of the prophet were inborn qualities of mind. His somewhat easy position at home, as well as his natural thoughtfulness, enabled him to obey the impulse awakened by the wave of excitement created by John the Baptist."

Some of the early writers affirm that John seems always to have led a single life. Ambrose positively declared that all the apostles were married except John and Paul. In the Middle Ages there were those who tried unsuccessfully to identify John as the one who was married in Cana of Galilee, and that on seeing Jesus turn the water into wine, he immediately became His disciple. What is clearly evident is the fact that John had a home of his own which after the death of Jesus also became the home of Mary, His mother. Behind John and his elder brother James there lay a very blessed home influence which must have shaped John's own home life. While we have no record of the impact his father, Zebedee, had upon his life, John must have been swayed by his dear mother's life and witness. Just when Salome became a disciple of Christ we are not told. Probably it was not till her two sons had received the call to follow Him. If it was part of John's record that he had brought his mother to Christ, then his heart must have been thrilled as he watched her sincere and growing devotion to Him.

3. A Disciple of the Baptist

To accomplish the will of God in the work of God, one must have a certain adequate spiritual preparation. Nothing worth while and permanent can be done off-hand. John began the preparation for his ministry for all nations and all ages, as a disciple of John the Baptist. How long he was with the preacher in desert places we are not told! All who came to him confessed their sins, were baptized, and confessed that he was a prophet sent from God. John's contact with the Baptist resulted in a spiritual crisis. As an earnest, thoughtful, pious Jew, John eagerly anticipated the coming of the Messiah, and when the Baptist declared that he had been raised up to prepare the way for the long-promised One, he believed.

What eventful days they were that John spent amid the crowd at Jordan, as he listened to the mighty preaching of the Baptist who had caught something of the spirit and power of Elijah! How deeply impressed John was by the strong character and forceful teaching of the Baptist! When the hour came and Jesus appeared, and the Baptist pointed to Him, saying, "Behold the Lamb of God!" how his heart thrilled at the sight of the Messiah. Familiar with the Old Testament, he knew all about the Passover Lamb, and the prophecy of the Messiah coming as such (Isa. 53:7). Thus, as the Baptist identified Jesus as the Lamb who had come to take away the sin of the world, John left John the Baptist, and followed Jesus. It is quite probable that the "other disciple" who was with Andrew was John, and that modestly he concealed his own name (John 1:35, 40).

It is evident that there was something in the call of the Baptist that touched the springs of all that was best in the being of those fishermen who had nursed the advent hope. As one writer expresses it: "The message of the earnest preacher met the deepest yearnings of the heart, and drew them in the train of the Stranger by an attractive force they could neither resist nor explain." From that hour the heart of John was captive, and the memory of seeing Jesus as the Lamb never left him. Such a truth became more vivid as he saw the Lamb led to slaughter, and crucified on a cross. "The Lamb, the bleeding Lamb," was to become the key-note of the gospel, epistles, and Apocalypse which he was to write. More than twenty times in the last book of the Bible John refers to the Lamb, and exalts Him as the central theme of the Everlasting Song before the Throne. The preaching of the Baptist was stern, and not characteristic of the gentleness John was to learn from Jesus, and which was to make him great as a preacher of the precious Lamb.

In the call and commission of John there were four stages in his spiritual development:

1. A convert and disciple of John the Baptist (John 1:35, 40).
2. An attachment to Christ as he left the Baptist (John 1:40). He was one of the first disciples to be called.
3. A discipleship under the Master's training (Matt. 4:21, 22).
4. An apostleship for well over seventy years (Luke 6:13, 14). John was one of the first apostles named (Matt. 4:18-22).

The purpose Jesus had before Him as He selected the apostolate after a night of prayer (Luke 8:12), was that of a transferred ministry. He knew that He was not to remain in the world to personally evangelize it. Such a task was to fall to His followers. If they failed, then the church Jesus envisaged would be seriously hindered in its growth. But, as the Acts prove, the apostles succeeded beyond their own hopes. The salvation of a lost, sinful world could be mediated only through the Savior — the evangelization of the world was to be the mission of those who were His witnesses. The choice of John as one of the first interpreters of Christ's saving message bore much fruit. Along with the rest of the chosen twelve, he did not have wealth, social prestige, or political influence, yet out they all went to preach a Gospel for the world rather than for a country or a province (John 3:16).

4. A Son of Thunder

What we have said in connection with this characteristic feature in our profile of James, is relevant here as we think of his brother John. Both brothers were intolerant, resentful of abuse and stern in their attitude toward offenders. They found it much easier to call down fire from heaven, than to remain meek under insult, and when footsore and weary, tramp on to another village. So John had to learn the lesson of humility. "Ye know not what manner of spirit ye are of." Impetuosity was not the Master's method, and must not be John's. By divine grace "the son of thunder" became a son of love. It would seem as if John was superior to Peter and James in courage, and ever remained a veritable "son of thunder" in presenting and pressing his claims upon the Lord, and the Lord's claims upon men.

When we come to John's vigorous denunciations of false views of Christ in his epistles, we are conscious of a strong and powerful vitality, an almost rigorous intellect able to face and cope with the most forceful assailants of truth. Dr. Elder Cumming tells us that he used to wonder why this new name, "son of thunder," which Christ gave John and his brother, was not used by John or James, as Peter used his name of *Simon*, but as the writer goes on to say, "I have come to see that it was *not* a 'new name,' but a name for the 'old man' of youth, who was to be cast out and give place to the 'new man' in Christ. A 'Son of Thunder' is a man who breaks out suddenly into a burst of passion, with loud voice and gleaming eye—a storm that passes in a few minutes. . . . The morning cloud, dark and ominous, passed away; the sunset was calm, clear, and beautiful exceedingly. The Son of Thunder had become the Son of Peace."

Calm me, my God, and keep me calm,
  Soft resting on Thy breast;
Soothe me with holy hymns and psalms,
  And bid my spirit rest.

5. *A Confidant of Christ*

Paul would have us covet earnestly the best gifts, and we find ourselves coveting John's place more than Peter's primacy or James' exalted throne. When the trio is mentioned it is "Peter, James, and John," but if Peter and James were first among the twelve, John was *first* in the affections of his Lord. Peter and James may have occupied chief place in the *apostolic college*, but John occupied the chief place *in the heart of Christ*. Thus, the most blessed and beautiful description we have of any disciple is that John was "the one whom Jesus loved." It is true that He loved all whom He had chosen (John 13:1, 2), but somehow Jesus loved John as He loved His own soul. John became a man after His own heart. In his company, the Master took deep delight because He found His kindred soul in him. While He played no favorites, He found in John the deep capacity of the mystic for spiritual truths, a quality of spiritual insight enabling him to understand His plan.

By beholding his Lord, John was changed into the same image from glory to glory. Further, if he was the disciple Jesus loved, then such a tribute implies that John was the disciple who best loved Jesus, and by force of his love for Him had a keen and true insight into his Master's thought and spirit. Leaning on the bosom of Jesus, John knew something of His heartbeat. Such a position was the coveted honor gained in the line of love.

John's admirable humility seen in the way he conceals his own worth and honor, comes out in his gospel, when he speaks of "the disciple whom Jesus loved." He omits his own name as the privileged disciple, leaving the reader to conjecture the one who was admitted into all the privileges and sanctities of Christ's friendship. Only one who had been His closest, most intimate friend, could have understood the love of His heart, and come to write of that love as no other. The whole teaching of John on *love* is vibrant with the deep heart-knowledge and experience of one who had sounded its depths.

The emphasis on our Lord's love for John is particularly striking, being found in five passages, four having one, and one the other Greek word translated *love*. The former word implies unselfish love, a love which does not seek for any return (John 13:23; 19:26; 21:7, 20-23; See 20:2). In each case it is most interesting to note that the literal rendering is "Whom Jesus kept on loving." The word John uses for *loved* at the resurrection is the same one he used when speaking of the Lord's love for Lazarus (11:3; 20:2). The affection and attention of Jesus for John went out continually and manifested itself in a variety of ways for the disciple's benefit.

Further, there was nothing unworthy in our Lord's yearning for a return of love. "Lovest thou me?"

(John 21:15). Years after John was able to write, "We love him because he first loved us." There is everything pure and true in Christ's desire to find Himself loved by His own. How comforting is the phrase, "Whom Jesus kept on loving," that is, with a clinging love for His is the love that will not let us go! We are "loved with everlasting love." How expressive are the lines of Charles Wesley on the privilege John experienced —

A Caesar's title less my envy moves
Than to be styled the man whom Jesus loves;
What charms, what beauties in his face did shine
Reflected ever from the face Divine.

The disciple whom Jesus loved! Is this not true of each, and of all, redeemed by His sacrificial blood? Love, if it is to be effective, must ever be singular and personal. Because Christ loved all and died for all, He loved and died for each. The *general* is translated into the *particular* and we exclaim with the apostle Paul, He "loved *me*, and gave himself for *me!*" (Gal. 2:20). When John described the betrayal of Jesus he portrayed himself when he said, "Now there was leaning on Jesus' bosom one of his disciples, whom Jesus loved" (13:23). Dr. J. B. Jones tells of a gardener who addressed a fragrant piece of clay in his garden: "What are you? Are you a rose?" "No," answered the clay; "but they laid me near a rose." Are we not thrice blessed if, like John, we catch the fragrance of the Lord, the Rose of Sharon, and know what it is as clay to become a rose?

Time, that affects all things below,
Can never change the love He'll show;
The heart of Christ with love will flow,
And we are loved.

A public and moving evidence of the holy intimacy of love existing between Jesus and John is seen at the cross where John seems to be the only apostle present, although Peter declares that he, too, was a witness of that hanging on a tree (Acts 4:15). Although in agony, Jesus sees His mother standing by the cross, "who by his death will be left without a son as well as without a husband, for the silence of history can only be accounted for on the supposition that Joseph was already dead." Concerned about the future of Mary, in the tenderness of His love Jesus commits her to the care of John whom He Himself loved beyond others, because beyond others he could receive His love.

The pathetic, solemn committal was a double one, for the loving heart of John would find, as well as give sympathy and support in the love of the mother. From that grim hour, the sympathy in their mutual loss would prove to be the source of love for each other. And, as we read, "from that hour" whatever home John had was shared with Mary. We cannot but wonder why Mary was not placed in the care of her other sons. Was it because of their attitude to Jesus, for at that time His own brothers did not believe on Him (John 7:5, 7)? We say that "blood is thicker than water," but the giving over of Mary to John's care proves that "spirit is thicker than blood." The truest bond between men is sympathy with Christ. Love to Him is the determining factor bringing into play the truest human sympathies. Thus, the opportunities given to John by his dying Lord of manifesting his love on His behalf, would be of great value in the development of his own character.

Surely, then, Jesus could not have given a more honorable testimony of His particular love for John, than to commit His own mother, whom of all earthly relations He held most dear, to John's trust and care. Can we not imagine how John stood by Mary, supporting her with a strong arm in the hour of her anguish, and then, when it was all over led her away to his own dwelling-place, which she was to share until her death? John could never forget this mark of love received from his dying Master. Was he not the last friend Jesus spoke to before He died? Jesus knew that John was fitted by strength of character, natural and acquired, to meet the demands He was placing upon the disciple He loved. The burden was put upon the right shoulders. The honor of the highest task was given to him who had most caught His spirit, and was most filled with His tenderness and compassion. May we never fail to remember that we can rise to no higher responsibilities than those for which we have been prepared!

6. *A Herald of Love*

The venerable Bishop Robert Lowth affirms that . . .

> God, who distributes His graces and gifts severally as He pleases, seems to have given John a peculiar insight into the mysteries of the divine love. He takes a particular pleasure in enlarging upon it, and he treats of it in a plain and unartificial style, but yet with such a lofty eloquence as is above the rules of human art, and can only be ascribed to that Holy Spirit which gave him utterance.

It is because of the love-life John shared with Jesus, and the prominence given to *love* in his writings that John earned the title of "the apostle of love." In his gospel and epistles, he gave to the world a definition of love not to be found in the writings of any other author, religious or secular, and such a declaration of love could only have been learned from close personal contact with the Lover of mankind

Himself. Through all his spiritual development, John knew that the love of the Master held him captive. This was why he could speak of himself with special emphasis, as "the disciple whom Jesus loved," as if resolving the Gospel as a theory of life as well as a practical experience into one grand principle of Love.

More than eighty times, John uses the term in his writings, and to him the love of which Christ spake was not a sentiment, but a principle, a life-transforming virtue. The substance of what John records of divine love can be classified thus:

1. God is One of Love (John 5:42; 15:10; See Luke 11:42).
2. God loved His Son (John 10:17; 15:9; 17:23, 24, 26).
3. God loved the disciples of Christ (John 16:27; 17:23).
4. God loves all men (John 3:16).
5. God is loved by Christ (John 14:31).
6. Christ loved the disciples in general (John 13:1-34; 14:21; 15:9, 10).
7. Christ loved individuals (John 11:5, 36; 13:23).
8. Christ expected all men to love Him and God (John 8:42; 14:23).
9. Christ taught that we should love one another (John 13:34, 35; 15:12, 13).
10. Christ emphasized that love is the sum and substance of the Law, and that the Law can be truly kept as one loves God and his fellows (Ex. 20:1-17; Matt. 22:36-40).

In addition to his other gifts, John had a passionate love, a spirit winged with love. If Peter was first in a primacy of order, John certainly had the primacy of love. To him, as he shows in his first epistle, love is life — love is the proof of love — the test of love is keeping Christ's commandments. God is Love, and as He *is,* so are we in this world. Deeply loved by Christ, John became an echo answering to such affection — a mirror reflecting an Image — a harp responding to the touch of a Master-hand. Had John known the expressive hymn of Horatius Bonar he would have sung with true heart-feeling —

Thy name is Love! I hear it from yon Cross;
    Thy name is Love! I read it in yon tomb;
All meaner love is perishable dross,
    But this shall light me through time's thickest gloom.

It is said that when John was at Ephesus, being aged he would be led into the church there to answer all inquiries concerning the faith, and that he would always answer with the same sentence, "Little children, love one another." When the people became impatient of this invariable admonition and asked why it was always the same, John would reply that it was the commandment of our Lord, and if this alone was observed, it would be sufficient. Beloved, let us love, for love is rest!

7. *A Witness of Integrity*

Bible writers seemed to have their own particular key-words, the repetition of which indicates truths they seek to emphasize. Another of John's key-words, recurring in his gospel, epistle, and the Apocalypse is that of *witness* (used some thirty times). But the cognates are partly concealed by the various renderings, *record,* used thirteen times, and *testify* and *testimony,* used twenty-five times. All three words are from one Greek root, and are akin to the term *martyr.* John introduces his gospel by laying stress upon the work of John the Baptist as a witness of the Christ as the Light,

and that through such a witness men might come to believe on Him. But the apostle magnified a far greater Witness (John 5:31-47). Having stood by and watched his Master die, John could write that his testimony of all he saw was true (John 15:27). Living with all he knew and loved in heaven, John had an unassailable testimony (John 19:35; 21:24). Christianity is a fact, and is based on a fact. John sets forth no fewer than seven forms of reliable evidence —

1. The witness of John the Baptist, forerunner of Jesus (John 5:32, 33).
2. The witness of Scripture (John 5:39).
3. The witness of the Father (John 5:37).
4. The witness of Christ Himself (John 8:14).
5. The witness of Christ's miracles (John 5:36).
6. The witness of the Holy Spirit (John 15:26).
7. The witness of the disciples (John 15:27).

The Gospel of the Person and work of Christ comes to us on the basis of assured divine and human testimony, and bids us believe and live (I John 5:7-11). Without doubt John was a seer, and premonitions of his visionary power are given us before the ascension of Christ. John was the first to see the fact of the resurrection, and as an accurate witness he described all he saw, even the position of the clothing left behind. Then, he was the first to discern his Lord's person on the lakeside when He appeared to the disciples after their fruitless toil, and, again, as a witness he described all that happened. But John's quality as a seer is at its best in the Revelation — a book that becomes more marvelous the more deeply it is studied. What a testimony it is to the Lord's ultimate conquest! In it, testifying to all he saw, John sets forth the fundamental realities of the Christian Gospel Rev. 1:4-8), and throughout the book, Christ is extolled as "The Faithful Witness."

Before John could bear witness to the world of the great truths God had chosen him to reveal, it was necessary for him to see in all His divine glory the Master whom he long loved and served (Rev. 1:10-20). What he saw and heard he wrote in a book, the contents of which can be summarized thus —

1. A vision of the Lord Jesus Christ in all His majesty
2. A vision of His church in all its reality
3. A vision of a lost world in all its hostility
4. A vision of eternity in all its glory.

For over seventy years John maintained a firm and fearless witness for his Master, creating, thereby, in the hearts of the saints of all ages both wonder and faith. Under all circumstances the apostle witnessed a good confession. His love was constantly centered on his Master, and his witness and work were always for His glory. In his gospel John witnessed to the fact that the Man of Galilee was God; in his epistles, that it was God who became Man; in his Apocalypse, that the ultimate universal victory over all forces of evil will be through and for the Lord Jesus — the God-Man. The effective witness of John in the apostolic age was fittingly described by the famous French theologian, Godét, in his fine estimate —

> The hour for work had sounded in the first place for Peter. He had founded the Church in Israel, and planted the standard of the New Covenant on the ruins of Theocracy. Paul had followed. His task had been to liberate the Church from the restrictions of an expiring Judaism, and to open the door of the Kingdom of God to Gentiles.

John succeeded them, he who was first to come, and whom the Master reserved to the last. He completed the fusion of these heterogeneous elements of which the Church had been formed, and he raised Christendom to the relative perfection of which it was then capable. It may be said, then, that —

> Peter *formed* the primitive Church,
> Paul *emancipated* it, and
> John *established* it.

8. *A Writer of Repute*

Sir Philip Sidney, 1554-1586, in one of his *Sonnets* has the phrase, "Fool, said my muse to me, look in thy heart and write." This is how John, who loved to use pen and ink and paper, wrote (II John 12; III John 13); and his writing is of the highest spiritual order because his heart was the palace of the King he loved and obeyed. It was Lucke, the theologian, who truly pronounced of John that, "He lives and will ever live by his writings, and the future belongs to him, as well as the past." The apostle who knew Christ most intimately, who had leaned on His breast, was spared through many years to write for the Christian Church as a whole, and for the world at large. In the main, John wrote as an eye-witness (I John 1:1). He had a most vivid way of describing persons and events. Running through his gospel, for instance, we have exactness of description, a representation of the whole scene photographed as it were upon the writer's memory, which is of greater weight than any number of individual quotations (Read John 1:38-51; 2:13-17; 20: 8-10). John remembers the days and hours when events occurred, for he was present, and writing from memory he knew what happened at the Tenth

Hour, the Seventh, the Sixth (1:39; 4:52; 19:14, etc.).

As to John's style and diction as a writer, Dr. W. Graham Scroggie reminds us that, "None of the Evangelists has so limited a vocabulary as the Apostle John, but none of them makes better use of what he has." Godét wrote of him, "If the author has only a few terms in his vocabulary these terms may be compared to pieces of gold with which great lords make payment." John's style is unique in many respects — a thing to be felt rather than to be defined. The most illiterate reader is conscious of this quality, says Dr. Plummer, "and the ablest critic cannot analyse it satisfactorily." In sentence construction, John usually makes his sentences stand by themselves, so that while there is continuity of thought, there is little in the form of expression. An illustration of this can be found in John 1:1-5 R.V., where we have ten statements with the only connecting link of a six times repeated *and*. Another feature of his writing is the repetition of a word or sentence to underline the thought communicated (5:31, 32; 10:11; 17:14-19, etc.).

Other characteristics of John's penmanship are fully dealt with in Ellicott's Commentary in his *Introduction to John's Gospel*, and in *The Guide to the Gospels*, by Dr. Graham Scroggie. As a whole, John's style is "contemplative, not controversial; calm, not militant; simple, yet profound; direct rather than oblique; transparent, yet deep; spiritual, rather than historical." Behind John's wonderful pen was a penetrative mind for he was a *thinker* equal to Moses or Paul. Visitors to the Metropolitan Museum of Art in New York are often fascinated by Francois Auguste Rodin, the renowned French sculptor's work, *Le Pensant*, The Thinker, a fine study

in stone of a figure, seated, bending forward, elbow on knee, chin on hand, gazing with eyes that search the realms of thought. Often John must have sat, pondering, reflecting, sifting matters which related to the person and performances and pronouncements of his Lord, until they assumed coherence.

We cannot read all John recorded without being impressed with the supreme position he assigns to Jesus. To him, his Lord was the sun behind all light — life before all existence — worker behind all energy. Sitting and writing, John's mighty thoughts as to the Godhead of Christ have reverberated all along the ages. Chrysostom cried, "Hear how John thunders!" Augustine commenting on the opening words of John's gospel wrote, "John has opened . . . as with a burst of thunder." Bengel says of the same portion, "This is the thunder brought to us by a Son of Thunder." John seems to have sounded the depths of revelation while others only ruffled the surface. He meditated until his Spirit-inspired imagination took wings and soared where he heard and saw beyond any other. Behind his powerful pen were reflection, imagination, intuition, and "the Spirit of wisdom and revelation of the knowledge of Him" he loved.

Admirably skilled in the language of his own nation, John translated from the Hebrew original, and what was wanting in any Greek finesse in his style was abundantly compensated for in the zeal of his temper, and the excellency and sublimity of his matter. Basil, the great Church Father of the third century, confessed that "among all the evangelical preachers, none like St. John, the son of thunder for the sublimeness of his speech, and the height of his discourses beyond any man's capacity to duly reach and comprehend." To this may be added the testimony of St. Cyril of Alexandria who said of John's written works:

> To the sublimity of his incomprehensible notions, the acumen and sharpness of his reason, and the quick inferences of his discourses constantly succeeding and following upon one another, must needs confess that his Gospel exceeds all admiration.

The mystics of an earlier age regarded John as "The Eagle Evangelist" *(A flying eagle,* the king of birds, Rev. 4:7), because with strong wing and steady eye he was able to soar into the open sky with a prophetic faith and bring from beyond the clouds in those dark days of crucifixion the secret of God. With open eyes and an ever-active mind, John gathered his figures and illustrations from the widest field. He was indeed the seer with eagle vision, bold imagination and poetic genius. Further, in medieval art, John is pictured with the face of a *woman,* for his clinging trust and direct insight made him specially the interpreter of the heart. It is not without reason he has been called "The Christian Plato." Alexander Whyte in his unique *Bible Characters* says, "John, fisherman's son and all, was born with one of the finest minds that has ever been bestowed by God's goodness upon any of the sons of men."

By the pen, the one-time unlearned Galilean became one of the immortals of the world. Yet it was not on his matchless books John prided himself. To him, pen, books, and fame were counted as the small dust of the balance, or dross. If men talked to him of his influence and work, his unfailing reply would be, "God forbid that I should glory save in this — Jesus loved even me!" No fewer than five books of the Bible came from John's pen

dipped in the ink of inspiration, and all of them are full of the marks of his personality, and although dead for many centuries, he still speaks. All of his five books are breathings pure and spiritual. As it is not within the province of our coverage of the apostles to give an exposition of each of John's written ·works, yet a brief description of each may be in order.

His gospel

Being characteristically modest John does not attach his name to this fourth book of the New Testament which is pre-eminently the "gospel of conversations," since it relates more largely than the other gospels the individualism of Jesus as expressed in His interviews. Altogether there are twenty-four conversations held with seventeen people, and they can be listed thus:

Nathanael the guileless.
The gentle Mary who treasured in her mother-heart the memory of the words of and about her divine Son — twice.
The perplexed scholar, Nicodemus.
The sinful but appreciative woman of Samaria.
A nobleman of Capernaum.
An impotent man at the Pool of Bethesda.
Talks with Philip, a blind man, Martha, Mary, John, Peter — four times, the high priest, an officer, Pilate, Mary Magdalene, Thomas — the last two being after the Resurrection.

These conversations were often brief monologues of Jesus and some were directions for His miracles, and were associated with a variety of conditions. In the A.V. of the gospel there are 879 verses, 419 of which contain words of our Lord, nearly half the gospel. John's definite statement as to the purpose and contents of his gospel is given toward its close: "These are written, that ye might believe that Jesus is the Christ, the Son of God; and that believing ye might have life in his name" (20:31). Two aspects John had in mind, then, are clear:

1. To lead to personal belief in the historical *Jesus as the Christ,* or *Messiah* (for the Jews), and as *the Son of God* (for the Gentiles).
2. To lead, by believing, to the possession of life in His name.

Clement of Alexandria calls this gospel by John, *a spiritual gospel,* by which he implied that it contains less of historical narrative than any other, and more of doctrine. It gives a fuller development of Christian truth, admirably adapted to confute various heresies, which, since the writing of the first three gospels, had sprung up respecting the person of our blessed Lord. The first eighteen verses of chapter 1 are a clue to the intention of the whole gospel. John's reminiscences dwell mainly on the spiritual side of Christ's person and teaching. S. D. Gordon calls these verses "the front key at the front door." Then "the side-door key" is in Chapter 16: 28 and "the back door key" in 20:31.

In John's gospel we are in a region of thought widely different from those of the other gospels, and as Ellicott observes, "Characteristic thoughts naturally express themselves in characteristic words." Some of these words, the special forms of which express the special thoughts which have come to us through John, are herewith cited:

Light — twenty-three times
Life — fifty-two times
Love — seven times (seventeen times in I John)
Truth — twenty-five times
True — (ideally) five times
Witness — forty-seven times (substantive and verb)
Believe — ninety-eight times
World — seventy-eight times
Sign — seventeen times.

The gospel of John has a character and a history that are alike unique. Commentator Lange called it, "The Diamond amongst the Gospels," while Van Doren wrote of it as, "The Gospel of the Gospels." Yet another said of it, "The Holy of Holies."

His first epistle

In what other book of the Bible does the exalted view of the love of God shine forth as brightly as in this first epistle of John? The first error disturbing the early church was the denial of the *human,* and not of the *divine* nature of Christ. To establish believers in sound views respecting the person and office of Christ, His human and divine nature, and His atonement was the burden of this epistle. But as in all John's writings this was done, not in the form of abstract discussion, but in a spirit of the most persuasive tenderness.

John particularly enlarges on the love of God in redemption, urging it as a motive to holiness and mutual love. This epistle is, throughout, especially useful, as offering many tests by which to try the sincerity of our Christian profession. (See I John 2: 4, 5, 15; 3:7, 15; 4:13; 5:4, 18). If, as Bishop Westcott suggests, this epistle was the last book of the New Testament in chronological order of writing, then there is a striking contrast between the opening words of the Bible and the closing statement —

In the beginning God — Genesis 1:1.

Little children, keep yourselves from idols — I John 5:21.

With characteristic reticence John conceals his name as the writer of this general epistle, calculated for all times and places. He knew that men would be more concerned about what it said, than who it was who wrote it. That it came from the gifted pen of John has never been questioned.

His second epistle

This further epistle, and the next, are actually short letters or notes of a few verses each, directed to particular persons. The doctrine, phrase, and design of these two letters testify to John's penmanship. His sentences are grave and simple, short and penetrating. Whether it was addressed to a church or to a family is an open question. Of the thirteen verses contained in his second epistle, eight are found in substance in the first epistle.

If it was addressed to a Christian mother, a lady of honorable quality, to warn her against the prevailing error of the times, respecting the person of our gracious Lord, then it implies the importance in the sight of God of a Christian mother, the earnestness with which she should interest herself in the spiritual welfare of her children, and the encouragement she will give to Christian ministers, and to the progress of truth, by so doing.

His third epistle

This short letter was addressed to the charitable and hospitable Gaius, so kind a friend to John, and so courteous an entertainer of all needy believers. Probably Gaius is the person mentioned by Paul (Rom. 16:23; I Cor. 1:14). Particularly renowned for his kindness to those who went about preaching the Gospel, John expresses his affectionate joy at this and other evidences of his piety. Ten times in John's three epistles, the word *Beloved* is found. This significant and beautiful expression expresses the attractive oneness in Christ between the apostle and Gaius.

As for Diotrephes, conspicuous for his ambition and turbulence, nothing is known of him beyond the brief sentence in which John clearly describes his character. A striking contrast is found in Gaius, for whom John uses his favorite term *Beloved* — the fourth time in this brief note. The apostle strongly recommends Demetrius to Gaius's friendship, as one well-known for his fidelity. The epistle closes with the deferment of other matters to when John and Gaius meet for a personal conversation.

The Apocalypse

There can be no doubt about John's authorship of this final book of the Bible. Withholding his name from his gospel and epistles, he uses it five times over in the Revelation (see 1: 1, 4, 9; 21:2; 22:8). Sir Isaac Newton wrote that, "No book of the New Testament has been so strongly attested, or commented upon so early as this: nor does any other equal it in the dignity and sublimity of its composition." The visions contained in it were given by Christ to His much-loved apostle, during his exile on the Isle of Patmos, and was published not long after his death, about the year A.D. 97.

All that needs to be said at this point about John's highly dramatic book is what D. M. Panton once wrote:

> The Book of Revelation is a shock to the sleeper; a sting to the carnal; a tonic to the good; a summons to the dead; by disclosing the things that as a matter of fact will happen, it places in our hands the master-key to every modern problem.
>
> It illuminates backwards like an electric flare; and by revealing their issues, it tears out the heart of the movements around us, so that our feet are shepherded forever in the narrow way.

9. *A Prisoner of Nero*

Our next chapter will deal with the traditions and legends associated with John's closing years and death. In this section we simply draw attention to the authentic record of what the apostle himself has to say as to the eventide of his ministry. In all probability after the death of Mary (for whom John faithfully cared in memory of her Son he dearly loved), he resolutely turned his back upon the house of ineffable and hallowed memories, and went out into the great, wild, wide vineyard of the Lord. Despite the centuries intervening we find the lonely majesty of John awe-inspiring. Paul had many traveling companions and dearly loved students, such as young Timothy around him, but the record of John seems to have so many blanks. After the ascension of Christ, the apostle must have had almost seventy years of service, yet the curtain is not raised very often on his long career.

When the curtain is raised for the last time, John is an old man in the isolation of exile on a desolate island. He commenced his life of suffering for Christ's sake when he was apprehended with Peter and put in prison (Acts 4:3), but he lived on after the martyrdom of Paul and Peter for some thirty years. The picture of his loneliness was painted by Browning in *A Death in the Desert:*

> It is long
> Since James and Peter had release by
> death,
> And I am only he, your brother John,
> Who saw and heard, and could remember
> all.
> . . . There is left on earth
> No one alive who knew —
> Saw with his eyes and handled with his
> hands
> That which was from the first, the Word
> of Life,

How will it be, when none more saith, I saw?

Then we have these further expressive lines from the Christian poet:

> Since I, whom Christ's mouth taught, was
> bidden teach,
> I went for many years about the world,
> Saying, "It was so; so I heard, and saw"
> Speaking as the case asked: and men be-
> lieved.

But the fine testimony of the last surviving witness to the life, death, and resurrection, and ascension of Jesus Christ had come. A new Emperor, Domitian, began a fresh course of persecution as he *vexed* the church. Someone had reported from Asia Minor that there was a prominent Christian there preaching the *way* of Christ. Soon an edict arrived from Rome that John should be seized and banished to Patmos. It seems ridiculous that anyone should be afraid of a man ninety years of age.

Such an old man needed loving care but in Patmos there was no one to watch over him. What hardship John suffered we are not told. History does tell us that in the marble mines on the Isle, "men worked chained to their slave barrows." Thinking of other saints enduring cruel persecutions, John could write to them as "your brother and companion in tribulation" (Rev. 1:9). Are you not tempted to ask why God allowed His most faithful to reach the age when activity had passed, and only the dregs of life seem to remain, to endure the mailed fist of Imperial Rome? Was it to prove yet once again that His strength is made perfect through human weakness?

Moses was eighty years old when the call came to do the greatest work of his life, and John, now ninety or so, was in Patmos, but he found himself "in the Spirit on the Lord's Day" and received the vision — glorious, inspiring, thrilling. Patmos was surrounded by the sea, making escape impossible, but John, while in the third heaven heard the message that "there shall be no more sea." A wonderful commission was given this old man. Prophets there had been, but it is not too much to say that so far as the future, especially the far future, is concerned, John in the Revelation foresaw and taught more than all the old prophets put together. As Elder Cumming has it —

> To no man was the time to come set forth so fully, so clearly, so graphically, so solemnly, so blessedly; but God had to wait till John was a very old man, almost done with the world, before He could trust him with such a charge. His eyes and heart turned naturally — perhaps I should rather say *spiritually* — to that future on which he was just entering.

John was a super-victor over the Roman antagonist who had taken the field against Christ and His church. Although there was seeming disaster there was no cause for fear, seeing Christ was in the midst of His church, and its leaders were in His right hand (Rev. 1:16-20). Thus, had it not been for John's imprisonment, the church would never have had the vision of Christ, as the Lord of Life, Warder of the Unseen, and Holder of the Keys.

As we are to see in the following chapter, many traditions gathered around John. There are legends, for instance, about his martyrdom. But some of the early fathers who had been John's disciples have left it on record that on his release from Patmos, he returned to Ephesus, where he fell asleep, and passed once more to the presence of his Master — this time forever. His grave, like that of Moses, is known only to God. As Daniel McLean so beautifully put it —

John died like a summer day, his heart expanding like the setting sun; the clouds spent of their thunder catching up the twilight glow of warm light as if the chariot of fire that bore Elijah into Heaven had returned in softened sweetness to bear aloft the beloved of the Lord. He crowned the Apostolic Age; he closed the book of inspired revelation with a sort of echo of the promise at Ascension, saying, "Even so come, Lord Jesus," and that coming ushered him into the full enjoyment of what he had formerly seen in thought. He now walks with Christ among the golden candlesticks.

The grave of D. L. Moody, the renowned evangelist, at Northfield, Mass. is marked by a stone slab upon which is cut his favorite verse, "He that doeth the will of God abideth for ever" (I John 2:17). When the apostle John penned these words he actually wrote his own epitaph.

10. *A Model to Copy*

We have a saying that "Example is better than precept." From John we are privileged to have both the example and the precept to emulate. Remarkable as his witness was in length and influence, the Lord did not exhaust all His power in the enduement of the one He loved. What He did for and through John, He is able to do for us if only we are determined to abide in the will of God as the apostle did. During his apostolate we see him at the Lord's Supper leaning on the bosom of Jesus and we have already hinted at the formation of character which brought him there. Would we have the same privilege of intimacy? Do we desire to live near enough — nearer to Him than all others — to speak and to hear Him reply? Then we must be disciples such as John was, for his secret can be ours.

The Christ John knew was the One

of experience — the One he had seen and heard and handled. To the apostle, He was a Friend, and Light and Love; and dwelling in Him, believers come to resemble Him. Perhaps the sum of John's teaching for your heart and mine is that heaven is to be in the presence of Christ, for the Christian who has become like Him can, therefore, see Him as He is. Further, John's life illustrates that the image of Jesus is most clearly seen and reflected by those who respond most to His love. How much we owe John!

He it is who leads us into divinest fellowship with our Lord. He it is who brings us to see His pity for us in our sin, and His sympathy with us in our sorrow and bereavement. He it is who shows us how to keep our love for the Master in the background, and that it is in our yielding to, and resting in, His love that we are blessed.

Then, can we not learn a most valuable lesson on the great theme of Divine Grace, as we meditate upon the most striking spiritual development which John experienced? We think of his intolerant party spirit, sectarianism and religious rivalry; of his resentful mood that would call down fire on the Samaritans, and of Christ's severe censure of such ill-directed zeal and fire-breathing spirit; of his short and easy path to honor and ambitious request for promotion. But, beholding his Lord, as in a mirror, John was changed into His image, for the love of Christ shone steadily above all the disciple's obscurations, and became like Him as the result of His transfiguring power and over-mastering love.

We may think of ourselves as being more unlikely and unworthy material for the Divine Potter to shape, but He is still able to transform the son of thunder until he becomes the incarnation of tenderness and pity. Christ can change the volcano into a fountain of gentleness and affection. The One who wrought a perfect work in a once raging, stormy, ambitious nature, subduing it all to His own sweet qualities, leaving in it the strength of the lion, but imparting to it the meekness of the lamb, is the same today. The question is, Are we surrendered to the divine will as John was? Are we willing to be transformed by the renewing of our mind?

Not what I am, O Lord, but what Thou
    art;
    That, that alone, can be my soul's true
      rest;
Thy love, not mine, bids fear and doubt
    depart,
    And stills the tempest of my tossing
      breast.

JUDAS ISCARIOT

THE APOSTLE WHO COMMITTED SUICIDE

The dark story of Judas is one of the most tragic and mysterious records in Scripture, with features we cannot explain. Always placed last in the lists of the twelve, he became the best known of them because of his infamy. It would have been better for this traitor had he never been brought out of obscurity. Jesus said of him the most terrible thing that could be said of any man, *It had been good for that man if he had not been born;* and for nineteen centuries the world has repeated that phrase of those who, being born, blasted their life. Judas Iscariot and Pontius Pilate are pilloried together as objects of the world's scorn, and as base men who won for themselves everlasting shame. Of course, the name of the base Judaean carries a heavier load of guilt than that of the Roman Governor who believed in the betrayed One's innocency.

All down the ages the treachery of Judas has been regarded as the foulest deed that was ever committed. Artists have described Judas as a subject for the delineation of the most hellish passions; and poets have conjured up all the horrors of the imagination to represent his fierce malignity and hideous ingratitude. Children who have the story of Judas read to them shudder at the thought of his crime. Because of the feeling of abhorrence of his crime, his name has become a byword for betrayal and treachery, and no good mother would ever give a son of hers the name of *Judas,* just as she would be loathe to call her daughter, *Jezebel.* Says Charles Stanford, "Of all the spectres that have ever haunted the poet in his imagination, or the sacred sleeper in his dreams, or iced the blood of the seer, there has surely been none like the awful ghost of Judas." There are forty verses in the New Testament in which there is a reference to the betrayal of our Lord, and in each of them the dastardly sin of Judas is recorded. A gifted writer of a past century in a striking portrayal of degeneracy of character, gives us a description which might well be a cameo of Judas:

> A perfect traitor should have a face on which vice can write no marks, lips which will lie with a dimpled smile, eyes of such agate-like brightness and depth that no infamy can dull them, cheeks that can rise from a murder and not look haggard.

As we read the gospels it would seem that the rest of the apostles were unsuspicious of Judas up to the very last. The thought of treachery from Judas never entered their heads until the dark deed was consummated. But after the sell-out, then they understood that the foul act of Judas had been premeditated and deliberate. Supreme, then, in world-wide detestation is the name no family in the civilized world would ever think of perpetuating. In Dante's passage through hell Judas is depicted as occupying the lowest circle with Lucifer, enduring his "worst punishment," banned and shunned even in the caverns of the damned.

The rest of the twelve Jesus selected were, in spite of their failings, covered with a glory not their own, but for Judas Iscariot who sold his Friend, Lover, Teacher, and Master for a paltry handful of silver, by such a diabolical deed he expelled himself from the shining ranks of "the glorious company of the apostles," and plunged himself into an abyss of scoffing and loathing; and the place of honor he might have won was exchanged for a suicide's grave and a universal and dreadful condemnation and notoriety. Purposefully and deliberately he sold his Lord, precipitating, thereby, His cruel death upon the cross; and then, conscious-stricken, he went out and hanged himself on a tree. Let us now try to set forth the facts, as given in Scripture, concerning this traitor among the twelve.

1. *He Was of Kerioth*

The given name of the betrayer of Jesus was Judas, the second name *Iscariot* being a form of a Greek word meaning, "a man of Kerioth," the town where he was born. Such a double name is given to his father, Simon Iscariot (John 6:71; 13:2, 26, r.v.). It may be that the *Iscariot* was attached to Judas, to distinguish him from six others of the same common name of the time. Shakespeare prefers to call Judas, "The base Judaean who sold a pearl richer than all his tribe."

Kerioth, or Nerioth, the town from which Judas hailed, has passed out of existence. He was the only disciple in the Galilean band representing this district around Jerusalem, and on this account he was never thoroughly at one with the rest. Traditionally, Jerusalem despised Galilee, but Judas scorned public opinion of the South and he joined the northern Leader to whom men were gathering from every quarter. Galileans were not regarded as pure Jews by their brethren of the South (John 7:52).

Kerioth is the same word as "*Kirjath*," and means a "city" as in Kirjath-Jearim; but the name is found standing alone for two towns. One of these is in Moab (Amos 2:2), and the other is in Judah, on the south-east border, close to Edom (Joshua 15:25). The consensus is that Judas was a native of the Kerioth that lay in Judah. All the other apostles came from Galilee, in the far north of Palestine.

2. *He Was a Disciple*

As the first Scriptural reference to Judas is his election to the apostleship (Matt. 10:4; Mark 3:19; Luke 6:16), we are not told when and how he became a disciple of Jesus. Probably he had been present at the preaching of John the Baptist at Bethany beyond Jordan (John 1:28), or may have met Jesus during His return through Judaea with His followers (John 3:22). Perhaps he was among those who received the call at the Sea of Tiberias (Matt. 4:18-22). While the circumstances under which some of the band were called are stressed (such as Matthew's case at the receipt of custom), a veil hangs over the first meeting of Judas and Jesus. As discipleship had to precede apostleship, there must have been qualities and capacities in Judas which Jesus recognized. It may be that his admiration for, and emulation of, the new Rabbi left nothing to be desired, and so Jesus called him as a disciple.

If the character of Judas was conspicuously defective on the sympathetic side, then this would explain the reserve that marked his conduct while with Jesus. When he joined Him it was more as a patriot or political leader than as a personal friend, and his mind interpreted the words and deeds of Christ through the medium of his own anticipation. Strong-willed, as well as conceited, Judas could not brook the idea of being mistaken in his first opinion of the new King. The other disciples had found a Teacher who awoke admiration and love, but with Judas it was different. Political ambition, love of place and power, prospect of the Kingdom being proclaimed were his main inducements in joining those who were following the King.

We would like to think that at the time of his choice to follow Jesus, Judas was no conscious or deliberate hypocrite, and that the fervor and enthusiasm he displayed were no sham;

that he was sincere in his initial discipleship, having an honest desire to follow Him. But the fact remains that while he may have been sincere, he was not *whole-hearted* in his decision. He did not leave all to follow, but offered Jesus a divided allegiance. The love of money had been in his heart from earlier days, and he was thus a double-minded man. Had he followed the Master fully he might have had the noblest of lives, and the most blessed of destinies, but he took his sin with him into the service of Christ until ultimately his habitation became desolate, and his bishopric was taken by another (Acts 1:20).

3. *He Was an Apostle*

As already indicated, nothing is said of the call of Judas: where it took place, or when, or in what circumstances. The first mention of his name comes when, after Christ's night of prayer, He chose the twelve and included Judas among them, and in each list he is always the last named — and no wonder! With the other apostles, Judas was elected to learn of, and act for, Christ. An apostle had to be one who had seen and heard Him, and shared His companionship. Doubtless Judas was empowered along with the rest of the band to preach, heal sicknesses, and cast out devils (Mark 3:14-19). Thus, in spite of the absence of deep grace in his own heart he was used as an agent in the promotion of the work of grace in the hearts of others. One wonders what Judas must have thought of the Lord's declaration about those who cast out devils in His name, but of whom He would have to say, "I never knew you; depart from me, ye that work iniquity."

As a pure Jew from Judah, Judas found himself nearly alone in the circle of the twelve, yet doubtless he was as zealous as the rest in supporting and furthering the cause of the Messiah. As one near to Him, Judas had often looked into that wonderful face of His and must have blushed as he thought of the sin that was poisoning his soul. If ever a man had the opportunity to become a saint, that man was Judas who, for over two years had lived with the holiest Man on earth. It is not always true that what a man becomes depends largely on his surroundings. Had it been so in the life of Judas, then the years in closest intimacy with the one perfect Being who ever walked the earth should have inspired Judas to grow daily better and nobler and holier. But the devil entered even an apostle, proving that even the most coveted religious privileges are powerless to save a man. Bunyan in the last sentence of his *Dream* tells us that he saw a way to hell even from the gates of heaven.

What a hard blow it was for Christ to bear when such betrayal came, not from an avowed enemy, but from one He had chosen as an apostle and who had enjoyed the intimacy of His friendship for so long! It is not difficult to see a prophecy of Judas in the portrait David etched of a deceitful friend:

> It was not an enemy that reproached me; then I could have borne it: neither was it he that hated me that did magnify himself against me; then I would have hid myself from him: But it was *thou,* a man mine equal, my guide, and mine acquaintance. We took sweet counsel together, and walked unto the house of God in company. Let death seize upon them, and let them go down quick into hell (Ps. 55:12-15).

Judas the apostle and acquaintance of of Christ went out into darkness (Ps. 88:18), and the mystery ever remains, Why did Christ choose him as an apostle? Did He think Judas was a different man than he turned out to be? Was He not aware of his character, and was He deceived as the rest of the apostles were? At the outset, let it be said that we totally reject the suggestion given by Professor A. B. Bruce that, "Iscariot was chosen merely to be a traitor, as an actor might be chosen to play the part of Iago." Such an incredible theory is altogether contrary to the guileless nature of Christ, and to His purpose in selecting the twelve. To affirm that Jesus chose Judas to be a traitor is to make Him responsible for His own betrayal by the apostle — an act that would exonerate Judas from all blame.

What the Scriptures do declare is that Jesus, as the omniscient One, knew what was in man, and therefore "knew *from the beginning* . . . who should betray him," that is, from the hour Jesus first saw Judas and decided to include him in the apostolate (John 2:24, 25; 6:64). Foreknowing, then, all that would happen, why did Jesus prayerfully and deliberately elect Judas to His service, entrust him with all His teachings and confidences and even send him out with the other chosen ones to preach, heal the sick, and cast out demons? Answers to such a question are not easy, for no matter what explanation is given we are left with "the insoluble problems of the origin of evil and of Divine Omniscience, combined with human free will."

This we do know, that Jesus made the choice He did:

Because it was His own sovereign will to do so. "Whatsoever the Lord pleased, that did he in heaven, and in earth" (Ps. 135:6).

Because it was needful to fulfill Old Testament prophecies concerning every aspect of His life and mission. Exposing the betrayal by Judas,

Jesus quoted Scriptures fortelling the same (Pss. 41:9; 69:25; John 17:12; Acts 1:20). Knowing the end from the beginning God was able to record what Judas would do, centuries before he was born. All prophecies, then, relating to the betrayer prove the *foresight* of Holy Writ.

Because the sell-out by Judas would reveal that association with the godly — even with Christ, who knew no sin — is possible, without regeneration being a fact of experience. One can be in Christ's service and yet not have Him in the heart as Savior and Lord. Judas lacked the essential. He was destitute of faith and love.

Because the money Judas sought for his terrible deed would demonstrate that "the love of money is the root of all evil." Judas will ever remain as a monument to the terrible snare and curse of money, and of how it can drown men in destruction and perdition.

Because Jesus desired to manifest His amazing forbearance and longsuffering. He did not expose Judas as He witnessed his gradual degeneration, but left him in his own time to reveal his true character. How restrained Jesus was on the night of betrayal, as bread was eaten with him who had lifted up his heel against Him! Was ever contrast so marked as was clearly seen on this occasion between the betrayer and the Betrayed?

Because the unique sorrow that was our Lord's at the outcome of His choice of Judas was necessary to the completion of His qualifications as High Priest over the House of God. In all points He was tested as we are, but became perfect through His sufferings (Heb. 2:10, 17, 18).

Coupled with the above possible explanations of the problem of Judas' choice is that although Jesus saw in him certain evil tendencies which might develop, He saw other finer qualities he possessed which might under His teaching and influence overcome the baser inclinations. Jesus was cognizant of the struggle going on in this man's heart between light and darkness, and prayed and hoped that the nobler side of Judas would be victorious. When at last Jesus saw that he was bent on his dreadful crime, He gave him up, saying, "What thou doest, do quickly." Covetousness, combined with other motives, dragged Judas down to his unnatural and truly infernal deed, earning forever the infamous title branded on his brow, "Judas Iscariot, who also betrayed him."

Efforts have been made to defend Judas, extenuate his crime, and even whitewash his character. Pleas on his behalf would have us believe that he was not so black as he is painted, that he erred more through lack of judgment than through criminal intent. Thomas de Quincey, for instance, suggests that his object was not to give Christ up to the power of His enemies, but to force Him to use His own miraculous power against them, or to compel Jesus to resort to force in the establishment of His Kingdom. When he failed to force the Master's hand, Judas was surprised and shocked, and because his calculations failed, he committed suicide. If there was any truth in such a defense, then Judas was an early Jesuit of the worst type who thought the end justified the most infamous and immoral means.

But any plea to justify Judas is cancelled out by the fact that when he covenanted to sell Jesus for thirty pieces of silver, Jesus spoke of him as "a son of perdition," and allowed him to die by his own hand, and pass out into the blackness of darkness forever. If ever Judas had loved Jesus, the love

of money smothered it, and the root of bitterness possessed him, for there is a trace of vindictiveness and a spice of revenge in his final act of treachery Taken up, as we have been, with the problem of why Jesus chose Judas, let us not fail to turn to ourselves and consider the equal problem of why Jesus called us into His service. What did He see in you and in me, constraining Him to set His love upon us! Do you never pause and wonder why Christ, in His matchless love, brought *you* into fellowship with Himself? Yes, and conscious of the ever-present inbred sin, do you not feel the need of constant attention to the solemn warnings? "Let him that thinketh he standeth take heed lest he fall" (I Cor. 10:12; Heb. 12:15).

4. *He Was the Treasurer*

Judas held a position of trust and confidence as the purse-bearer of the apostolic band. He was not dreamy like John or impulsive like Peter, but he had economical habits, aptitude for finance, love of bargaining — qualities often associated with love of money. Wealthy women contributed to the maintenance of Christ and His disciples (Luke 8:3), and Judas was made treasurer and administrator of that fund. The very fact that he was given this responsibility proves that the other apostles had faith in his honesty, and a confidence which remained unshaken up to the very night of the betrayal. He carried "the bag" — a secular position requiring a good business man, not necessarily one who was saintly. With his ability in this direction, Judas might have nursed a secret ambition of becoming "Chancellor of the Exchequer" in the New Kingdom, about which his Master preached.

But the tragedy was that he took advantage of his position, and as John tells us plainly, Judas "was a thief, and had the bag, and bare [kept] what was put therein" (John 12:6). What a mean act! Surely conscience — an accuser never silent — must have warned him of his avarice; that what he thought was hidden from unsuspecting eyes was known to his Master who read the secret thoughts and knew what was in man. Could it have been that the greed and suspicion which He saw working and growing in Judas prompted Him to utter warning words about covetousness, and of how hidden things would be brought to light? Greed made Judas a thief, and in the end, a traitor guilty of the blackest crime in history which ended in a hangman's rope.

An impressive feature of the relationship of Jesus with Judas is the way He repeatedly tried to warn him, directly and indirectly, of the peril he faced. Judas did not rush blindly and ignorantly to his terrible fate. Again and again in our Lord's constant teaching about the love of money and its effect upon character the warning note was sounded. This teaching Judas often heard. With deep concern about Judas' soul, He said in his hearing, "Ye cannot serve God and mammon." Do you not think He looked at Judas when He said, "What shall it profit a man to gain the whole world and lose one's life?" Was it not for his benefit that Jesus uttered the parable about the farmer and his barns and storehouses bursting at the seams, but who with all he had gained, had an unprepared soul when smitten with sudden death?

In the feet-washing episode with its lesson on humility (John 13:1-20), Jesus made premonitory allusions to the fact that a traitor was among the twelve, hinting that they were not all clean, insinuating, thereby, that there was one of them who knew and would

not do. "He knew who should betray him" (John 13:10, 11, 18). When Jesus finished and explained the service of love, He immediately proceeded to the unwelcome task of making an announcement of His betrayal. His spirit must have been troubled at the thought of His painful duty, and He must have shuddered in the presence of satanic wickedness. At the Supper, He indicated the particular individual by saying that the traitor would be the one receiving the sop or morsel after He had dipped it in the wine.

Even toward the last when Jesus said, "That thou doest, do quickly" (John 13:27), far from being a command to Judas to go out and finish his dastardly work, it was rather an awful warning, a declaration to Judas of Christ's foreknowledge of his wickedness and preparation for it. It was therefore peculiarly calculated to deter Judas from his fatal purpose. But all warnings went unheeded and Judas "went immediately out" — out of the apostolate of which he had been an unworthy member. The wonder is that such a man ever got *in*. We now come to a classification of references to Judas in the gospels and the Acts, for an arrangement of the setting of his dreadful crime. It would seem as if there are three main features in the tragedy of one who had been a member of the inner circle.

5. *The Bargain Planned*

While there were circumstances that changed Judas from a *possible* into an *actual* traitor, he was a traitor at heart from the outset. The petty pilfering from the meager treasury of the apostles was a sure sign of a mean, sordid soul. While the gospels do not explain but only record the wickedness of Judas, it is easy to discern his character from the narratives.

Instigated by Satan

Behind the traitor was the tempter, for Judas was but a dupe of the devil, as the references to his satanic possession clearly indicate. It is John who emphasizes the part Satan played in the betrayer's crime. How pointed is the assertion of Jesus, "Have not I chosen you twelve, and one of you is a devil?" (John 6:70). Judas was possessed, not by a *demon* but a devil, as the Greek implies.

Satan entered Judas as the originator of a cruel and wicked purpose, "The devil having now put into the heart of Judas Iscariot, Simon's son, to betray him" (John 13:2). Then Satan possessed Judas as the source of diabolical action, "After the sop Satan entered into him (John 13:27).

It would seem as if the morsel given to Judas was more than a mark of confidence and trust and honor; it was the last act of Jesus to save Judas from the committal of his great crime. When the sop had been eaten and the honor which it conferred had failed of its purpose, there was nothing to be done short of compulsion. Satan, not Jesus, had taken possession of the heart of Judas, and in spite of all the privileges of apostleship, Judas gambled with destiny and "went to his own place." Satan had failed to get the Master into his power, but he succeeded in getting His apostle who was not spared a drop of humiliation and distress. Judas had to drain the cup of bitterness to the last dregs.

As Jesus desired to spend His last hours in the tender, confidential fellowship of His faithful ones, without the presence of a deadly enemy, He did not wait till it pleased Judas to leave the company. Jesus, asserting His authority over Judas, even though he had prostituted his privileges and sold himself to Satan, commanded Judas to leave the company and complete his foul deed. Jesus had failed to arrest the estranged mind of Judas "before the Devil Doubt became the Devil Deed, before the alienation of feeling had passed into open desertion. Judas had come to the Supper with a guilty secret in his heart and with a bribe in his hand, and must have been most uneasy under the eye of Him who was able to see him through and through."

Ambitious, greedy Judas had sold his soul to the devil like Goethe's *Faust* to Mephistopheles. Gamblerlike, he hazarded his all and lost, and nothing was left to him but to expiate blood with blood. His ambition overreached itself, and he fell headlong and burst. But while the devil was the evil figure behind the betrayal, wicked though he is, he must not be blamed for everything. When the devil came to Jesus with suggestions alien to the divine purpose, He could say, "Get thee behind me, Satan!" Judas, however, left an avenue open to the devil, and the disgraced apostle's own greed and avaricious nature, revealed in his pilfering of apostolic treasury, enticed the devil to secure a firm hold on the thief.

Who would have thought that stealing a few little coins from a bag when no one was looking would open the door to Satanic possession, and result in a most monstrous crime and a suicide's grave? We can never be too careful about shunning so-called little sins, for *sin* has an awful power of growth.

> Thought becomes Act,
> Act becomes Habit,
> Habit becomes Character,
> Character shapes Eternity.

Bitterly opposed to the Savior and His cause, Satan was the prime mover in the effort of Judas to speed up the death of Jesus. Had the enemy of souls known all that would result from the cruel death of Jesus at Calvary, he probably would have been less zealous in his haste to bring Him to the cross. As the slain Lamb, He will finally destroy Satan and his works, and reign supreme. It is comforting to remember that the schemes of Satan are often, as in this instance, overruled for the accomplishment of the holiest purposes.

Arranged by Judas

There are several aspects of the dramatic episode that prove how heartlessly and cruelly Judas acted in carrying out his foul deed. His crime is never represented as a blunder, nor Judas himself as a blunderer. Scripture certainly regards what he did as a veritable mystery of iniquity, but represents him as being cool and calculated in the crime he committed. As Allen Poole puts it —

> In some respects Judas seems to have been the most farseeing member of the band, certainly the one most capable of reading the signs of the times on the sinister side. He sensed the craft that tried to entrap Jesus, that watched His actions, that weighed His speech, that hardened into hate and plotted His murder. Here we have a clue to the frequent references to the cross, until at last Judas sensed the end of everything for which he had accepted and continued in the apostolate. . . . The disclosures at the Last Supper settled his purpose, and precipitated his decision to betray his Lord.

1. A convenient arrangement

Both Matthew and Mark record how cunningly Judas watched for a fitting opening to sell Christ: "He sought opportunity to betray him" (Matt. 26:16). "He sought how he might conveniently betray h i m" (Mark 14:11).

Judas did not act in a moment of passion or insanity. His dark deed was quietly and deliberately planned. He waited for the opportune hour to secure his blood-money. Seeking the door to hell, he waited for it to open, and when it did, Judas sinned against light and love. Oh, how wicked can man become! Men still wait for a convenient season to get rid of Christ, and His salvation and claims.

2. A cowardly arrangement

Judas had often trodden the sacred pathway to Gethsemane, and listened to the hallowed teaching and heartfelt prayers of Jesus, for John tells us that Judas "knew the place." Now he used his knowledge for the purpose of handing over his Master to His enemies. He sank to the deepest depths of wickedness when he used the Garden for his cruel purpose. Satanic influences can make a soul oblivious to the most sacred considerations. Sacrelige reached its fullest development when Judas betrayed his Master in Gethsemane. Though he knew this hallowed place, he was always *out of place* when in it. Ultimately, Judas had "his own place" (Acts 1:25), but it was not Gethsemane.

Both Luke and John remind us of the cowardice of the betrayer who had little respect for the sanctities of life.

"He promised, and sought opportunity to betray him unto them in *the absence of the multitude*" (Luke 22: 6). "He . . . went immediately out: and *it was night*" (John 13:30). Judas carried out the satanic task in the absence of the multitude because he feared what the crowd, made up of the common people who heard Jesus gladly, would do to him. He was afraid of the people mauling him to pieces if his dark deed was discovered. His scared conscience made him a coward. Then John's touch, "it was night," implies the same scared frame of mind. The darkness was not only the time when few people were about, but afforded him the opportunity of covering up his movements.

Luke reminds us that Judas fell so low as to act as guide to the party of Roman soldiers in the pay of the Pharisees who were sent to apprehend Jesus (Acts 1:16). How suggestive is the alliance here! Physical force, ecclesiastical authority, and an unfaithful disciple joined hands against the Lord's Anointed. Judas was the blackest sinner of that group, for he was sinning against light and knowledge. Having received good at the hand of the Lord, he now requited Him with treachery.

3. A callous arrangement

A *kiss* has always been a token of love and friendship, a symbol of fidelity, but the kiss of Judas was a profane one, marking out Jesus for arrest. Often he had felt singled out from the rest of the apostles under the powerful teaching of Christ, and being sensitively alive to insult and destitute of love he had no defense against vindictiveness. Thus, "a private grudge, like a spark from Hell, set his withered heart on fire, and brought him at the head of a torch-lit band with a scorching kiss on his unholy lips."

"Whomsoever I shall kiss, that same is he" (Matt. 26:48).

"Judas . . . drew near unto Jesus to kiss him" (Luke 22:47).

There is a fable of a man who took a poisonous reptile to his kindly bosom to be warmed but it rewarded its benefactor by striking its deadly fangs into his flesh. As Judas approached Jesus, and made to kiss Him, He lovingly called the traitor, "Friend" (Matt. 26:50), and doubtless reciprocated the kiss, for divine love never retaliates. But heaven and hell met in that embrace — there the Son of man spoke His last word to the son of per-

dition; the eternities united in that strange moment of a kiss on which history looks back with horror and pity.

A kiss from John as he leaned on Jesus would be sweet, but from an apostle who had become a mortal enemy, such a token of affection was abhorrent and abominable. That kiss was not necessary for the success of the plot Judas had hatched. The soldiers had torches, and could have been guided by some other sign as Judas kept himself in the background. But no, still believing that Jesus was his Master he acted as a bosom friend but murder was in his heart and kiss.

Jesus wished to spare Judas the part of his treachery, representing the last aggravation of sin, namely, from offering the hypocrisy of *the traitor's kiss*. There was no need for Judas to point Him out, and Jesus tried to forestall the token of betrayal by saying to the soldiers who came to the Garden —

"Whom seek ye?" They answered:

"Jesus of Nazareth." Then He replied;

"I am he" (John 18:4, 5).

But Judas would not take advantage of the offer — or shall we say, Satan would not let him take it? Judas must drink the dregs; he must grovel in the dust. So he "came to Jesus, and said, Hail, Master; and kissed him!"

Welcomed by the priests

The hatred the Scribes and Pharisees had for Christ made them eager to jump at the proffered help of Judas to betray Christ unto them. "And when they (the chief priests) heard it, they were glad, and promised to give him money" (Mark 14:11). The fallen apostle had given Satan inroad into his life. As Judas sold the Christ whom Satan hated, he found the grinning faces of hell most willing to pay the price agreed upon. Those joyful enemies of Christ must have had a low opinion of Judas. Hypocritical though they were, they must have had contempt in their hearts for a renegade disciple who was willing to sell his Master.

Internal, external, and infernal foes are glad the moment we climb down from the pinnacle and become less Christian. The forces of hell are all glad when men are willing to sell Christ for the sum of this world's pleasures and possessions. Lower the flag, compromise, become a good mixer, and semi-religious people will be ready to hail you as a "good fellow."

6. The Bargain Completed

We have now reached the heart of our sad and sordid story. The betrayal and arrest of Jesus struck terror into the hearts of the other disciples, and they forsook Him and fled (Matt. 26: 56). Jesus was led away to face the High Priest and the Sanhedrin, there to suffer false accusation, shame, and indignity. But by this time the hellish bargain had been clinched, and the betrayed One was safe in the hands of those who more than once had tried to kill Him.

The purchase price

If greed of money was the motive of betrayal, then the sum received was most paltry. Perhaps it was a down payment on an agreed larger sum to be paid later. When Judas protested against the waste of a quantity of perfume on Jesus, he asked, "Why was not this ointment sold for 300 pence?" As a Roman penny was the ordinary daily wage of an agricultural laborer at that time, 300 pence would be a sum equivalent to the wages of a laborer for 300 days — an amount sufficient to excite the covetousness of Judas. Yet he bargained to betray the Son of God for 30 pieces of silver, not half the amount represented by 300 pennies. All Christ was worth to Judas

was the price of a slave when killed by a beast (Ex. 21:32). "They took the thirty pieces of silver, the price of him that was valued" (Matt. 27:9).

The very meanness of the bribe of money offered must have been an insult to Judas, but he took the miserable sum without demur. If anyone had told Judas on the day of his election to apostleship that one day he would sell the One who had called him for thirty pieces of silver, he would have been indignant with horror at such a suggestion. But he kept the sin of avarice in his heart, and it grew until it drove him to commit a monstrous and unspeakable crime for which he is still despised. His lust brought forth sin, and the sin when full grown brought forth a terrible death. What horrible deeds men will do for money!

Ezekiel speaks of polluting God "for handfuls of barley and for pieces of bread" (13:19).

Amos describes those selling "the righteous for silver, and the poor for a pair of shoes" (2:6).

There are still those who sell honor and truth, barter away their souls for money, sacrifice religion and any hope of heaven for material gain. As with Judas of old, their consuming lust for gold brings eternal loss. Jesus taught that the soul of man is worth more than all the wealth of the world, yet His worth was estimated as being around $10.00. To John, who had discovered the preciousness of his peerless Lord, His price was above rubies. Never was so little paid for so much.

We must guard ourselves against undervaluing Christ. If we deem Him to be our most valuable possession then there will be little fear of selling and betraying Him, or exchanging for lesser treasure. Around us are far too many who part with Him and with a peaceful conscience for the round of pleasure, ungodly companions, their darling sin, for pride of appearance and the praise of the world. The thought that one of His own chosen twelve had sold Him to His deadly foes for a slave's ransom pierced Jesus to the quick. "He was troubled in spirit, and testified and said, Verily, verily, I say unto you, that one of *you* shall betray me." May we be delivered from returning treachery for love, and piercing the Savior's soul anew!

It may not be for silver, it may not be for
    gold,
But yet by tens of thousands the Prince
    of Life is sold,
Sold for a godless friendship, sold for a
    selfish aim,
Sold for a fleeting trifle, sold for an empty
    name.

Sold in the mart of science, sold in the
    seat of power,
Sold at the shrine of fortune, sold in plea-
    sure's bower,
Sold for your awful bargain none but
    God's eye can see,
Ponder my soul the question, shall He be
    sold by thee?

Sold! Oh God, what a moment! stilled is
    conscience voice;
Sold! and a weeping angel records the
    fatal choice,
Sold! but the price accepted to a living
    coal shall turn,
With the pangs of a late repentance deep
    in the soul to burn.

The pitiless purchasers

Smitten with remorse, as he saw Jesus delivered over to Pontius Pilate, Judas tried to return the blood-money received from the chief priests and elders, confessing all too late that he had betrayed innocent blood, but they only mocked him. These religious haters of Jesus had no concern either for His fate, or the tortured conscience of Judas.

"What is that to us? See thou to that" (Matt. 27:4). If the guilt of

Judas was deep, the mockery of those who taunted him was deeper still. Who knows? Perhaps if Judas had received sympathy and counsel from those who, because of their profession should have given it, he might have been saved even at that last hour.

How true to pattern is the response of those who used Judas to bring Jesus into their evil hands! They held Judas to the bargain mutually agreed upon. Too often, when men sell Christ for their mess of pottage, and then come to bitterly regret their treatment of solemn issues, they are treated with scorn and indifference by their godless companions. No sympathy is shown to the repentant by those whose passion is to get rid of Christ. Their attitude is, "You should be left to bear the fullest penalty of your own sin." They mock and sneer at those who, at last, have seen the error of their ways. One wonders what would have happened if Judas had had the opportunity of pleading the anguish of his tortured mind before Jesus instead of before the heartless priests and elders?

7. The Bargain Repented

We now come to a review of the dreadful consequences accruing from the terrible bargain Judas made with those religious leaders, and as we do so we cannot fail to see how descriptive James' words are of the career of the betrayer. "Every man is tempted, when he is drawn away of his own lust, and enticed. Then when lust hath conceived, it bringeth forth sin: and sin, when it is finished, bringeth forth death" (James 1:14, 15).

A tortured conscience

Again and again we hear the cry of repentant hearts — *I have sinned!* We may readily assent to the general statement of Paul that, "All have sinned, and come short of the glory of God"

(Rom. 3:23), but how many are there who raise their own hands to heaven, and say, "I have sinned a great sin" (Ex. 32:30)? King Saul, who in some respects is the *Judas* of the Old Testament, cried out of a smitten soul, *I have sinned* (I Sam. 15:30; 26:21). It was also the moan of Job (7:20; 33:27). Matthew tells us that Judas *repented himself* which was not a repentance toward God. As he heard the sentence of death passed on the head of Jesus the pangs of remorse sickened the soul of Judas, but there were no tears like those of Peter who "wept bitterly" over his denial of the Master. At last, the memory of the betrayed became a scorching fire as he thought of friendship dishonored, and in his repentant mood, attempted to retrieve the crime on his conscience by a confession of guilt and a renouncement of his sordid gains — but to no avail!

All who betray innocent blood sooner or later discover the enormity of their sin. Before their sin, it was gain they saw — after the sin, guilt and self-reproach. Poor Judas, he lost Christ, he lost his fellow apostles, he lost his ill-gotten bribe, and finally he lost his soul and heaven. Would that multitudes of sin-blinded men and women could realize that the price they pay for sin is not worth it! If they do not rue the day they slighted Christ, then unending remorse will be theirs in the place where the worm never dies.

A tarnished name

We have already seen that wherever Judas is mentioned, he wears the label, "Who also betrayed him." His dark deed is bound to his name, so that men can always combine the two. *Judas Iscariot* ever recalls the man who stained his hands with the blood of the most perfect Man who ever lived. As long as the world stands the name of Judas will be remembered for one thing — he sold his Lord! All else about him is forgotten.

The most dreadful description of the traitor, however, came from the lips of the One he betrayed. Jesus called Judas, *The son of perdition*, that is, one worthy of perdition (John 17:12; see Matt. 23:15; II Thess. 2:3). Professor A. B. Bruce reminds us that:

> The infirmity of sincere disciples Jesus could patiently bear with; but the Judas-character — in which correct thinking and fine sentiment are combined with falseness of heart and practical laxity, in which to promise is put in place of performance, and to utter the becoming word about a matter is substituted for doing the appropriate deed — such a character His soul utterly abhorred.

Our Lord's reference to Judas as "the son of perdition" is translated by Martin Luther as "the lost child." Actually, he became "the lost apostle." He was indignant over what he called "waste," (everything was *waste* which did not enrich *him*). The word Jesus used, *perdition*, is the same word in the Greek for *waste*. Greed gradually sapped the finer traits of his character, and he died as *waste*. "The name of the wicked shall rot" (Prov. 10:7). One of our hymns has the line, "Sowing the seed of a tarnished name." May we seek to live leaving behind a name as fragrant as ointment poured forth! "The memory of the just is blessed" (Prov. 10:7).

A tragic end

There are those scholars who suggest that Judas entertained the hope that Jesus would perform a miracle and escape out of the hands of His captors, and because He did not, he went out and committed suicide. But Judas killed himself because he knew that his lust of money ultimately killed the Master. "He... hanged himself" (Matt. 27:5). "His bowels gushed out" (Acts 1:18). Could it be that his confession about betraying innocent blood was prompted by the Law of Moses, with which, as a Jew, Judas was familiar? "Cursed be he that taketh reward to slay an innocent person. And all the people shall say, Amen!" (Deut. 27:25).

What a tragic accompaniment to the crucifixion was the suicide of Judas, who was bad enough to do the deed of infamy, and good enough to be unable to bear the burden of his guilt. As Jesus said, it would have been better for Judas had he never been born. Disowned by the pious, crafty priests, who laughed over his scruples about taking their money, and goaded by the anguish of an intolerable hell in his own heart, so long hard-hearted but at last broken-hearted, he ended his own life. A moral suicide as well as a self-murderer, Judas destined himself to an immortality of shame. Sin has a dreadful end. What stories of a sold, rejected Christ there must be behind the tragedy of so many suicides and murders today!

How fitting are the verses of W. Blane —

THIRTY PIECES OF SILVER

Thirty pieces of silver for the Lord of life they gave,
Thirty pieces of silver, only the price of a slave:
But this was the priestly value of the Holy One of God;
And they weighed it out in the temple, the price of His precious blood.

Thirty pieces of silver laid in Iscariot's hand,
Thirty pieces of silver and the aid of an armed band:
Like a Lamb that is led to the slaughter brought the humble Son of God,

At midnight from the Garden, where His sweat had been like blood.

Thirty pieces of silver burns on the traitor's brain,
Thirty pieces of silver — oh, it is hellish gain:
"I have sinned and betrayed the guiltless," he cried with a lowered breath,
As he threw them down in the Temple and rushed to a madman's death.

Thirty pieces of silver lay in the House of God,
Thirty pieces of silver, but oh 'twas the price of blood.
And so for a place to bury the strangers in they gave,
The price of their own Messiah, who lay in a borrowed grave.

A terrible eternity

If, by taking his own life, Judas thought he could end the misery of his conscience, he made a terrible mistake. When sin and trouble gang up on a person, and he despairs of life, and thinks of suicide as a way out of his inner remorse, he is cruelly deceived of the devil, for if he dies outside of Christ, he goes out to an eternity of contrition. Luke says that, "Judas by transgression fell, that he might go to his own place" (Acts 1: 25). John has the arrestive phrase, "He... went immediately out, and it was night" (13:30). Jesus said of the traitor, "Good were it for that man if he had never been born" (Mark 14: 21). The very name used of the coming Antichrist is the very one Jesus used of Judas, "The son of perdition" (II Thess. 2:3). Do not these solemn descriptions indicate that because Judas failed to cry aloud in his extremity to the Savior of sinners, he died in his sin and went out to the place corresponding to our Satan-possessed life?

Dante, in his *Vision of Hell*, placed Judas in the lowest circle of the damned, as the sole sharer with Satan himself of the very uttermost punishment. Judas went out and it was night. Is it not always so? For all who die without the Light of the world in their heart, there is the blackness of darkness for ever, even if they seek oblivion in suicide. Origen, one of the early church fathers, suggested that possibly there mingled with the agony of Judas, some confused thought that in the world of the dead, behind the veil, he might meet his Lord and confess his guilt to Him. But Jesus would never have said of Judas that it would have been better for him had he never been born, if there was forgiveness for his dastardly crime in another world. This son of perdition was lost to Jesus for ever. Judas's life, which for almost three years had been under the highest influences, and might have reached the sainthood of John, went out into eternal night.

Jesus could say, "I go to prepare a place for you" (John 14:1-3). What a different place this is from the one to which Judas went! For all who die in Christ, there is the land of pure delight, a place of eternal peace. But for those who live and die without the Savior, they go to their own place — a place of eternal pangs. Although Jesus said it would have been better for Judas had he never seen the light of day, yet he had parents who thought it good to bring him into the world, and who rejoiced over his birth. Perhaps their early training of their son was defective, and his tendency toward avarice was not checked. Had the work of salvation begun in the home with evil tendencies being checked by loving discipline, Judas may have been saved from a suicide's grave. Parents must ever remember that spiritual training of children cannot begin too soon, and that God-directed discipline cannot be too firm.

As we turn from the tragic story of Judas, what are some of the lessons to be learned from his character and crime? Immediately there comes to mind the exhortation of another apostle who finished his course with joy, "Let him that thinketh he standeth take heed lest he fall" (I Cor. 10:12). Paul then goes on to say that no matter how we may be tempted, there is always a way of escape — which somehow, Judas missed! We must guard ourselves against laxity and indifference regarding the subtle workings of Satan and sin — "Lest any of you be hardened through the deceitfulness of sin."

We must never tamper with even the thought of sin; since thought issues in acts, and acts create habits; habits formulate character, and character determines destiny. Judas might have ranked with the best of the twelve and had his name engraved on one of the foundations of the Holy City, but instead of becoming a noble ideal of Christian service, his name became the deadliest insult that one man can offer to another — *traitor!* My soul, come not nigh his dwelling!

Further thoughts arising from the biography of Judas can be mentioned. For instance, we must not be too surprised when a bad man is found in church — there was one among the twelve apostles. It is no proof against the reality of Christianity when a professor of religion turns out to be a hypocrite. The defection of Judas did not leave a stain upon the name of Jesus nor disprove the loyalty of the rest of the disciples. One black sheep does not make a black flock. Outwardly, Judas was a disciple — inwardly he was a devil, and he warns us that even privileged nearness to Christ does not mean we have a holy character. He lived for three years in intimate fellowship with Christ, heard His words and saw His works, lived in the atmosphere of love, instructed and unchanged. Yet honored as an apostle, he became guilty of black treachery, and his corpse is flung across the threshold of the church for warning and instruction.

It is sadly possible to be reckoned among Christians, go to church, say prayers, read the Bible; to have a name that we live yet be spiritually dead; to lie on the bosom of Christ yet have a heart sealed against the entrance of His love. Judas fell because he followed Christ with a divided heart. His mind was on what he might *get* rather than upon what he had to give. This son of perdition did not rise to the high-water mark of Peter, the son of impulse, "We have left all, and followed thee." His tragedy was that he carried the world into his witness, and was more ruled by the prince of the world than by his rightful Master. Although promoted to the apostolate, Judas was content with mere association. The message he proclaimed as he followed Christ found no place in his own heart and life. Professing much, he possessed nothing — not even the silver for which he sold his soul.

From the high pinnacle of privilege, Judas fell to a terrible depth. Yet he was not the creature of circumstance although, probably, the creator of it. His very closeness to Jesus should have changed his heart, but it only turned distrust into dislike. He had the same privileges as John but with adverse effects. The means of grace may be a blessing or a curse, according as they act as a spiritual stimulus or a narcotic, or irritant poison; grace makes the good, better — the bad, worse. The traitor is not alone in sacrificing the highest for the lowest. We may shrink in horror from the treachery of Judas, yet repeat it in other forms. We must get on, maintain our position in life, keep up with the Joneses. We cannot afford to be singular and such a course usually ends in treachery to all the sanctities of life.

Another lesson to be gleaned from the tragic story of Judas is that love is ever the crucial test of a disciple, the touchstone of sincere profession. Without a deep and ever-deepening love for Christ, all is vain (John 21: 15-17). A heart-experience of His power to save and sanctify can alone aid us in the conflict between the trinities of evil and of good around us in the world. When Jesus said to the twelve gathered at the table, "One of you shall betray me," He did not point an accusing finger at Judas, although the statement was meant for him. Each of the other disciples, knowing the weakness of his own heart, was smitten with fear and asked, "Lord, is it I?" No one of the eleven said, "That is meant for Judas." No, each looked into the bottomless pit of his heart, feeling that *he* might be the traitor Jesus was exposing. Each felt guilty of such a possibility. *Lord, is it I?* I must treat this warning as if it were meant for me, and learn that only divine love can transform a treacherous heart into a palace worthy of the King.

A further warning to heed is that repentance may come too late. In his remorseful state of mind, Judas knew he could not set back the clock. He had passed *redemption point.* He might cry, "I have sinned," but Christ was not near to say, "Thy sins be forgiven thee." Judas had reached the point in the history of his soul when his Lord and Lover was not at hand with His interposition. Through the years, Jesus had stood between Judas and his fatal sin. The Master had honored him, even at the threshold of his treachery, even greeting him as "Friend," and suffering the touch of his deceitful lips. Loving him to the last, Jesus let Judas go because He was no despot forcing or coercing Judas to repent. Love, and not force, is His weapon of conquest.

How dreadful is the thought that at last some souls are so completely abandoned to evil that divine mercy falls upon deaf ears! Incarnations of evil and the evil one, they go out to their own place, not because they were not loved of God, and not constantly warned of their peril, but in spite of all the renewing, ennobling influences brought to bear upon them by heavenly influences. "None of them is lost, *but* the son of perdition." Death, then, is the real test of life. Each sinner writes his own biography in the sentence, "He went to his own place." All men do, saints and sinners alike. Precious in the sight of the Lord is the death of His saints, because they go to be with Him in the place He prepared for them (John 14:1-3). But the prostitution of the soul must end in perdition. The contrast between the death of Jesus and Judas runs into eternity. Heaven or hell. Paradise or perdition — the choice is made this side of the grave.

MATTHEW

The Apostle Who Wrote a Great Gospel

The choice of Matthew by the Master is a further proof that He attracted men from every walk of life, often from a class which might not have been expected to supply Him with followers. He met with sympathy where we would not have looked for it. Do not the actual disciples of Christ surprise us? Because He came as the One, holy, harmless and undefiled, we would not have been surprised to see the pious of the land, such as godly Simeon and Anna,

supplying Him with adherents. But who would have looked among the *publicans* for an apostle? The warped nature of Matthew, which became harder under the scorn and loathing heaped upon him because of his trade, would surely make him immune to divine influences!

But the marvel is that as soon as Matthew heard the call, he responded, and his surrender to Christ is one of the most inspiring incidents in the gospel, and full of encouragement for those who labor for the salvation of souls in most unlikely places. Perverse in life, selfish of gain, Matthew adopted a profession arousing the ill-will of his fellow Jews. Doubtless he was the heartbreak of his godly parents. Yet when he looked into the holy face of Jesus, sinner and Savior became one forever. John Keble in his poem on *Saint Matthew* in his "Christian Year," has familiarized us with the way Jesus "took the things which are not to bring to nought the things that are."

The saintly poet writes of the way Jesus "bade the meek publican his gainful seat forsake," and goes on to describe those who in —

. . . this loud stunning tide of human care
    and crime —
        Carry music in their heart
Through dusky land and wrangling mart
Plying their daily task with busier feet
Because their secret souls a holy strain
    repeat.

When Jesus affirmed that He came, not to call the righteous to repentance, but sinners, He indicated that He would find His jewels in most unlikely places. How He loves to mend the broken earthenware of life, and to transform even rebels into kings and priests! Wherever Jesus went preaching it was "the publicans and sinners who gathered themselves together for to hear him." Later on, another most unlikely convert was to write "that not many wise men after the flesh, not many mighty, not many noble are called."

I take Thee as my Wisdom too,
    For Wisdom's sum Thou art;
Thou, who dost choose the foolish things,
    Set me henceforth apart,
That I may speak and work for Thee
    As Thou shalt work and speak in me.

Among the twelve Jesus chose there was not one rich man, not one of noble birth, not one of acquired culture and education. Perhaps Matthew had more money and education than the rest. Over half of them were humble, unlettered peasants and fishermen of Galilee. When He called Matthew to follow Him, He set every consideration of worldly prudence at defiance, and disregarded the maxims of worldly wisdom. The eye of Jesus was single as well as omniscient, and thus He looked on the heart, having respect solely to the possibility of spiritual fitness. His love has a deep look as

can be gathered from His contact with the rich young ruler whom beholding, He loved.

1. *A Hebrew Son*

A fact that must not be forgotten in any study of the twelve apostles is that they were all *Jews*, and that, belonging to the house of Israel, they were probably familiar with Old Testament Scriptures from their earliest days (II Tim. 3:14, 15). Therefore when Jesus appeared as "the glory of [His] people Israel" (Luke 2:32), hearts, longing for His coming, instinctively recognized Him as the Promised One, as did Bartholomew or Nathanael (meeting Him, they greeted Him as the King of Israel). Matthew came from a pious parentage, and the *gospel* he came to write reveals how conversant he was with the Old Testament and also the traditions of the rabbis. The masterly way in which Matthew sets forth his material on *The King and His Kingdom*, proves that he had been carefully instructed in all that pertained to the Jewish religion, and that he had enjoyed a general education well above the average.

While we learn practically nothing about Matthew *himself* from the gospel he wrote, his knowledge of the history and noble traditions of his race appears on almost every page. Once Matthew fully committed himself to Jesus and heard Him expound the Scriptures, he became a fiery herald of the coming glory the King of Israel would bring. His very name, *Levi*, related to the priestly order, indicated his membership in the tribe set apart for the worship and service of God (Num. 3:6; Deut. 10:8, etc.). According to Mark and Luke, his birth name was *Levi* — which means "joined" (Gen. 29:34) — a reference to the adherence to Aaron for priesthood ministry (Num. 18:1, 2). The apostle speaks of himself as *Matthew,* but Mark and Luke used his old name *Levi,* being unwilling even after thirty years or so to identify him with Matthew the apostle. But he made the identification to prove that by divine grace Levi the customs officer, became Matthew the apostle (Matt. 9:9-13; Mark 2:13-17; Luke 5:27-32; Acts 1: 13).

It was likely, after his call by Jesus, that his name was changed from Levi to the Greek name Matthew, *Levi* being his national name as a Hebrew, and *Matthew,* his Christian name – a name commemorating the triumph of Christ in his life. *Twice-named* men are common in Scripture – Jacob became Israel, Simon became Peter, Bartholomew was Nathanael, Joses became Barnabas etc. Anxious to magnify the goodness and mercy of God in his salvation and election to apostleship, the apostle preferred to refer to himself under the dishonorable term of "Matthew the *publican*"– the symbol and memorial of the most important transformation wrought by Christ in his heart and life.

Probably a Galilean and born at or near Capernaum, Matthew was the son of Alphaeus and Mary, the latter possibly being a relative of Mary the Virgin. Matthew's pious parents must have been heart-broken when their *Levi* chose a profession of ill-repute, as orthodox Jews deemed that of a *publican* to be. As he sat at the receipt of custom, adding up his ill-gotten gains, Levi must have been haunted by the vision of the haggard face and dry-eyed grief of his noble father and the tense quivering features of his saintly mother over their son's despicable position. To think that their son, who had brought them such joy when he was born into the world, had, because of his love for mammon, taken the hire of the alien and found himself bound fast by the gilded fetters of the Roman state, must have been a heavy cross for his loved ones to bear.

2. A Roman Taxgatherer

If it be true that the average Jew can add to his wealth where a man of another nationality would die in penury, then, if the love of money was Matthew's besetting sin, the fatal flaw in the marble of his character, we can understand how his ruling passion brought him to a most unworthy way of amassing riches – even to that of being a pariah of the worst type, an outcast from the Jewish synagogue and society. Levi became – not a priest – but a *publican.* Who or what was a publican? The profession of a publican represented the profession of a tax-collector. Caesar's tollmen were usually Roman gentlemen sent into the provinces of the Empire to collect the tribute for the Emperor.

The officials responsible for the security of the Roman revenue were called *publicani,* from the Latin *publicanus,* because of their close relation to the public purse. The *pasha* system that was common to Egypt came very near the *publicani* type of operation in Ancient Rome. "The Publicani of Rome were active workers at the digging of the grave of the Empire," because of their corrupt ways and gross injustice in the modes of levying dues. All who undertook this odious work had their reward in that they could extort for their own benefit more than the caesars demanded. It was for this reason that they were known as *leeches,* seeing they were allowed to gorge themselves in their task. In his confession to Christ, Zacchaeus, the rich chief of the publicans, hints at the terrible extortion that had produced his wealth when he spoke about

restoring *four-fold* to the poor he had
robbed (Luke 19:8).

The Jews who chafed under and
deeply resented Roman domination,
held that if any one of their nation
took on the office of *publican* for the
Romans, he was disloyal to God and
outside the pale of decent society,
and must be classed as a sinner. Matthew became a customs officer in the
territory of Herod Antipas, and earned
the contempt of his fellow Jews among
whom excess taxation was the badge
of foreign servitude and was especially
galling to all their inherited hopes.
Any Jew, then, entering the *publicani,*
was regarded as "a social outcast, a
renegade from the national faith and
a betrayer of the Messianic hope."
Added to the fact that the Romans
diligently sought Jews, who were not
averse to collecting taxes from their
own people, to fill such a post, was
the dishonesty of both the greater
publicans like Zacchaeus, and the
smaller ones, like Matthew. Wealth
procured by dishonest taxation was
hinted at by John the Baptist when
publicans came to him for baptism
and asked of him "Master, what shall
we do? He said unto them, Exact no
more than that which is appointed
you" (Luke 3:12, 13).

No men were more detested in Jewish communities than Roman tax-collectors and so, when a Jew accepted
such an office, he was looked upon as
one who had sacrificed his patriotism
and sold himself for gain to his Roman
masters. It was not surprising then
that in popular sentiment a tollman
was classed with the most disreputable
of people. This is why "publicans and
harlots," and "publicans and sinners"
are grouped together (Matt. 9:11).
A common proverb among those who
hated these pests of society was —

"Take not a wife out of that family
wherein is a publican, for they are

all publicans, or thieves, robbers,
and wicked sinners."

In his desire to gain tainted money,
think of what Matthew lost. He sold
his home circle, and placed himself
outside the fellowship of his loved
ones, orthodox Jewish friends and
acquaintances. He sold *his country.*
His kinsmen writhed under the tyranny and oppression of Rome, and when
he entered its service, the flame of
pure patriotism he had known was
quenched by a baser love. He sold
his conscience for he knew that, generally, tax-collectors represented a
most dishonest profession, a set of
unscrupulous extortioners. Lust for
money stifled the warning of the inner
bell. He sold *his faith.* His very name
Levi was a link with a godly ancestry,
running back through a long line of
priests to the son of Jacob. Emerson
is credited with saying that "The
worst of money is that it so often costs
so much to get it." Money cost Matthew separation from his tribe and
nation, and exclusion from the synagogue with all the anathemas of the
religious vocabularies.

In a great book Victor Hugo portrays the chief character as having a
gigantic wrestle with himself about a
man whom he knows is liable to be
sent to the galleys as an escaped convict. Valjean knows himself to be the
convict; he knows the man charged
to be innocent. He salves his conscience by specious reasoning, and
decides to save himself at the expense
of the other. He proceeds to destroy
all links with the past, hearing an "internal burst of laughter." He is assured
that though men will see his mask,
God will see his face; although his
neighbors will see his life, God will
see his conscience. Then he remembers "a little wood near Paris, where
lovers go to pick lilacs in April." He
enters the town which gives its name

to the wood. The streets are silent. Silent men lean against the walls. Behind every tree, every door, round every corner, stands a silent man. Earth is gray; heaven is lead! He beholds a naked horseman with a heavy, supple wand, who rides into the silent town to chastize its inhabitants. In horror Valjean leaves the town, only to be followed by the crowd, who at last recover their lost voice. This is what they say: "Do you not know that you have been dead for a long while?" Valjean would have killed himself in destroying his conscience: that is Hugo's great lesson.

Matthew had been dead for a long while because honor had been sold, and conscience had been all but stifled!

Dr. W. Graham Scroggie suggests that we may see traces of Matthew's former occupation in his use of the word *tribute* for money, instead of *penny*, and in his recording the miracle of the Stater (Matt. 17:22-27; 22:19 with Mark 12:15). Then there is more frequent mention of money in Matthew's gospel than in any of the others, and more and rarer coins are introduced. Mark refers to three coins only, and these the poorest: *mite, farthing, penny*. Luke refers to the *mite, farthing, pound;* but Matthew, who was in the habit of handling money, refers to the coins of highest value at the time — *talent,* for example, which was worth about sixty times as much as the *pound*. Whereas Mark speaks of *brass*, 6:8, and Luke of *silver*, 9:3, Matthew speaks of *gold, silver and brass*, 10:9 — a great deal of which he handled while sitting at the receipt of custom.

3. A Sacrificial Convert

It is most interesting to observe how and where the Lord met those He challenged to enter His service.

The call came to them right where they were. They did not have to dress up and go to church to meet Him. Peter and Andrew were casting their nets, and James and John were mending their nets when, as Jesus was walking by the Sea of Galilee, the miracle happened and they became His disciples. Saul of Tarsus was on his way to Damascus to persecute the saints of God there, when at noon on the highway, the Christ he rejected appeared to him and instantaneously his rebellion ceased, and he found himself charmed and captivated by the voice divine. And here is the story of Matthew who was sitting at his table attending to his business as customs officer at Capernaum on "The Great West Trunk Road from Damascus and the Far East to the Mediterranean Sea," where he heard all the news that was going. All at once, the Stranger of Galilee he had heard about appeared, and approaching the tax-man, commanded him to rise and follow Him.

In all probability Matthew may have been one of the eager listeners as the new Teacher preached His memorable Sermon on the Mount, and His all-penetrating glance may have caught Matthew's eye as He underscored the tax-collector's besetting sin, "Ye cannot be a bond-servant to God and mammon." What is evident is that when Jesus met Matthew at the receipt of custom, He read the secret of his heart in his face, and knew there would be no hesitation about the response to His appeal, "Follow me!" Such a brief appeal or regal command found Matthew prepared. Without a moment's delay he rose, left his business and associates and followed Jesus; and as he did so he stepped into liberty and peace. Immediately, the pent-up forces of his nature were emancipated, the accumulated guilt of years removed, and his head anointed with the oil of gladness.

For all we know Jesus may have had Matthew under observation for awhile, and as He watched him at the tax-booth, saw in him capacities He could discover and use, when his feet, swift to run in the wake of mammon, would be made speedier as a herald of the Prince of Peace. The double call of Christ came to Matthew simultaneously, *Believe* and *Follow* — "And he arose, and followed him." There can be no doubt that he understood the condescension of the Master's call, and how, by it, he was being exalted to the peak of privilege after having touched the depths of degradation. Having sold himself to the highest bidder in the Roman Empire, he now gives himself up to the service of the King who was greater than Caesar. Instead of greedily counting his silver and gold unjustly secured, he was now to experience the spiritual wealth the Master offered.

What a searching test it must have been to leave his most lucrative occupation, and follow Jesus with no prospect or promise of material support! It is true that the other disciples had made sacrifices in their surrender to His claims, but it is quite probable that Matthew had more wealth to forsake than the rest. Before, he had a public post and office, books, accounts, profits, and perhaps employees. Yet with rapidity of judgment, strength of will, clearness of vision, he gave up everything in response to Christ's call which was to put on him the hallmark of grace. Out he went to experience that it was no cross to bear the cross of Him who had made him His disciple. The immediate reaction to the divine appeal resulted in the new birth of the whole man, and with the vigor of a mind touched by Christ, and the energy of a body quickened

by Him, Matthew rose from his desk and moved toward the Master.

Richard Glover, in his most profitable commentary on *Matthew*, suggests many marvels associated with the Master's call and the Publican's response. Here is the outline, worthy of development by a preacher:

Its Solemnity. It calls to sacrifice of wealth, occupation and habits, for an unknown and perilous future.

Its Mercy. For none would have fellowship with a publican — yet Jesus offered Himself as the Savior and Friend of such a sinner.

Its Promise. Apart from Christ, Matthew was on his own. Christ's call to follow Him was a promise of salvation, fellowship, guidance and protection.

Its Light on Transformation. Yesterday, Matthew was a companion of sinners; today, a disciple; tomorrow, a prophet of the kingdom.

Its Honor. The call testified to the way Jesus honored a sinner to become His fellow-worker, and an apostle.

Its Essence. At the heart of the call, *Follow Me,* is the surrender to a Person, not a creed. Obedience to, confession of, and fellowship with Christ are all involved in the Master's command.

We read that Matthew arose, *left all,* and followed. Telling his own story, Matthew ignored the sacrifice. Thus we note these benefits of obedience to the call —

The courage and vigor of his decision.

That the bravest are the easiest courses.

The wisdom of it. It led to salvation, peace, and honor, for Matthew came to write a gospel which has blessed millions all down the ages. If Matthew had turned from Jesus as the rich young ruler did, how much the church would have lost! But he obeyed. *Have we?* Christ still needs the Matthews, who rise up and leave all at a word, in the assurance that it comes from One who can make life supremely blessed under any condition.

Jesus is calling in accents of tenderness,
   Jesus is calling, my brother, to thee,
Just as of old, by the waters of Galilee,
   Fell from His lips the command,
          "Follow Me!"

4. A Grateful Host

Before he ostracized himself from his godly home and the synagogue, Matthew must have read the Psalms many times and have been familiar with the exhortation, "Let the redeemed of the Lord say so, whom he hath redeemed from the hand of the enemy" (107:2). Now delivered from the power of his enemy, Matthew redeemed from his greed and guilt wanted to "say so" to as many as possible. Having experienced the joy of sins forgiven, he sought to tell others the good news, and he chose a novel way of doing so. Now that the revenue dues had been left behind for someone else to collect, the transformed tax-collector arranges a feast on a grand scale and begs Jesus and the disciples, and also a great company of his fellow-collectors to come. Matthew himself puts it, "Behold, many publicans and sinners came and sat down with him and his disciples" (9:10). Luke is more descriptive and says that "Levi made him a *great feast* in his own house: and there was a *great company* of publicans and of others that sat down with them" (5:29).

The large number of those who were still outside the pale of honorable society would not find it hard to accept an invitation to a feast given by one who had been one of them for so long. Matthew did not turn his back upon those he had labored with in the service of Rome. He wanted these men, warped and twisted by

their business, to share his joy, and follow the One who was his Master, and he saw to it that it was not an occasion for mourning, but of joy and gratitude. We can imagine how Matthew gave Jesus the seat of honor at the table. Jesus joined in most heartily at the feast, for it was at His call that Levi arose as Matthew, "God's free man." With his newly found faith, Matthew wanted the men among whom he had lived, and who knew the seamy side of his life, and whose low ideals he had shared, to be there as he confessed his faith and its Author, in whose presence he was not afraid.

Altogether, there are five feasts in which Jesus took part: at the house of Simon the leper (Mark 14:3); with the woman who was a sinner (Luke 7:37); unwashen hands (Luke 11:38); taking the chief seats (Luke 14:1); and here, in Matthew's house. Of all these feasts Jesus attended, perhaps none was so completely dear to His heart as Matthew's, seeing that it was the feast-offering of a grateful soul who with gratitude wanted to tell his "raptures all abroad." This was Matthew's way of showing that he had forsaken his old life, and that he was not ashamed to own the One who had made all things new. His was indeed a true missionary spirit. This, then, was *a feast* — not a funeral. Matthew and all invited could eat, drink, and be merry, for the lost was found, and the dead lived again. One wonders how many of his old confrères also rose up and followed Jesus. There are several aspects of this great feast worthy of notice:

1. It was arranged in Matthew's own house which must have been a large establishment to hold a great company, and all the tables and couches necessary for them. This was no poor man's house. Both the house

and lavish entertainment testified to the affluent life of Levi. Before long, however, he knew what it was to share the poverty of his Master.

2. The invited present a strange selection. All the publicans and sinners in town were there. It is more than likely that Matthew's relations and his one-time religious friends were also urged to come, for he wanted all to meet the Savior who could do the same for them, as He had done in restoring his soul. This was his way of introducing Jesus to his old associates and other present who needed salvation. That glad day, other outcast souls heard the voice of Jesus say, "Come unto me and rest," and, as Dr. J. D. Jones expresses it: "Of Matthew's house and Matthew's feast it will be declared in The Great Day — that this and that soul was born there."

3. There were discordant voices. By eating and drinking with publicans and sinners, Jesus laid Himself open to misrepresentation but He braved the ignominy of the self-righteous. To the joy of Matthew the publican and to the chagrin of the Pharisees, Jesus sat down with the pariahs of society, and met the charge first formulated here that He was the Friend of publicans and sinners. The Scribes and Pharisees murmured against the feast. These religious hypocrites shut up in their own conceit and narrow sectarian jealousy had to learn that Christ came not "to call the righteous, but sinners to repentance." His presence at the feast was a fulfillment of His mission in extending to outcasts the offer of forgiveness. So with impatient scorn Jesus turned upon His accusers in ridicule, charging them with ignorance of the true spirit of divine sympathy. Accusing them of the lack of the simplest elements of grace and godliness, Jesus told them to go and learn the message

of Hosea, "I will have mercy, and not sacrifice" (6:6).

Jesus suffered shame gladly for the sake of Matthew and his friends, and such an attitude must have resulted in the sudden deepening of Matthew's own spiritual life. The Pharisees grumbled — they always do! "When Jesus is born into a world of publicans and sinners, *all worlds marvel.* When He admits them to His Communion table, they marvel still more. When He takes publicans and sinners, saved by grace, to feast with Him in heaven, they marvel at it most of all."

4. The Pharisees were not the only ones to censure Jesus. The devout disciples of John the Baptist were also disturbed over His presence at a feast. Perhaps it was only natural that the followers of the austere "Apostle of the Wilderness" should wonder why there was feasting instead of fasting. A comparison of the gospels suggests that the Pharisees, knowing of the misgivings of the Baptist's disciples, stirred them up to ask the questions they did (Matt. 9:14, 15; Mark 2:18; Luke 5:33). It will be noted that there was no rebuke for John's followers — such as there was for the Pharisees — but a wonderful explanation in which Jesus vindicated the freedom of His own disciples. Two principles were laid down by Jesus:

a. *The natural* is a legitimate guide in all things harmless and innocent.

b. *In religion,* the mixture of incongruous elements is to be avoided (Matt. 9:15-17).

Out of the Feast, there came some of the Lord's most precious sayings, more valuable than pearls of great price. Rich truths fell from His lips. These helped to make the feast which Matthew gave more memorable still. Go through the records of this feast and make a list of the rich utterances of Jesus and you will find that supreme among them is the announcement of His mission, "They that are whole need not a physician, but they that are sick. I came not to call the righteous, but sinners to repentance."

5. *A Humble Apostle*

Matthew came to possess a self-effacing humility enabling him, even as an apostle, to lose sight of himself in adoration of his Hero. In his record of the names of the twelve apostles, Matthew is careful to attach to his name the epithet — *the publican* — as a reminder of his debtorship to divine grace (Matt. 10:3). There was no need to mention this fact, which does not appear in any of the other lists of the apostles. As Elder Cumming reminds us, "There was almost a reason for not saying anything of it, for it took from the dignity of the others, and almost of the Master, that one of the unpopular servants of Rome should be one of His apostles." But it was a characteristic mark of Matthew's true and honest spirit that he added the record of his unflattering past to his name: He wanted it never to be forgotten or overlooked that he had been a sinner. It kept him from pride to be reminded of all he had been before Christ came his way. Are you not grateful that the name of a once sinburdened and guilty sinner is found among the twelve? Then he further presents a bright example of humility in the way he describes his abandonment of every worldly prospect. You would think it was someone else who wrote, "As Jesus passed forth from thence, he saw a man, named Matthew, sitting at the receipt of custom: and he saith unto him, Follow me. And he arose, and followed him" (Matt. 9:9). This manner of presentation suggests to us the prayer for grace to forsake as Matthew did, all

covetous desires and inordinate love of riches, and the willingness to follow the same Lord. A characteristic feature of the writers of the gospels is their silence as to many details respecting their own personal history. Nowhere do they make themselves prominent. Their theme was not themselves, but Christ Jesus their Lord. Dr. William Cave in his volume on *The Apostles* reminds us that what appears to be the most remarkable virtue of Matthew was his humility. He was "mean and modest in his own conceit, in honour preferring others before himself. Whereas the other Evangelists, in describing the Apostles by pairs, constantly place him before Thomas, Matthew modestly places him before himself."

Matthew says little about his experiences among the other disciples. Whether the recollection of his former life restrained him, or a natural timidity prevented him from saying much about himself, we do not know. What is evident, he made much of Jesus in his gospel. With the rest of the evangelists, Matthew was sublimely unconscious of himself as he wrote. "No other authors whom the world has known have so completely lost and hidden themselves in their subject as these men," remarks Greenhough. And Matthew, more than the rest, kept his own person and thoughts in the background, telling us nothing, directly or indirectly, about himself. He wanted the One who had done so much for him to be exalted. His ambition can be summed up in the lines —

Not I, but Christ, be honored, loved, exalted,
    Not I, but Christ, be seen, be known and heard;
Not I, but Christ, in ev'ry look and action,
    Not I, but Christ, in ev'ry thought and word.

6. *A Gifted Author*

In the choice of Matthew we have evidence of the far-seeing discernment of Christ who knew what was in men. Seeing the tax-gatherer at his task, He could see that the literary gifts of such a man who, although then disreputable, would render invaluable service in His cause. Although we have no record of Christ committing any of His messages to writing, it was part of His divine wisdom to choose those who would be able to take careful note of all He said and did, and then, under the inspiration of the Holy Spirit, He was to bring all things to their remembrance, to write and preserve a careful account of all the Master said and did. Thus in His choice of Matthew as an apostle, He secured a *choice* biographer.

Trained to systematic methods, and gifted with his pen in connection with his old trade, Matthew was to learn how his Lord would consecrate these faculties to higher use. It would be most interesting to learn when the first hint of the divine use of his pen reached him. Did Matthew, we wonder, see Luke taking notes one day, and learning the physician's purpose to write a gospel, determine to do the same? In his remarkable *Bible Characters*, Dr. Alexander Whyte says that, "When Matthew rose up and left all and followed our Lord, the only thing he took with him out of his old occupation was his pen and ink." How grateful we are that he did take his pen and ink to write for posterity the glorious gospel that bears his name! After the record of the great feast which Matthew provided, he disappears from history; but in the gospel he wrote he lives on to comfort and gladden the souls of men.

Whether it was by observation or intuition, inspiration or command that Matthew came to write his record of Christ, and unveil His Glory as Israel's King, this fact is certain: he never dreamed, when he rose up from tabulating taxes, the use the Master would make of him in after days. We may not have the privilege of writing a gospel about the King, but we can live and labor for Him, allowing Him to liberate undeveloped powers within us, and consecrate them to holy purpose. We can become epistles of Christ written not with ink, but with the Spirit of the living God, and shine, thereby, as lights in the world (II Cor. 3:3).

It was, then, from Matthew's consecrated pen that there came the first gospel in our Bibles which has been referred to as "The most important book of Christendom," and as, "The most important book that has ever been written." Written around A.D. 70 *Matthew* met the need of early Christians for a record of the life and teachings of Christ. Churches were multiplying and the apostles were passing away, thus eye-witnesses of all He accomplished were obliged to recall the past. In passing, let it be noted that although Matthew, because of his alliance with the Roman Government, was practically a social outcast as far as the Jews were concerned, yet he must have been a man of education to work with Romans and Jews as he did when a tax-collector. His shady past by no means implies that he was uncultivated or had no learning. He must have been acquainted with the Aramaic and Greek languages. Matthew wrote his gospel in Greek, although Aramaic was the popular language of the time.

The gospel of Matthew was written expressly for the Jews of Judaea, probably under pressure of the last agonies of Jerusalem under Titus in A.D. 70. This gospel is the link between the Old and New Testaments, and its first sentence proves that the writer was well acquainted with the Jewish character, religion, and hopes and set out to commend Christ to the Jews. Christ came as the Son of David, and was the Heir of the kingdom; He came as the Son of Abraham, and was the Heir of the Blessing. These facts influenced Matthew in the selection of material for his gospel, which has many Hebrew characteristics, making it "The Hebrew porch of the New Testament."

Tradition is unanimous in the affirmation that the gospel was for the Jews, as its complexion and content prove.

Irenaeus said of it, "Matthew issued a written Gospel among the Hebrews. . . . The Gospel of St. Matthew was written for the Jews."

Origen observed, "St. Matthew wrote for the Hebrews."

Eusebius also held that "Matthew . . . delivered his gospel to his countrymen."

Of the four Gospels, Matthew is the one Jewish gospel, written by a Jew for his brother Jews, and reveals how he was immersed in the Jewish thought of the Old Testament. To him the Christ of history was the Christ of prophecy. Further, his gospel is Galilean, and more than the other evangelists, dwells upon the Galilean work of Christ. Matthew alone quotes the great promise given by Isaiah, "Galilee of the Gentiles; the people which sat in darkness saw great light; and to them which sat in the region and shadow of death light is sprung up" (Isa. 9:1, 2; Matt. 4:15, 16).

For the coverage of every phase of the contents of the gospel, the reader is referred to the remarkable section in Dr. Graham Scroggie's *A Guide to the Gospels,* dealing with *Matthew.* All that we can do in our profile of the apostle is to touch briefly upon one or two aspects of his gospel. Characteristically, it is the gospel of discourses; of types in history, law, worship, prophecy, and the kingdom. Prominent throughout the book is the idea of retribution. We might title it *The King and the Kingdom.* Further, Matthew has the qualifications of love of truth, sensibility to the mercy of God and misery of man; and he was an eye-witness of the events he described, and an eye-witness of the discourses he recorded. Thus Matthew magnifies the Lord. Of the 1071 verses forming the gospel as we have it in the A.V., 644 verses (or more than three-fifths of the whole gospel) contain words of our Lord. As there is much in it not found in the other three gospels, how impoverished we would have been if Matthew had not written his gospel, or if it had been lost.

The keynote of the gospel of Matthew is *righteousness* — the words "righteous" or "righteousness" occur sixteen times in the book. Christ came to fulfill all righteousness (3:15; 5: 17), that is, to fulfill all the requirements of law and prophecy. Our Lord was the embodiment of every precept and every requirement of the ancient Law. Taken as a whole, then, Matthew presented the image of the Messiah as it fell upon him — a Messiah who was to bless the whole world through "the chosen people — a Messiah who would realize the world hopes. Thus, Matthew's gospel can be divided into three parts —

1. The Early Days of the Messiah (Chapters 1 - 4:16)
2. The Signs and Works of the Messiah (Chapters 4:17-16:20)
3. The Passion of the Messiah (Chapters 16:21 - 28:20).

In conclusion, Matthew will ever remain an inspiration, as long as his gospel is read. His transformed life is a reminder to the outcasts of society today that they can also experience the power of Christ to change the foul current of life. Then the apostle wrote all he did about the Savior that his readers might experience in their lives His power ever able to make them disciples. This is the individuality of the Gospel we must not lose. If we cannot tell all that Christ is, we can tell all we have seen and experienced of His grace, and our representation of Him in life and witness will prove to be a guidepost to others who have lost their way. May your life and mine present as faithful a portrait of the King, even as Matthew's gospel does!

PETER

THE APOSTLE WHO WAS HOT-HEARTED

Studdert-Kennedy wrote "Rough Thymes of a Padre," and, in one of them, reminds us that:

There's nothing in man that's perfect,
  There's nothing that's all complete,
He's nobbut a big beginning,
  From his head to the soles of his feet.

Is it not in this fact that our tragedy and also our hope are found? From "a big beginning" we can sink back into perdition or move on to completion as did the apostle we are now to consider. If a man is being considered for a responsible position the question asked is — Which way is he going, *up or down?* It is not so much where he is *now* as where he is headed. He cannot stand still or remain static. If he has the ambition to journey on from his beginning, then his ascending ambition will carry him far. Too often, men go up in material things at the cost of moral and spiritual values, and meet their own soul coming down. As we are to discover, Jesus saw in Peter "a man of large ascending ambition, which if given proper objectives would carry him far"—a man who would not rest at the beginning but who would go on unto perfection. True, Peter had his faults, for he was intensely human, but failures and triumphs were but stepping stones by which he reached higher heights. This is why the fascinating story of Peter is so encouraging for others who seek to climb the upward way from their "dead selves to higher, better things."

1. *An Apostle Who Was Once a Fisherman*

If we combined what Scripture, tradition and legend have to say of Simon Peter, it would take a large canvas to paint a life-size portrait of this outstanding figure among the apostles. Quite a gallery of pictures would be required to represent all the stirring scenes in his history. None of of the twelve bulks so largely in the New Testament as Peter, and, because of the complexity of his nature, no one is less understood. Dr. Alexander Whyte reminds us that —

> The four gospels are full of Peter. After the name of our Lord Himself, no name comes up so often as Peter's name. No disciple speaks so often and so much as Peter. Our Lord speaks oftener to Peter than to any other of His disciples: sometimes in praise sometimes in blame. No disciple is so pointedly reproved by our Lord as Peter, and no disciple ever ventures to reprove his Master but Peter. No other disciple ever so boldly confessed and outspokenly acknowledged and encouraged our Lord as Peter repeatedly did, and no one ever intruded, and interfered, and tempted Him as repeatedly as Peter did.

> Peter's Master spoke words of approval, and praise, and even blessing to Peter the like of which he never spoke to any other man. And at the same time, and almost in the same breath, He said harder things to Peter than He ever said to any other of His twelve disciples, unless it was to Judas.

Of the background of such a dominant personality, we know little. All that the gospels tell us about Peter before he met the One who was to make him the channel of mighty blessing he became, is that he was a son of Jona, and a native of the small town of Bethsaida (John 1:44), on the shores of Galilee, a town where Jesus often worked and taught. Although we know him as *Peter*, the name given him after he came to know Jesus, his original name was *Simon*. Let us glance at the significance of the names he bore (Matt. 10:2; Mark 3:16; Luke 6:14; Acts 15:14).

Simon Bar-Jona

"Simon" is the common form of his given name. *Bar* means "son" and *Jona*, "John," and so the spirit of this designation in English would be, *Simon Johnson*. "Simon" was a Jewish name in the latter days of the history of Israel. Although not found in the Old Testament, in the Inter-Testament period it was used and with the opening of the New Testament "Simon" appears as *Simeon* (Luke 2:25). James the Lord's brother calls Peter "Simeon" (Acts 15:14). An old translation of Second Peter gives "Symeon Peter" in the opening salutation. "Simeon" is the form of "Simon" in the Old Testament, there being a tribe so called after one of the sons of Jacob (Gen. 49:5).

From the time of the Maccabees, "Simon" was one of the most common Jewish names. Among the twelve apostles there were two Simons and two Judases. In fact, there are nine in the New Testament bearing the name of *Simon* —

Simon Peter,
Simon Zelotes,
Simon of Cyrene,
Simon the leper,
Simon, a brother of the Lord,
Simon the Pharisee,
Simon Iscariot,
Simon Magus,
Simon the tanner.

Both Simeon and Simon are from the Hebrew *Shimeon*, which signifies "listening." Simeon was widely used as a name in the Middle Ages and again after the Reformation but it is not common now. Simon, the better known English form of *Shimeon*, was most popular in the Middle Ages, because of the renown of the Apostle Simon Peter at that period. After the Reformation, because of the emphasis of Roman Catholicism on Peter as the first Pope, the name Simon went out of fashion, but gradually came back into favor.

Peter

When Andrew brought his brother to Jesus, He met him with a strange salutation — "Thou art *Simon* the son of Jona; thou shalt be called [*Kephas*] (as it should be pronounced), which is by interpretation, a stone" (Petros, or Peter). Here we have three names—

Simon, Jewish;

Kephas, Aramaic or Syriac;

Peter, a descriptive Greek name — which is the name by which we best know the apostle — the Man of Rock. It must not be forgotten that this was his nickname, or "given name," bestowed upon him by Jesus. As we are to see, this was a strange given name for this unstable son of Jonas who appeared to have in him nothing of the steadfastness of a rock. But divine grace transformed him into the "Rock-man." Born *Simon,* under the hand of the Master who chose him and the Holy Spirit who came to control him, the "given name" was justified, and Peter became a *Rock* — a strong, firm character, on whom one could rest — a stone chosen by the Builder, to be laid upon the Rock and built upon; yet he had a certain hardness, not to be easily melted.

Peter, being born into a Jewish home, as a boy would have gone to a synagogue school, where he would learn portions of the Law and the Prophets. Long after, when he became a notable apostle, he was able to quote portions from memory. In his youth and young manhood Peter would go on the Sabbath days to the synagogue which a rich Roman centurion had built for the Jews in Capernaum. Coming from a fishing family, Peter and Andrew his brother had a fishing-boat of their own. These brothers, along with another pair of brothers, James and John, the sons of Zebedee, were in partnership, and shared the fish they caught.

Accustomed as he was to the free life of a fisherman, Peter must have sacrificed much when he accepted the control and discipline necessary as one of Christ's disciples. Something of the pleasure and comfort he left behind can be detected in his question, "We have left *all,* what shall we have?" Further, although both Peter and John became classified as "obviously uneducated and untrained men." they yet had the ability to confound the Jewish Council at Jerusalem (Acts 4:1-22). The description given does not mean that they belonged to the ignorant, lower class but that they had not received special scholastic or rabbinical training. Living in "Galilee of the Nations," Peter was able to converse in Greek as well as in his native Aramaic.

When Peter left his home in Bethsaida, he had his own house at Capernaum which, with its spacious courtyard, capable of holding many people, was an indication of his social standing as a prosperous fisherman. It was here that Peter lived with his wife whose mother lived with them (Matt. 8:14; Mark 1:28, 30). We should have liked to have known his wife's name, and whether any children were born to them. Evidently his wife loved the work of the Lord, and accompanied Peter on some of his missionary journeys, for Paul speaks of her in this way. Bruce remarks that "The likelihood is that married disciples, like married soldiers, took their wives with them or left them at home, as circumstances might require or admit . . . We find the *mother* of James and John in Christ's company far from home." Although Peter is the only apostle named as having a wife, evidently he was not the only one among the apostles who was married (I Cor. 9:5).

A human touch is given to Peter's

home-life in that his mother-in-law was stricken with a violent fever (Luke 4:38), proving as Cave puts it that, "No privileges afford an exemption from the ordinary laws of human nature; Christ, under Peter's roof did not protect this woman from the assaults of a fever. Here was a fresh opportunity for Him to exert His divine power. No sooner was He told of it, but He came to her bedside, rebuked the paroxysms, commanded the fever to be gone, and, taking her by the hand to lift her up, in a moment restored her to perfect health, and ability to return to the business of the family, all cures being equally easy to Omnipotence."

Before coming to the spiritual crisis that changed Peter from a fisherman into a follower of Christ, a word or two might be in order as to his personality and physique. Someone has said, "There is more human nature in Peter than in any other of the Lord's apostles." When the men Jesus chose became apostles, they never lost the individuality of their manhood in the spirituality of their apostleship. Even the inspiration that rested upon them partook in its effects of their peculiarities. In *The Greatest Faith Ever Known,* by Fulton Oursler, a remarkable book dealing with "The story of the men who first spread the Religion of Jesus and of the momentous times in which they lived," the gifted author has this vivid portrayal of the apostle we are now considering:

> This tall man appointed to destiny tramped the hills and valleys in the Palestinian spring-time — a big man all over he was, with a head round as a globe and with the pugnacious jaws of a fighter — but the largest thing about him was his great loving heart. . . . There are likenesses of Peter preserved until this day, the oldest being an early third century bronze medallion showing Peter with

rounded head, uncompromising jaw-bones, and thick curly hair and beard. Two later portraits of Peter are to be found in the Catacombs, very like the head on the bronze medallion, and out of these, steps barefoot into our hearts a living and very human man. . . . Essentially Peter was a man of brawn and action.

His hour of decision

Archangel Gabriel, in announcing the birth of John the Baptist, prophesied that when he appeared and took up his ministry in the spirit and power of Elijah, that he would turn many of the children of Israel to the Lord their God (Luke 1:16,17). Conspicuous among the Baptist's indirect converts was Peter, who was made ready for the service of the Lord Christ through John's influence. As we saw from our study of Andrew, Peter's younger brother, it was he who, along with other Galileans, went down to the Jordan valley to hear John the Baptist preach the message of repentance and of the coming Christ. When He appeared, and John exclaimed, "Behold the Lamb of God!" Andrew and another seeker followed Him. Every good, orthodox Jew looked for the Messiah who was to come, and Andrew, thrilled over his discovery of the Christ, hurried home to Peter with the good news, "We have found the Messiah, which is, being interpreted, the Christ." And then we read, "Andrew brought Peter to Jesus," and the miracle happened:

I looked at Him,
He looked at me,
And we were one for ever.

As soon as Jesus looked at Simon, He knew that this was the man upon whom He could rely to build up His church, which He was to purchase with His own blood, and said to Peter, as Westcott put it in his rendering of the Greek, "Thou art the son of

Jona; hereafter thou shalt win the name of Cephas, a rock or stone" (John 1:35-42). Everything, then, began afresh for Peter that day when his brother led him to Jesus, and his introduction to Him, his subsequent call, the decision to follow Him, was the beginning of everything for good and great for the rugged fisherman. Although not conscious of it, Peter was destined to achieve eminence in the ranks of the One who saw great possibilities in him.

The declaration with which Jesus greeted Peter was both a revelation and a prophecy. *"Thou art . . . Thou shalt be."* Was this not an evidence of our Lord's omniscience? Here was an insight penetrating to the deepest recesses of Simon Peter's nature, and a wisdom revealing that He could not expect more from Peter than he could give, but also a faith that once all the angularities of his character had been rounded off, he would be a vessel unto honor. Thus it was love that bore with Peter's limitations as he emerged from his old life. Grace pardoned his failures, and he became an apostle to leave the impact of utter devotion to Christ upon succeeding ages. The latent possibilities under the surface of Peter's nature, then, were read by Christ with prophetic insight into a forecast of his true character, and the new name of Cephas, or Peter, He gave him was "the first flash of divine inspiration in the ministry of Christ." As Daniel McLean so fitly puts it:

> At the introduction of the brother of Andrew to Jesus the divine instinct rose into the region of inspired intuition, and in view of the undeveloped resources of the rough fisherman of Bethsaida the prophetic mind of Christ saw in embryo the brilliant advocate of Jerusalem. The possible Cephas, or Peter, was enshrined in the actual Simon.

It was Andrew who brought Peter to Jesus, but there the brothers seem to part. Andrew exhausted his power of usefulness in such a loving, brotherly act, but now he must leave the spiritual development of his more forceful brother to others and the Lord. Andrew had introduced Peter to the Lord, and He now took over, and read what His new disciple would grow to and become. *Thou shalt be called,* on Christ's lips, could only mean, *Thou shalt be, Thou shalt become.* And as we are to see, the Teacher never lost heart over His pupil, but kept right on until His prophecy was verified when Peter became the rock-like character whom Luke depicts in the *Acts of the Apostles.*

Just how long a time elapsed between Simon's first contact with Jesus and his subsequent call to discipleship and apostleship, we are not told. It would seem that after that initial, memorable interview with Christ, both Simon and his brother Andrew returned to their fishing, and it was while they were working that the call came; and when the summons reached ear and heart, they obeyed, and from that hour there was no turning back. Perhaps Simon was not easily won for Christ and His cause. The *stone* resisted pressure. Dr. Elder Cumming suggests that it needed *two,* and probably *three,* calls to induce Simon to cast in his lot with the Man of Nazareth:

> Matthew tells us, before the Sermon on the Mount (Matt. 4:18), of a call given by Jesus to the four disciples, Peter and Andrew and James and John, who were *fishing.* Luke tells us of a call given by Jesus to the same four when they were *mending their nets,* on which occasion Jesus addressed a multitude from Peter's boat, and thereafter wrought a great miracle.

At the close of the story the Evangelist tells us that four disciples "forsook all and followed Him" (Luke 5:1-11). We are not sure whether these two descriptions refer to the same event or not. If not, it needed three calls of Christ to persuade Peter to give up his business and follow the Master fully.

The *first* call was to believe; the *second*, a call to follow occasionally; the *third*, the call to have no other Master, and to surrender everything to Jesus.

At last, the fisherman of Galilee became a fisher of men on a most extensive scale, and under divine inspiration gathered multitudes into the church of such as should be saved. By his life and work, and his two epistles, Peter is still casting his net into the sea of the world and bringing an unending haul of disciples to Him who had the happiness of being numbered among His first followers.

Although Peter left the sea for the Savior, and left catching shoals of fish for the saving of souls, the sea remained much with the one-time fisherman. It is interesting to gather together the sea-episodes in Peter's career. For instance, no narrative is more self-revealing than the one when Jesus, eager to teach the assembled crowds on the sea-shore, commandeered Peter's boat. Along with his partners, Peter had been out all night, rowing, hauling, casting nets, but had nothing to show for it. Spent with toil, and perhaps faint with hunger, the partners were about to wash their nets and go home for a meal and rest.

The sun was rising, and Jesus turned to Peter with what seemed an unreasonable demand, "Launch out into the deep and let down your nets for a draught" (Luke 5:4). Can you not imagine the old Adam rising in poor, tired Peter, as with a touch of sarcasm he replied, "Master, *we* have toiled all night, and have taken noth-

ing." Peter was a craftsman, and knew that as the sun was now shining upon the water, it was not the time to catch fish. It was asking too much of his loyalty to fish at such a wrong time. Only a novice would suggest such a thing. Surely Jesus knew nothing about fish and their habits to make such a request. Why, if he obeyed and let down his nets in the gleaming sun, he would become a laughing-stock among those on the shore.

When Peter said, "Neverthless, at *thy* word I will let down the net," it was not in accents of loving unquestioning obedience, but with a touch of fiery impetuosity, as if to say, "Well, it's not the right time to fish, as You ought to know, but if You say so, here goes!" This sea-incident represented a major crisis in Peter's experience, for the miraculous catch of fish brought the fisherman to realize that the One who had commanded Him to cast his net was no mere man, but the Master of ocean, and earth, and sky. Henceforth Jesus became his Lord. Conscience swept his soul as with a searchlight, as he saw himself a sinful man daring to question the knowledge and power of the sinless Lord. Humiliated to the depths, and crushed with a sense of guilt, he cried, "Depart from me, for I am a sinful man, O Lord!" But Jesus did not leave the sinner, but stayed with him to the end. Peter became conscious of the presence of a Power beyond his knowledge.

Another sea-episode was the one associated with the finances of the apostolate. The money-bag was empty and there was no money to meet the Temple-tax demand. But the resourceful Master told Peter to take a fishing line to the nearby lake where he would catch a fish with the required amount in its mouth. Again, Peter learned that his Master was the Lord of nature. Incidentally, this miracle throws light on the poverty of our Lord and His disciples. We take our Lord's words in their literal sense, and believe they were literally fulfilled. How the fish happened to be at the spot where Peter threw his line, with the exact amount of tax-money in its mouth, was the Lord's secret (Matt. 17:24-27). A parallel of this miracle is the well-known story of the ring of Polycrates, the tyrant of Samos (Herod. 111:39-45).

Then there is the record of the storm at sea which must have reminded Peter of the old days when, as a fisherman he experienced many a dangerous squall (Matt. 8:23-27). You know the dramatic story. Peter is the pilot of that boat on the Galilean lake which carried the Destiny of the world asleep in the back of the vessel. Up comes a raging storm defying the steering skill of the man at the helm. Peter looked at the Master fast asleep and wondered how He could sleep in such a storm. In desperation he awoke the slumbering One with the rebuke, "Carest thou not that we perish?" Jesus arose and rebuked the wind and the sea in the calm majesty of His power, and Peter with the rest bowed in humiliation and adoration at the feet of their majestic Lord. Two phrases stand out in this sea-incident. *The storm arose — and he arose.* For the rising of the storm there is always the rising of the Master who alone can silence it.

Another experience Peter had on the sea was when Jesus told His disciples to go by ship to the other side, and He would meet them there after a season of prayer in a mountain. While He was communing with His Father, the disciples encountered turbulent waves which threatened their safety. But Jesus saw their peril and coming down the mount, *walked* on the sea.

Seeing Him, the disciples thought it was some kind of a ghost, then they heard the assuring voice of One they knew so well. Fear brought out into strong relief the adventurous confidence of Peter. So he requested liberty to meet Christ on the troubled waters in something like bravado. "He walked on the water, to go to Jesus" (Matt. 14:22-33). While Peter kept his eye on Jesus he could walk, but looking down at the boisterous waves, he began to sink. His experiment exposed Peter's presumptuous spirit, and his baptism in the sea was a salutary lesson on the nature of faith, and a further reminder of his Lord's sovereignty over nature. The outstretched hand of the Master came to Peter's relief as he cried, "Lord, save me!" This manifestation of divine power resulted in a noble testimony — almost a perfect creed — "Of a truth thou art the Son of God."

The last sea-episode in which Peter, the one-time son of the sea, is connected, was after the resurrection of Christ. The apostles were evidently awaiting the coming of the Master and as He did not appear, Peter, impetuous as always, said, "I go a-fishing." The rest said, "We also go with thee" (John 21:1-14). Then came another fruitless night's work, Jesus' sudden appearance on the shore and His question about having anything for breakfast, the miraculous draught of fish, the meal Jesus had all ready for them when they returned, and the abiding vision the apostles had of the omnipotence of their Risen Lord. After that meal, which nail-pierced hands had prepared, Peter was recommissioned for his great task ahead in saving multitudes of souls. J. K. Nitting wrote a simple poem on this incident which he called *Simon Stone.* The last two verses read:

Oh! he swam for life, and he swam for
  love,
  Till he stood on the shore with the Lord
  alone.
Who knows, but he and the Lord above,
  How the Lord spake sweet to Simon
  Stone.

Then tell me if ever you loved like him,
  If ever you felt like Simon Stone;
"Whether I run or fly or swim,
  I must have a word with Jesus alone."

2. *An Apostle the Master Moulded*

When Peter and his brother, Andrew, received the call to leave their fishing and follow Jesus, they heard Him say, "I will make you *fishers of men*" (Matt. 4:18-20). As the Divine Potter, He was to undertake the molding of these followers for the supreme task of evangelism. Andrew is never conspicuous in this field, as far as the sacred record reveals, but Peter became the greatest soul-winner in the early church, as we shall presently discover. The emphasis in the command is on, "I will *make* you." He was to have the sole responsibility of shaping them after His will. In the process of developing the characters of those He had chosen, it seemed as if He had poor material with which to work, but He succeeded in conforming them to His image — with the exception of Judas who, as hard clay, resisted the will of the Potter, and was discarded.

As for Peter, Jesus knew that he would grow in grace and in the knowledge of Himself, as the apostle came to write in II Peter 3:18. Under His training, He saw that he would become a workman who had no need to be ashamed, and so He set about developing Peter. Of course, the scholar in the divine school was constantly making mistakes and the Divine Teacher had to correct them, and guard against their return. Jesus never lost heart over His pupil, but kept on with the tuition until His prophecy of a rock-like character was verified in the life of the disciple. Slowly the Master's anticipations were realized. He knew both the strong and weak points of Peter's make-up, but His love would not let him go, and Peter came to repay all the loving care, understanding, and patience Jesus had shown in his spiritual development.

No other Bible character provides us with the same evidence of our Lord's training technique with one He desires to raise to prominence in His service, as Peter, the "simple-hearted, impetuous and lovable Jew," whom Jesus chose for the leadership of the apostolic band. As J. Oswald Sanders expresses it in *Men From God's School*, "Peter's vivid personality, forthright utterances and deep devotion combine with the greatness of his strength and the magnitude of his mistakes to make him an ideal test-case for the methods of the Master."

Peter, at the time of his call, along with the rest of the humble fishermen of Galilee, had much to learn and unlearn before the high requirements of Christ were satisfied. The majority of them were unlearned, superstitious, and full of Jewish prejudices, misconceptions and animosities. But, above all, they were honest men, and "the soil of their spiritual nature was fitted to produce an abundant harvest," as it did in Peter's dynamic ministry after the resurrection of Christ. Having left all for Christ's society and service, the men of Galilee revealed by such a surrender, an indefinite capacity of spiritual and mental growth.

The variety of personality which Jesus had to bring into harmony with His mind and will is another aspect of His training of the Twelve which we should note. It is clear that they were not all out of the same mold. But the Potter knew how to work with *each* lump of human clay. His methods with Peter varied from those He used to prevent Judas from his dastardly deed. In the portrait gallery of the apostles, then, "the thoughts of many hearts are revealed," and the Lord had use for the differences which made them individual and distinct from each other. "Duplicates do not count, except in swelling the figures of the census; and there are none around Jesus in the gospel story." Once molded by Christ, through the variety of types there ran an infinite order, adding unity to variety.

The violent and extreme contrasts in Peter's own nature are clearly evident. While he had his moments of rapture and high vision, he yet was conscious of depths of sin within his being. He could give utterance to sublime utterances and yet have the lips of a denier and blasphemer. He was able to soar to great heights yet sink to the depths of contrition. One day Peter pronounced a magnificent eulogy of Christ, the next day he sought to rebuke Him. At one time we find him a companion of the Master on the blessed Mount, but later on we have him swearing he never knew Him. Peter forsakes all to follow Christ, yet at the end forsakes Him in the Garden. Is not this picture drawn from life? Are not the same almost unbelievable contrasts descriptive of many saints today?

As we approach, then, an understanding of some of the necessary lessons Peter had to learn, we concede that "the complexity of his nature easily lends itself to exaggeration or one-sided treatment, and his somewhat erratic career renders it difficult to obtain a fair all-round view. He has the virtues and vices of creative minds, the lights and shadows of sanguine temperaments, the inconsisten-

cies of genius: and it is no easy task to grasp the stable principle of all his varying moods and exhibit in clear-cut outline the various elements of a character so full of striking contrasts." Let us give ourselves, then, to a survey of outstanding incidents in the "Big Fisherman's" life and trace the gradual unfolding of a richly-endowed nature under the educational influence of divine grace. It has been suggested that his history may be grouped into three sections under the well-known names —

Simon,
Simon Peter,
Peter.

Lesson of restraint

Because Peter was naturally impetuous and forceful it may be that the hardest lesson he had to learn under the tutelage of Jesus was that of *restraint*. And as we know, He succeeded in harnessing the Niagara forces within the fisherman's vehement nature for dynamic service among the lost sheep in the House of Israel. Peter's exposed life on the sea accentuated his rough-edged impetuosity, and made him forthright and outspoken. Conspicuous among his traits was an intuition enabling him to pierce instantly to the heart of a situation, and then to act decisively, promptly and without hesitation. Indicating some of Peter's unmistakable footprints, Alexander Whyte says that he was "hasty, headlong, speaking impertinently and unadvisedly, ready to repent, ever wading into waters too deep for him, and ever turning to his Master again like a little child."

Perhaps his somewhat impetuous temperament was inherited from his father Jonas, and as Peter developed into manhood, his unbridled heart became harder to control. But, as Alexander Whyte goes on to tell us, "by degrees, and under the teaching, the example and the training of his Master, Peter's too-hot heart was gradually brought under control till it became the seat in Peter's bosom of a deep, pure, deathless love and adoration for Jesus Christ." Regardless of consequences, Peter was frank, outspoken and generous in his impulses, even when mistaken. At times, he was utterly wanting in personal reserve, and his hot-headed impatience got him into trouble. Caring little for conventional propriety, or for difficulties blocking his way, Peter acted on the rule, "When in doubt, speak." Yet in spite of his reckless tongue, heedlessness of prejudice, and lack of caution, Jesus chose him as an apostle.

Our Lord's rebuke of Peter's lack of restraint was always free of bitterness, and just and timely (Matt. 16: 22, 23). With a gentleness of firmness, He censured Peter for not understanding His plan. In fact, Peter received the severest censure of any of Christ's followers — yet, withal, the highest praise. When he denied his Lord, Peter fell a victim to his own impulsiveness, and "the backstroke of his own sword wounded his soul, and the old fisherman habit of swearing came back to confirm his utter degradation." When Jesus was arrested by the band of men who had been guided to Gethsemane by Judas, Peter drew his sword and impulsively leaped before his Master, ready to thrust at the first enemy daring to injure his Lord. Although this was a generous deed, and an exhibition of sincere human devotion willing to take risks, Jesus had to lovingly rebuke the impetuous action of His disciple, and tell him to sheath his sword. Peter had to learn that the cause of Christ could not be advanced by the weapons of worldly warfare. Fleshly zeal but hinders such a cause (John 18:36).

The volcanic, explosive, and impulsive nature of Peter, whose hot heart often ruled his head, and who could do nothing by halves, was not "the kind of flower that is born to blush unseen," says Dr. J. Stuart Holden in his study of Peter. He was "quick, impulsive, impetuous — a man who must express his feelings; a man who, if he sees anything, must say so — must suit his actions to his perceptions. Adjournments were no part of his make-up. He was 'quick on the trigger,' a man who does things first and then thinks over them, sometimes sadly, later on. Such a man will make mistakes, but he'll make other things too!" Was it Abraham Lincoln who said that, "He who never makes a mistake, never makes anything"?

Was Peter the kind of man who "didn't wait to watch which way the cat would jump," or was he the kind of man who invariably makes "the cat jump his way"? Under the Master's teaching he came to learn how to curb impulse by judgment, and to restrain action by wise calculation of consequences. Patience and self-restraint became his. Jesus succeeded in mastering Peter's soul, as the teaching of First and Second Peter clearly indicate. The prophecy was fulfilled: *"Thou art . . . Thou shalt be."* At the outset, Peter was a man of the strongest, the most willful, and the most wayward impulse which, if not controlled, would lead to destruction. But as he continued to live under Christ's control the lion in Peter became more lamb-like.

Lesson of humility

In many of his announcements, as well as in some of his answers to Jesus, Peter made generous use of the personal pronoun. The *I* is prominent. The middle letter of SIN is *I*, and self-confidence is indeed the armor-bearer of sin. Self-confidence, which is related to self-conceit, can blind one to his own ignorance and to his own weaknesses. Poor Peter had to learn, "Not *I,* but Christ." Confidence in himself made him rush in where angels would not tread. He valued too highly his own importance, and this made him venture when he should have drawn back, and utter magnificent promises which he afterwards shamefully broke. Over-rating himself, he presumptuously tried to rebuke and correct his Master — the only disciple who dared to do so — as if he knew better than the all-wise One. Had he possessed more of the humility he came to write about he would have been silent when tempted to be outspoken. Peter was tempted, as we all are, to rely upon self and not be wholly dependent upon the Lord.

With his most extraordinary self-confidence he had to learn to pray with the psalmist, "Keep back thy servant also from presumptious sins; let them not have dominion over me" (Ps. 19:13). Confidence in himself turned Peter into an idle boaster and led him to throw caution to the winds (Matt. 26:33, 34). Strong, forceful and masterful, Peter had complete and perfect confidence in himself. "Though all men should be offended in thee, *I* will never be offended," but before the night had passed this boastful, self-reliant disciple denied his Lord three times. It was this self-confidence which, as chaff, had to be sifted from the wheat of Peter's character, and by painful trials and sad failures, he learned humility through suffering.

Yet this conspicuous vice became a conspicuous virtue, for the very self-confidence which betrayed Peter and made him too forward was the element, when sanctified, which helped to fashion him into the early church leader he became. The masterfulness — the direct and immediate cause of some of Peter's bitterest humiliations — constituted him the mighty spiritual force we see him to be in the first twelve chapters of the Acts. Under divine training Peter came to learn that the secret of victorious strength in service for Christ is self-distrust, "When I am weak, then am I strong." Through his pride, through his overweening self-confidence, Peter fell, but there is one verse in his first epistle, addressed especially to those who are self-reliant, "Be sober, be vigilant; because your adversary the devil, as a roaring lion, walketh about, seeking whom he may devour." From Jesus, Peter learned the lesson of self-abnegation. The Master died to self before He died for sin. "Reviled, he reviled not again." This was the example which Peter the braggart came to follow (I Peter 2:21-24). Along a hard road he came to experience that "God resisteth the proud, and giveth grace to the humble" (I Pet. 5:5).

One has read of a household returning home only to find that the house had been burglarized. The thief had taken all the valuables he could find. But in one room there was a silver crucifix which remained in its place. Before the thief could touch anything, however, he set the face on the crucifix to the wall. He could not steal with the sorrowful eyes of Christ fixed upon him. Peter's deliverance from self-trust came as he allowed Christ to look into his heart and reveal how ugly and repulsive such a self-centered life was.

Lesson of grace

Peter was forever asking questions. There was the pointed one he put to Jesus about the matter of forgiveness, probably because he found it difficult to forgive his enemies as the Master was instructing His disciples to do.

What a new and subduing conception of the forgiving grace of Jesus Peter received in reply to his question, "Lord, how oft shall my brother sin against me and I forgive him? Till seven times?" How grateful we are that the disciple's thoughts on forgiveness differed from those of the Master! Peter had to learn to forgive as his Master forgave. What is the measure of divine forgiveness? It means more than getting rid of a resentment or grudge. It represents a complete reconciliation. "As far as the east is from the west, so far has he removed our transgressions from us." Christ's forgiveness of us cost Him all the shame and sacrifice of the cross.

It would have been a poor outlook for Peter himself had there been any natural or numerical limit to forgiveness. Had Jesus accepted Peter's limit of forgiveness, he would never have entered the inheritance of the saints in light. Sinning Simon needed the grace that never wearies of forgiving, and will forever remain a monument of the patient and pardoning love of Christ. Sinning and falling again and again he needed the seventy times seven (Matt. 18:21, 22). He came to prove that—

"Unwearied in forgiveness still,
His heart can only love."

Unable, perhaps, fully to understand that the divine commandment is "exceeding broad," Peter might have felt that there must be some limit to the way of dealing with a brother who had sinned against him (Matt. 18:15)), and so used the sacred number suggesting a limit. Did Peter have in mind the prophet's reference that "for three transgressions . . . and for four" (Amos 1:3), punishment should not be turned away? But Christ's reply, "until seventy times seven," in-

dicated that no line should be drawn in our forgiveness, just as He recognizes no numerical standard. As there is no boundary to God's forgiveness of us, there should be none in our forgiveness of others. After this lesson on matchless grace, Peter, anticipating the words of the gospel poet, must have said to his soul, again and again—

"O to grace how great a debtor
Daily I'm constrained to be!"

Lesson of sacrifice

The twelve in general, and Peter in particular, had further to learn that there is no easy way to dominion and a crown. Is this not the truth enshrined in Christ's rebuke of the apostle when, in his characteristic impetuous fashion, he rebuked the Master for taking what Peter deemed to be unnecessary risks (Matt. 16:22-23)? What contrasts he presents! One moment he was on the mountain peak of revelation being chosen of God to be the first apostle to see the glory hidden behind the veil of his Lord's humanity, but the next moment he becomes a spokesman for the devil. Christ had begun to reveal to the twelve His coming rejection, the agonies of the cross, the victory over the grave, and final exaltation. But impulsively Peter countered this talk about supreme sacrifice with the assertion, "Be it far from thee, Lord, this shall not be unto thee."

The striking feature of this episode is that Jesus did not reply directly to Peter but to the devil who was making a flanking attack on Him through Peter's personality. Unknowingly, in his effort to keep Jesus from the cross, Peter allied himself to his Master's adversary who was using Peter's lips.

"Get thee behind me, Satan!"

Jesus did not brand Peter as being *Satan,* but He directly rebuked His arch-foe by name for his use of Peter in prompting him to seek service without sacrifice, a crown without a cross. Peter had to learn that the kingdom cannot be advanced by any and every means short of the cross; that service is only successful when sacrificial; that there can never be an Easter and a Pentecost without a Calvary. To his credit, let it be said, Peter came to experience that it was the way of the cross that led home, for at the end he hung upon a tree.

O Cross, that liftest up my head,
   I dare not ask to fly from Thee;
I lay in dust life's glory dead,
   And from the ground there blossoms red
   Life that shall endless be.

Lesson of a new society

Immersed in the aspirations and hopes of Judaism, Peter, as a Jew, looked for the coming of the Messiah to establish a kingdom on earth. But with an isolationist's point of view this Galilean, believing that salvation was of the Jews, looked upon the Messiah more as "the glory of His people" than as "a light to lighten the Gentiles" (Luke 2:32). It was this restricted outlook of the divine plan that God corrected in the vision Peter had of the great sheet let down from heaven (Acts 10:1-22). Godly Cornelius, renowned officer in the Roman army, and a *Gentile*, desired a deeper knowledge of the Lord and fellowship in the church. A convert to the faith of Israel, he sought those who were able to lead him to a higher life and in a vision was guided to Peter.

But Peter had to be taught that the distinction between Jew and Gentile had been done away in Christ, and that His Church embraced *all* who had been born anew by the Spirit. Hence the vision he received at Joppa of the great sheet let down to earth wherein were all four-footed beasts — even the swine that were used as food by the Gentiles. Humbly, Peter confessed that he had learned the lesson which the vision had taught him, namely, that God was not the God of the Jews only, but the God of the Gentiles, and that He was willing to receive all men — even the most outcast Gentile. This was the composition of the Church which Christ called, *My Church*. Peter first heard about this from the lips of his Master in response to his heaven-inspired revelation and declaration of His Messiahship and deity (Matt. 16: 13-20).

The twelve had been with Christ now for more than a year and had studied His life and felt the impact of it on their own lives; they had witnessed His life as miracle followed miracle; they had listened to His incomparable discourses. Our Lord knew how they felt about Him, but He asked them how the people at large regarded Him. What were they saying about Him? Peter, making a series of swift mental comparisons, thought of some of the saintly heroes of the past, and in reply to Christ's question, "Whom do men say *I* am?" Peter said, "John the Baptist"; "Elijah"; "Jeremiah"; "one of the prophets." Then, with His eye resting upon Peter, Jesus asked of him, "But whom say *ye* that I am?" Swiftly as echo follows voice, Peter replied, "Thou art the Christ, the Son of the living God." In a flash, he saw how He dwarfed all the spiritual giants of the ages.

Such a revelation of the glory hidden behind the veil of Christ's humanity was received, not by intuition, or acquisition, but by the Holy Spirit, who is ever the Interpreter of God to men. This was the first Christian creed. Peter had reached the mountain peak of revelation, and received the benediction of the One revealed to his mind: "Blessed art thou, Simon

Bar-jona: flesh and blood hath not revealed it unto you, but my Father which is in heaven. Then followed our Lord's first mention of the new society He had come to found — *My Church* — which Peter was to be conspicuous in establishing and extending. This brings us to a consideration of our Lord's words which have been grossly misinterpreted by the Roman Catholic Church, "I say also unto thee, That thou art Peter, and upon this rock I will build my church; and the gates of hell shall not prevail against it" (Matt. 16:18). What our Lord went on to say about Peter having the keys of the kingdom is dealt with separately in our next section. Just here, let us seek to understand the significance of the *rock* of which our Lord spoke.

The *mecca* of Roman Catholics is St. Peter's in Rome, which is supposed to be built on the spot where Peter died and is buried. Not so long ago Rome affirmed that it had identified the apostle's bones. This is a symbol of Rome's heresy, namely that the Church is built on Peter, as Jesus said it would be. So in *The Unity of the Church,* Father M. J. Legoc translates our Lord's words in this way, "Upon thee — Peter, whom I made a rock — I will build My Church." Peter is the head of the Church, was the first to preach the Gospel in Rome, established his throne in the city of Rome. Yet that most famous and reliable Roman Catholic historian, the Abbé Duchesne, in his *Early History of the Church*, refutes the claim of his church. Here is what he wrote:

Whose hands had sown the Divine seed in the ground, that is, Rome, *we shall never know.* Conjectures built upon foundations *too insecure to be sanctioned by history,* takes the Apostle Peter to Rome during the first years of Claudius, A.D. 42. . . . About the time St. Paul gained his

liberty, St. Peter came to Rome. He had, perhaps, been there before: this is possible. *But it cannot be proved. We have no information whatever* as to Peter's apostolic work in Rome.

When we think of the somewhat stained record of the church of Rome *it* might have been founded upon poor, failing Peter, but *the* Church, which Christ called, My CHURCH (the Church of the living God, I Tim. 3: 15) has Christ alone as its foundation. "For other foundation can no man lay than that is laid, which is Jesus Christ" (I Cor. 3:11). The dynamic preaching of Peter was the means of the first mass conversions of Jews and Gentiles, and as his labors established and extended the Church, in this sense he can be spoken of as its foundation (Acts 2:41; 10; 15:7). Paul refers to Peter as one of the *pillars* of the Church (Gal. 2:9), and "the household of God" as being "built upon the foundation of the apostles and prophets, Jesus Christ himself being the chief cornerstone" (Eph. 2:20; Rev. 21:14).

What, then, is the true significance of our Lord's word about building His Church on a *Rock?* The two Greek words for "rock" differ in gender. The first one used of Peter is *petros*, meaning a fragment of stone chipped from the rock-face; the second word is *petra*, implying the whole rock itself. As already indicated, association with Jesus transformed *Simon* into *Peter,* and he came to have a rock-like character, but he is not *the Rock* upon which His Church is built. Peter was a Jew and with his knowledge of the Old Testament would know that *Rock* throughout the Hebrew Scripture is never used symbolically of man, but always of God. "The Hebrew word is *Tsur,* and we find it occurring at least forty times figuratively in the Old Testament. Twice it is used of false gods as in Deuteronomy 32, as they are put in contrast with the Rock of Israel, who is the Living God. In every instance the figurative use of the word applies to God."

The crux of the matter is that the true Church is built not upon Peter as an individual, but upon what Peter had just confessed — "Thou art the Christ, the Son of the Living God." Peter saw the Son of God as the Administrator of the will and way of God, bearing a unique relationship to God, and it was to this ultimate fact that our Lord made reference when He said, "Upon this rock — (My deity and Messiahship) — I will build my church." He is the great and wise Master-Builder of the Christian Society — the Rock on which it is built (I Cor. 10:4; I Pet. 2:4-6). The implied contrast, then, can be expressed thus: "Thou art the Rock-Apostle; and yet not *the* Rock on which the Church is to be built. It is enough for thee to have found the Rock, and to have built on the one Foundation."

Augustine, Bishop of Hippo, A.D. 396, put into the mouth of Jesus the following form —

> Upon this rock I will build My Church, not upon Peter whom thou art, but upon the rock whom thou hast confessed, saying, "Thou art the Christ, the Son of the Living God . . . Upon Me I will build thee, not Me upon thee."

Chrysostom, Patriarch of Constantinople, A.D. 398 in a sermon on Matthew 16:18, expressed it this way: "I say unto thee, Thou art Peter, and upon this rock I will build My Church, that is to say, upon the faith of confession. He did not build His Church upon the man, but upon his faith." Both Augustine and Martin Luther held that the Church was built upon the heaven-inspired revelation of Christ, to which Peter gave utterance (see

Gal. 1:16; I John 4:2, 3). Of this new society, Jesus declared that "The gates of hell [or hades] shall not prevail against it." The language here implies aggressive strength of a Church at war, conquering sin, overcoming sorrow and therefore triumphant over death. The world at large looks upon the organized church as a weak force indeed, unable to do much against the rising tide of iniquity, international and national strife and war, and the multiplying problems of our age. May God so re-vitalize His Church, that once again she will be as terrible as an army with banners!

Lesson of love

In one of his *Sonnets*, Shakespeare would have us remember that —

Roses have thorns, and silver fountains mud;
Clouds and eclipses stain both moon and sun,
And loathsome canker lives in sweetest bud.
All men make faults.

Peter certainly had his faults, thorns among his roses, but with all his clouds and eclipses, we love him still. The lack of a warm, emotional, and generous nature, however, was not one of his faults. Beneath his rugged exterior there was a loving heart. Dear old Alexander Whyte has a paragraph well worthy of repetition in his character study of Peter:

> Blame Peter as much as you like; dwell upon the faults of his temperament, and all the defects of his character, and the scandals of his conduct, as much as you like; I defy you to deny that, with it all, he was not a very attractive and a very lovable man. "The worst disease of the human heart is cold." Well, with all his faults, and he was full of them, a cold heart was not one of them. All Peter's faults, indeed, lay in the

heat of his heart. His hot heart was always in his mouth, and he spoke it all-out many times, when he should have held his peace.

His sense of sin, and bitter tears over his sin, reveal Peter's innate tenderness. He was the only one of the whole apostolic company to fall at the feet of Jesus and cry, "Depart from me, for I am a sinful man, O Lord!" What a crushing sense of guilt, of remorse, Peter manifested! Such an "exquisite sense of sin" is surely an evidence of a heart easily touched by a tender hand. Is it not this deep consciousness of utter unworthiness that has gained a place for him in the hearts of all who have no false ideas of their own value and importance (Luke 5:8)?

Peter's heart was always in the right place. What it needed was a firmer control, and this was slowly experienced under his Master's tuition. His concern for the coming rejections and sufferings of Jesus filled him with indignation and pain (Matt. 16:22), and the peril and insults to which Jesus was exposed made Peter boil over with uncontrollable wrath (John 18:10), all of which revealed him as a man of deep feeling. The curing of his mother-in-law's fever was not only a special mark of favor for Peter, but a proof that under his rough exterior there beat a warm and loving heart.

At the Sea of Galilee, the risen Christ met His disciples with a new and larger call to service, and it was at this private interview so wisely held in silence that Peter is singled out for a further sifting process. Jesus is faithful and tender in His questioning of Peter. Then there rang out the confession of his heart, "Thou knowest that I love thee." In the moving story of this conversation between Jesus and His erring disciple Jesus asked him the question, not once, but thrice,

"Lovest thou me?" Peter's old name was used, *Simon*, and his triple confession succeeds his threefold denial — "He denied him thrice." Probed to the quick, Peter replies, each time avoiding his Master's use of a word denoting intensive affection, deliberating, choosing a word implying deep regard rather than love. In the end, he used the word Jesus did and answered, "Yea, Lord, Thou knowest that I love Thee!"

Satisfied with His disciple's outburst of passionate, burning love, Jesus recommissioned Peter for future service. From now on, he knew what his work was to be and how he would die (John 21:15-19). No wonder in after days, when Peter came to write his epistles, he declared that, "Love covereth a multitude of sins" — and it still does! Daniel McLean reminds us that:

> Peter's sun had been eclipsed but never put out, and it shone out with genial warmth as soon as the shadow was gone, so that we accept the opinion of Chrysostom, "Christ loved John exceedingly, but by Peter Christ was exceedingly beloved."
>
> Simon, the disciple of promise, through this confession opens out into the heroic Peter. From this point he enters on a brilliant career of usefulness, and the wealth of his sanctified genius is consecrated to the service of the faith.

"Lovest thou me *more than these?*" By *these* we are to understand not only the fishes, boats, and nets — his old calling — but the other disciples who were present. The obvious reference is to Peter's own comparison of himself with others in the confidence of love which he thought would never fail (Matt. 26:33; Mark 14:29). Has the same searching question reached our hearts, "Lovest thou Me *more than these?*" — and has the reply been that of Peter's, "*Thou knowest* that I love Thee"? Better than wealth, better than health, better than fame, better than the nearest and dearest? Peter came to love much, because, like the woman who bathed Christ's feet, he had been forgiven much. Is this our personal experience?

Lesson of disciplined courage

Peter was naturally and constitutionally of an enthusiastic and sanguine temperament. How can we define enthusiasm? "What is it but the heart, and the imagination, and the whole man, body and soul, set on fire?" It was the quality that helped Peter to manifest unmistakable courage and because the bravest men are subject to a temporary lapse into panic and cowardice, we must not chide Peter for yielding to such a mood. Ignominiously Frederick the Great ran away from his first battle. Both Elijah and John the Baptist were undoubted heroes, but, as we know, the heart of one failed in the desert, and the heart of the other in prison. Essentially, Peter was a brave man, as his effort to walk on the sea proves. This was not a rash act: only a brave man would have attempted such a feat. Then, only a fearless man would have stood up against the company of soldiers who came out to take Jesus prisoner. When he said to Jesus, "I am ready to go with thee to prison and to death," Peter meant it, and if the trial had come that moment, out he would have gone with Jesus. But this natural courage was mixed with softer material, and needed to be disciplined, purified by fire, strengthened by a higher spirit of trust and devotion to become rock-like. Pentecost brought about such consecration of courage, making it "deep-springing, strong-flowing, divinely-purified, and divinely-directed," so much so, that when Peter stood up and condemned the rulers, elders, and scribes with the crime of history, they marvelled at his boldness (Acts 4:5-13).

> Since I must fight if I would reign,
>   Increase my courage, Lord!
> I'll bear the toil, endure the pain,
>   Supported by Thy Word.

3. An Apostle Who Received the Keys

After his sublime revelation, which elicited the benediction of Jesus, He gave Peter a solemn charge and commission, which, because of its misinterpretation by the church of Rome, deserves our consideration. It reads, "I will give unto thee the keys of the kingdom of heaven: and whatsoever thou shalt bind on earth shall be bound in heaven: and whatsoever thou shalt loose on earth shall be loosed in heaven" (Matt. 16:19). Legend depicts Peter at the door of heaven having keys to admit to eternal bliss those he deems worthy. It was this false idea Lord Byron embodied in his poem on *Vision of Judgment* —

As he drew near, he gazed upon the gate
Ne'er to be entered more by him or Sin,
With such a glance of supernatural hate
As made Saint Peter wish himself within;
He falter'd with his keys at a great rate,
And sweated through his apostolic skin;
Of course his perspiration was but ichor,
Or some such other spiritual liquor.

Roman Catholicism, claiming Peter as its foundation, interprets these *keys* as symbolizing the unique power given to Peter. But as Dr. J. D. Jones expresses it, "Christ bestowed upon Peter no lordship or authority over his brethren. For the Roman theory of an official primacy there is not the slightest shadow of foundation, but the fact that Peter exercised a primacy among the twelve sprang from his own bold, masterful and impetuous nature is written large upon every page of the New Testament." What must not be forgotten is the fact that the very same words of authority as our Lord spoke to Peter, about binding and loosing, are spoken to individual believers. Peter was the first to use the keys, but not the only one to do so (Matt. 18:18). The last important reference to Peter in the Acts is where he made reference to his use of the keys, in his plea for Christian liberty, before the Jerusalem Council (Acts 15:7-9).

The mission of a key is to turn a lock and open a door, and once the door is open, the key has no further value, unless the door should shut. Peter's presentation of the keys simply means that he was to have the privilege of unlocking the door, or to proclaim Christ who is *the Door*, and invite Jews, Samaritans and Gentiles to enter the Door and be saved. This Door has ever remained open, and all who are willing can enter (Acts 2:14-40; 8:14; 10:34-48). Once Peter used the keys, he faded from the picture and left the door wide open for whosoever will. Paul distinctly tells us that Peter's special mission was to be the apostle of the circumcision, to the Jews. Yet in the house of Cornelius at Caesarea, Peter used the key Christ put into his hands, to open the door of faith to the Gentiles.

In the first twelve chapters of the Acts, Peter dominates the scene as he inaugurates great Christian enterprises, opening doors for sheep to enter, then feeding the sheep as the Master had commanded him to do. The apostle had the privilege of opening the treasure-house, and bringing forth things new and old, but in this service he was only a representative of all true believers, each of whom has the privilege and joy of opening doors for Jesus. Origen, one of the early fathers, rightly observes that, "He who has Peter's faith is the rock of the church,

and he who has Peter's virtues keeps the keys of the kingdom." A key is a badge of power or authority (Isa. 22: 22; Rev. 3:7), and such authoritative power is at the disposal of every born-again child of God (Matt. 28:18-20).

4. An Apostle Prominent as Spokesman for the Twelve

It is interesting to compare what James has to say about the little member, the tongue, and the necessity of its control as we think of Peter's rashness of speech. "Out of the same mouth proceedeth blessing and cursing" (James 3:10). Peter both blessed and cursed with his tongue. He became the mouthpiece of his Father in heaven, and alas! the mouthpiece of Satan (Matt. 16:17, 23). But Pentecost brought about a mighty change for Peter who, thereafter, spake as the Holy Spirit gave him utterance.

What impresses one in the gospels is the way Peter functioned as "The Mouth of the Apostles," as Chrysostom put it. Peter was always frank and outspoken, speaking his mind regardless of consequences. Throughout the gospel narrative he appears as the spokesman of the apostolate, asking the questions all felt, but hesitated to express; giving the answers and making the confessions which were in their minds, but which they had not courage or decision to utter. He asked the questions for the twelve; he makes suggestions for the twelve; he expresses opinions in the name of the twelve. Think of Peter as he boldly asks Jesus questions about —

The tribute money (Matt. 17:24).

The meaning of His parables (Luke 12:41).

The number of times forgiveness should be shown (Matt. 18:21).

The reward to be given to those who follow Jesus (Matt. 19:27).

It was also voluble Peter who made —

The first great confession of Christ's Messiahship and deity (Matt. 16:16).

The reply for the rest of the apostles when Jesus asked, "Will ye also go away?" (John 6:67, 68).

The statement about feet-washing in which Peter speaks out the reluctance which was in the minds of the rest (John 13:6).

When we come to the Acts, how prominent Peter is as the fearless preacher! What a tongue of fire the Spirit gave the apostle! At last, he was the "perfect man" with a God-controlled tongue "bridling the whole body," and as a "fountain" yielding "sweet water" for multitudes of sin-thirsty souls (James 3:2, 12).

5. An Apostle Who Became Chief in the Apostolate

It was his whole forceful personality that brought Peter to primacy among the apostles. Lloyd C. Douglas titled his entrancing novel on the legendary Peter, *The Big Fisherman*, which is apt, seeing the son of Jona was *big* in every way and destined for leadership. It is somewhat interesting to observe that the earliest lists of the twelve whom Jesus chose begin with the words, "*The first,* Simon, who is called Peter" (Matt. 10:2). At the outset, he stands out from the rest, and stands out *first* in order. His name also heads the other lists. Whatever Matthew meant to convey by the above phrase, whether it was his own opinion, or the general sentiment of the other eleven apostles, or the feeling of the Church at the time he wrote his gospel, the accuracy of the statement stands. Simon Peter is "The First," and his place was usually in the center of the picture. *First* in the lists of apostles, next in the affections of saints in every age.

A phrase in the Acts suggests the leadership the apostle exercised. "In those days Peter stood up in the midst of the disciples." Discounting altogether the absolute supremacy of Peter which the church of Rome claims for him, we know that the New Testament recognizes his precedency or foremost place among the twelve. On almost every page are proofs of his primacy — a supremacy conferred upon him by nature herself. Of the twelve Jesus trained, Peter is by far the most striking, impressive figure, and he kept his forward position to the last. Peter was "the natural prince and leader of the apostolic company," and he had the indisputable title to the place of primacy, although he did not have any spiritual prerogative or privilege his associates in the apostolic college did not have. Rome falsely claims that unique powers were conferred upon Peter by Christ after his great confession. But the official primacy, lordship and authority which the church of Rome gives Peter is not of Scripture.

Of some of the other apostles we have nothing but their names, but the record of Peter is detailed, vivid, life-like, and commanding. Dr. William Cave, in his volume on *The Apostles* wrote of Peter:

> His age, and the gravity of his person, more particularly qualifying him for a primacy of order amongst the rest of the Apostles, as that without which no society of men can be managed or maintained. Less than this, as none will deny him, so more than this, neither Scripture nor primitive antiquity do allow him.

First among equals, Peter was the first to declare his faith in Christ's supernatural mission and the first to see the risen Christ on the first Easter. Peter's eminence is suggested by the phrases, "Go . . . tell his disciples *and Peter*"

(Mark 16:7). "The Lord is risen indeed, and hath appeared *to Simon*"
(Luke 24:34). Then Paul, recording
the various early appearances of the
risen Lord, says, "He was seen of
Cephas, then of the twelve" (I Cor.
15:5). After the ascension of Christ,
Peter dominates the scene as the apostle, particularly, to the Jews. The first
to behold the Lord's glory, he was
given the honor of being the first
herald of his Lord's grace. With
Peters' arrest in Herod's reign, his
story seems to end (Acts 12), and Paul
comes upon the scene as a more dominant figure still in early Christianity.
Peter retained the foremost place in
the apostolic church till Paul arose,
and as Alexander Whyte affirms:

> Peter, remarkable and outstanding
> man as he was, had neither the na-
> tural ability nor the educational ad-
> vantages of Saul of Tarsus. His mind
> was neither so deep nor so strong
> nor so many-sided nor at all so fine
> and so fruitful as Paul's incompar-
> able mind. And as a consequence he
> was never able to come within sight
> of the work that Paul alone could do.
> But, at the same time, and till Paul
> arose and all but totally eclipsed all
> the disciples who had been in Christ
> before him, Peter stood at the head
> of the apostolate, and so leaves a
> deeper footprint on the pages of the
> four gospels at any rate, than any of
> the other eleven disciples.

6. *An Apostle Who Denied His Lord*

The sad crisis in Peter's life when
he failed his Lord in the hour of His
agony ought to humble every one of
us before God, seeing that it reveals
the weakest of even the strongest of
men when relying on their own
strength. Insincerity was not one of
Peter's faults and when he said, "I
will lay down my life for thy sake,"
he meant it. No one can suspect Peter

of being a hypocrite. He meant what
he said, and said what he meant, but
alas! he was unconscious of his own
weakness. Here was a man who, only
a few hours before drew a sword in
defense of his Master, but his lips became soiled with profanity and lies
at the accusation of a mere slip of a
servant girl. What a revelation these
opposites are of the angel-heights and
devil-depths in the best of men, who
are but men at the best! The low
swamps of evil are always adjacent
to the grounds of the most holy. The
noblest and purest men are often
tempted by evil thoughts and per-
plexing doubts.

And none, O Lord, have perfect rest,
For none are wholly free from sin;
And they who fain would serve Thee best,
Are conscious most of wrong within.

Within us all there are possibilities
of virtue and likewise possibilities of
vice. When we would do good, evil
is ever present with us, and the more
highly endowed the nature is, the more
lamentable its sins. "The corruption
of the best is the worst." Thus, it
came about that Peter, saluted as
blessed by the Master, goes out to
deny that he had ever known Him.
Apostle though he was, he passed from
beatitude to blight. But the *sifting*
time for him had come when the chaff
would be separated from the wheat
— when the vain, self-confident, self-
willed, impetuous Simon, son of Jonas,
would be taken from the devoted,
chivalrous, heroic, rock-like Peter
(Luke 22:31, 32). It was during the
conversation at the Last Supper that
Jesus, turning to Peter, said, "Satan
hath desired to have you, that he may
sift you as wheat; But I have prayed
for thee, that thy faith fail not."

Then came the assurance that after
this sifting process, Peter would be a
source of strength to the rest of the

disciples: "When thou art converted —
turned back again to me — strengthen
thy brethren."

This discovery of his weakness,
made Peter strong. His over-weening
self-confidence vanished, and more of
the wheat of utter dependence upon
the Lord appeared. When he came to
write his two epistles, Peter had pertinent warnings for strong and self-
reliant men. We are all familiar with
the tragic triple test that came to
Peter. He went into the High Priest's
house to see "the end" (Matt. 26:58).
Peter thought that his Master's arrest
and death would be the end of all
things he had deemed worth living
for.

Satan's subtlety to destroy Peter's
faith is seen in that he began his
sifting of the apostle, not with a soldier's taunt, but a maid's off-hand
teasing question — a question related
only to his bodily whereabouts, not
with his spiritual allegiance. To parry
an off-hand question, Peter told an
off-hand lie.

J. Oswald Sanders reminds us that
the verbal blunderings of Peter afforded Jesus occasions to teach His
disciple invaluable lessons. Peter had
made a *threefold confession* of Christ's
deity:

"We believe and are sure that thou
art the Son of God."
"Thou art the Christ, the Son of the
living God."
"Depart from me, for I am a sinful man, O Lord."

Peter had also made a three fold
boast:

"Though all men shall be offended
because of thee, yet will I never
be offended."
"Though I should die with thee,
yet will I not deny thee."
"Lord, I am ready to go with thee
both to prison and to death."

Peter meant all he confessed but
was unconscious of his own weakness,
and so the Master pressed home *three
solemn warnings:*

"Satan hath desired to have you
that he may sift you as wheat,
but I have prayed for you."
"Get thee behind me, Satan, for
thou savourest not the things
that be of God but those that
be of men."
"Before the cock crow thou shalt
deny me thrice."

But even these red lights failed to
arrest Peter or prevent him making a
three-fold denial, the inevitable issue
of his self-confident boasting:

"I know not what thou sayest."
"He denied him again."
"I know not this man."

Let us review that unworthy exhibition of cowardice on Peter's part
in a crucial moment of testing. What
a strange combination of courage and
cowardice he manifested! Courageously he had followed Jesus, and
had taken his stand against everything the world values, and defended
his Lord with a sword! Yet a question
of a servant-maid in the High Priest's
kitchen made Peter turn white, tremble, and lie, afraid to let his discipleship be known. Hotter than fire, as
were the searching eyes of the maid,
Peter sought refuge and coolness in
the outside porch. Then came a second question, and a second denial left
his lying lips. When accosted the
third time, poor Peter reverted to
type and forgot his discipleship, his
vows, his Master — everything but
his peril.

Like a sow, Peter returned to wal-
lowing in the mire for he not only
lied but *swore.* Falling under the
power of an old habit, he became
the wild, profane Peter, the fisherman

of the lakeside. "He began to curse and to swear." It is so hard to believe that Peter came to call upon God to curse him if he is a disciple, or has aught to do with the Master. What a wound for the heart of Christ such a profane denial must have been! Surely Simon Peter was at the very lowest rung of the ladder when he, "the *first*" of the apostles, had sworn with many oaths that he did not even know the Jesus of Nazareth who had been taken prisoner and was, at that moment, before the High Priest. We do not condone nor condemn Peter for all he did. We know our own hearts only too well.

Although Peter sinned with his lips, we believe his lips that lied were less profane than the lips of Judas that kissed the sacred face. Certainly we deeply deplore the lapse of faith that resulted in Peter's fall. Following Jesus afar off paved the way for his relapse. Had he not promised Him that he would follow Him, no matter where He went? (John 13:36-38). "Follow far off and you will not follow long." Too much of the discipleship of today is of this distant kind, and lacks the glow and power of nearness to Christ. Two things awoke Peter to the consciousness of his guilt. *First,* there was the crowing of the cock, which Jesus had prophesied: the signal He gave Peter. *Second,* there was the look of Christ. The *cock* waked him, and the *look* softened Peter.

In describing the apostle's repentance, Luke tells us that, "The Lord turned and looked upon Peter" (22: 61), and if there is such a thing as the language of a look then that look of Christ seemed to say, "I have prayed for thee, that thy faith fail not." Love, compassion, and forgiveness in the eyes fastened upon the erring disciple moved and melted Peter. As Jesus passed out of the High Priest's house after being unjustly condemned, He turned and caught Peter's glance, and such a beseeching, almost heart-broken look stands out as one of the strongest incidents in the whole story of Peter. That look awoke self-reproach and broke his heart in repentant tears. Out from the place of judgment he went to weep bitterly. As the eyes of his accused Master turned to him at the cock's crow, Peter remembered His prophecy of his denial and of His concern for him. Remorse was his for he had fallen into a sin he did not love. Peter had suffered an eclipse of his faith, not its extinction. Blessed is the heart whose repentance comes so swiftly and strongly.

What a contrast there is between Judas and Peter! The repentance of Judas was without tears — it was a worldly sorrow with a remorse of conscience ending in suicide. Peter's sorrow was of a godly sort (II Cor. 7: 10). Love to Christ caused him to weep. "Peter at heart was a child of God; Judas, in the core of his being, had been all along a child of Satan. Therefore we may say that Peter could not have sinned as Judas sinned, nor could Judas have repented as Peter repented."

Peter's bitter tears were the beginning of a repentance that never ended. They melted a heart that might readily have hardened. Those tears became his telescope through which he saw his Lord more clearly. How appealing are the lines of Elizabeth Browning, as she sings with spiritual appreciation:

Two sayings of the Holy Scriptures beat
Like pulses in the church's brow and
     breast;
And by them we find rest in our unrest,
And heart-deep in salt tears, do yet entreat
God's fellowship, as if on heavenly seat.

The first is, "Jesus wept" — wherein is
  prest
Full many a sobbing face that drops its best
And sweetest waters on the record sweet.
And one is, where the Christ, denied and
  scorned,
Looked upon Peter. Oh, to render plain,
By help of having loved a little and
  mourned,
That look of sovran love and sovran pain
Which he, who could not sin yet suffered,
  turned
On him who could reject but not sustain.

The terrible thought of denying the Master whom he so passionately loved and revered must have haunted Peter with spectral fears during the dark days after the crucifixion, so completely had he misinterpreted himself in such a shameful episode. We can imagine how one sound would ring in his ears to the end, namely, the cock whose crowing heralded the dawn; and how one sight would abide in his memory, namely, the pleading, loving glance of his Lord as He passed by. But all was not lost in Peter's lapse. With the news of the resurrection of the Lord, there came a special message from Him for His repentant disciple, "Go tell my disciples *and Peter.*"

Visiting the empty tomb, Peter leaves his grave-clothes behind as the chrysalis bursts its prison to find its wings. Out of the tomb of his own repentant heart he rises again a new man, a mighty "Rock-Man" for his Master. You will recall how Tennyson in *Idylls of the King* writes of Sparrow-hawk, the rebel, who —

    Came to loathe
His crime of traitor, slowly drew himself
Bright from his old dark life, and fell at
  last
In the great battle fighting for the King.

It was so with Peter as the result of Christ's forgiveness and re-commission. A triple confession of love succeeded the three-fold denial, and Peter receives a three-fold commis-

sion for future service. The Acts tells how after his abysmal fall, Peter became as a polished shaft in the Master's hand. The cursing fisherman became the preacher of the most vital sermon ever preached in the history of the Church (Acts 2), and performed the first apostolic miracle after the ascension, (Acts 3:1-4). The Psalmist's prayer, "Remove from me the way of lying" (119:29) had been answered for Peter, and with anointed lips he proclaimed with power the Gospel of redeeming love and grace. Those flame-kissed lips were vocal in praise and proclamation until silenced by death.

There is a message in the fall of Peter for us. If we have sinned, or fallen from the heights, there is mercy and pardon, if sin is forsaken and divine forgiveness sought.

  Manlike it is to fall into sin;
  Friendlike is it to dwell therein;
  Saintlike is it for sin to grieve;
  Christlike is it all sin to leave.

7. *An Apostle Who Was Crucified*

Boastingly, not knowing the full import of what he was saying, Peter told his Lord that he was ready to go to prison and to die for Him. In time, he was to experience both, for some remarkable prison experiences were his as he suffered for the Master's sake. Through many years, he labored, most sacrificially, in an extensive evangelistic ministry during which he was the means of turning multitudes to the Savior. While we are sure of the *fact* of his death, we have no certainty as to the *place* of his end. Our Lord predicted that Peter would die by crucifixion (John 21:18). Lactantius, one of the early fathers, recorded that:

  Execrable and noxious tyrant as he
  was, Nero determined to destroy the
  heavenly Church and to abolish righteousness; and becoming the persecu-

tor of God's servants he crucified Peter and slew Paul.

When we come to our chapter dealing with legendary information concerning the service and martyrdom of the apostles we hope to record some of the appealing stories concerning Peter. Meantime, it can be said that as his crucifiers came to end his honored career, he pleaded with them to hang him upside down because he deemed himself unworthy to die in the same position as his Lord had done. How the trumpets must have sounded on the other side as the martyred fisherman entered and was reunited with the Lord he had loved most sincerely and served so sacrificially.

As those who follow the same Christ, we never tire looking at the portrait of Peter because he was so thoroughly human, "not too good for human nature's daily food." He reminds us so much of our own failings, and we instinctively feel that what Christ accomplished for him, He can do for us. If He could make something great of this imperfect mortal — make a strong, fearless, mighty apostle of this combination of iron and clay, fire and water — there is both encouragement and hope. The world has yet to see what God can do through a life utterly yielded to His sway. Peter will ever remain a lesson to us all in that he teaches us the answer to human frailty, and how the weak can become strong and the fearful be made bold. The secret of transformation is in the mighty Spirit who, at Pentecost, became the believer's reservoir of unfailing power, courage, and wisdom.

8. An Apostle Who Wrote Two Epistles

As the life and varied experiences of David are reflected in the Psalms

he was inspired to write, so in the two epistles of Peter, we can discern references to the events of his career as recorded in the gospels and the Acts, as well as indications of the lessons he learned from his trials and triumphs. It is clearly evident that the apostle in his own writings never attempted to apologize for the sin (which it was well known he had committed), of denying his Lord. This failure overshadows some of his warnings. In these two letters of his, Peter continues using the keys to unlock many of the treasures of truth for the enlightenment and edification of Christ's sheep. Lardner observes that — "Peter's two epistles, with his two discourses in the Acts, and the multitudes who were converted by these discourses, are monuments of a divine inspiration, and of the fulfilment of Christ's promise to Peter, 'Follow Me, and I will make you fishers of men'." Whence had this poor fisherman such wisdom and power, but from God? It is not within the range of our study to give a thorough and detailed exposition of Peter's epistles, but let us simply state a few guideposts for preachers and teachers to follow in their exhaustive exposition of the same.

The first epistle

Ostervald said of this epistle that it is "one of the finest books of the New Testament." Probably written for both Jewish and Gentile converts scattered throughout Asia Minor, the letter is peculiarly characterized by energy and dignity (1:1, R.V., 2:9, 10). Written about A.D. 63 it has been well described by Leighton as:

A brief and yet clear summary, both of the consolations and instructions needful for the encouragement and direction of a Christian in his journey to Heaven; elevating his thoughts and desires to that happiness, and strengthening him against all opposition in the way, both that of corruption within, and temptation and afflictions from without. The heads of Doctrine contained in it are many; but the main that are most insisted on are these three —

Faith, Obedience and Patience:
to establish in believing, to direct in doing, and to comfort in suffering; often setting before those to whom he wrote the matchless example of the Lord Jesus and the greatness of their engagements to follow Him.

It is most profitable to compare the portrait of Peter in the gospels and his pronouncements in his epistles. How amazingly and gloriously different they are! In the gospels, Peter had the privilege of seeing his Lord transfigured; in his epistles, Peter is before us transfigured by the matchless, boundless grace of God.

In the gospels, we see Peter impetuous, courageous, quick to meet personal slight, ambitious of earthly power, self-confident yet cowardly.

In his epistles, we see Peter subdued, patient, forbearing, humble, loving, with all his old buoyancy and courage purified and ennobled.

Among the most notable of the key words and thoughts of this first letter which was delivered by the hand of Silas, one of Paul's companions (5: 12), mention may be made of the following:

Precious. Many of the writers of the Bible had their favorite expressions. With Peter it was the term "precious," which he uses some seven times —

Precious Faith (I Pet. 1:7; II Pet. 1:1).
Precious Blood (I Pet. 1:19).
Precious Stone (I Pet. 2:4, 6).
Precious Christ (I Pet. 2:7).
Precious Quietness [of great price] (I Pet. 3:4).
Precious Promises (II Pet. 1:4).

Hope. Peter was present that day in the upper chamber when Jesus said, "I will come again and receive you unto myself" (John 14:1-3), and likewise witnessed Christ's ascension and heard heaven's confirmation of Christ's promise given by the two men from heaven, "This same Jesus ... shall so come in like manner as ye have seen him go" (Acts 1:10, 11). Again and again in his preaching after Pentecost, Peter referred to "the blessed hope," and it was this advent truth that made him radiantly buoyant. If Paul is, outstandingly, *The Apostle of Faith;* John, *The Apostle of Love;* Peter may be called *The Apostle of Hope,* who believed that the Coming of Christ was as a light, shining in a dark place.

"A lively hope" (1:3).
"The appearing of Jesus Christ" (1:7).
"The revelation of Jesus Christ" (1:13).
"Your faith and hope" (1:21).
"To whom coming" (2:4).
"A reason of the hope" (3:15).
"The end of all things is at hand" (4:7).
"The day star arise in your hearts" (II Pet. 1:19).

The Lord Jesus Christ in First Peter.

While First Peter has a practical design, it is as evangelical as if it had been chiefly doctrinal. How rich it is in Christology! It points everywhere to Christ:

To His atonement foretold by prophets, contemplated by angels;
To His resurrection,
To His ascension,
To the gift of His Spirit,
To His example as a suffering Savior,
To the awful solemnities of the Last Judgment.

To the great doctrines of the Gospel as the great motives to holiness and patience,

To the incorruptible Word as the appointed means of the Christian's growth in sanctification.

Look at 1:2, 18, 19; 2:21, 24; 3:18; 4:1; II Peter 1:8; 3:18.

Suffering. As this word, and its equivalent, occurs twenty-one times in this short epistle, it emphasizes the message and purpose of the book. The sufferings of Christ are referred to in all five chapters, and are used to console the saints amid the sufferings they may have to endure. So much of the epistle teaches us to suffer patiently, joyously, and to the glory of God. The chief object of Peter in writing this letter is expressed in 5:12, "I have written briefly, exhorting and testifying that this is the true grace of God wherein ye stand." To prove that Peter never forgot the lessons learned in the school of Christ compare 1:17 with Acts 10:15, 34; 2:4-8 with Matthew 16: 18; 2:25 with John 10:1; 4:19 with Luke 23:46; 5:2 with John 21:15, 17; 5:5 with John 13:4, 5. As for a general outline, we have

Introduction 1:1, 2.
1. General Exhortation to Love and Holiness 1:3-2:10.
2. Particular Exhortations on Specific Duties 2:11-5:12.
Conclusion 5:12, 14.

The second epistle

Penned when Peter knew himself to be drawing near to his martyrdom, this short epistle derives a solemn interest from such a fact. As the apostle faced the kind of death Christ had predicted for him, holiness was important to him as he anticipates a glorious immortality. Notice how Peter dwells upon the perfections of God, the glory of Christ, the tremendous consequences of sin, and the grandeur of coming judgment. After a life of suffering, and with the immediate prospect of the agonies of crucifixion, Peter rejoices in the choice he made of the service of Christ. Thus his last and abiding exhortation to the church of which Peter had been a strong pillar was: "Grow in grace, and in the knowledge of our Lord and Saviour Jesus Christ." His last testimony to the deity of his Lord, is found in the doxology — "To Him be glory both now and for ever. Amen" (II Pet. 3:18).

Although the apostle has his signature at the beginning of this second epistle (II Pet. 2:1), perhaps there is no other New Testament book the authorship of which has been so called in question as this one. It is not our purpose to go into the pros and cons of the objections raised to Peter's authorship. These facts are satisfactory as far as we are concerned:

The writer was an apostle of Jesus Christ 1:1.

The writer was one of the privileged three on the Mount of Transfiguration 1:16-18.

The writer had written a previous epistle to the same people 3:1.

While Peter's style and language are different from that used in his first epistle, we must understand that the purpose of each is different. The *first* was written to encourage and support believers under trial and persecution; the *second* was designed to warn believers against false teachers and their corrupt and corrupting doctrines (see 1:4; 2:12, 19, 20). Three divisions may be noted:

1. Moral Corruption. 1:1-14. Key verse 1:4.
2. Doctrinal Corruption. 1:15-2:22. Key verses 2:1, 2.
3. Stedfastness amid Corruption. 3. Key verse 3:17.

Characteristic features of the epistle are:

Description of the Christian graces. 1:5-8.

Value of a knowledge of the Lord. 1:2, 3, 5, 8; 2:20; 3:18.

Necessity of diligence. 1:5, 10; 3:14.

Blessings of remembrance. 1:12, 13, 15; 3:1, 2.

Eulogy of Paul's epistles. 3:16.

Touching reference to Peter's old age and impending death. 1:14.

Because Peter dominates the gospels and the first part of the Acts, our coverage of his ways, words, and works has been more lengthy than the attention given to many others among the twelve. We love his company — he is so much like ourselves. But Peter lives on, not only in the Biblical record of his life and labors, and in the precious epistles he wrote, but also in the countless thousands of males who bear his honored name; and likewise in the unknown number of churches that carry the title of St. Peter.

PHILIP

THE APOSTLE WHO WAS SLOW-WITTED

One cannot read the books of the Bible without observing that these forty or so writers were both annalists and analysts of high order, seeing they wrote under the inspiration of the Holy Spirit (II Pet. 1:21). They were economists of space, and were not given to recording unimportant facts. All that was necessary for the world to know, they set forth in a way of information that can be readily understood. At times, we may feel that some of the biographies are scanty, yet sufficient is recorded for us to distinguish the features of one character from another, and to read a good deal between the lines.

It will also be noted that what one writer may omit from his portrait of a person, another writer adds in a few touches to give us a more complete picture. Thus, as Daniel McLean reminds us:

The first three evangelists deal mainly with the eternal facts in the life of Christ, whereas the author of the fourth gospel uses the historical data as a substratum for working out the picture of the Divine Teacher, slowly unfolding from beginning to end the greatest spiritual conception of the kingdom of God. The synoptists are annalists, recording the external evidence of work and word in proof of the divine mission of Messiah, whereas John's aim throughout the record of miracle and parable is to show the great principle of divine life in its unfolding under these outward conditions.

This principle is most noticeable in connection with all we know of Philip, whose distinctive character John alone records. All the first three gospels state of Philip is the inclusion of his name in the lists of the twelve apostles whom Jesus chose. It is John who fills in sketches of Philip's witness omitted by the other writers, and who also enriches our knowledge of others of the apostolic circle such as Nathanael and Thomas. Although Philip is mentioned in the four complete lists of the twelve (Matt. 10:3; Mark 3:18; Luke 6:14; Acts 1:13), it is interesting to observe that John is the only writer to tell us all that is to be said about Philip, yet he is the only one out of the four evangelists who does not quote the list. The first three evangelists give us his name and acquaint us with the fact that he was an apostle, but John loses sight of the dignity of the office that Philip filled and gives us a profile of the man himself with his own individualities and peculiarities. Though the facts respecting him are few, they are quite sufficient to study with profit (John 6:5-7; 12:20-23; 14:8).

1. *A Native of Bethsaida of Galilee*

We gather from John's record that Philip was born in Bethsaida (1:44-51; 12:21), the city of which our Lord had sad things to say (Matt. 11:21), for the people there had rejected the truth which Christ Himself declared unto them, and which was authenticated by His mighty works. The result of such rejection was tragic for the most terrible language of the doom of His rejectors came from the same lips which previously had proclaimed glad tidings. Yet it was from this city that Philip came to be a witness of the Lord, and Bethsaida had the privilege of hearing the truth that he had the greater privilege of knowing and declaring. The One his own fellow-townsmen had rejected, Philip preached. How true it is that faithful witnesses for Christ sometimes come

from unlikely places, like the saints in Sardis who escaped the pollution of the city in which they lived (Rev. 3:4).

Is there not a key to Philip's spiritual history in the announcement, "Now Philip was from Bethsaida, of the city of Andrew and Peter"? This is more than a geographical note, or the notice of Philip's postal address. The important part of John's sentence is not only that Philip was born in Bethsaida but that it was the city of Andrew and Peter. Experiences sanctify events and places, and Bethsaida represented to Philip not only his dwelling place, but what is infinitely more, his *friendships*. Two saints of God lived in Bethsaida: the brothers, Andrew and Peter. They were the friends of Philip, and helped to prepare him for his apostolic calling.

Under God, Philip owed his soul to Andrew, and in the gospels they are closely associated. It was to Andrew that Philip found his way when difficulties arose, for he was his father in the faith. As expectant souls, Andrew and Peter looked for the hope of Israel, and through the example and influence of Peter, Philip caught the contagion of holy expectancy. In a noble sentence Augustine said, "The Church would never have had Paul but for the prayer of Stephen." In like manner, we can say, "The Church would never have had Philip but for Andrew and Peter." If we could ask Philip how he came to sit on one of the twelve thrones judging Israel, and to have his name inscribed on one of the twelve foundations of the Eternal City, doubtless he would reply, "I was born in Bethsaida, the city of Andrew and Peter." Can we say that our lives are a means of blessing to those who live under the same roof with us, or live on the same street, or in the same town as we? As "the salt of the earth," are we acting as a preservative against surrounding corruption and pollution?

Perhaps it is as well, at this point, to indicate that the *Philip* we are considering — Philip the apostle — must not be confused with Philip, the deacon-evangelist, of whom we read in the Acts. Although namesakes, they are different persons. Philip the evangelist was the persuasive interpreter of the Old Testament who led the treasurer of Queen Candace of Ethiopia to Christ, and in turn brought Christianity to that part of the world (Acts 6:5; 8:5-40). An interesting fact to bear in mind is that we never read of the deacon Philip *before* the day of Pentecost, and that we never read of the Apostle Philip *after* such an historic occasion.

Further, when Philip the deacon was mightily used of the Lord among the Samaritans, he sent for two of the apostles from Jerusalem, to visit the scene, so that by apostolic hands the converts might receive the Holy Spirit. This act of the evangelist would have been wholly needless, if Philip himself had been one of the apostles (Acts 8:1). Where and how Philip the apostle was serving the Lord during the evangelistic ministry of Philip the deacon we are not told. Each in his own office and way, lived and labored for the same Lord.

2. A Jew With a Gentile Name

In *King Henry IV*, Shakespeare exclaims, "I would to God thou and I knew where a commodity of good names were to be bought." *Good* names, however, cannot be bought, but only inherited or earned. The attractive name of *Philip*, which means, "a lover of horses," is one of these *good* names which, alas! has not always been borne by *good* men. As *Philip* is a Greek name, it would seem as if the apostle had Greek connec-

tions, which may explain why he acted for the Greeks at the Passover, and why the Greeks who sought Jesus first approached Philip. The apostle's name is reminiscent of the history of the Macedonian conquest of Asia by Alexander the Great, the son of King Philip of Macedon. It was a common custom in 'some parts of the Roman Empire to name children after the reigning prince, and it is possible that Philip's parents named him thus after Philip the Tetrarch of Galilee officiating at that time.

A singular feature is that we know the apostle by no other name. He must have had a Jewish name, for all the apostles were Jews. His father's name must have been in use as a family name, but the same has not been revealed to us. Wearing a Gentile name, however, made no difference to Philip's Messianic outlook. He was thoroughly Hebrew in religious conviction, and early felt the touch of the rugged prophet's teaching on the banks of Jordan.

3. A Seeker Who Was Found

John tells us that the day after the call of Andrew, Jesus was minded to go into Galilee, and that, finding Philip, He said unto him, "Follow me" (1:43). What a pregnant phrase this is, "Jesus . . . *findeth* Philip"! Scripture is fond of this verb transitive, *find*. The first person Jesus sought was Philip, and he became His disciple. *Findeth* implies a diligent and concentrated search. "Seek and ye shall *find*." Jesus sought and found Philip, but it is evident that Philip must have sought for Jesus also, for he said to Nathanael, "We have *found* him" (1:45). The seeking was mutual, and so also would be the joy of finding.

Many of us, looking back to the commencement of our Christian life, can say, "I sought the Lord and He heard me." Others are obliged to confess, "Jesus sought me when a stranger." In the one case Jesus was wanted, in the other He wanted us. Andrew heard John the Baptist say, "Behold the Lamb of God!" and immediately he went out and found Him. He owed his apostleship to his seeking after Christ. Philip, however, owed his presence in the apostolate to Christ seeking after him. "*Jesus . . . findeth Philip.*" The Shepherd found the sheep; the Physician, the patient; the Savior, the sinner. But whether we seek, or are sought, makes little difference. The all-important matter is that salvation must precede discipleship.

Jesus . . . findeth Philip. This "first-called disciple" was not found by accident, or haphazardly. In divine dealings there is no room for chance or luck. It was inevitable that Jesus and Philip should meet, and it was through direct contact that Philip was brought in. No friend interposed, no human voice directed him. As one who, like Simeon, looked for the consolation of Israel, Philip's ear was open, and his heart ready, and once the divine voice was heard saying, "Follow me," the Savior and the sinner went off together. Among saints today there are those who were acted on by Christ, without any known instrumentality of men, and they became His, there and then, as Philip did. Philip had the prerogative of being the *first* called to discipleship, and was thus the first-fruits of our Lord's disciples. While Andrew and Peter were the first to come to Christ, they returned to their trade, and about a year later they were called to discipleship. But Philip, as soon as he was found, followed.

It is profitable to note the order of *seeking* and *finding* that John records. After having *found* the Messiah, An-

drew *findeth* Simon. Later, Philip *findeth* Nathanael. Throughout the Bible the connection between *seeking* and *finding* is regarded as possessing all the rigor and inevitableness of a natural law. The one is regarded as the invariable and necessary sequence of the other:

"If thou seek him, he will be found of you"

"Ye shall seek me and find me, when ye shall search for me with all your heart"

"Seek and ye shall find"

"I am found of them that sought me not"

"Seek ye the Lord while he may be found."

Thus, as certainly as day follows night and summer follows winter, so he that *seeketh, findeth*. What else could Philip do as soon as Christ found him, but run to his friend Nathanael, and cry, "We have *found him,* of whom Moses in the law, and the prophets, did write!" Here, then, is a search that *never* fails. Would that ours was a *seeking* age! In one sense it is, for the multitudes seek sin, pleasure, wealth and self-satisfaction, but not Him who is the secret Source of every precious thing. "They that seek *me* shall *find* me." How thrice-blessed we are if out of a grateful heart we can sing —

I was lost, but Jesus found me;
Found the sheep that went astray.

4. *A Convert Who Became a Soul-Winner*

Once he was found, Philip went out to *find*. Answering Christ's call, out he went and became instrumental in Nathanael's conversion and call. As a yearning heart, an inquiring mind, an anxious soul, found their goal when Jesus met Philip, so it was with Philip's first convert as he came into contact with Jesus. As He set out to gather disciples around Him, it was common for each new disciple to be on the track either of a relative or friend, and seek him out for the Master. Dean Farrar says that Philip, in seeking out Nathanael, "exercised the divinest prerogative of friendship." What an incentive to personal evangelism we have in the call of those first disciples!

The new convert became an evangelist, for now *saved,* Philip *served.* Zealous to tell others the good news, he never lost a moment. He went out, not to bring the worst of his acquaintances, but the *best,* even the one Philip found reading his Bible and praying under a fig-tree. It was over his dear friend and companion that Philip's heart yearned. Among the first disciples there was a kinship binding them together, before they were united by their Lord in a higher fellowship. The same word is used of Philip's zeal of early love as of his own initial contact with Christ. "Jesus . . . *findeth* Philip," "Philip *findeth* Nathanael." Having taken possession of Philip, Christ became an active principle, fermenting and diffusing Himself, and through His "first-called disciple" brought the glad tidings to another seeking soul. Thus, Nathanael, a person of fine character, was drawn into the happiness his friend had come to experience. There are those expositors who suggest that Philip and Nathanael, or Bartholomew, were brothers. If this was so, then as Andrew went to find his brother, Philip went out to find his (John 1:40-46).

When Nathanael received the good news that Philip so enthusiastically proclaimed, the guileless man asked for proof that the One who had found Philip was actually the Messiah. But Philip, conscious of his limitations to argue, answered his friend's scruples with the urgent appeal, *Come and see!*

As an effective messenger he could say, "Jesus found me," and therefore he was able to urge the great experimental argument, Come and see! Philip had seen Jesus as the Messiah, and was satisfied, and knew that the best evidence that he was right could be furnished by sight. To Nathanael's credit, let it be said that he promptly complied with Philip's request, and seeing Jesus likewise became His disciple. In the mass evangelism of our time, we seem to have lost sight of the necessity and effectiveness of personal evangelism. Those early converts represented a one-by-one band. One set out to win another for Jesus. Peter certainly became the leading figure in mass evangelism as we find in *The Acts,* but he himself represented hand-plucked fruit for it was his less prominent brother who led him to Christ.

5. *A Companion of One With a Brighter Mind*

In the three lists of apostles found in the first three gospels, Philip is always bracketed with Nathanael as a companion and fellow-worker. While they were both Galileans, we have no information as to how they came to be paired. The fourth list of apostles in Acts 1 connects Philip with Andrew, possibly as the result of the change in Thomas's standing and position after his remarkable confession of Christ's deity.

The twelve are divided into three quartettes, and in each list, Philip heads the second quartette, and is followed by Nathanael, or Bartholomew. Philip always stands *fifth* in the lists. Andrew, Philip and Nathanael appear in this order in each list. When two of them are mentioned we have Andrew and Philip. Philip's gift for friendship not only drew Andrew to him by soul affinity, it was revealed in his solicitude for Nathanael. Charles Kingsley, the renowned English cleric and novelist, was once asked: "What is the secret of your life? Tell me, that I may make mine beautiful too." Humbly, Kingsley replied: "I had a friend," and his biography reveals the one to whom the novelist owed more than words could express.

Philip might have said, "I had friends whose counsel was sweet, whose confidence was freely given, whose companionship was ever choice. We loved and served the same Lord, and each was richer for the others. Andrew on the one side, and Nathanael on the opposite — no three in Bethsaida were so blest as we." While all this is true we cannot but be impressed with the differing personalities of the apostles. What opposites are paired together! Take Philip and Nathanael, for instance, as an illustration of extremes in fellowship, and as a proof that Christ has a place for each of us with all our personal peculiarities.

Philip was a plain man, slow in arriving at a decision, reluctant to act on his own initiative. Simplicity of heart and mind is shown in his every appearance in the gospel story. Although he had a Greek name, he had none of the brightness in perception, and incomparable cleverness of a Greek. He is revealed as a slow-witted plodder.

Nathanael was cast in a different mold from that of his friend. He was of quick wit, alert intellect, seeing at a flash the objections to any statement. It was thus he felt that nothing could come out of a place like Nazareth. He was able to debate Scripture, and knew sufficient of it to be satisfied that Jesus was the One filling the expectation of the ancient prophecies. Yet although their natures differed, the Lord sent them out together — the man of slow wit and the man of quick wit, having need of both, and each having need of the other. We read that Jesus sent forth His apostles *two by two*. This principle of togetherness was to be maintained, for two together would mutually encourage each other, and correct each other's faults.

It has been said that "One-and-one are more than twice one." Shared responsibility means increase of power. Isolation in Christian service is often the cause of inefficiency, so fellowship in adventure is a divine principle. For Moses there is an Aaron, for Elijah an Elisha, for Paul a Barnabas. Peter and Andrew, the two sons of Jonas, are sent out together, for the Lord needed both and they needed each other, and each supplemented the other's defects. The Master needs the man of foresight, as well as the one of insight. Contrasts are exhibited, then, in the pairing of the apostles. What one lacked, the other supplied, and out of two half-men, one whole man was made.

6. *A Scholar Who Was Dull*

While by no means the brightest among the apostles, Philip was yet chosen by Jesus and therefore had a place in His plan and purpose. What were the conspicuous characteristics of this native of Bethsaida? Although the gospels do not tell us very much about Philip, enough is recorded to give us a consistent portrait of him. At the outset, we see him as a man of an inquiring mind. In his testimony to Nathanael he said: "We have found him of which Moses in the Law and the Prophets did write." Andrew and John followed Christ on the testimony of John the Baptist and at the bidding of their own hearts. Philip, however, accepted Christ and followed Him because he found that Christ satisfied all the prophecies and descriptions given of Him in the Old Testament.

But though Philip came to live with Christ he somehow failed to grasp the truth that He came as the full revelation of God, and as the One having omnipotence. His grade of spiritual intelligence was not high, yet the Lord had use for the dull as well as the bright in His service. J. G. Greenhough describes Philip as being practical and prompt in decisions, but whose spiritual perception was low:

> His mind was precise, methodical, and almost mechanical — the mind of a plodding, accurate, conscientious business man—but with no originality. He had little moral imagination, and was slow to understand and slow to believe what he could not see.

That Philip had a cool rationality, and a materialistic trend of mind is manifested in his association with the miracle of the feeding of the multitude on the eastern shore of the Galilean lake. The popular excitement created by the works and words of Jesus brought an eager crowd of admirers to a place removed from supply-sources of food, and being concerned about the human need of those who thronged Him, Jesus presented the problem to Philip: "Whence shall we buy bread, that these may eat?" (John 6:5).

Why did the Master single out this scholar of His and interrogate Philip? It was not for the sake of information, for Jesus knew how the need would be met. It was for the sake of instruction. The question was an educational one. Jesus asked it to *prove* Philip (John 6:6). This word *prove* means "to try, or put to the proof." Here was Philip and the rest, in a place where there was no bread, and the circumstance was a trial of his faith in the power of Christ. But the disciple was slow on the up-take, and the result of the inquiry was unbelief. Investigating, Philip found that only

"two hundred pennyworth of bread" was available to feed the multitude, and such a small amount was useless to feed so many hungry mouths. Two hundred pennies represented the whole store of money contained in the common purse and cool, calculating Philip knew that such a meager sum was insufficient to buy the required bread.

Naturally cautious and practical-minded, Philip was hesitant about making a move unless he could see the way to go. He was "a man who knew too much arithmetic to be adventurous." Somewhat slow in spiritual apprehension, he would only cut his coat according to his cloth. Christ's design in this miracle was to test Philip's faith and deepen his grasp of the divine side of His mission, but His disciple's perplexity over the solution of the problem on hand revealed that He had failed in His training of this slow-wit in His school. The test found Philip defective "in spiritual imagination, in the power of intuition and in consequence was somewhat slow in attaining to the apocalypse of faith."

Philip had been singled out not only for a test of his faith, but to meet the challenge of a great opportunity. Suppose he had met Christ's question about bread for such a crowd by saying, "Well, Lord, you know how. You are the Omnipotent One and more than able to furnish a table in this wilderness," how he would have glorified Jesus! But no, Philip resorted to mental calculation to solve a problem to which deity alone had the answer. Poor Philip, he lost his opportunity and his blessing, for Jesus turned to another — even to a small boy, to prove no need is ever too great for His power. Philip was a man of little faith, and in his reply to Christ's question revealed a radical weakness of faith in divine omnipotence. This episode exposed him as "the materialist of the band, and [he] needed Christ's most patient and forbearing teaching to develop in him the spiritual mind." Doubtless he came to learn that nothing is impossible to almighty power, when pleased to exert itself. If any measure of commercial sagacity is ours, let us not fail to reckon upon the Divine Provider. There is the divine way, as well as the common sense way of looking at things.

7. *A Guide Who Could Not Lead*

The next glimpse we have of Philip occurs in connection with a company of Greeks who came up to worship at the feast (John 12:20-22). These Gentiles, with a true desire to see the Christ they had heard so much about, approached Philip with the request, "Sir, we would see Jesus." But somehow he could not make up his mind to introduce these seeking souls to Jesus even though they had applied to him for such a purpose. He had had former experience to guide him for did he not seek out Nathanael and introduce him to Jesus? But now in the position of a go-between he hesitated. Perhaps Philip wondered whether Jesus would receive these Gentiles, so, afraid to make the venture he put the onus on Andrew, his partner.

Approachableness might well have been one of Philip's characteristic features, and the Greeks, impressed by his genial manner, felt he would be the right one to whom they could express their heart-felt desire. But the fact remains that he bore a Greek name and so they possibly thought that like themselves he was of Greek origin. Says Lange: "Their turning to Philip depended upon a law of kindly attraction." As no mediators are required between the soul and Christ, those Greeks could have gone straight

to Him. Further, it was not any sense of modesty that prevented Philip being the mediator between those seekers and the One they sought, but a certain lack of self-reliance that made him turn to Andrew for advice.

Perhaps there was some excuse for Philip's hesitancy in a man with his type of mind. He remembered the caution of the Master, "Go not into the way of the Gentiles," but though he lived on the borderland of their country, and had secret sympathy for their outcast condition, he lacked the courage to introduce the strangers to his Master. Thus he almost lost another opportunity of serving Him. Fortunately, Philip consulted Andrew, and together they went and told Jesus of the request of the Gentile proselytes. As both of these apostles had been inquirers, they had an inquirer's sympathy with those seeking their intercession. Is it not gratifying to see these two apostles who had known one another in their early years, working together in such close unison? They were privileged to be the means of the mystic truth Jesus came to proclaim about His death and resurrection. How overwhelmed they must have been by heaven's answer to the request of Jesus, "Father, glorify thy name," and how grateful they were that they had been the guides of those Gentiles — the first-fruits of the glorious ingathering. Little did they realize that they were the unconscious agents in the tremendous crisis of a great transition in the history of the world, namely, the guiding of the outstretched hands of heathenism in its search for God.

8. *A Disciple Who Lacked Spiritual Insight*

It was during the sad hours spent in the Passover chamber that Jesus revealed Himself as the Mediator between man and God (John 14:6). He declared Himself to be one with His Father, and the manifestation of His virtues and purpose. Then Philip asked, "Lord, show us the Father, and it sufficeth us" (John 14:7-12). Here, again, Philip is the practical calculator who had little patience with anything mystical. To him, "Seeing is believing." He failed to remember that as an apostle it should have been, "Believing is seeing." Can you not see Philip wince as Jesus replies, "Have I been so long time with you, and yet hast thou not known me, Philip?" Strange, is it not, that the one Philip had led to Christ at the beginning had the inner revelation of who He was as soon as he saw Him? Nathanael exclaimed, "Thou art the Son of God! thou art the King of Israel" (John 1:49). Sad Philip, he had not discerned at the end of his sojourn with Christ, what Nathanael had seen at the outset of his discipleship.

Philip was certainly true in speaking of the vision of the Father sufficing us, but he had missed the vision and received his Lord's loving rebuke, "He that hath seen me hath seen the Father; how sayest thou then, Show us the Father?" Note the kind use of the name—Philip—the familiar friendship which adds it just here. While there was sorrow in the heart of Jesus over Philip's remark, the Master's rebuke was tender and gracious. Philip had failed to discern in Jesus the culmination of the revelation of the Father; that though they were distinct in personality, they were one in power, pity, wisdom, purpose, grace and love. How ashamed Philip must have been for failing to see in Jesus the express image of God's Person (Heb. 1:3), and the essence of the Father! After such a revelation, Philip had no doubt that the Jesus he knew was

indeed the *Way* to the Father, the *Truth* about the Father, and the *Life* from the Father (14:6).

The only sight of the Father was in the face of Jesus, and Philip had been gazing upon that face for almost three years, yet failed to see the treasure he wanted. He had followed Christ, worked for Him, been taught by Him, and had been privileged to witness for Him, yet in Him was the Father, and Philip did not know it. He asked for what he already had.

In *Thee* most perfectly expressed,
  The Father's glories shine;
Of the full Deity possessed,
  Eternally Divine:
Worthy, O Lamb of God, art Thou
That every knee to Thee should bow!

A. B. Bruce in *The Training of the Twelve* says that the ignorance and spiritual incapacity of Philip so late in the day was disappointing to Jesus, but that He was "with characteristic patience, not irritated. He took no offense either at Philip's stupidity, or at the contradiction he had given to His own statement." The demand to have the Father shown him was both unnecessary and impertinent on Philip's part. After almost three years of spiritual education under Christ's discipline and tuition, Philip was an ignorant scholar — ever learning but never coming to the knowledge of the truth of God manifest in flesh. After so long, he was still in the bondage of sense, desiring some ocular demonstration of the divine. Was it not altogether unworthy of the education in spiritual thought Philip had been privileged to enjoy through the years of his discipleship, that he wanted some material proof of God's reality? He failed to see that God was in Christ.

In a way, there was both *bad* and *good* in Philip's request, "Lord, show us the Father, and it sufficeth us!"

Bad, in that Philip had the mistaken idea that God can be seen with the material eye. Yet though God in Christ had been standing before Philip, he knew Him not. *Good* was also in Philip's request for it revealed an inner craving, the longing for One who would satisfy his longing and rest his heart. As the Greeks who came to Philip wanted to see Jesus, so Philip himself desired to see God, the chief joy of man's soul. True, Philip missed much, did not understand, was spiritually blind, but yet he had his heart set on seeing Him who is invisible, and the center of all life and truth. "Blessed are the pure in heart for *they* shall see God."

9. *An Apostle Who Went Forth to Serve*

A brother of low degree among some others of the apostolate, Philip came to rejoice in the exaltation that came to him after the truth of all that Christ was, in Himself, possessed his heart. While much of the story of his later life is not known to us, we have sufficient to convince us that he overcame the initial defects in his character, and fulfilled nobly the charge that his risen Lord laid upon him and the rest of the apostles, before His ascension. Philip went forth to preach the Gospel, conscious that the Lord was with him confirming the Word with signs (Matt. 28:16-20; Mark 16:19-20).

Philip's name appears in the list of the apostles gathered in the upper room for prayer and supplication, and was one of them to receive the mighty baptism of the Holy Spirit on the historic day of Pentecost, enabling him to preach the Gospel in the language of the people who had gathered together out of every nation under heaven (Acts 1:13; 2:1-7). Philip was one of the Galileans who pro-claimed the wonderful works of God (Acts 1:11), and his name adorns one of the twelve foundations of the Holy City (Rev. 21:14). As we leave our meditation on *Philip,* it is with the encouragement that the Lord has use for the dull as well as the bright in His service. As we look around those who form His Church we see that He has need for all grades of intelligence. If, like Philip, we are conscious of imperfect faith and limited knowledge, let us follow on until full light is ours. "He that followeth me shall not walk in darkness, but shall have the light of life."

If Jesus Christ is a man,
    And only a man, I say
That of all mankind I cleave to Him,
    And to Him will I cleave alway.

If Jesus Christ is a God,
    And the only God, I swear
I will follow Him through Heaven and
    Hell,
    The earth, the sea, and the air!

SIMON THE CANAANITE

THE APOSTLE WHO WAS A REVOLUTIONIST

This next apostle bears the label, "The Canaanite" or "Cananaean," in the apostolic lists to distinguish him from "Simon, who is called Peter" (Matt. 10:4; Mark 3:18). Luke names him *Simon Zelotes* (Luke 6:15; Acts 1:13). The R.V. calls him "Simon, the Zealot." It may help us if we can understand the significance of the terms used to describe Simon. *Cananaean* has been wrongly interpreted as coming from "Cana" or from "Canaan," implying that Cana was Simon's birthplace, or that as a Canaanite, he had Gentile blood in his veins, and was not therefore wholly Jewish. *Cananaean* is an epithet derived from a Hebrew word, *Kana*, which means "to be ardent or zealous," and is the exact Hebrew equivalent of the word for *Zealot*, which Luke gives us. It is not, then, a geographical term, but a distinguishing one connecting Simon with a radical and revolutionary party among the Jews.

The Greek name *Zelotes* describing "The Zealots" and Simon's connection with them is the *only* thing the Bible tells us about him. Yet in this one word, *Zelotes*, we see a Jew of flaming zeal and burning enthusiasm. Through one small peep-hole one may behold a landscape, and this one word enshrines a revelation. Designate a man a *communist*, and there comes to mind immediately an ideology with its cruel and godless principles. So the *Simon* we are now considering, a mere name in the apostolic lists, a silent figure in the circle of the twelve, is a name more suggestive of the social conditions of the times, than another in the list of twelve. Further, no name with its label bears a more striking evidence of the comprehensive purpose of Jesus in the selection of His disciples, than that of *Simon the Zealot*.

Efforts have been made (but with-out conclusive evidence) to identify Simon with Simon the brother of Jesus (Matt. 13:55; Mark 6:3), or with Nathanael (Bartholomew). But beyond the fact that he became an apostle we have nothing but his name, and a nick-name by which he was familiarly and commonly talked of and known. Unlike his great namesake, Simon Peter, who became the prince and primate of the twelve, not a single word Simon the Zealot ever said, or a single deed he ever did, has been recorded for us. The particular adjective, *Zealot*, applied to Simon, is yet significant and by it we can recognize what kind of a man he was. Sir Richard Owen, the renowned zoologist, affirmed that from one bone he was able to sketch the structure of an animal long since extinct. In the absence, then, of any personal history what kind of a man was Simon the Zealot?

1. *A Lover of His Country*

John Gay, 1685-1732, in his *Epistle to a Lady*, wrote of one who was "always zealous for his country's good." Simon's appendage, "the Zealot," suggests that he was an enthusiastic patriot. There was a Jewish nationalist party prior to A.D. 70 known as *the Zealots*, but whether Simon was a member of such a group we have no way of knowing for certain. However, "Simon the Zealot" gives him a character of his own, and probably suggests something about his former life.

For a thorough understanding of *the Zealots* the reader is referred to the account of Josephus, the Jewish historian. The distinctive existence of the body seems to date from the time of the Maccabees, when a determined stand was made against foreign influence in religious life. "Be ye zealous for the Law, and give your lives for the Covenant" (I Mac. 2:50).

These Zealots were *the Pharisees* of the Pharisees, the strictest sect of the rabbinical schools, insisting upon the literal obligation of traditional renderings of the Law. They looked for a Messiah who should restore the Kingdom again to Israel with all the glory of the old theocracy. The red-hot and flaming patriots banded themselves under Judas of Samala to deliver Judaea from Roman dominion, and the history of the crimes they were guilty of in the cause of patriotism makes sad reading.

These fanatical Jews declared that Rome had not merely destroyed the independence of Israel, but had made it difficult for them to observe many of the ceremonials prescribed by the Law of Moses. From their headquarters in Galilee, they stirred up sedition and rebellion and at every opportunity, seized upon any pretext to inflame the people against their conquerors. Elder Cumming says that these Zealots were a distinct party and —

> *Not Pharisees,* actual Pharisees, who were much more indifferent, if their own worship was not interfered with;
> *Not Sadducees,* who were more sceptical and careless as to their interpretation of the Law;
> *Not Essenes,* who abstained from all share in public movements;
> *Not Herodians,* who took part with Herod.

The Zealots stood alone, and were always ready to resist, even with arms, the pretensions of Roman power. About the time of Christ, several of their leaders were put to death. At one time they were a great power in Jerusalem, and exercised a deep influence on state affairs. Having no law, they became a law unto themselves, finding in their aims and ambitions justification for their infamous "Jewish Wars," the horror and repugnance of which Josephus describes. Barabbas was one of these Zealots, who was cast into prison for sedition and murder. When the Roman Eagles under Titus ransacked Jerusalem, divine retribution overtook these fanatics, and the sacred temple in flames was the holocaust of Zealot infatuation. God struck the misguided party with fatal effect; with the temple it entirely disappeared.

If Simon the Zealot had been of these "irreconcilables" of Judaea, then he may have taken part in some of those terrible revolts marking the course of Roman rule in Palestine. He may have been ready to draw his sword and die for her deliverance, earning, thereby, his designation. The epithet given him is a vista, then, through which is seen the national aspiration working out by intolerant methods the problem of deliverance. But Simon came to experience a more glorious deliverance through the marvelous magnetic influence of Christ who was a Zealot of the higher order. And, as you shall see, Simon's inclusion in the apostolate is an evidence that the Gospel of grace is able to make even of a "rebel," a priest and a king. Simon as a *Zealot* loved his country and was prepared to die for it. But he found Christ, loved Him sincerely, and, if legend be true, died for Him as a martyr.

2. A Lover of a Better Leader

What a mighty transformation took place when Simon left the control of the fanatical Judas of Samala for the sweet yoke of Jesus of Nazareth! Through amazing grace the fiery patriotism of Simon became refined to a deep and lasting zeal for Christ and His kingdom. But how he came to meet Christ we are not told, for all that is recorded of Simon is his name and distinguishable feature. What is implied in the gospel history are certain facts we can with confidence assume respecting him.

He must have had some fitness for the Master's service, otherwise He would not have chosen him as an apostle.

He became one of the Master's companions, and must have rendered service to Him in such a capacity.

He took his share in the mission-work of the twelve, when the Master sent them forth two by two.

Jesus caused no small stir by His revolutionary messages and methods. Hearing of this new spiritual Zealot who had appeared upon the horizon, Simon met Him and was attracted to Him, perhaps thinking that He was heading up another revolutionary cause — withal of a different nature. Hearing of what He said about a kingdom, Simon probably followed Jesus thinking that He would be the one to overthrow Rome. What exactly prompted Simon to leave the fanatical *Zealots* we are not told. All we do know for certain is that it was a happy exchange for him when he left the insurrection party for the Prince of Peace. If he was one of the adherents of the crushed Judas of Samala, the fire of discontent still smoldered in the breast of Simon. But when Christ and he met, there took place a union of hearts, for Simon recognized in Jesus the promised Messiah of Israel. At the outset, he doubtless shared the prevalent hope that He would espouse the cause of the Jews, and deliver them from Rome in an earthly and human manner, but through the constant teaching of the Master, Simon came to learn that His kingdom was not of this world. Simon entered a new world for here was a Leader who had no use for the bloodshed, hatred, cunning and deceit *the Zealots* prac-

ticed. Here is One talking of the love of God, and the vindication of His truth, of loving your enemies, of doing good to those despitefully using you; that the greatest snare of Palestine was not the Roman Empire, but the nation's sin and departure from God. Thus, the miracle happened, and the ardent, violent revolutionist laid his zeal at the feet of Jesus to become a fiery herald of His Gospel.

A fact to be remembered is that after Christ chose Simon as an apostle, he never ceased to be known as *the Zealot*, even though he came to learn that emancipation must first be won in spirit and in truth. Perhaps we have wondered why Jesus chose a man like Simon to be an apostle, and why Scripture records nothing of him but his name. We would have thought such a reckless zealot would not be a safe man to have as an apostle lest he might cause dissatisfaction among the rest, and render his new Leader an object of political suspicion. But Jesus disregarded all prudential wisdom, for His ways are not our ways. The Author of our faith knew what He was about, and that through Simon He would be able to reach the dangerous classes, as other apostles would influence despised classes, so that different elements could be represented among His disciples.

While we hear nothing more of Simon after his choice for the apostolate, we can believe that in his development and growth, there was no one among the twelve with a warmer enthusiasm and a willingness to face danger or death for the Master, than Simon Zelotes. With his tendency to violence and use of worldly weapons restrained, he likely became one of the boldest and strongest followers of the Son of David. A one-time fierce and untamable patriot, through the transforming and reconciling power of

Jesus Christ, Simon became a rich trophy of divine grace, and the forerunner of another rebel who, on his way to Damascus, was suddenly arrested by the Lord and made His slave. Viewing the twelve apostles as a whole we see how they form "a practical exposition of the function of the Church, the only qualification for entering into its fellowship being the consent to the appeal of Christ, and obedience to the royal law of self-surrender."

3. A Lover of a Holier Cause

In his expressive poem, *Rugby Chapel*, Matthew Arnold has the lines:

Somewhere, surely, afar,
In the sounding labour-house vast
Of being, is practiced that strength
Zealous, beneficial, firm.

Simon the Zealot came to practice such strength, as he served the Lord during His sojourn on earth, and after His ascension. Simon had come to know Him who is the Truth, and his soul was free from the old-time fanatical patriotism, and he found a blessed cause in "the glorious fellowship of the apostles." In the past, his zeal was not according to knowledge when he plotted with others for the overthrow of Rome. Now his ardor and passion were curbed and consecrated, being directed into another channel, namely, the introduction of the kingdom of God. A purer flame was now burning upon the altar of Simon's heart and like the fire burning upon the altar long ago, it never went out (Lev. 6:13). A consuming zeal was now his to further the cause of Christ, and with the inner flame of his ardent spirit fed by constant contact with Him, Simon could say with Him, "The zeal of thine house hath eaten me up."

When Christ took Simon into His service, He did not eradicate his passion, but enhanced it and made it glow with a heavenly light. It has been said that, "Nothing great or good was ever done without passion." Was it not the highest form of passion Jesus manifested when He offended the Temple money-changers by sweeping them from its courts with a scourge of small cords? In any realm of life *enthusiasm* is the motive-power of success, for it gives one the full register of working power, and the zeal tempered with grace Simon came to display enabled him to obtain spiritual results, and carry the palm for a consuming ardor among the twelve Jesus selected to work with and for Him. Witnessing the holy and untiring zeal of the Master, Simon sought to bear this mark of his Lord. It was said of Sir Walter Raleigh that, "He was a whole man to one thing *all the time.*" This came to be true of Simon who had one object in life, namely, to pursue with a quenchless and indomitable enthusiasm the cause of righteousness in which he had enlisted. Like his Master, he came to believe that there can be no toleration of evil in the Gospel of the grace of God.

The secret of the Church's inadequacy as she faces a world of dire need, is her lack of spiritual enthusiasm. Impotent, nerveless, and helpless, the church is in sore need of Zealots who are not afraid nor ashamed to fling the cross in the face of a godless world. What God-inspired revolutionists those early saints were as they turned the world upside down! How willing they were to hazard even their lives for the Gospel's sake! The Church must experience another baptism of fire if she is to warm a cold, cold world. What an impact she would make if only every member within her fold could be a Simon the Zealot!

Come Holy Spirit, Heavenly Dove,
With all Thy quickening powers,

Kindle a flame of sacred love
In these cold hearts of ours.

4. *A Lover of an Inner Peace*

Henry Drummond, who was so greatly used of God among students in Edinburgh, and whom D. L. Moody came to highly respect, once said that "it is better not to live than not to love." The Apostle John would have us know that love is evidence of the possession of life: "We know that we have passed from death into life, because we love the brethren."

Surveying the apostles as a whole, we see how deep-seated antagonisms vanished and men of utterly divergent views became comrades in their service for Christ. There was love among the brethren. We have been thinking of Simon as a *Zealot*, first against Rome, then for the Redeemer, but looking at him as Simon the apostle, we know that he became the possessor of an inner peace enabling him to love others, especially after becoming a spectator of the Love that died upon the cross. Thinking of the opposites making up the apostolate we can see how He who came as our Peace, bound the twelve disciples together in a bond of peace.

Is it not amazing to place two of these members of the band together? For example, put Simon the Zealot and Matthew the Publican side by side — tax hater and tax-gatherer — and see how, although they represent extremes, they meet together in a close and peaceful fellowship. Simon had been a Jewish patriot, chafing under a foreign yoke, and sighing for emancipation. Matthew was an unpatriotic Jew who degraded himself by becoming an agent of the Roman rulers, whom Simon sought to destroy. Yet in Christ there came about a union of opposites. Before they both met Christ, they hated each other, but

through the call of Christ, Simon and Matthew were brought together and made to love each other and to be at peace among themselves. You see, Jesus loved each, and each loved Him, and so it was a short and easy step to love one another. The religious puritan and the social pariah became so closely attached to Jesus the Great Reconciler, that their former feuds were forgotten in common unity of action and in their united promotion of the Gospel of peace.

It may seem impossible to reconcile and bring into perfect harmony such extreme antagonisms characterizing the apostles before Christ chose them as such, but all things are possible to Him. Writing of Simon the Zealot, J. G. Greenhough concludes his profile by reminding us that Simon and Matthew —

> Were men divided from each other by a wide, deep gulf of thought and feeling, and even of impassioned hatred. Yet the publican and the zealot clasped hands and joined hearts at Jesus' feet. In the furnace of His love these opposites were welded together. It was a picture and prediction on a small scale of what would come to pass in the greater Church, where walls of partition were to be broken down, where national antipathies were to be crucified and buried with Christ and rise again transfigured into the glory of a uniting faith and charity, and where there were to be neither Jew nor Greek, Barbarian, Scythian, bond nor free, but Christ all and in all.

As we look back on the Master's training, not only of Simon and Matthew, but of all the apostles, what are some of the practical lessons for our hearts today? Well, the *first* is that no type of mind and character is excluded from the kingdom, or required to transform itself into another type to be acceptable to Christ and useful in His service. As the God who loves variety, He delights to have it in the church, as well as in the world of nature. We speak about "measuring our wheat in another man's bushel," but we are not called to become mechanical robots, but with all our varying personalities and gifts to serve Him devoutly who made us all (I Cor. 4:4-13).

The *second* lesson is that we serve Christ best, not by singling out someone who is most like us, and who will respond most quickly to our preferences in action and our ways of thought and feeling, but one who is opposite and unlike us in disposition and temper and who will be able to supply, in the long run, our defects of insight and activity. The Lord ever seeks to send us forth together in such unities of diversities.

Peter, enthusiastic in his faith —
Thomas, a doubter, in spite of the intensity of his love —
John and James, the sons of thunder —
Philip, a man of practical, calculating wisdom —
Nathanael, a soul so full of gentle devotion —
Simon the Zealot, whose natural vehemence made him rebel.

Christ brought them together, imperfectly fit as they were, and made them what they became, Judas excepted.

The *third* lesson is that when we become Christ's we are not to be "the graceless Zealots" that Alexander Pope wrote about, but like *Seraph Abdiel* whom John Milton describes, "His loyalty he kept, his love, his zeal." Yes, and we are to be warned by the tragic confession of the disappointed servant of the crown, whom Shakespeare depicts for us in *King Henry VIII:*

Had I but served my God
with half the zeal
I serv'd my King, he would
not in mine age
Have left me naked to mine
enemies.

If the defect rather than the excess of zeal is our shortcoming, then may the fiery enthusiasm of Simon the Zealot, inspire us to emulate his example! Let each of us pray for the fresh enduement of the Spirit of Power, for the robust energy of apostolic times, that we, too, may aspire to the creative energy of the early church and manifest something of the zeal of those who made its later history immortal. May ours be the inextinguishable flame!

THADDAEUS

THE APOSTLE WHO HAD THREE NAMES

In the record of creation we read that God made the sun and moon as two *great lights;* the sun, the greater light to rule by day, and the moon, the lesser light to rule by night: *He made the stars also* (Gen. 1:16-18). God has made other lights also, spiritual lights, and has set them in the firmament of His Holy Word to give light to men. Bible characters are these lights, giving light, not of themselves, but of God. The Lord Himself is the Source of Light, the Light of men, the Light of the Word (John 1: 4; 8:12), and those who are His reflect His Light, as lights — lesser lights — of the world (Matt. 5:14).

As among the heavenly bodies, there are greater and lesser lights — the lesser lights, as distinguished from the two great lights, the sun and the moon — so among the characters of Scripture there is a like distinction. Great lights there are such as Moses, David, Isaiah, Daniel, standing forth most prominently, and shining most brightly, but there are lesser lights too — minor personalities we know little about. Yet whether great or small, each has his own special office. Just as not one of the stars that spangle the sky could not be removed without being missed, so not one of the lights of Scripture can be disregarded. Each life and character teaches us its own lesson. Guidance and example come from the unknown as well as the known.

A further comparison is that often the greater in our reckoning is not always the greater. The greater lights in the sky, with the moon lesser than the sun, only seem greater to us than the stars. Astronomers tell us that the moon is a mere nothing compared with some of the far-distant lights; that the sun is actually less than many a twinkling star millions of miles away. Is this not likewise true with some of the less-known saints on earth who may be great in the sight of God as the greatest, shining in His presence above (Matt. 11:11)? Many a humble, obscure saint, unknown to the world, will shine brightly as the brightest in heaven. What surprises will be ours when we reach there!

Dealing, as we are, with the apostles, we are discovering how they are made up of greater and lesser lights. Peter, for instance, was a blazing sun, and more conspicuous than any other disciple in the gospel story. But apostles like Simon the Zealot, and now Thaddaeus, are lesser lights, yet they had their place in the plan of Christ. All we know of this apostle is that he had three names and asked Jesus a sixteen-word question. Yet he was among the twelve the Master chose after a night of prayer, and He sent him forth to preach His message and assist in His miraculous ministry. As for his full record, it is on high.

1. *A Man With Three Names*

While some of the apostles have double names, Thaddaeus is the only one described as having three names. As to his genealogy, he was "the son of James," as the r.v. calls him, and not *brother* as the a.v. puts it (Luke 6:15, r.v.). There are at least four men who were named *James*.

James, the son of Zebedee, brother of the apostle John.

James, son of Mary, brother of our Lord.

James, the son of Alphaeus, also known as James the Less.

James, the unknown father of Thaddaeus, or that Judas who was neither the Iscariot, nor the near relative of Jesus. Whoever this James was, he kept his loyalty. Efforts have been made to identify Thaddaeus, or Judas, with the Judas, or Jude, who was one of our Lord's brothers, and who wrote a brief epistle. But as our Lord's family circle rejected His claims and accounted for them by concluding Him to be insane and were not converted until after His Resurrection, Judas, not Iscariot, or to give him his other names, Thaddaeus and Lebbaeus, could not have been one of the family, seeing Jesus chose him early in His ministry as an apostle.

As an ancient philosopher would have us know that "the beginning of the instruction is the study of names," let us take a look at the somewhat puzzling variety of names this apostle possessed.

Judas (Luke 6:16; John 14:22; Acts 1:13)

Doubtless this Hebrew name derived from Judah, meaning "Jehovah leads," or, "He will be confessed." This was the original name, or surname of this three-named disciple. John carefully distinguishes him from the traitor by the parenthetical remark, *not Iscariot* (John 14:22). There was the necessity of this distinctive title to mark him clearly off from the other Judas who had basely dishonored the cause of Christ. One Judas was true, the other traitorous. Thus, the Betrayer is called by the name of his birthplace, and *Iscariot* was, in his case, the brand of shame. The Judas before us, however, known by his two epithets, remained devoted to Christ.

Thaddaeus (Matt. 10:3; Mark 3:18)

Ellicott comments, "*THAD*, in later Hebrew, meant the female breast, and may have been the origin of *Thaddaeus*, as indicating, even more than *Lebbaeus*, a feminine devotedness." This Greek form of a Jewish name, then, can mean, *breast-child*.

Lebbaeus (Matt. 10:3)

Possibly derived from the Hebrew, *Leb*, implying "the heart," and representing warmth and earnestness of character, this Greek form suggests "heart-child." Another meaning given to this name is "the courageous one," and may have been indicative of his character. Perhaps *Thaddaeus* and *Lebbaeus* were added to the name he originally bore, as a term of endearment in his childhood, or as descriptive terms to mark his special features after his discipleship commenced because of the quality of tenderness he possessed. Apparently both Matthew and Mark avoided the name *Judas* because of the traitor-apostle having the same name. Matthew uses *Lebbaeus* only as a marginal background interpretation of *Thaddaeus*. Taking the three names together, they suggest the thought that he was one of the youngest of the twelve, and was looked upon by the others with an affection which showed itself in the two nicknames added to *Judas*.

2. A Man With a Question

All we are told about this apostle apart from his three names is that one day he asked Jesus a brief question:

"Lord, how is it that thou wilt manifest thyself unto us, and not unto the world?"(John 14:22).

On the same occasion in the Passover Chamber, Thomas had asked the question "How can we know the way?" (14:5) — and these questions remind us of others that were asked —

"How can these things be?" (John 3:9).

"How were thine eyes opened?" (John 9:10).

There are questions that cannot be answered in words. A child asks its mother, "How much do you love me?" The most devoted parent cannot fully answer a question like that. In His reply to the question proposed by Judas our Lord repeated much of what He had said before. There was no explanation of the method such as the questioner desired. How much time is wasted in useless speculation! John, who heard the question asked, thought it worth recording, not because it contained any light or wisdom, but because of the gracious answer which it drew from Jesus.

Without doubt we learn by asking questions, and Judas here showed the marks of a true disciple; for the true disciple is always ready with questions, eager to learn and deeply conscious of his need of teaching. Further, a question often reveals the questioner more than anything else, in that it shows the stage of thought the mind has reached, and reveals the bent of mind in looking at a subject. Judas had heard his Lord's answers to Thomas and Philip, and tried to grasp the secret of them without success, and so his own questioning thoughtfulness found voice in a request about the method of Christ's promised manifestation of Himself. The question asked revealed the frankness of an honest mind, which did not understand and was not ashamed to confess its ignorance. Such an ignorance darkened all the disciples, and was a source of grief to the Master.

If, as we have suggested, one of the names of Judas implies "courage," it required a little of this quality to ask the question he did, for it almost amounted to a contradiction of the Master's word. Had He not just told them that He was the revelation of the Father, and that He would show Himself to His disciples, though the world would not see Him as they could? Up came Judas with a somewhat bold challenge, "How can it be that thou wilt manifest thyself to us, and not unto the world?" As with the rest of the disciples, Judas had followed Jesus with great expectation and hope, but whatever kind of hope was in his mind, it needed the visible presence and power of Christ for its realization. Jesus had been talking about leaving the world and of no longer manifesting Himself to it, and to Judas' spiritually dull mind such language was mystifying and meaningless.

In His reply to the question of the apostle Jesus could not explain Himself fully then. He never gratified the curiosity of His disciples on divine things, "simply because the reign of faith is shut to sense and the method of God is only known to responsive hearts." Thus, at this stage He did not explain the method of His manifestation as His disciple required. After the resurrection and Pentecost, however, none of the apostles required explanations for truths which Jesus uttered while He was with them. At last, they came to believe that the secret of the Lord is ever with them who fear Him. While pursuing their spiritual education in the school of Christ, they seem to remain earthbound in their understanding of His Messiahship, but His ascension enabled them to see light, in His light.

The answer Jesus did give to Judas, not only throws a gleam of light on the heart and mind of the apostle, but was one he came to understand fully: "If a man love me, he will keep my words: and my Father will love him, and we will come unto him, and make our abode with him." Jesus saw in His disciple an earnest spirit of love and obedience, and knew that such would reveal in due time what, at that time, he could not appreciate (John 14: 23). The word *manifest,* which the questioner used, indicates a spiritual hunger within his mind which was not satisfied with simply hearing and seeing the Master, who replied to an unspoken thought by saying that "the manifestation which is made of itself by love, is understood by love alone."

Love is the key unlocking the gates of obedience, and likewise the key of entrance into blest communion with the three sacred Persons of the Trinity. By *love* we become the mystic cabinet of the Trinity. "If a man love me, he will keep my words: and my Father will love him, and we will come unto him, and make our abode with him" (John 14:23). Surely, there is not a more blessed word in all the gospels than this one, and we should ever be grateful to Thaddaeus-Lebbaeus-Judas for eliciting it by the question he put to the Master, as in it he revealed the groping of his own mind after deeper truths.

In passing, it will also be noted that, along with Thomas and Philip in the chapter, Judas began his question by calling Jesus, *Lord* (John 14:5, 8, 22). Such a form of address indicates that he was a devoted and obedient disciple, and that he had received a certain amount of revelation concerning the nature and purpose of Christ. Did not Paul write that no man can call Jesus, *Lord*, but by the Holy Spirit? Another Judas — the Iscariot who betrayed him — is never found calling Jesus, *Lord*, even though he was one of the chosen twelve.

May we not be slow to learn as "Judas, not Iscariot" did, that the root of discipleship is the *love* that secures obedience resulting in fellowship with the Father and the Son! It is only as we love, that we can obey; and obeying, we experience unbroken communion with heaven. It is from the apostle who asked Jesus a question, then, that we discover that love is the secret of obedience, and that obedience is the secret of blessedness.

> Trust and obey,
> For there's no other way
> To be happy in Jesus,
> But to trust and obey.

3. *A Man Who Lived in Obscurity*

As already expressed, apart from his three names and the one short question he asked, we have no other information regarding the apostle before us. We literally know nothing of his occupation before he met Christ, or under what circumstances he was called to discipleship, or what he accomplished for the Master, either befor or after the ascension. A dead silence surrounds his life and history, with the sole exception of the one question he asked. By deduction, we know that Judas, also known as Thaddaeus and Lebbaeus, was included whenever *the twelve* are mentioned in the gospels; that he was among those who shared in the ministry for whom Jesus set the apostles apart; that he was re-commissioned with the rest to go into all the world to preach the Gospel; that he was one of the number in the upper chamber prayerfully awaiting the coming of the Holy Spirit to mantle him with power for service; that his name is inscribed on one of the twelve foundations of the Holy City which John describes in the Apocalypse. Later on, we shall find that tradition has something to say about him.

The fact remains that like James the apostle, Judas the apostle's distinguishing feature is *obscurity*. An outstanding feature of both is that they were not men of mark. But because they were inconspicuous, simple men and models of mediocrity does not mean that their place in the sacred record has no interest or value for us. Obscure, they were yet obedient and went where they were sent, fighting the good fight, keeping the faith, and finishing their course with joy. Although their names are graven on the pages of gospel history, they, themselves, are hopelessly obscure men. Little space is allotted to their record, as if to suggest they did little worthy of mention. Yet they were never unnoticed, for He who had called them to His side knew all about their capabilities, and if they had known the lines of John Milton they would have said —

Yet be it less or more, or soon or slow,
It shall be still in strictest measure even,
To that same lot, however mean or high,
Toward which Time leads me, and the
    will of Heaven;
All is, if I have grace to use it so,
As ever in my great Taskmaster's eye.

No matter how obscure James and Judas may appear to have been, they were not solitary, for they had the signs of the Lord's presence. They had received His promise, "Lo, I am with you always," so out they went to live and serve, "the Lord working *with* them." With such assurances no obscure toiler need be lonely. Conscious that he is within range of the Lord's eye and within touch of His hand, the lonely, unnoticed servant is content. Regarding the silence of Scripture with reference to these two apostles, Dr. Alexander Maclaren says that after all the apostles were not the real workers in the Church, but *Christ*. Had they been all-important we should have had minute and detailed accounts of their careers. Thus, one reason for silence as to their life and work is that the Holy Spirit, who inspired Scripture, wished to concentrate attention upon the Lord Jesus as the all-important Person. The figure of any man is not allowed to obscure the prominence of the Savior. The excellency of any power the apostles may have had was not of themselves, but of God. Alas! we often magnify the importance of the human instrument.

It would seem as if there are, at least, three lessons we can glean from these obscure apostles whom the gospel just mentions and then dismisses almost without a word:

Although unknown they were not unfaithful

When chosen, all of the twelve ventured forth with Christ without any financial guarantees. How they were to be supported was the responsibility of the One who had called them, and devotion to Him must have sorely tried their fidelity. But they were faithful, with the exception of the one who betrayed Jesus; and after His ascension, they were destitute of everything we regard as being essential to success in Christian enterprise and evangelism. Even such obscure apostles as James and Judas had their share in turning the world upside down, even though their part may not have been as conspicuous as that of Peter. Having no history, they were yet among the real history-makers of the world.

Even though others did not notice them, they did their best, and lived as unto Him. It is often comparatively easy to do one's best in a conspicuous sphere where all eyes are on us, but the triumph and final achievement of fidelity is to do our best, and be at our best, when no eye save God's is watching.

Some of the greatest and most sacrificial work in the world is done by those whose names are unknown and who will never figure in any *Who's Who*. They do not cease to labor if suitable recognition is not forthcoming. For them, the motto is not *fame*, but *faithfulness*. They know that at the Judgment Seat when every man's work is to be tried by fire, of what sort it is, that the Master's commendation will be theirs, "Well done, good and faithful servant; thou hast been faithful over a few things, I will make thee ruler of many things; enter thou into the joy of thy Lord." Their humble, obscure service may have gone unrecorded of men, but certain recognition and recompense are theirs as they stand before Him whom they were content to serve in obscurity to receive their reward. In heaven, the first are last, and the last, first. Many of the unnoticed names of earth are among the most glorious names above. *Unknown* to the records of earth, they are *well known* in the books of heaven. Thomas Gray, the renowned English poet, 1716-1771, gave us his immortal elegy, in which he gives pathos to the thought of humble and heroic fidelity passing away unnoticed. After musing in a churchyard he wrote:

Perhaps in this neglected spot is laid
  Some heart once pregnant with celestial
    fire;
Hands that the rod of empire might have
    swayed,
  Or waked to ecstacy the living lyre.

Full many a gem of purest ray serene,
  The dark unfathom'd caves of ocean
    bear;
Full many a flower is born to blush
    unseen,
  And wastes its sweetness on the desert
    air.

These lines may be true of some people as they live out their life on earth. Their sweet and gracious lives may pass unnoticed by the world, and seem as if their sweetness is wasted. But no faithful witness is ever wasted, neither overlooked or forgotten in heaven. Human praise and plaudits they may have missed, but their unfailing loyalty came up before God as an acceptable service, an odor of a sweet smell, and from Him they, at last, receive the recompense of the reward. As we linger amid the shadows, whether we are conspicuous or obscure, may we be found living to the limit as the Lord would have us do in a world of wickedness and woe.

Some little joy I have in doing still
The humble work He bids me do for Him;
A tender gladness when 'tis mine to fill
Again some empty chalice to the brim.

THOMAS

THE APOSTLE MOST MALIGNED

The idea behind the proverb, "Give a dog an ill name, and his work is done," is certainly true in connection with Thomas, for whom expositors and preachers have hardly a good word to say. Rarely has a man been so pilloried and maligned on such insufficient grounds. Surely Thomas commands our sympathy for the mistreatment accorded him. For the most part, adverse criticisms of the apostle are mere echoes of one another, following a beaten track, simply because it is beaten, with some expositors balancing their lack of independent judgment by piling up rebuke for Thomas. Here are a few criticisms we have gathered. All restate much the same thought in different words; repeated, they thereby help to perpetuate a series of misconceptions, expressing in varying terms the stock objections to Thomas. The following quotes from high sources do him less than justice:

"Thomas is very much to be blamed for his unbelief, in that he compares very unfavorably with the rest of the Upper Room."

Again, "Thomas was a man of choice spirit, only he was kept very low."

Again, "If ever a dismal, sombre note was to be struck, you could depend on Thomas to strike it."

Again, "A man of warm heart but melancholy temperament."

Again, "A man of much love and little faith."

Again, "A man of candor and resolution but inclined to subordinate the invisible to the visible."

Alexander Whyte, for whom we have a profound admiration, evidently had his far-fetched appraisal of Thomas in mind as he read old Richard Burton's *Anatomy of Melancholy*, written about 1600:

All my joys to this are folly
Naught so sweet as Melancholy

for here is Whyte's description of the Apostle Thomas: "The character of Thomas is an anatomy of melancholy. If 'to say man is to say melancholy,' then to say Thomas, called Didymus, is to say religious melancholy. Peter was of such an ardent and enthusiastical temperament that he was always speaking, whereas Thomas was too great a melancholian to speak much, and when he ever did speak it was always out of the depths of his hypochondriacal heart."

Candidly, we dissociate ourselves from such an estimate of the temperament of Thomas, just as we do from others in which he is regarded as the skeptic among the apostles — a man of materialistic mind and mold — a man who lost his faith in a panic of fear and found it difficult to recover, one who had to be brought back to abandoned privilege by a special manifestation of the Lord. It is high time that a striking character like Thomas

was studied independently, without bias or blinkers, with a desire to see him as he really is. Certainly, Thomas may have had doubts — so do the saintliest of men! I do not believe for one moment that Thomas was among those "born sad," whose heart was "the home of sorrow," who "looked upon life with sad eyes," and "carried about with him everywhere a heavy heart." Neither do I hold that the *Mr. Fearing* whom John Bunyan portrayed in *Pilgrim's Progress*, is the picture of Thomas drawn to life.

Perhaps, in no others in the apostolate is individuality more marked, for although Thomas' character appears complex in its related elements, "yet it is so consistent in its action that it is possible to understand his temperament with some degree of accuracy."

1. The Significance of His Name

His Hebrew name *Thomas* with its Greek equivalent *Didymus*, means "a twin." Evidently, it was customary with the Jews when traveling into foreign countries, or associating with the Greeks and Romans, to assume to themselves a Greek or a Latin name, either of great affinity, or having a connection with their own birthplace. Thus our Lord was called *Christ* answering to His Hebrew title, *Mashiach*, or The Anointed. *Tabitha* is called *Dorcas*, both names signifying "a goat."

"Thomas which is called Didymus." *Thomas*, according to the Syriac importance of his name, had the title of *Didymus* — both names meaning "a twin" — the same name expressed in different languages. The Syriac version renders the phrase, "Thauma, which is called Thama." Several expositors have busily employed their imagination trying to find a twin brother for Thomas in various New Testament personages. Because his name is paired with that of Matthew, there are those who suggest that they may have been twin brothers. Others go the length of implying that Thomas was a twin brother of the Lord Himself.

Who the twin of Thomas was we should very much like to know; and whether he or she also became a follower of Jesus Christ. A feasible suggestion comes to us from an old tradition saying that the other twin was a sister called *Lysia*. Other inferences are just as imaginative. For instance Trench affirms that "the coincidence between the name and his twin-mindedness is remarkable (James 1:8; 4:8). In him the twins, unbelief and faith, were contending one with another for mastery, as Esau and Jacob in Rebecca's womb." There is a sort of dual consciousness in all of us, "When I would do good, evil is present with me." Where Scripture is silent, we should preserve the same silence, and not let our imagination run riot. We take Thomas' name at its face value, namely, that he was born a twin, and carried this name into the circle of the twelve without any index of character, or as a key to the assumed twofold aspect of his nature. Eusebius, one of the earliest historians of the church, says that Thomas' real name was *Judah,* and that his nickname, "Twin," may well have been used by his companions to distinguish him from the two other Judahs — the brother of James, and Judas Iscariot.

2. The Record of His Call to Apostleship

Altogether there are some eight passages in the New Testament in which Thomas is mentioned, of which four are in the lists of the apostles. Although the references may be somewhat scanty they are usually characteristic, and from them can be gained a fair conception of the style and character of the man (Matt. 10:3; Mark 3:18; Luke 6:15; John 11:16; 20:24, 26; 21:2; Acts 1:13). As far as gospel history is concerned we know absolutely nothing about the kinsmen of Thomas, his place of residence, or occupation. The first three gospels give us nothing but his bare name, and, as we have seen with Philip, we are indebted to John for the few but interesting particulars, investing Thomas with flesh and blood, making him stand out before us a real man, with those distinct and impressive qualities from which we can learn much.

That Thomas was a Jew is certain, and in all probability he was a Galilean (Acts 1:11). From legendary material we gather that he was born of poor parents, who brought him up to the trade of fishing, and who gave him a useful education, instructing him in the knowledge of the Scriptures, whereby he learned wisely to govern his life and manners. As we shall presently see, apocryphal literature is rich in references to the later ministry and death of Thomas. The New Testament is silent as to when and how Thomas was called to discipleship. The first mention of his name is when our Lord chose the twelve and sent them in pairs. It is John who, in his gospel, saves Thomas from oblivion, and makes him a reality, surrounding him personally with an undying interest in the three facts about him which John records. Yet the little he does tell us about Thomas is sufficient to help us understand him, and to make us feel that we know more about him than some of the other apostles of whose lives we have more information.

Thomas shares with Simon the Zealot and Judas Iscariot, appearance on the sacred page without reference to circumstances of their call to follow

Christ. At some time, Thomas must have listened, with the multitudes who thronged Him, to His voice and teaching, and stirred by the Holy Spirit, surrendered his life to the claims of the Savior, leaving all to follow Him. Then He must have seen something in Thomas constraining Him to select him as an apostle. Elder Cumming would have us know that:

> The absence of all detail about his conversion and call is of no purpose. It serves a double end. It shows how varied is the way in which sinners are brought to salvation, some giving a testimony thereto that stirs up others as by a trumpet, and some giving very little. There is a vast variety of character among the children of God, and this variety shows in their new birth, as well as afterwards. Nay, there are many who cannot give a definite account of their conversion. They know that it has taken place, but they do not know when or how. And all such cases are covered by the silence wrapped round the great change in the case of such an apostle as Thomas!

Life was changed for Thomas from the hour he met Christ. And he went forth a messenger of the Master, a herald of the Highest, receiving power over all kinds of diseases, rejoicing that even the demons were subject unto him, but rejoicing more that through grace, his name was written in heaven — equally with those of the seventy that Christ likewise chose (Luke 10:17-26).

Our first glimpse into Thomas's character is supplied by the law of association. In the lists of the apostles the names appear in pairs — an arrangement inspired by the Spirit, showing how like drew to like, each man finding his kindred spirit. Thus we find bracketed together the names of Thomas and Matthew, not because, as some expositors suggest, they may

have been brothers, but because they had much in common, and drew together in consequence. Comparing the lists given of the apostles it will be noticed that while Luke and Mark give their order *Matthew* and *Thomas,* Matthew in his list with characteristic humility puts *Thomas* before himself.

Matthew and Thomas, then, will be found side by side, with a common experience and a personal sympathy helpful to both. These two were inseparables, the one clinging to the other, as his shadow. Of this we can be certain that the Lord who sent forth His disciples two by two, saw to it that they were not unequally yoked together. Allan Poole asks the question, "Was Matthew the original of the Parable of the Prodigal Son? Surely he was Christ's miracle of mercy within the circle. In the fact of that renegade Jew being chosen to the apostolate lay Thomas's point of contact with him. For it was ever a wonder to Thomas that he should have been selected to become 'a vessel unto honor, meet for the Master's use!' " This was probably the thought uppermost in Thomas's mind, and helps to explain much in his attitude to the Lord.

3. *The Fearlessness of His Devotion* (John 11:16)

It is to John's gospel we turn for the three sketches he gives us of Thomas the apostle — who is first seen in his speech to Jesus when He expressed His intention of going into Judea again; at the Last Supper when he acknowledged his ignorance of the place to which Jesus was going, and asked Him the way there; then, following the resurrection when, after he saw the Lord, he made the astounding confession, *My Lord and my God!* We are taking these three episodes separately, and hope to find that Thomas is truly representative of all of us who have believed in the Lord Jesus for salvation.

Thomas had not journeyed far in his apostleship before he manifested an eminent instance of his hearty willingness to undergo the saddest fate that might attend all the twelve, namely, fellowship in the Master's death. Learning of the death of Lazarus, Jesus resolved to go to Bethany to raise the friend He loved, but the rest of the apostles sought to dissuade Him from going into Judea because of the religious leaders there who plotted to kill Him. But Thomas spoke up and said that they should not hinder the Master doing what He desired, though it might cost them their lives. "Let us also go that we may die with him!" This brave decision implied that instead of raising Lazarus from the dead, they themselves might go with Jesus to their own graves.

Do not the words of Thomas glow with a love, deep and true, for the Master? We dissociate ourselves from those who infer that Thomas gave way to pessimism when he felt that there could be no other issue of the rash journey Jesus was to take than the death of them all. One writer calls Thomas *"an heroic pessimist,"* and a few other expositors follow the same mistaken idea of the decision of Thomas. Even though he did not know the full import of what he said, his utterance was that of a loyal and loving heart and implied, "We will not desert: we will go too; and, if need be, we will die with him." How different was the boast of Simon Peter, "Lord, I am ready to go with thee to prison and to death." But those were mere words, which were not followed up by the deed. With Thomas it was a declaration backed by deed for he crossed Jordan with Jesus, and went up to Judea, where he expected only death for himself and the rest.

It is always well to be identified with Jesus, even though it be at the risk of life (Acts 15:26; Rev. 12:11). Thomas thought of death: Jesus thought only of the glory of God (John 11:4). Thomas saw only the dark side, certain death – as afterward he saw no possibility of resurrection (John 20:25). While we may detect a touch of fatalism in his resolution to follow Jesus, even at the cost of life, Thomas may have shrunk from the thought of death, but he had no thought of flight. His attitude at this juncture in Christ's ministry was a sign of his attachment and devotion to Him, and marks him as having a love both deep and strong as that of any other disciple. His was a love that counted no sacrifice too great, and, as one of the bravest of the brave, he was willing to go into the very jaws of death in the company of his Lord. Love would make it sweet for Thomas in such blessed company. Perfect love expelled fear for the time being. His high courage in an hour of peril is expressed in the lines we often sing –

Where duty calls, or danger,
Be never wanting there."

The Master has always had among His followers those who have seen, as if by inspiration, what ought to be done; who have been swift to see where duty led, and what devotion to Christ ought to lead to; and Thomas remains as the forerunner of them all. Let us, therefore, cease maligning Thomas, accusing him of morbid fear, gloominess, and pessimism. He was a choice spirit, with a nobility and worth of character some theologians have not fairly recognized. His chief characteristic was that of a deep and devoted love ever ready to leave all for Christ, dare all for Christ, and die with Christ.

Like those brave knights in attendance upon the blind King John of Bohemia, who rode into the Battle of Crecy with their bridles intertwined with that of their master, resolved to share his fate whatever it might be — so Thomas, come life, come death, was resolved not to forsake his Lord, seeing he was bound to Him by a bond of deep and enthusiastic love. Would that we had his devoted and consecrated heart, and passionate and heroic love! "Let us also go with him, that *we may die with him.*" Jesus had taught His disciples that unless they were prepared to hate their own life for His sake, they could not be His disciples. All praise to Thomas for hating *his own life also!* Christ's demands went deep, but devoted Thomas knew no reserve, and instead of accusing him as being "an anatomy of melancholy," let us seek to imitate his heroic spirit and begin to live the life that is life indeed.

4. *The Quest of His Mind for Knowledge* (John 14:1-6)

The next reference to Thomas brings us to the Supper Room where our Lord had His own gathered around Him. It was a sorrowful occasion for the idea of parting from Jesus lay on their hearts like a nightmare, and the shadow of separation at first struck them dumb. But He spoke to their troubled hearts about the joys of heaven and of the place He was going to prepare for them, that they might follow Him. He would not leave them as orphans but would come again for them. They knew both the place whither He was going, and the way to reach it. Then it was that Thomas spoke up and said that they knew not whither He was going, much less the way to such a sphere.

While our Lord spoke cheerfully of His return to His Father's home, Thomas could see nothing cheerful in the hopeless separation before them, and so his reply, like all his recorded words, has a touch of sadness about it: "Lord, we know not whither thou goest; and how can we know the way?" (John 14:5). When at last Jesus was crucified, Thomas must have felt that the powers of darkness had prevailed in tearing the beloved One from those who loved Him. Each time he is mentioned he "plays upon his bass" and is kept very low. All that Jesus had said about mansions in glory did not grip his mind, all he knew was that his dear Lord was to leave him, and that he wanted ever to be with Him. Thomas may have been slow of mind, over-cautious in accepting truth, thereby coming the hard way to believe, but beneath the surface of this hesitant, quiet apostle, a fierce fire burned, the eruptions of which no one could foretell. Some of the apostolate began well, but disappointed Christ. Thomas went steadily on, however, showing little quality at first, but surprising those around him both by his zeal and faith as they came to know him better.

When Thomas seems to contradict what Jesus had just said, we must not condemn him with a lack of faith or with utter failure in understanding the teaching of his Lord. He is among those who miss information because they assume a knowledge they do not possess. It has been said that, "If there be art in concealing what one does not know, there is wisdom in revealing one's limitations. What is knowledge at best but ignorance — *with a library?* Knowledge at best is relative—the limits of it are so quickly reached." We are slow to learn that there is always great hope for the mind conscious of its limitations and imperfections; but there is next to

none for the mind content with its
area of darkness.

The question of Thomas, "How can
we know the way?" reveals him as a
seeker after fuller truth, and was like
Goethe who, yearning for expansion
of knowledge, cried, "Light — light —
more light, give us more light or we
die!" The natural, cautious temperament of the apostle did not close his
mind to further knowledge. Perhaps
his very anxiety to understand what
Jesus had said, created a temporary
confusion of thought. From what He
said to Thomas it would appear that
he knew more than he thought he
knew, for he must have gathered from
many things Jesus had said that He
would be put to death, and after His
death, return to His Father. For all
that we know Thomas may have tried
to make himself believe that he had
misunderstood the Master's teaching,
and came at last to think he was ignorant upon a subject about which he
had no wish to be clear, because of his
Master's coming departure from him.

What is evident is the fact that in
His reply to the statement and question of Thomas, Jesus gave utterance
to one of the most sublime revelations
of Himself to be found in Scripture.
How can we know the way? Only
One could supply the answer — *The
Way*, Himself, who is the sum-total of
all that we need to know, to believe,
to love, to follow. He is all we need
for time and eternity. We can never
have more than He is; we must never
be satisfied with less. So Thomas's
quest for deeper knowledge was satisfied, and he must have been thrilled
to learn that his Lord was:

The Way to God — The Way without which there is no *going*.

The Truth of God — The Truth
without which there is no *knowing*.

The Life from God — The Life without which there is no *living*.

5. *The Demand for Facts About His Lord* (John 20:24-29)

While Thomas, called Didymus,
was one of those to whom the Risen
Lord revealed Himself (John 21:2),
and is named in the apostolic list of
those present at the pre-Pentecost
prayer meeting (Acts 1:13), the dramatic episode of the fear-stricken disciples assembled together and Jesus
suddenly appearing in their midst after His Resurrection, is the last occasion we have of Thomas speaking
about, and then to, the Savior. The
very day when He arose, He made His
way to the house where His distressed
disciples were and gave them sufficient evidence and assurance that He
had really risen from the dead and
was alive forevermore.

At this first meeting with the disciples, Thomas was absent (John 20:
24), and his subsequent conversation
with them and their animated rehear-
sal of seeing and hearing the Risen
Master, while not altogether convincing him of the truth of the resurrection, induced Thomas to be among
the apostles eight days later (20:26).
As we feel that many preachers and
teachers have misinterpreted his absence from the rest at the Master's
first appearance; and then his refusal
to accept their testimony as to seeing
Jesus — let us try to exonerate Thomas
from much of the blame wrongly
heaped upon him. First of all, take
the matter of his absence from the
rest after the sad experience of Calvary. One common explanation is that
he had fallen into a state of religious
despondency, and so refused, obstinately, to keep with the other disciples.
As a result, he missed the first appearance of Christ. Then, the application
is made that if we absent ourselves

from a prayer meeting without a valid reason, we are bound to lose a blessing. Certainly, Thomas missed much through absence on that memorable first Lord's Day (John 20:24).

Let it be made clear, however, that we do not know the reason why Thomas was not present, nor can we guess why he alone was absent. Feeling, as the rest of the apostles had done, that the sealed sepulchre was the grave of all hopes, Thomas may have retired to some quiet spot to shed his tears alone and hold aloof in solitary sadness. Like Peter before him, he may have wanted to get away to be alone with his grief. Perhaps his old fear of the Jews kept him away (John 11:8, 16). Probably he had not recovered the company of the other apostles, after their last dispersion in the Garden, when everyone's fears prompted him to consult his own safety. Is it not wrong to affirm why Thomas was absent, when the Scripture gives us no reason whatever for his empty seat in the house where the others were gathered?

We have been guilty of another error — that of misinterpreting his attitude toward his fellow-apostles when they came to him with the glorious news of the resurrection. Thomas refused to accept their evidence, meeting their excited testimony with the declaration that he would not believe unless he saw for himself the nail-pierced hands and feet of Jesus. Had they not been mistaken once before, about His appearance when He walked to them on the sea? Now they might equally be mistaken; instead of His body what they saw might have been a spirit (Matt. 14:25). All he demanded was the same evidence they had received; when he could see and handle the person of his Lord for himself, then he would set no bounds to his faith.

Surely such a characteristic of Thomas should be commended and not condemned! The news he had heard seemed too good to be true, but he did not reject what he heard. He simply desired to test all truth by evidence. It was his sincerity which prompted him to stand aloof from the rest of the apostles until he had attained to personal conviction regarding the resurrection. The same sincerity was to draw from him the greatest testimony ever made of Christ. But think of the injustice we have been guilty of in nicknaming him, "Thomas *the doubter*," and of remembering nothing about him save his supposed doubt, and of calling any person who may not accept a certain fact, a *doubting Thomas*. Yet his chief characteristic was not *doubt* but a deep and devoted love for the Master.

Thomas said, "Except I shall see . . . I will not believe" (John 20:25). Before we castigate him as a determined doubter and one guilty of gross unbelief, let us remember that the other apostles did not believe in the resurrection till *they had seen* the Risen Lord Himself. So we cannot separate Thomas from the rest and stand him up as the sole monument of doubt and unbelief. *All* of the disciples were the "fools" Jesus spoke of who were slow of heart to believe all the Prophets, and He Himself had spoken concerning His death and resurrection and glorification (Luke 24:25, 26).

What we must not forget is that Thomas was a broken-hearted man, and that the reservation he had regarding the news of Christ's resurrection was not of the head but of the heart — not the result of intellectual difficulty, but of *great sorrow*. "In the shadow of a great affliction, a soul sits dumb" — and Thomas had sat thus for a week, and so found it hard to accept the good news. Thomas was no "flippant doubter." Any doubt he had was the doubt of one who *wanted to believe*. There was nothing he yearned so much for as another sight of his much-loved Lord. Tennyson would have us know that —

"There lives more faith in honest doubt,
Believe me, than in half the creeds."

What are the marks of *honest* doubt? Well, it is first of all an agony, then it pants and yearns for the light, and being *honest*, comes into the light. Augustine put it, "Thomas doubted that we may never doubt." Robert Ellis Thompson says that, "The story of Thomas proves, if proof were needed, that the apostles were not a set of silly devotees, who were ready to believe whatever was told them, for there was at least one among them who insisted on proof and evidence, as might a Tyndell or a Huxley."

While we do not condemn the action of Thomas, we hasten to say that it was not ideal because faith should not rest on demonstration, but on a venture of the heart and mind, growing out of a personal trust. "Do not fear to doubt," says Coleridge, "if you wish to believe." All honest doubters end where Thomas did, on their knees before the Master in praise and adoration. What a glorious occasion that was when eight days after His first appearance, He came again into the presence of His own, and that this time Thomas was present — not to have any intellectual doubts which he may have entertained solved, but to experience the tender healing of his broken heart over the apparent loss of his Lord.

The Master proclaimed *peace* three times over as He dispelled the fear of His disciples, and each utterance is significant:

The first is associated with His a-

toning work, for it is said that when He had uttered the words, "Peace be unto you" (John 20:19), "he showed unto them his hands and his side." The ground of peace is the blood of the cross (Col. 1:20).

The second utterance of the word of peace is associated with a commission given to the disciples to go forth in the name of Christ. They were to be messengers of peace, therefore, He said, "Peace be unto you" (John 20: 21; Acts 10:36; Eph. 2:17).

The *third* utterance of this word of peace was heard on the second Lord's Day, when Thomas was present with the rest of the disciples. His unbelief was doubtless a source of disquiet, but in the midst of his cautiousness the Master speaks the word of peace. Thomas himself quickly participated in the blessing of such peace passing all understanding (John 20:26).

Singling out Thomas, our Lord entered into one of those notable conversations of His which were often brief monologues revealing Him as the perfect Conversationalist. After giving the excited band His benediction, Jesus in His invitation to Thomas to handle Him for evidences that He was indeed alive, revealed His omniscience. Adopting the language Thomas had used, He asked His cautious disciple to examine His wound-prints for the evidence he wanted. Lovingly He rebuked Thomas for his weakness of faith. "Be not faithless but believing." All Thomas had heard from the lips of His Lord regarding His death and resurrection ought to have been sufficient without the aid of sight. Surely it would have been better even to distrust his senses than to discredit His Word.

Further, was it not somewhat sad that Jesus should have to speak of an apostle in the terms He had used in the denunciation of the world? The word *faithless* employed here is the same the Lord uttered in rebuking the prevailing unbelief of His time (Matt. 17:17). But the rebound of Thomas was as magnificent as it was immediate, "MY LORD AND MY GOD!" He is the only person in the New Testament to address our Lord as *God*. John's gospel is, of course, in a special sense the gospel of our Lord's *deity*. The compassionate Savior did not take advantage of His disciple's refractory unbelief, but urged him to satisfy his faith by a demonstration from sense, and quickly convinced of his error, Thomas acknowledged his Risen Master to be the omnipotent One. What a thrill must have been his to see how his Lord had triumphed over death!

At last, Thomas had reached the sunnier side of his cheerless cautiousness, and, after almost swearing that he would not accept the resurrection, he is already sure that he is standing before Jehovah Himself, giving a wonderful testimony that must have satisfied His own heart — "My Lord and my God!" Truly, this is the grandest, strongest and shortest witness in the New Testament to what Jesus was, and is; and it is the more remarkable as coming from Thomas. Rapidly he ascended from the deep Valley of Humiliation and the grounds of Giant Despair to the Delectable Mountains and the height of celestial vision, to live, thereafter, a life strong in faith, giving glory to God. With the first ascription of deity Thomas came to experience the rest of Tennyson's poem, *In Memoriam* —

. . . Thus he came at length
To find a stronger faith his own;
  And Power was with him in the night,
  Which makes the darkness and the
    light,
And dwells not in the light alone.

The spectres of the apostle's mind had vanished. Conscious of his honest de-

sire to believe, Jesus with pitying tenderness accommodated the revelation to Thomas's state of mind, enabling him to give the brightest witness to His deity yet given by any disciple which put Thomas into "the front place of all believers at that momentous crisis of the world's history." With this great apostolic confession came the Master's thrilling benediction: "Thomas, because thou hast seen me, thou hast believed: Blessed are they that have not seen, yet have believed"(John 20:29). Henceforth, a living faith must ever be a personal faith, standing in the power of a Spirit-given demonstration to the conscience and consciousness, and ever centered on Christ. Are we not among the number who have not seen, yet have believed? We were saved by faith through grace, and endure as seeing Him who is invisible.

Jesus, these eyes have never seen
  That radiant form of Thine;
The veil of flesh hangs dark between
  Thy blessed Face and mine.

Now we take our leave of the most attractive Thomas who, although he was a cautious, slow man and apt to take a dark view of events, was yet a man who could not be persuaded by others of what he did not see for himself. What he lacked in natural buoyancy of spirit, he made up for in indomitable courage and entire unselfishness. What deep significance there is in his declaration, "Except I shall see in his hands the print of the nails . . . I will not believe." Any religious system or philosophy failing to bear those nail-prints is to be rejected. Those Calvary marks are a sure sign of authenticity. Further, as the Lord's "sent ones," it is essential for us to bear those marks of His (Gal. 6:17). When the godless around "see the print of the nails" in our life and living, they cease to be "faithless" and become believers, and with us pass into a radiant confidence and joy.

I want to be marked for Thine own,
Thy seal on my forehead to wear;
And have that new name on the mystic
white stone,
Which none but Thyself can declare.

II. THE OTHER APOSTLES —
THE WIDER CIRCLE

Whenever we think or speak of *the apostles* quite naturally we have *the twelve* in mind, whom Jesus chose at the outset of His ministry that they must be with Him and trained for future service. Frequently the apostolic band we have just considered are spoken of as "the disciples" or "His disciples," but they were not His only disciples, or for that matter, the only apostles. There was an ever-widening circle of those whom the Master drew to Himself. There were, for instance, the "other seventy also," whom He appointed and "sent . . . two by two before his face, into every city and place, whither he himself would come" (Luke 10:1). Added to these were the many women who followed Him and ministered unto Him of their substance. As disciple means "a learner," Mary was a true disciple who sat at Jesus' feet and heard His word (Luke 10:39). After Pentecost, the disciples multiplied abundantly (Acts 2:41; 4:4).

It was thus with apostleship, which the early church did not restrict to *the twelve*, although their position must ever remain unique. Sometimes we wonder why prominent saints, named in the gospels and the Acts, who appeared to have the necessary qualifications for apostleship, were not included in the apostolate — men such as Mark, Luke, Stephen, and Philip the Evangelist. Coming to the Acts

and the epistles, let us seek to enumerate those who are added to "the glorious company of the apostles." Here, again, we deal with those who were thus called, alphabetically, as we did with *the twelve,* remembering as hitherto explained that the term *apostle* means "one sent forth," or "a missionary."

The apostles we are now to consider were in no sense inferior to *the twelve*. True, there were differences among them — differences due to natural talents, to personal acquirements and experience, to spiritual gifts. Thus, Peter and John were more distinct than Thaddaeus or Simon the Cananaean, just as Paul stands out greater than Barnabas. Apostleship, denoting as it does missionary service, was measured by its seals, and Peter and Paul were prominent in these. The apostolate, then, was not "a limited circle of officials holding a well-defined position of authority in the Church, but a large class of men who discharged one — and that the highest — of the functions of the prophetic ministry (I Cor. 12:28; Eph. 4:11). It was on the foundation of the apostles and the prophets that the Christian Church was built, with Jesus Christ Himself as the chief corner-stone (Eph. 2:20). The distinction between the two classes was that while the prophet was God's spokesman to the believing Church (I Cor. 14:4, 22, 24, 30, 31), the apostle was His envoy to the unbelieving world" (Gal. 2:7-9).

ANDRONICUS
THE APOSTLE OF NOTE

In Paul's portrait gallery of the saints he sought to commend ere he finished his course, was *Andronicus* who, along with Junia, the apostle described as being "of note among the apostles" (Rom. 16:7). In fact, Paul gives us a four-fold sketch of these fellow-laborers —

"My kinsmen —
My fellow-prisoners —
Who are of note among the apostles —
Who also were in Christ before me."

Kinsmen is a title Paul gives to six persons in this chapter, and probably implies that they were members of the same nation — Jewish as Paul was.

My fellow-prisoners is a phrase suggesting that at some time or another they shared imprisonment with Paul. They had been, as Bishop Moule puts it, Paul's "fellow-captives in Christ's war."

Who are of note among the apostles, can mean one of two things: either they were distinguished *as* apostles themselves being included in "all the apostles" (1 Cor. 15:7), or Andronicus and Junia were most highly esteemed by the apostolic circle, being honored above others for their toil and their character.

Who also were in Christ before me. When these two apostles were converted to Christ we are not told, but from them Paul had heard of such a transaction. Bishop Moule has the comment, "Not improbably these two early converts helped to *goad* the conscience of their still persecuting kinsman, and to prepare the way of Christ in his heart" (Acts 26:14). Andronicus was one of "the traveling evangelists or missionaries who preached the Gospel from place to place," and was likely one of the most prominent and successful of these itinerant envoys of the Early Church.

APOLLOS

The Apostle Who Was Eloquent

When Paul wrote about the apostles who were made a spectacle unto the world and to angels and to men, he seems to include Apollos along with himself in the wider apostolate (I Cor. 4:6, 9). This cultured and educated Jew of Alexandrian race (Acts 18:24), came into contact with Paul while he was in Ephesus during his third missionary journey. Luke gives us a full account of the remarkable ability of Apollos to expound the Scriptures, and how, after his private tuition from two godly souls, Aquila and Priscilla, he mightily convinced the Jews of the Messiahship of Jesus (Acts 18:24-28). Paul seems to allude to Apollos' eloquence, wisdom, and letter of commendation in defense of his own position as an apostle with authority (I Cor. 3:1-8, 22). The last glimpse we have of Apollos is when he is recommended along with Zenas the lawyer to Titus (Titus 3:13), who was then on a missionary journey through Crete and was probably the bearer of this *epistle* addressed to him by Paul (Titus 1:5).

There has been a tendency to represent Paul and Apollos as rivals based on Paul's stricture regarding the folly of partisanship. "Are you for Paul or Apollos?" But the hearts of these two workers were knit together in a bond nothing could break. These two apostles experienced a friendship withstanding the greatest of temptations among preachers — envy! Paul heard of the crowds in Corinth flocking to the Bible-lectures eloquently given by Apollos, and he rejoiced. The two had worked separately in Ephesus and Corinth, then together in Ephesus.

That there must have been something refreshing about the unique ministry of Apollos may be gathered from the way both Luke and Paul compared him to water. Luke, the historian, thought of Apollos as "boiling hot" in earnest spirituality for this is what the word *fervent* means; Paul, the great missionary statesman, spoke of Apollos' words as cool streams upon a burnt-up garden, "Apollos watered" (Acts 18:25; I Cor. 3:6). The drooping converts of Corinth, so spiritually parched, revived under the preaching of Apollos, "and his fellow-apostle, Paul, rejoiced in having gained such a capable partner." Within the Church today there are many drooping, withering plants in dire need of watering, but their case is forlorn if the pulpit lacks an Apollos who can water God's garden.

BARNABAS

THE APOSTLE OF COMFORT

Our abiding impression of Barnabas is that of a man of tender heart — pitiful, forgiving, and wonderfully kind — *the son of comfort*. In a beautiful way, Luke sums up his character in the expressive words, "He was a good man, and full of the Holy Spirit and of faith." And then an item full of meaning follows—wherever he went, "much people was added to the Lord." Goodness was his persuasive power, and he is deemed worthy to be enrolled in "the glorious company of the apostles."

Luke links Paul and Barnabas together as *apostles* (Acts 14:1-14). Tradition has it that Barnabas was one of *the seventy* whom Jesus sent forth (Luke 10:1). Clement of Alexandria, an early Church Father, asserted that as one of *the seventy*, Barnabas possessed one of the distinctive qualifications of the apostolate, in that he had seen the Lord Christ, and followed Him during His earthly ministry. If this is so then it is more than likely that he was one of the 500 brethren of whom Paul speaks, who had seen the Risen Christ (I Cor. 15: 6), the majority of whom were still alive when he wrote his epistle to the Corinthians. But the New Testament gives no hint of the previous discipleship of Barnabas before Pentecost. He first appears in the setting up of the Christian community in Jerusalem, which may suggest that he became a Christian as the result of the great flood-tide of fervor and conversion which began on the historic day of Pentecost. We can briefly summarize the facts and features of his career in the following way. The reader will find additional material in the author's work on *All the Men of the Bible* published by Zondervan.

1. Although Barnabas was not one of *the twelve,* he stands out as the most important early Christian apostle to the Gentiles with the exception of Paul. He is the central figure in the affairs of the infant church (Acts 11: 19-15:41), and receives frequent mention in Paul's epistles (I Cor. 9:6; Gal. 2:1, 9, 13; Col. 4:10). Francis Bourdillon in his work on *The Minor Characters of Scripture*, places Barnabas among "The Lesser Lights." But we cannot leave him in such a category, for he shines as a star of first magnitude. He is prominent as one of those —

Whose bright faith
Makes feeble hearts grow stonger.

Barnabas struck the men of Lystra as
being like God. In fact, the Lystrans
had a legend that if the "Father in
Heaven" came down to walk on the
earth, He would be very like Barnabas. For whatever reason and however mistakenly, "they called Barnabas
Jupiter." A similar effect was produced at an earlier date. The people
of Antioch were deeply impressed
with the personality of this apostle,
for as he lived and preached with the
newly converted Saul of Tarsus in the
polluted streets of the city, the title
by which we are now privileged to
call ourselves, *Christians,* or "Christ-
men," was then coined to convey the
impression of the likeness of Barnabas
and his companions to the Master they
preached.

2. It would seem as if Barnabas
was a Jewish Hellenist from a Cypriot
family who joined the Jerusalem
church soon after Jesus' death. Many
Jews had settled on the island of
Cyprus, and although this country is
not mentioned by name among the
countries whose people heard the
apostles speak in their own tongues
on the day of Pentecost, there were
doubtless people from countries not
expressly mentioned. Do we not read
that there were then those "dwelling at Jerusalem Jews, devout men,
out of *every nation* under heaven"?
A probability is that Barnabas had
come from Cyprus to be present at
the Feast, and hearing Peter preach
the Gospel in his own native tongue,
was among the 3,000 who repented
and believed (Acts 2:41). That a deep
work of grace was wrought in his
heart is evidenced by the leading part
he took in all that followed that marvelous Pentecostal experience. Whether he went back to Cyprus to witness
among his countrymen we are not

told. It would seem that he remained
in Jerusalem where he became a notable figure, and that he was among
those disciples who were scattered
abroad in consequence of the persecution, following the death of Stephen
and who took part in spreading the
Gospel throughout Judaea and Samaria (Acts 8:1).

3. Although *Barnabas* is the name
by which we know this apostle, his
original name was *Joses,* or "Joseph,"
and he was surnamed "Barnabas" by
the apostles, after he became a Christian (Acts 4:36). As a Jew by birth,
and of the tribe of Levi, Joseph was a
fitting name for one who was to become famous as *Barnabas,* which interpreted means "the son of encouragement," or "the son of exhortation," or "the son of consolation." A
Hebrew name, according to common
usage in the Hebrew language, it
means a person great in the gifts of
prophecy or exhortation. The exact
English of Barnabas means "a son of
prophecy." Luke says that being interpreted the name implies "the son
of consolation," and there is no confusion here, for "being interpreted"
means being translated from the Hebrew language into the Greek — the
language in which the book of Acts
was written.

In Greek the same word is used for
both exhortation and consolation. It
may be that the apostles who gave
Joseph the name of *Barnabas,* meant
both of these qualities by it. Certainly
his character agrees with both. As "a
son of the power of the Paraclete,"
we find him offering new converts
"comforting counsel to keep close to
Jesus" (Acts 11:23). Barnabas was
able to give such "comforting stimulus" because he was full of the Divine Comforter. The folk in Jerusalem
called him "the son of comfort," in
the fullest sense of the word — *comfort*

indicates strength as well as tenderness. Says J. G. Greenhough of his pre-eminently suggestive name:

> The disciples gave him that name because his heart and life were brimming over with kindly thoughts, generous impulses, and helpful love. He was a man whose self-forgetting and noble spirit was free from every tinge of envy and jealousy, as his whole relationship with Paul proves, and he must have been full of that forbearing, long-suffering, all-forgiving, charity of which Paul wrote so grandly. It was that which made him take the side of the sinner in the dispute which eventually parted the two men.

Barnabas was a true "son of consolation" by which we are to understand that he had a warm heart and an open hand. There was always a close relation between his character and the complimentary title the apostles gave him, for his whole career shows evidence of a disposition peculiarly considerate and kind. He was known in the church in the character of John Bunyan's *Great-heart*. Barnabas does not strike us as having much brilliance of intellect, nor anything of original or constructive ability, as his friend Paul possessed, yet he moves in the narrative like the good angel, always loved and trusted, always on the side of sympathy with the broad interests of humanity, and therefore wielding a social influence which lifts him into great eminence in the early days of Christianity.

4. It is not without significance that Joseph was surnamed Barnabas by the apostles at the remarkable display of sacrifice when those of one heart and of one soul decided not to call what they possessed their own, but sold all to create a common fund from which each could draw an equal share (Acts 4:32-37). A landowner, Barnabas sold all his land and handed over the exact money received to the apostles. Ananias and Sapphira suffered tragic deaths for acting as if they had sold all and *given all*, but had been guilty of keeping back part of the price (Acts 5:1-11). Pride of ownership can become deep and absorbing, but the former Joseph, as a Levite, knew that by the Law, Levites were forbidden to hold estates, and now, as *Barnabas* he sold all his property, gave away the proceeds, and thereafter, like Paul, toiled at a trade that he might earn an independent living while preaching the Gospel free of charge. Paul makes significant mention of the fact that Barnabas, who had willingly impoverished himself in the interests of the church, was found laboring with his own hands to support himself on his missionary journeys.

It was after Peter and John had been released from prison following their arrest for the healing of the cripple at the Gate Beautiful, that a praise meeting was held and *Christian communism* was organized — a foregleam of the Utopia to be realized when peace and righteousness cover the earth as the waters cover the sea. We must not confuse the community of goods which the apostles instituted with the atheistic *communism* of our time which controls the lives of millions.

5. Barnabas is also notable in that he was the first to offer Paul true Christian friendship after his dramatic conversion on that Damascus Road. It was Augustine who said that "unless Stephen had prayed Paul had not preached." It is likewise true that unless Barnabas had drawn back the bolts Paul had found no open door for the Gospel. Alexander Whyte compliments Barnabas for entertaining the lonely Saul in this way, "No proud householder of them all can ever steal this honour from Barnabas, that he

was the first man of influence and responsibility who opened his heart and home to Saul of Tarsus, when all Jerusalem was still casting stones at him" (Acts 9:20-31).

The disciples in Jerusalem, who had only known Saul as a fierce persecutor of the saints who had "breathed out threatenings and slaughter against the disciples of the Lord," were afraid of him, and could hardly believe that the wolf had been tamed. But Barnabas, revered by the saints, came forward and showed great kindness toward him, although the rest shrank from Saul in fear and suspicion; Barnabas introduced him to the apostles, told the story of his miraculous conversion and how he had preached with power at Damascus (Acts 9:27). We cannot but admire this gracious conduct of Barnabas in sponsoring Saul who, when he became known as Paul the apostle, ever remembered the generous spirit "the son of encouragement" had shown.

Taking Saul under his wing, as Barnabas did, and becoming his first friend, made possible the great ministry he was to exercise. How grateful Saul must have been that his first Christian companion was a man of a large heart such as Barnabas! Out they went together to open up a larger world for Christ. In a measure, Paul came to eclipse Barnabas for he was greater in intellect and force of character than his colleague and fellow-soldier. Yet in the Acts when the two men are spoken of together, Barnabas is placed first. That was evidently the position assigned him by the church which had sent him forth. These were the first apostles to grasp the full extent of Christ's all-embracing, saving plan, and so the first to venture forth into the unknown wastes of heathendom to claim the whole world for the Master.

Such a mighty enterprise had its origin in the heart and mind of Barnabas, and then Paul embodied it and gave it expression in his wider and grander labors. Such a conbination reminds us of Martin Luther and his friend, Philip Melancthon. The latter, the less-known man, had the first vision of the Reformation, and the former man of greater energy worked the vision into fact. To Barnabas, the light came first, and securing Saul, these two became messengers "to the regions beyond, being willing to "hazard their lives for the name of the Lord Jesus" (Acts 11:25; 15:25, 26; Gal. 2:1-10).

As Paul came into greater prominence, Barnabas quietly fell back into second place, and before long dropped out of the story. There came that serious conflict between them over John Mark (Gal. 2:11-13; Acts 15:36-41), which led to a definite breach between them, with Barnabas returning to Cyprus (Acts 15:39). The last reference to him was the one Paul made a few years later when it would seem as if they were friends again and together in harness (I Cor. 9:6).

EPAPHRODITUS

The Apostle Who Risked His All

One cannot read the epistles of Paul, studded as they are with the names of saints to whom he has given everlasting remembrance, without realizing what a genius for friendship he had. Thinking of the New Testament as a whole, no man made fiercer enemies than Paul, but few men in the world had better friends. They cluster around him so thickly, specially in *Romans*, that we are apt to lose their personality in their devotion. As Alexander Whyte expresses it, "Paul so eclipses every one of his contemporaries that it is with the utmost difficulty we can get a glimpse of any one but Paul." But Paul, in his generous mention of friends who swarmed around him as bees around a honey-pot, compels us to think of the striking figures who followed in his train.

The staff officers of this great soldier of the cross were themselves quite capable of leading a victorious campaign, or doing efficient service independently, and it is most profitable to consider some of these loyal followers separately, to restore to them their golden and unbroken circle of fellowship and service. One of these was *Epaphroditus* who was bound to Paul by the cords of love. It was William Penn who, centuries ago, described the seven features of deep-hearted friendship in this way:

"A true friend unbosoms freely,
Advises justly,
Assists readily,
Adventures boldly,
Takes all patiently,
Defends courageously, and
Continues a friend unchangeably."

As we are to see, Epaphroditus answers this drastic test without flinching. To Paul he was a friend sticking closer than a brother. As a friend in need he was a friend indeed. While he was one of Paul's choice companions, and we are including him in the enlarged band of apostles, it has been questioned whether he should be numbered among them. In his commendation of Epaphroditus, Paul refers to him in writing to the saints at Philippi as "your messenger" (Phil. 2:25-30).

Both words, *messenger* and *apostle*, are the same original word in the Greek, and the margin of the R.V.

gives "your apostle." Some expositors have suggested that Epaphroditus was the bishop or chief pastor of the Philippian church, but there is no example of a pastor of a church ever being called its *apostle*. Among "the messengers of the church," Paul included Titus, and here again the R.V. gives us "the apostles of the church" (II Cor. 8:16-24). While we do not know whether Epaphroditus had the essential qualifications for original apostleship (Acts 1:21, 22), of this we are certain, he possessed all the *spiritual* virtues as "one sent forth" to witness for the Master, and was part of "the glory of Christ" which Paul speaks of in Second Corinthians 8:23 (R.V. margin).

All we know of Epaphroditus, the gallant Macedonian, is recorded in two vivid passages in Paul's cheery letter to the Philippian church, but from these brief sketches we gain a good deal of insight into the life and character of this saint who was so precious to Paul the aged. Although *Epaphras* is a contracted form of *Epaphroditus*, we must not confuse him with the messenger of the Philippian community we are presently considering. Epaphras was indeed another friend and co-laborer of Paul whose imprisonment he shared (Philem. 23). Epaphras was the missionary by whose instrumentality the Colossians were converted to Christianity (Col. 1:7; 4:12). Paul manifested his regard for him by designating him "our dear fellow-servant" and "a servant of Christ Jesus" — a description Paul uses several times of himself but only once of another besides Epaphras (Col. 1:7; 4:12; Phil. 1:1).

Paul initiates us into the true character of Epaphroditus, who was one of the most loyal and devoted servants of the Lord mentioned in the Pauline epistles. The apostle's love toward true believers knew no bounds, and we have a manifestation of his intense love for the Philippians in his attitude relating to Epaphroditus, who was one of their number, and who, at the risk of his life, had undertaken the hazardous journey to Rome that he might convey a substantial gift to God's imprisoned servant. The strain of that journey had brought on a sickness so serious that for some time Epaphroditus was at death's door; but God graciously granted him recovery that he might be able to perform further acts of Christlike love. Thus, we are brought to his two-fold value:

1. *His Value to Paul*

The apostle testified in a four-fold way to the quality and qualifications of his much-loved friend. The first three designations are arranged in an ascending scale and in the Greek are closely joined together and form a kind of climax. Each of the names Paul has for his friend begins with a prefix and implies a tie of some sort — "a brother in love"; "a partner in work"; "a comrade in fight." Here are common sympathy, common works, common danger and suffering. Paul, then, praises Epaphroditus for his tenderness, his industry, his courage. It is rare indeed to find these three qualities in combination. The tender man is not always industrious, nor the strong man always tender, yet this trinity of graces possessed the soul of Epaphroditus and his fellow-believers saw his "beautiful actions and glorified his Father in Heaven," according to Christ's prophecy in the Sermon on the Mount.

My brother (Phil. 2:25)

This was a relationship based upon regeneration. In all likelihood Epaphroditus was a convert of Paul, or possibly of Luke, and, as a believer, all

others with a similar experience of Christ's saving grace and mercy were his brothers and his sisters. Thus Paul thought of his friend as a brother in a common Christianity. Having received the spirit of adoption, this Philippian apostle could call God his Father, and Paul his brother. One interpretation of the name of Epaphroditus is *lovable,* and he certainly made for himself a singular place in Paul's affection who, with deep feeling could speak of him as, "My brother."

My companion in labor (Phil. 2:25)

Useful in his ministry, he earned the reputation of Paul's fellow-worker in the service of the Master. If the first good point speaks of Paul's unreserved love and fellowship, this second quality reveals the cordial help and courage received from his "brother." When C. H. Spurgeon pastored The Metropolitan Tabernacle, London, a lone old woman used to sit, Sunday after Sunday, picking out a score of strange faces in the congregation for whom to pray during the week. Anyone seeing her would have thought that she was of little use to her pastor, but when Spurgeon officiated at her funeral he gratefully referred to her as his "best helper." Epaphroditus was one of Paul's best helpers, being among those gifts of the Lord to His Church, which the apostle describes as *helps* (I Cor. 12:28).

My fellowsoldier (Phil. 2:25)

What an expressive picture this is! My comrade in arms. Here Paul praises his companion for his endurance and championship, "My fellow-soldier who was sick unto death," and then goes on to dwell upon his unflagging constancy saying that, "he made up for the services you were not here to render." Epaphroditus shared in the hardness of daring and suffering, which the warfare of the cross implies (II Tim. 2:3, 4). There has never been a more gallant knight than the apostle Paul, or ever a more puissant defender of the faith; and at such a flame, Epaphroditus lit his candle. In him, Paul found a kindred spirit, and so called him "a soldier like myself."

In Rome, these noble companions were under the shadow of pagan gods, and when the true God was blasphemed or the cross reviled or the Scriptures assailed, could these two co-workers in arms keep silence? A thousand times, *No!* As fellow-soldiers they stood with shields over-lapped and lances poised for the defense of truth and righteousness. Bishop Lightfoot, in his illuminating *Commentary on Philippians* reminds us that an inscription at Philippi bore the name of *Gaius Clodius Epaphroditus,* and suggests that possibly a similar association of names might identify the Epaphroditus of Philippi with *Gaius,* the Macedonian companion of Paul who worked together with Aristarchus was caught in the Ephesian outbreak, and escaped murder by a hair's breadth (Acts 19:29). If this is so, we have a further illustration of the gallantry of Paul's fellow-fighter.

My minister (Phil. 2:25)

What a heart-warming phrase this is!—"He that ministered to my wants." We have seen the significance of "your messenger," or *apostle.* So we have the spectacle of one apostle ministering to the needs of another apostle. Is there not a sacrificial solemnity about this word *minister?* It is a word having sacred and patriotic associations and is the root of our word *liturgy.* This suggests that Epaphroditus went to Paul's relief in Rome with the feeling of a priest carrying an offering, both

fragrant and acceptable to God and man (Phil. 2:25; 4:18).

2. His Value to the Church

That Epaphroditus was held in high repute by the saints in Philippi is evident from what Paul says about his unselfish service on behalf of the church there. Briefly stated the situation described was this:

While at Rome, Epaphroditus was taken desperately ill, being "nigh unto death." His sickness was the result of his earnest devotion to the work of Christ. He was homesick for Philippi, longing to see the saints there again. Somehow his friends at Philippi were advised of his illness and were sorrowful on that account.

Epaphroditus heard of their sorrow and because of his love for them was full of heaviness. His recovery was due to a special mercy of God.

He was now returning to Philippi. He and Paul with all his other friends would unite in thanksgiving to God. Paul besought for him that the church should receive him with joy and hold him in honor, as we are most sure they did because of the way he had disregarded his life to supply that service of love which they had been unable to manifest through lack of opportunity.

There are two or three phrases in the cameo which Paul sketches of Epaphroditus that call for closer examination. For instance, the two clauses, "Longed after you all", and "was full of heaviness" are distinct from each other in the decision of Paul to send his friend home. The original of the first clause is strong and implies, "because he was continually longing" (1:8; 2:26; 4:1) — he had such a yearning to see the saints at Philippi again. "Full of heaviness" suggests that he was *distressed and uneasy,* because of the anxiety which the news of his apparently fatal illness had caused.

But the miracle was that although "he was sick nigh unto death," yet "God had mercy on him," then note, "and not on him only, *but on me also,* lest I should have sorrow upon sorrow" — the latter clause meaning that Paul did not want the sorrow of losing one who had risked his life for his sake, to be added to the sorrow of his captivity (2:27, 30). As an *apostle,* Paul had power to heal, yet such a power, great as it was, was not his own, to use at his own will. Miracleworking, "the sign of an apostle," was given at special times (Acts 19:11; II Cor. 12:8-10). In the sickness of Epaphroditus, "the apostle could not, as our Lord would not, work miracles for His own needs," as Ellicott comments. "Thus, in this case, deeply as Paul sorrowed for Epaphroditus, there is no hint of his exercising that power on his behalf. He could only pray that God would have mercy on him, and thank God when that prayer was heard."

Further, there is a wealth of significance in the phrase, "He was nigh unto death, *not regarding his life*" (2: 30). J. B. Phillips expresses that last phrase, "*He risked his life* to do for me in person what distance prevented you all from doing." Mason in one of his fine character studies, *The Truants,* depicts Anthony Stretton hazarding life and love in recovery of an endangered ideal.

"There will be great risks," said his friend.

"I have counted them," Stretton replied.

"But there is a prize too proportionate to the risks. Take the risk halfheartedly and your boat's swamped. But take it with all your heart and there is the prize to your credit. It will have been well worth waiting for."

And out he goes into the night, with this as his watchword —

One must take one's risks.

Was it not this counting of the risk, and facing it whole-heartedly, which greatly impressed Paul in the service of Epaphroditus? Between the lines of his praise of this devoted companion of his, we can read something of the personal risk involved in bringing the generous gift from the church at Philippi to Paul. Epaphroditus was not only ill but suffered from poor health in general; but such a disability had no terror for this man of high motive and holy daring (Phil. 2:30). He knew all about the risk, but staked his life with calmness, if only he could be at Paul's side to comfort him. So out he went and faced the hazards and found a prize proportionate to the risk — the reward of Paul's great delight at seeing him and in receiving fruit from his prized garden at Philippi (Phil. 2:25; 4:10, 17). Apparently unhealthy, he squarely faced the possibility of death, but came out in the end triumphant (see II Cor. 11:9).

There is still a further thought arising out of the phrase Paul uses in his report to the Philippians about Epaphroditus, "not regarding his life." This phrase, in the original, is the word *Paraboleuomai,* and means, "to throw aside"; "to expose onself to danger"; "to hazard one's life." The R.V. gives us "hazard" here in Philippians 2:30 and the term is akin to Paul and Barnabas who "hazarded" (risked) their lives for the name of the Lord Jesus (Acts 15:26). This same word *Paradidomi* is given as "betrayed" in connection with Judas' foul deed (Matt. 17:22). It the betrayer entertained the thought that Jesus would perform a miracle and deliver Himself out of the hands of those who paid the fatal price, he took a great risk — and lost!

Ellicott's most reliable *Commentary*

says that the phrase, "not regarding his life," as given in the A.V. can be given the sense, "having hazarded his life," or literally, *having gambled with his life,* not merely having staked it, but staked it recklessly. There may be a possible allusion here to the *caution money,* staked in a cause to show that it was not frivolous and vexatious, and forfeited in the case of loss. Epaphroditus, risking his life through over-exertion in the cause of Christ, as a prisoner awaiting trial, actually *gambled with his life* for such a notable purpose. The journey made by this kind-hearted man to relieve the need of an old minister who had worn himself out in the service of Christ, involved a tremendous risk, but it paid off!

In *Paradise Lost,* John Milton wrote of —

United thoughts and counsels equal hope,
(And hazard in the glorious enterprise.)

Well, Epaphroditus knew all about hazarding his life in the most glorious enterprise of all, the service of his Master. This utter disregard of his own life was akin to the quality of abandonment of which Shakespeare reminds us in *The Merchant of Venice*:

Men that hazard all
Do it in hope of fair advantages:
A golden mind stoops not to show of dross.

Again, there may be an association between this sacrificial act and the name he bore — *Epaphroditus,* which was a common one in the Roman Period and occurs often in both Greek and Latin inscriptions. Harrington Lees suggests that we have here one of those touches of humor which marked the earnest apostle who played on his friend's name. Such play on personal names was frequent in Eastern life. For instance, Zacharias in his *Benedictus* plays on the names of his wife — *God's oath;* his son — *Jehovah's mercy;* and himself — *Jehovah's memory,* in the words, "To perform the mercy, and to remember his covenant, the oath which he sware" (Luke 1:72, 73). Then we know how Paul, in his tender letter to Philemon, played on the name of Onesimus, the runaway slave, which means, *the unprofitable.* Although he had been so unprofitable to his master in the past, now a Christian through Paul's ministry, Onesimus would prove most *profitable.*

When Paul wrote his letter to Philippi he implied, "Epaphroditus is a regular gambler where his life is concerned" (Phil. 2:30) — a jest on his name, for *Epaphroditus* is a gambler's word. With the Greeks and the Romans *Aphrodite* or *Venus* was the goddess of good luck at games of chance. The highest throw with the dice was called the *Aphrodite* or *Venus;* and the man who was lucky in play was called *Epaphroditus* or *Venustus,* because he had incurred hazards and come out a winner seeing his hand had been guided by a heathen deity. So Paul, possibly with a smile on his lips, wrote that Epaphroditus, his fellow-soldier, had risked his life on a throw, and came out of the risk successfully because the hand of God was in it. Those like Zebulun and Naphtali and Barnabas and Paul and Epaphroditus, "Men who have jeopardized their lives unto the death in the high place of the field," are proofs of the watching eye and protecting hand of God (Judg. 5:18; Acts 15:26; Phil. 2:30).

In the Middle Ages there was a band of godly men who for Christ's sake took their risks and went into plague-infected houses to minister to the sick, and who called themselves

Parabolani — "The Gamblers," confident that the Everlasting Arms were their sufficient shelter. Wyclif's old rendering of Joseph's issue from his risks is suggestive, "The Lord was with him and he was a lucky fellow" (Gen. 39:2). As soldiers of the King we are frequently faced with the necessity of taking risks: we are God's gamblers, but He holds our hands as we throw the dice, and we win.

Before we leave our meditation of *The Apostle Who Risked His All,* a word is necessary as to the choice language Paul uses to describe the gift which Epaphroditus had risked his life to bring to Rome. Unknown sickness laid its grip upon his overworked frame and nearly carried him off, but "God had mercy upon him," and he was able to finish his course with joy. It was said that Alexander, the Macedonian conqueror, carried everywhere with him a statuette of Hercules, the demi-god of strength and triumph over difficulties and dangers, the hero of twelve successful campaigns. But Epaphroditus, another Macedonian, set *the Lord* before him, confident that in Him all risks would be surmounted, and his task completed.

To the laboring church at Philippi the news came that Paul was a prisoner in Rome, after shipwreck and loss of all his personal effects, and the question was raised concerning his comfort and supplies, but no one seemed to be available to send at the time. "You thought about it, but had no opportunity" (Phil. 4:10). Later on, Epaphroditus volunteered to represent the church as their accredited messenger or apostle, "to make up for the services it was not theirs to render" (Phil. 2:25, 30, margin). The monetary help he brought to Paul cheered the apostle's heart. "Your thoughtfulness for me has just burst into bloom

again." Acknowledging the gift Paul wrote, "I have all, and abound: I am full, having received of Epaphroditus the things which were sent from you, an odour of a sweet smell, a sacrifice acceptable, well-pleasing to God" (Phil. 4:18).

The language here seems to indicate that Paul offered the gift to God before he used it. Somehow it was tinged with a double sacrifice, namely, that of the church that gave it, and the great physical risk on the part of the one who brought it to Paul. The word he employed for *sacrifice* implies the idea of propitiation, "a bloody sacrifice" (Rom. 12:1; I Pet. 2:5). How long Epaphroditus remained with Paul after delivering the tangible token of the affection and concern of the Philippian church, we are not told. Whether the days were few or many, it must have been a time of hallowed fellowship with Paul helping his kinsman, by "breathing in thoughts that burn."

JAMES, THE LORD'S BROTHER

THE APOSTLE WHO PREACHED PRACTICAL MORALITY

Because *James* was a common name in New Testament times, and some four bearers of the same are mentioned, speculation has gathered around the exact identification of the James we are now considering. He should not be confused with the two apostles enumerated in the list of those chosen by the Master, namely, James, the son of Alphaeus, and James, the son of Zebedee (Matt. 10:2, 3), both of whom we have already considered. Neither of them could have been the Lord's brother, because Scripture states quite definitely that Jesus' brothers did not believe on Him during His earthly ministry.

However we are convinced that the James with whom Paul counseled (Gal. 1:19; 2:9) was not one of the twelve, and is only called an apostle as Barnabas and others were in the wider circle with which we are now dealing. Let us gather together the references to this James who is famous in Jerusalem and see if they can tell us much of his character and witness.

1. A Brother of the Lord

What a definite and descriptive statement this is that Paul gives us in the account of a visit to Jerusalem some three years after his remarkable conversion! "But other of the apostles saw I none, save *James the Lord's brother*" (Gal. 1:19). What an arrestive phrase this is to pause at and ponder over! Both Matthew and Mark give us the family circle in the home where Jesus lived for the first thirty years of His life: "Is not this the carpenter's son? is not his mother called Mary? and his brethren, James, and Joses, and Simon, and Judas? And his sisters, are they not all with us?" Matt. 13:55, 56; Mark 6:3). Can we not conjure up the happiness of that home at Nazareth — Joseph and Mary, four sons, and at least two daughters,

and Jesus! Some commentators think they were children of Joseph by a former marriage and therefore all older than Jesus, and having no blood-relationship with Jesus. Another theory held the "brethren of the Lord" to be His *cousins,* sons of Mary, the wife of Alphaeus, "brother" here implying merely kinship as Abraham calls himself and his nephew Lot "brethren" (Gen. 13:8), and Laban calls Jacob, his sister's son, his "brother" (Gen. 29: 15). The Roman Catholic Church teaches Mary's perpetual virginity, implying that she never married, and had no other children apart from Jesus, whose conception was miraculous.

It is clearly evident, however, that Mary had other children, for Jesus is referred to as "her *first-born* son," or the first to whom she gave birth. According to Rome's contention this should have read "her only son" (Luke 2:7). We believe that Jesus was miraculously conceived in Mary while she was yet a virgin and that, thereafter, the four sons and daughters followed in due course, along the avenue of natural generation as a reward for her willingness to become the mother of our Lord whom she dedicated to God from the womb (see I Sam. 1:20-28; 2:1-11, 18-21). As the sons and daughters came one by one and grew up with Jesus, and passed through the phases of childhood, youth, and womanhood or manhood, what an honored family it must have been with Jesus in the midst. We know that He was subject to His mother and to His foster-father, and set an example in holy living for the younger children to emulate. His four brothers are named, but His sisters are unnamed, and all, at least seven of them, grew up together side by side.

As we are thinking of James, one of His brothers, we wonder how he grew up under the influence of a godly home and of a perfect Brother. Was he molded by such a holy atmosphere, created by his elder Brother who was holiness incarnate, who had a perfect character at each age—a perfect child; a perfect youth; a perfect Son; a perfect brother; a perfect man? Elder Cumming paints this beautiful picture of that privileged Nazareth home:

> Unseen, that home was full of angels, who had begged of God to be allowed to come and look on! Unheard, their sweetest songs and praises were sung there; unheard, except by God! What a light was there, sweeter than that of an evening star, yet lonelier than the star of morn! What love was there, tenderer than a mother's, yet stronger far than woman's! What truth was there; what a study of the Word, which we call the Old Testament, there in its roll written on both sides, which He never wearied in reading! What times of prayer, as the young voice sounded through the closet door, pleading, praising, rejoicing, weeping for sinners, taking hold of God!

2. *An Adversary of the Lord*

As Jesus was about thirty years of age when He left the home in which He was sheltered for so long, His own brothers and sisters experienced a most intimate association with Him as He "increased in wisdom and stature, and in favour with God and man" (Luke 2:52). Were His own kith and kin loved into holiness of life by such a Brother at their side? The astounding fact is that in spite of His life and witness all through the years they were together, His brothers did not believe in His Messiahship (John 7: 3-5). They sneered at Him and once they concluded that He — their own Brother — was mad, and sought to arrest Him and convey Him away from Capernaum lest He should cast

further reflection upon the old home (Mark 3:21, 31).

It was this adverse treatment on the part of His own family that led Him to declare openly, "My mother and my brethren are these (those around waiting spellbound upon His message) which hear the word of God and do it" (Luke 8:21). Then can we not detect the significance of His further declaration that "A prophet is not without honour, save in his own country," and note the suggestive clause, "and *in his own house*" (Matt. 13:57). As Christ was applying the whole verse to Himself, the deduction is that He was referring pathetically to the unbelieving attitude taken toward Him by those in the home He had left behind. A further sorrow is that there is not a single trace, even in tradition, that His own dear *sisters* ever embraced the true faith which their illustrious Brother embodied and enunciated.

We cannot but believe that Jesus was good in the eyes of His brothers and sisters. They could find no fault in Him as He went about doing His heavenly Father's business. What, then, is the explanation of the rejection of His witness? Perhaps there were two factors responsible for their unbelief. First of all, they may not have been prepared to follow Him in the entire committal to God He manifested. He was without sin, and lived by a standard too severe for them. No compromise with the evil of the world, opposition to every form of sin, perpetual self-denial, and utter devotion to God represented a high level of living they could not endure. His presence in the home was a perpetual rebuke to those brothers and sisters who were among "his own [who] received him not" (John 1:11).

The second reason for their unbelieving attitude may have been His constant claims as the Messiah predicted of old, and who had been hoped for by all past ages in Israel. To His brothers and sisters it seemed incredible that He would be able to perform miracles, which He did at every stage of His career. Tradition relates many fanciful miracles He performed even as a boy at home. Not present at His first miracle at the marriage in Cana after leaving home, His own family must have heard about it from Mary who was there. Yet they were not persuaded that He was indeed the Messiah that should come. From then, on, His brothers and sisters became more intimately acquainted with His marvelous works and mighty words, but it would seem as if they remained in unbelief right up until the cross was reached. We all know from our own observation that often the most ungodly children come from the most godly homes, and they become foes of their own saintly household.

3. A Convert of the Lord

The record is that Calvary and the resurrection brought about a wonderful transformation in the brothers of our Lord. But because of the omission of His sisters in the mention of the women gathered in the upper room after the resurrection, it would seem as if they continued in their unbelief (Acts 1:14). Convinced by so tremendous a demonstration of Christ's victory over the grave, His brothers joined the company of believers, entering, thereby, His Church. James was won to faith by a special manifestation of the Risen Lord (I Cor. 15:7)— and what a trophy of divine grace he became. James became one of the earliest witnesses to the resurrection. What a moment that must have been when the Risen Lord and James met, not only as one-time brothers, but now as Master and disciple. "He was seen of James." When Paul penned this phrase the one *James* he had in mind was "James, the Lord's brother."

Why did our Lord make a special appearance to *him?* Well, he would be of all men best qualified to know whether Jesus was the same man he had known so well, and convinced he was, he repented of his unbelief and became a believer. As for his other brothers, Joses and Simon and Judas, whether James had influenced them likewise to accept Christ as their Savior and Messiah we are not told. What is evident is that they, too, were converted at the same time as their elder brother, for *all* the brethren of the Lord are found assembled together with the church with one accord and supplication waiting for the promise of the Father, and that on the day of Pentecost all four brothers were among those disciples to whom the Holy Spirit gave utterance to preach the reconciling Word. From this time on, James stands out from his brothers, and became an apostle.

4. An Apostle of the Lord

After the death of James the brother of John, Peter was thrown into prison, and after his miraculous release, requested that the news be sent to James, the Lord's brother, and to the brethren in Jerusalem (Acts 12:17). This implies that by this time James had become an authority in the church there and figures in the capacity as bishop or leader on three occasions.

A. Three years after his conversion Paul went up to Jerusalem to interview Peter, and, though he stayed there for fifteen days with Peter, Paul saw no one else except James (Gal. 1:18, 19). The eminence and authority of James were equal to Peter's.

B. After an interval of fourteen years Paul went up again to Jerusalem. This was the occasion of the historic conference regarding the terms on which the Gentiles should be admitted into the Christian Church. The speech of James on this occasion expressing his sympathy with the religious needs of the Gentile world, and his desire that formalism should raise no barrier to their moral and spiritual advancement, indicated that he was a man who loved peace more than faction, and the spirit more than the law, and a harmony in which all, in spite of different forms of observance, might live and labor together in common allegiance to Christ. His presidential speech was unanimously accepted (Acts 15:14-34; see Gal. 2:1, 9).

C. It was to James, acknowledged as the head of the church at Jerusalem, that Paul returned from his third missionary journey to recount in the presence of the elders, of the Lord's doing. At this meeting Paul was admonished for exceeding the orders he had received at the first Council (Acts 21:17-21).

From First Corinthians 9:5 it has been inferred that James was married. But this is only a conjecture, for the passage speaks about those "who led about a sister, a wife." As far as we know, James did not travel about, but remained in Jerusalem all his life. As we shall discover in our next chapter, tradition has much to say about the Apostle James, surnamed "James the Just."

5. A Scribe of the Lord

The remaining feature to dwell upon is the well-established fact that "James, the Lord's brother," was the writer of the epistle bearing his honored name. It is interesting to observe how he commences his epistle, "James, a servant (that is, *slave*, the lowest kind of servant) of God and of the Lord Jesus Christ" (James 1:1). Here we have an indication of his character in styling himself not the *brother*, but the slave of his Master; a mark of modesty in that although he was the brother of the Lord, he had no wish to insist on his relationship after the flesh. He was adverse to making capital out of such a privilege.

Although James did not believe in Jesus in the days of His flesh, he must have listened attentively to His teaching, for his references to Him reveal how steeped his mind was not only in the substance of such but also in its phraseology. We have been reminded by one expositor that "James says less about the Master than any other writer in the New Testament, but his speech is more like that of the Master than the speech of any one of them. There are at least ten parallels to the Sermon on the Mount in this short Epistle, and for almost everything that James has to say we can recall some statement of Jesus which might have suggested it. When the parallels fail at any point, we are inclined to suspect that James may be repeating some unrecorded utterance of our Lord. He seems absolutely faithful to his memory of his Brother's teaching. He is the servant of Jesus in all his exhortation and persuasion."

Twice over James gives his former Brother His full title: *The Lord Jesus Christ* (1:1; 2:1), and several times he used the term *Lord*. Doubt once ruled his mind as to the Messiahship of Christ, but now James magnifies Him as the sole object of faith, and as the "Lord of glory" (2:1) — which ascription is offered to each of the Persons of the Trinity, but to no one else. Whenever he uses the designation *the Lord*, we are safe in assuming that "the Lord Jesus" is meant. Thus we have these expressive aspects of all He is in Himself:

The Promiser and Giver of Eternal Life (1:12; 2:5)

The God of Providence (4:15)

The Hearer of Prayer, and Restorer of the Sick (1:5; 5:15)

The Coming Lord (5:7)

The Righteous Judge (5:9)

The Inspirer of the Prophets (5:10)

Is it not a wonderful triumph of grace that James, who lived at the side of Jesus day and night for almost thirty years, and yet failed to see His glory as the only-begotten of the Father, should come to think and write of Him as he did? What a testimony! "James, the brother of the Lord" had become "the slave of God, and of the Lord Jesus Christ, the Lord of Glory."

As we examine the epistle which James wrote, we cannot but observe the remarkable resemblance in its language to the speech he gave before the assembly in Jerusalem, and how the same casts light upon the character of the writer. Going back to the address he gave, and to the letter drawn up and his suggestion, note these verbal resemblances in the language of his *epistle*. Compare —

Acts 15:23 with James 1:1

Acts 15:17 with James 2:7

Acts 15:13 with James 2:5

Acts 15:20 with James 1:27

Acts 15:29 with James 1:27

Both his *address* and *epistle* show the thoroughly Jewish as well as Christian character of James, who in his *epistle* makes faith the essence of true religion and urges upon "the twelve tribes scattered abroad," a spiritual interpretation of the ancient Law. Written by a Jew to Jewish Christians, there is a good deal that is distinctly Jewish in the style and spirit of the *epistle*, which has an air of patriarchal authority about it, seeing it came from the pen of the father of the church at Jerusalem. Thus it is thoroughly Hebrew in tone, feeling, and lang-

uage. The following short coverage of *James* may help to whet the appetite of the reader for a more extensive study of this epistle which more than any other epistle deals with the *external* life of a believer, whether Jewish or Gentile.

Its date

Biblical authorities are coming to agree that we have in *James,* the *first* of the New Testament epistles, of which there are twenty-one. If it was written between A.D. 45 and A.D. 53, then such a date is of vast importance. The idea was held that James wrote his epistle to combat the Pauline view of justification by faith, as unfolded in *Romans,* but as *James* was written some years *before* Paul wrote *Romans,* this could not have been Jame's purpose in writing his epistle. Martin Luther felt that James stressed *works* contrary to the grand doctrine of justification by faith in Romans, that he felt called upon to champion. So he called *James,* "A right strawy Epistle, having no true evangelical character." In after years, the Reformer saw differently and held that James is really the complement of Paul. As Dr. A. T. Pierson puts it, "Paul and James do not conflict. They stand not face to face, beating each other, but back to back beating off common foes."

Its purpose

Jews, representing the twelve tribes scattered abroad because of bitter persecution, were facing severe trials and temptations, and James writes to comfort and encourage them. There were likewise a few grave disorders in some of the early Jewish Christian assemblies, and in his letter James sought to correct them. Then there was a tendency to divorce faith and works, and so James endeavored to show that the only true *hearer* of the Word is the *doer* of the Word: that the Word of God is a *mirror* to reveal what manner of man we are, and to influence character and conduct (1:22-25). Every true inward grace must bear outward fruits.

This is the reason why there is little doctrine in *James,* but plenty about practice and morals. This indicates how exceedingly practical the apostle was — and he lived what he preached! The *key words* of the epistle are "works," occurring thirteen times; "faith," twelve times; "doer," five times. The *key verse* reads: "For as the body without the spirit is dead, so faith without works is dead also" (2:26). This then is an epistle on *holy living,* with great stress laid upon works, not apart from faith, but as both the proof and fruit of faith. It gives us the morality-side to the Gospel of grace. As those redeemed by the blood, we cannot live as we like, only as the Redeemer dictates. Our liberty in Christ does not mean license. Although a man of a theological cast of mind, James was likewise decidedly practical. While he does not deal with the great fundamentals of faith, they are in the background of his thinking as he affirms that all profession and every creed which do not make their holders good and holy men are a delusion. James was fully persuaded that faith which brings a man to God is a faith which lives and works in a world of need.

Its outline

The epistle does not lend itself to a clear-cut division of contents. Like *Proverbs,* it is somewhat fragmentary and disconnected, like so many scattered pearls of truth. Yet as Robert Lee suggests, on closer inspection a beautiful order is discernible —

Christian Greeting 1:1
Chapter 1:2-21

Faith tested and shown by our temptations
Chapters 1:22-2
Faith shown by our works
Chapter 3
Faith shown by our words
Chapter 4
Faith shown by lives of unworldliness
Chapter 5:1-12
Faith shown by our patience under cruel wrong
Chapter 5:13-20
Faith shown by our believing and effectual prayers

JUNIAS, or JUNIA

The Apostle Whom Paul Praised

As Junias is paired with Andronicus, all we have written about him (see page 183) is applicable to Junias, seeing Paul's greeting at the close of his epistle to the Romans was addressed to them both (16:7). Like his companion, Junias was among the first converts after Pentecost, or "early disciples" such as Mnason of Cyprus (Acts 21:16). Both of these men were well known to the apostolate circle, and are distinguished as *apostles* — the term being used in the widest sense as missionaries (I Cor. 15:7). The prophetic ministry of the early church consisted of apostles, prophets, and teachers (I Cor. 12:28; Eph. 4:11). Some apostles functioned as missionaries being sent out to different areas by particular churches (Acts 13:2, 3; II Cor. 8:23; Phil. 2:25). Both Andronicus and Junias were faithful and sacrificial envoys of the Gospel, as Paul's description of them testifies.

MATTHIAS

The Apostle Chosen by Lot

Visitors to Venice are familiar with the Doge's Palace, and with one of its peculiar features. On the Council Chamber there is a medallion or frieze of figures famous in the history of the sea-born Republic. In this series of remarkable portraits running around the wall there is a noticeable gap, as if one of the pictures had fallen or been removed. In this empty space is a black tablet with this inscription — *This is the place of Mariono Falieri beheaded for his crimes.* That blank in the cornice of the Venetian Valhalla marks the disgrace of the traitor, and the epitaph on the empty space records the national detestation of the betrayer.

This striking memorial of the disloyal Doge well illustrates the omission of the name of Judas Iscariot from the portrait gallery of the twelve, which Luke gives us in the Acts, where only *eleven* figures are presented in his list of the original apostles (Acts 1:13). The *twelfth* niche is empty, and notice is plain — *This is the place of Judas Iscariot who played a leading part in the greatest tragedy of human history.* The absence of his name from the apostolic list indicates that the Cain brand was stamped upon his character and the tragic crime had thrown back its ominous outline of his memory. But the rest of the apostles gathered in the upper room at Jerusalem to fill the gap with another portrait to complete the twelve. "His bishoprick let another take" (Acts 1:13-26; see Psalm 109:8). From a study of the ancient prophecy the apostles knew that the vacant place must be filled.

What is clearly evident about the choice of a successor to Judas is that it was the Holy Spirit who prompted David to predict that a successor to the betrayer must be found who had all the qualifications necessary for the office of apostle. The question is, was Matthias the successor whom Christ

called (for He it was who called the twelve as He entered His ministry)? The Holy Spirit was not yet given, by whose immediate dictates and inspirations the apostles were to be chiefly guided from this point on. They were still in the upper chamber praying and waiting for the promise of the Father. Seeking to fill the vacancy in the college of the apostles, Peter stood forth and, rehearsing the tragic deed and death of Judas, pressed upon the rest the necessity of choosing a successor — one who had been a constant companion and disciple of Jesus, and who was able, consequently, to bear witness to His life, death, and resurrection.

Among the many who were well-known to the apostles as fulfilling these qualifications — for Peter said, "Wherefore of these men which have companied with us all the time that the Lord Jesus went in and out among us" (Acts 1:21)— two were appointed, namely "Joseph called Barsabas, who was surnamed Justus, and Matthias." As to *Barsabas*, we have no knowledge of his personal history apart from the fact that after being an adherent of John the Baptist, he was one of those who followed Christ — probably one of the seventy He sent forth, and that he satisfied all the qualifications for apostleship. The Judas Barsabas who along with Silas was chosen by the rulers of the Church at Jerusalem to accompany Paul and Barnabas to Antioch, is reckoned to have been a brother of Joseph Barsabas, nominated along with Matthias to be voted on to fill the vacancy in the apostleship (Acts 15:22-23). It is likewise true that we have no clue as to the identity of Matthias, the one chosen (he is never mentioned again in the New Testament).

The problem is, Can Matthias be reckoned, by divine right, as the twelfth apostle, even though he is included in the twelve of whom Luke speaks (Acts 6:2)? The validity of the whole proceeding by Peter has been questioned upon several grounds. The small company of believers approved Peter's suggestion that a successor to Judas should be chosen by lot, and Matthias was elected. But although the election to office was an honest transaction, it was nevertheless a human choice, being made by the eleven apostles themselves who acted on their own initiative to appoint a successor. It would seem as if there is not sufficient reason to believe that they were divinely directed in their action, that they were premature in such, seeing Jesus had constantly laid emphasis on the fact that the disciples were His choice and His alone, "Have not *I* chosen you twelve?" "Ye have not chosen me, but *I* have chosen you" (John 6:70; 15:16; Acts 1:2).

Can it be, then, that the apostles undertook to do what Jesus had kept in His own power? Quoting David's prediction about another filling the place of Judas, they concluded that they should act upon the matter, and so resolved to appoint a successor. Doubtless they thought that a man should be appointed in time to partake of the promised blessing of Pentecost when it came, but there is no hint that they sought guidance from God before the choice of the two candidates who were presented. Evidently they took it for granted that He would approve, and only prayed when a decision of choice was necessary: "Show whether of these two *thou* hast chosen." Does this not imply that, having made *their* choice of Barsabas and Matthias, they were *giving God the choice between the two*, without submitting to Him the questions, whether anyone was to be appointed

at that time, or whether there was any other whom He thought best?

Alas! are we not guilty of the same fault? We make up our minds to do certain things, and ask God to bless them and bring good out of them. We go to Him, not *before* a course of action, but *after* we have decided upon it. We do not ask Him what to do, but to bless what we are doing. We do not want Him to take charge of the springs of action, but only to direct their results. Are we like those eleven in the upper chamber who presented their choice of two out of many disciples, then asked Him to show which of the two He has chosen, when the truth was that they had chosen both themselves? Do we act and then pray?

The answer to their prayer as to which of the two should take the vacancy in the apostolate was to be decided *by lot*. While Barsabas and Matthias were on the same level as far as qualifications for apostleship were concerned, we wonder how far the eleven were guided more by their own preference than by the guidance they sought from the Searcher of hearts? The usual way of casting lots in such cases was to write each name on a tablet, place them in an urn, and then shake it till one came out — a practice recognized by the Law (Lev. 16:8). The lot fell upon Matthias, or his name fell out of the urn first, and "he was numbered with the eleven apostles," but was he God's choice as the last of the twelve?

We strongly discount the argument that the silence about the future history of Matthias proves that his election of office was hasty and premature on the part of Peter and the rest. Because his work finds no record, and he secured no place on the master-roll of fame, such silence, in itself, is no evidence that his election was unendorsed and unsanctioned by the Lord. Few of the disciples in the Upper Room where the lot was cast for a successor to Judas won through to fame. History is silent as to the labors of Simon the Zealot, for example. After the roll call of the apostles before Pentecost, not a syllable is written of more than half of them. Are we to conclude therefore that the wisdom of Jesus erred? that His prescience was at fault? that He selected the wrong men to be His witnesses? The conclusion that the appointment of Matthias was settled, more or less, by the apostles, must be reached in another way.

We have no doubt whatever that Peter acted in all good faith when he proposed that the gap in the ranks caused by the death of Judas should be closed, and that the consequent plan of selection was carried out in all sincerity. Further, although we have no further mention of either Barsabas or Matthias, both of them were as faithful to the cause of Christ *after* Pentecost, as they were before it. Chosen and unchosen alike they had been chosen of the Lord when as disciples of John the Baptist they came to behold Jesus as "The Lamb of God."

Who was the divinely-chosen successor to Judas? Solomon reminds us that "the lot is cast into the lap (as we see when the apostles drew lots); *but* the whole disposing thereof is of the Lord" (Prov. 16:33). How did the Lord dispose of the matter? Were His ways higher than those of the apostles in their choice of Matthias? We think they were in that the Lord quietly ignored the action of the apostles and filled the vacant place in the apostolate Himself in His own wise way, without human aid, by calling Saul of Tarsus whom the Church has recognized as the divine choice. Saul was

thus the last apostle to be chosen by Christ Himself, just as He had chosen the twelve personally. There may be some reason for thinking that Paul is referring to the transaction of the eleven in the Upper Room, when he more than once emphasized that he himself was an apostle appointed *directly* by the Lord.

How decidedly Paul wrote of himself to the church at Galatia — "Paul, an apostle, *(not of men, neither by man,* but by Jesus Christ . . . ")" (Gal. 1: 1). It was from the Son of God that Paul received his apostleship, and in numerous places he reiterates this privilege (Rom. 1:1, 5). Although, at the time of the transaction of the eleven, Saul was a fierce persecutor of the church, he became a Christian shortly after Pentecost, and would doubtless learn in due course of the election of Matthias, and thus affirm that he had seen the Risen Christ also, and so looked upon himself as "the least (can we say *last*) of the apostles" (I Cor. 15:8, 9). This Corinthian epistle is heavy with Paul's claim as a divinely elected apostle. "Paul, called to be an apostle of Jesus Christ through the will of God" (I Cor. 1:1; 9:1).

As soon as the miracle happened on that Damascus Road, the Lord, who arrested and saved him, declared to Ananias of Saul, who became Paul, "He is a chosen vessel unto me, to bear my name before the Gentiles, and kings, and the children of Israel" (Acts 9:15), and forth he went to become the mightiest figure, apart from Christ, in church history. We thus believe that Paul will occupy the twelfth throne of Israel which Judas forfeited; and that his illustrious name will adorn the twelfth foundation of the Holy City, thus replacing Judas, as the twelfth apostle of the Lamb (Rev. 21:14).

PAUL

The Apostle Extraordinary

The above caption is like Elisha's axe head — *borrowed!* It happens to be the title of one of the most recent appraisals of the character and message of the apostle Paul. In his *Apostle Extraordinary*, Dr. R. E. D. White, Lecturer of Greek and Philosophy in The Baptist Theological College, Scotland, has given us a most illuminating study of Paul: "A modern portrait" as this most helpful volume is described. The purpose of this portrait, Dr. White tells us, is to present the most renowned of all the apostles as

> The Greatest of Christians,
> Profoundest of Teachers,
> Staunchest of Friends,
> Most Intrepid of Adventurers,
> Most Dauntless of Sufferers,
> Most Winsome of Saints —
> Paul of Tarsus, Soldier and Slave and Lover of Jesus Christ our Lord.

That the author succeeds most admirably in his task, is evidenced by the way he has made the extraordinary first century apostle live again for the ordinary disciples of the twentieth century.

To paint a full portrait of Paul requires a large canvas indeed which, alas, we were not able to provide for such a saintly adventurer for Christ. Who is there with gift sufficient to perfectly delineate this magnificent personality whose "conversion was violent and dramatic, his roving life full of action and danger, and whose achievement was to transform Christianity from a small Hebrew sect into a world religion," as Ernest Hauser so aptly expressed it in the January 1967 issue of *The Reader's Digest*. We have more biographical matter on Paul than on any other New Testament personality —our Lord excepted. How he seems to dominate *the Acts!* As for his own priceless letters, they are likewise well documented with glimpses of his trials and triumphs. His "many crises, quick decisions, narrow escapes and sporadic outbursts of violence" make his career "one of the greatest adventure stories of all time."

Do you not often wonder what this remarkable first Christian theologian was actually like? Although artists have tried to depict him, no contemporary portrait of Paul survives. All we have from the fourth century is a diptych and a large medallion from the Roman cemetery of Domitilla, as well as a glass dish in the British Museum, London. From these sources, and from ancient writings, Fulton Oursler in *The Greatest Faith Ever Known*, has given us this unique picture of the "Apostle Extraordinary" —

> He was not more than three cubits tall, and since a cubit was a foot and a half of our measuring, Paul, who breathed forth fire and slaughter, was less than five feet tall. But he was broadshouldered. Early athletic victories had hardened his well-condi-

tioned body. He was sinewy and graceful in spite of his prematurely balding head and the early gray that encroached on the close-knit eyebrows and thick beard in this his thirtieth year. Yet it was not his stalwart figure, nor his fair complexion, nor the decision suggested by the long, aquiline nose, not yet his impelling manner that held the crowded synagogue silent.

What transformed Paul, bespelling his hearers, was his fire of faith, a zeal that flashed and flared in those enormous eyes that were like two draught windows in a human furnace. He who often conceded that his bearing was not impressive stood in the Damascus synagogue and impressed everyone within sound of his voice, beginning there a ministry for Christ that was to last thirty-nine years.

As to his physical appearance, we are not left without means of knowing it fairly well. It was not prepossessing, and neither attractive nor dignified. A small man, feeble, plain, nearsighted, and early in life bald-headed. An account in the apocryphal second-century *Acts of Paul* says, "He was a man of little stature, partly bald, with crooked legs, of vigorous physique, with eyes set close together and nose somewhat hooked." His enemies said that "his bodily presence is weak, and his speech contemptible" (II Cor. 10:10). He said of himself:

"I was with you in weakness, and in fear, and in much trembling" (I Cor. 2:3).

"Rude in speech" (II Cor. 11:6).

"Without were fightings, within were fears" (II Cor. 7:5).

"Through infirmity of the flesh I preached the gospel" (Gal. 4:13).

"If it had been possible, ye would have plucked out your own eyes, and given them to me" (Gal. 4:15).

"I desire to be present with you now, and to *change my voice*" (Gal. 4:20).

All these features indicate that the apostle had a frail body which groaned under the demands made upon it, barely able to meet them. Yet the fire of zeal glowed and burned in his feeble frame, and consumed him with its fervor. How God magnified His grace and power by placing such treasure in a cracked yet clean earthen vessel.

The most fascinating record of Paul, which Fulton Oursler goes on to tell in his heart-gripping volume, is one no preacher of the Gospel should miss. All that we can do in our simple sketch is to indicate a few focal points in the life of this apostle, about whom more books have been written than any other Bible character, apart from Christ. The total of Pauline books must be enormous. Paul may have been short in physical stature, but he stands tall, a commanding figure second only to the Master Himself in the history of the Christian faith and in Christian literature down the ages.

1. *A Man of Tarsus*

The history of the Church proves that in a time of crisis God knows where to find the man He needs as His weapon of war. As in the past when He required epoch-making men for the Old Covenant, He raised up Abraham and Moses, so with the New Covenant, God knew where to lay His hand on great men, who proved to be His best gifts to the Church and to the world. The record of Christianity is the biography of those whose background eminently fitted them to advance its cause in a world of need, and the brightest star in such a firmament is the apostle Paul whom God arrested and by His grace and power fashioned into the magnificent hero of aggressive Christianity and the preacher whose message ever is — the Gospel of salvation as God's gift to a sinful world.

We thoroughly agree with the sentiment that "without the consecrated labors of this Christ-intoxicated man it is debatable whether Christianity would ever have become a universal religion. No figure in church history stands as high or has had such far-reaching influence as this apostle to the non-Jewish world. Centuries have not dimmed the luster of his personality nor changed the significance of his place in Christian history. Whenever and wherever the impact of a secular world and the spread of unworthy religious practices have left the Church in need of revitalization, it is to Paul that men have turned, as to a fountain from which again the pure water of the evangelical faith could be drawn and the essence of the Christian Gospel republished."

The background and former training of Paul is gathered from the Acts, and from his own epistles. These are the facts given principally by himself

1. A Jew of Tarsus, a city of Cilicia (Acts 21:39).
2. A free-born Roman citizen (Acts 22:28).
3. A Pharisee, and the son of a Pharisee (Acts 23:6).
4. A Hebrew of the Hebrews, of the tribe of Benjamin (Phil. 3:5)
5. A pupil of Gamaliel, taught according to the perfect law of the Fathers (Acts 22:3; Gal. 1:14).
6. A student of Greek, as well as Jewish literature (Acts 17:28; Titus 1:12).
7. A man with a changed name (Acts 13:9).

Paul is thus distinguished from the rest of the apostles as a man of learning and culture, and pre-eminently designed and fitted by birth, education and earlier experiences to fill the peculiar place in the establishment, extension, and edification of the Church. How well trained he was to be the chief interpreter of his Master's thoughts and purpose. Because of his unique background and past relationship, he was better prepared than the men of Galilee to take a comprehensive view of the Savior's mission and aims. A brief survey of the facts that Paul relates about himself are necessary for a full understanding of all he became and accomplished.

I am a Jew (Acts 22:3)

It was shortly after the beginning of the Christian era that Paul was born of a Jewish family of strict Pharisaic persuasion, descended from "the tribe of Benjamin," which closely associated him with the center of Judaism in Jerusalem. The Jews of Tarsus were related to the business life of the city. As Paul was a tent-maker it is likely that he followed his father's trade. Many of the Jews of Tarsus were Roman citizens, some by bestowal, others by purchase. Jerome, in the fourth century, held that Paul's parents were from Gischala in Galilee, and that his father obtained his Roman citizenship after going to Tarsus as a prisoner of war.

When the Roman centurion was about to scourge Paul, the apostle protested, "Is it lawful for you to scourge a man who is a Roman citizen?" Queried further, Paul said, "I was born a Roman citizen" (Acts 22:24-29). Such a citizenship was valuable, for it carried with it special rights and privileges, including immunity from scourging or crucifixion. When in his later days, Paul desired to journey to Rome, it was his Roman citizenship that made the journey possible, even though he went there as a prisoner (Acts 19:21; 25:11, 12).

Exercising his privilege of Roman freedom, Paul cried out in court, "I appeal to Caesar," and under Roman law, the provincial authorities had no other alternative but to reply, "To Caesar you shall go!" Dr. White's apt comment is worthy of repetition —

Paul never forgot his citizenship in Israel; he never undervalued or repudiated his citizenship of Rome; but he held at all times as first priority his membership of the city of God, and found at last, after a glorious career of which the world was not worthy, that the Christian's dearest citizenship is indeed in Heaven.

In spite of the fact that Paul's family were Roman citizens, they remained loyal to their Jewish faith and practice. Thus young Saul was raised strictly after the manner of the Jews, attending the synagogue school and learning with devotion and brilliance as his epistle to the Romans proves, all that was required of him as a student of the Scriptures and the Law of his Fathers. "Study to shew thyself approved..." (II Tim. 2:15). His mind was ever alert to the contrast between the strict moral and religious behavior expected of him and the generally loose ethical life reflected in an environment given over to idolatry (Rom. 1:20-32). In writing to the Philippians Paul described himself as "a Hebrew of the Hebrews" (3:5). Here he was re-affirming his proud heritage which reached back to the Father of the Jews, Abraham, the patriarchs and the first Hebrew. Thus he referred to himself as "a descendant of Abraham" (Rom. 11:1), and although he became the apostle to the Gentiles, being delivered from the narrow patriotism of the Palestinian Jew, Paul never lost his love for, and keen interest in, his own kinsmen (Rom. 9:2-5). When he came to read the Jewish Scriptures with Christian eyes, he was more certain than ever of their divine authority, hence the repeated phrase, "It is written," with which he clinched every argument and closed every discussion.

Further, we are told that Paul, as *Saul*, was "A man of Tarsus," and it was as such that he is first introduced to us, when he is found, not in his home town, but in Jerusalem (Acts 8:1; 9:11). As J. Patterson Smyth expresses it in *The Story of St. Paul's Life and Letters*, "Unexpectedly, suddenly, out of the unknown, Saul of Tarsus makes his first appearance on the stage of history. The curtain rises on a howling Eastern mob and stones hurtling through the air and a young Jewish rabbi in the background with white robes piled at his feet."

What effect did his birthplace of Tarsus have on the life and character of this young Pharisee as he watched Stephen murdered by the stones of a frenzied mob? In the first century, Tarsus was the capital of Cilicia, a province of Asia Minor. Being built at the mouth of the Cydnus River, it commanded a place of considerable importance commercially because of its location on one of the most important overland trade routes of the ancient world — a meeting place for East and West with commerce going in both directions, land and sea.

Tarsus was also known as "A Free City," its liberty being granted by the Roman general, Mark Anthony, in 42 B.C. As a free city it was not required to pay the usual tribute of conquered cities to Rome. Although part of a Roman province, Tarsus was self-governing. The city was also a famous meeting place for philosophers and poets. As a university city, Tarsus was a center of culture and became famous for its Stoic teaching. *Stoicism* owned no personal God, and Paul, with his knowledge of its psychology, knew how to combat it, as he did in his teaching on divine grace. Strabo, the famous Greek geographer, contemporary of the Emperor Augustus, praised the Tarsians highly for their interest in education and philosophy and compared the city favorably with Athens and Alexandria.

To Paul, *Tarsus* was "no mean city," and its sights and scenes left an indelible mark upon his mind. Having grown up in this illustrious city where he had spent the formative years of boyhood and youth, he never forgot his experience there, as allusions in his writings indicate. He had witnessed the slave markets of Tarsus and watched the ownership marks seared on the foreheads and hands of slaves being sold there. With such in mind, he could write in later years, "I bear in my body the marks of the Lord Jesus" (Gal. 6:17). Then, as he thought of those branded slaves sold to a master, he adopted the Greek term *Doulos*, meaning, a "bond-slave" to illustrate how in his relationship to Christ his Master, he was utterly surrendered to His will and control. As a lad, he often saw Roman soldiers with their helmets, armor and spears, and came to use many military metaphors in his preaching and writing (II Cor. 10:4; Eph. 6). From the athletic center in Tarsus, Paul learned the language of athletics which he employed with great effect (I Cor. 9:24-26).

Further, when Paul sketches his character in those early pre-Christian days of his, he tells us that he lived after "the strictest sect of his religion" and was a *Pharisee* and that as "touching the righteousness which is in the law," he was "blameless" (Acts 23:6; 26:5-11; Phil. 3:4-8). What a claim to make for himself! "The Pharisee movement came into prominence to defend all that was distinctively Judaist against the inroad of Greek and Roman paganism," says Dr. R. E. O. White, "and it served the nation well in the maintenance of religion, law and morality." But by the first century

Phariseeism had decayed into self-righteousness, hypocrisy and "an unsympathetic and mechanical legalism."

Paul, however, was a typical Jewish youth, of the best kind, and through his home and synagogue training, had an outward conduct, not only reputable, but free from stain. He fully met the ceremonial requirements of Moses, ever striving to wear "the white flower of a blameless life." When he became a Christian his zeal for holiness was intensified, not as a slave of the Law, but of the Lord who came as the Fulfiller and Fulfilment of the Law. If he had been "more exceedingly zealous of the traditions of his fathers," profiting from Judaism above many equals in his own nation (Gal. 1:14), once Christ had claimed Paul as His own he exceeded all others in sacrificial service in the Christian Church of his day, dying daily for His dear sake.

Brought up at the feet of Gamaliel (Acts 5:34; 22:3)

Paul may have been short of stature but what he lacked physically, he made up for mentally. Without doubt, he was head and shoulders above the rest of the apostles in intellect. What a master mind he had! His remarkable powers of reasoning occasion no surprise when we remember that he studied under Gamaliel, the most famous rabbinic teacher of his day, a man liberal in mind and tolerant in spirit. This teacher of Paul was the eminent doctor of the law who advised the Council to let the apostles alone (Acts 5:33-39). The Jews celebrated Gamaliel as "The Glory of the Law" and he was the first to be designated as "Our Master." He was the son of Rabbi Simeon, and grandson of Hillel, and became President of the Sanhedrin under Tiberius, Caligula, and Claudius. He died eighteen years before the fall of Jerusalem.

The training of this famous teacher "held in honour by all the people" involved a rigorous study of the Jewish Scriptures together with the extensive comments of the learned rabbis concerning them. As a pupil of Gamaliel, Paul applied himself assiduously to his rabbinic studies as his later devotion to the Law and his frequent use of the rabbinic method reveal. The students of Gamaliel were required to learn a trade so that they could eventually teach without becoming a burden to the people. Paul likely followed a typical Tarsian industry, making tents from goat's-hair cloth, and his skill in this occupation came to prove a great boon to him in later days in his extensive missionary work.

Paul's knowledge of language also added to his intellectual superiority and to his prowess as a preacher and writer. As "a Hebrew of the Hebrews," meaning a Jew of pure descent, he had an intimate grasp of his own native tongue. He also learned Greek and probably Latin. In his famous sermon on Mars Hill, Paul quoted a line from Aratus, a Stoic philosopher-poet of Cilicia, who died long before Paul's day. "As certain of your own poets have said, *For we are also his offspring*" (Acts 17:28). In his epistles and speeches, the apostle habitually quoted from the Old Testament in its Greek version; thus Dr. Whyte suggests, "that Greek was his mother-tongue and Hebrew only a second." It was his fluency in the Greek language that gave Paul "a sovereign command of the colloquial tongue of most of the known world" — a most valuable asset for the world missionary of the first century. Doubtless it was his cultural background and linguistic ability that gave him access to and the confidence of the High Priest (Acts 22:5).

The manifold qualifications of the apostle also brought him to a seat in the Sanhedrin. Before Paul became a Christian, he was present when Christians were tried before this governing body, and "gave his vote against them" (Acts 26:10, R.V.). As such voting power was restricted to those who were married men, the implication is that Paul seems to have been married. It is said by some writers that we may have a trace of the dead wife in a message given in Romans, "Salute Rufus chosen in the Lord, and *his mother and mine*" (16:13). The natural conclusion drawn from this salutation is that Rufus' mother was the mother of Paul's wife. In this case she was a daughter of Simon the Cyrenian (who was compelled to bear the cross of Jesus to calvary). He was the father of Rufus (Mark 15:21).

Saul, who is called Paul (Acts 13:9)

The change is somewhat significant. *Saul,* "Shaul," as it is in Hebrew, was the name given him at his birth by his parents possibly after Israel's first king, Saul. But *Paul* was the Roman name he chose and is the one by which he has been revered through the centuries. This change of name after his conversion appears to have been made in Cyprus (Acts 13:4, 9), perhaps as a compliment to Sergius Paulus, the proconsul of the island who was converted to Christianity. *Saul* means "asked for," while *Paul* signifies "small" or "little one," which has led a few writers to suggest a connection with his small stature. At Lystra, Paul was taken for Mercurius, a god sometimes described as small and vivacious (Acts 14:12).

2. A Persecutor of the Church

Paul is first mentioned in the New Testament as a young man about thirty years of age at whose feet the witnesses laid their garments on the stoning of Stephen, and who was therefore consenting to that martyr's death (Acts 7:58-60; 22:20). It is more than likely that Paul was one of those alluded to from the synagogues of "the Libertines and Cyrenians . . . *and of them of Cilicia*" (his birthplace), who "disputed with Stephen," and who joined in the decision to kill him as a blasphemer. Thereafter he became the chief agent in the fierce persecution of the young and fast-growing Church, having come to the front in Jerusalem as an unwearied member of the party of ecclesiastical authority. This arch persecutor of the saints showed no mercy as he hunted them out of their homes (Acts 8:1-4; 9:1-2).

The factors responsible for the Pharisees' outburst of anger against the early Christians are well known. Among orthodox Jews a new sect appeared, *The Nazarenes*, who followed Jesus of Nazareth, whom they affirmed to be the Messiah predicted of old. They believed themselves to be the new and true "Israel of God," the people of the New Covenant, bringing to fulfilment all that God had purposed for His people and inheriting all the promises given in Hebrew history to the people of the Old Covenant.

These audacious claims on the part of a few unlearned peasants of Galilee, particularly those of a crucified and risen Messiah, were contrary to the Jewish training and rabbinical studies that Paul had received. With other Pharisees, he looked for the promised Messiah, but not for one who would die as a felon on a wooden gibbet. God's anointed One would come in all His glory as the King, was Paul's expectation. Thus, this new teaching of "the sect of the Nazarenes" (Acts 26:9-11) threatened the essential features of Judaism as the Pharisees understood them, and must therefore be exterminated. Out went Paul

to destroy this blasphemous heresy root and branch. Such a determination became the supreme passion of his life (Gal. 1:13). Blinded by his prejudice, he surmised that it was the will of God that he should oppose with all means at his disposal and pursue to death all who followed this *way*, and lay waste the Church (Acts 8:3).

Intensely hostile to the Christian faith, and specially opposed to some of its (to him) revolutionary doctrine, Paul was thorough as he sought to sweep away such heresy and silence the preaching of the apostles. With the spirit of a savage on the warpath, he was at white heat in bitter resentment as the saints baffled his plan of conquest by carrying into exile their unrecanted faith in Jesus of Nazareth, as the Messiah from heaven. Hearing that Damascus was becoming a Christian asylum for the Nazarene fugitives, Paul sought authority from the High Priest to pursue the retreating enemy into the Syrian capital. The method in his madness is seen in the way Paul carefully managed his plans, and armed with a warrant for search and arrest, started out as the fiery leader of a commission of inquisition to bring back the Nazarenes to face trial for heresy.

It is Emerson who reminds us that, "The history of persecution is the record of endeavours to cheat nature, to make water run uphill, to twist a rope of sand. The martyr cannot be dishonoured. Hours of sanity and consideration are always arriving to communities as to individuals when the truth is seen and the martyrs are justified." The bitter animosity of Jewish orthodoxy called into force the whole resources of the Sanhedrin against Stephen's bold defense and the fearlessness of those who had embraced the Christian faith, but its representative — Paul, the fire-breathing persecutor who witnessed the triumphant martyrdom of Stephen — was to illustrate in himself, that "the blood of martyrs is the seed of the Church."

The cause of Christianity never looked darker than at the start of Paul's extradition expedition to Damascus. We can imagine how the saints there trembled as word was received that their fierce antagonist was on his way to destroy them. But, as we are to see, "Man proposes — God disposes," for though Paul reached Damascus, his documents from the religious authorities in Jerusalem to arrest all the followers of the Nazarene were never used. His breathing out threatening and slaughter on a persecuting errand suddenly stopped, for on the way to Damascus a miracle happened to this saint-hater and blood-thirsty blasphemer — and what a miracle!

3. A Convert of Christ

As soon as Paul was miraculously converted he was ordained of the Lord, and instructed immediately by Him, a chosen vessel to bear His name before the Jews, and more particularly before the Gentiles. He continued thus laboring for some thirty years until A.D. 66 when it is believed he was beheaded by order of Nero at Rome (Acts 9:3-8, 15; 13:46; 22:21; Gal. 1:1; 2:8, 9). Dr. R. E. O. White's opening paragraphs in his chapter on Paul's marvelous transformation are most impressive and well worthy of repetition —

> Out of the many thousands of conversions in Christian history, only one — that of Paul — is celebrated with an appointed Feast Day in the Church's Calendar. Next to the Birth, Death and Resurrection of Jesus and the Day of Pentecost, it is of course the most significant event in the New Testament story, and nothing in the subsequent history of the Church parallels its importance for all time and for all the world.
>
> That brief but astonishing encounter outside Damascus won for Jesus His most attentive disciple, His greatest apostle, His most devoted servant. It removed at one stroke the Church's ablest and most violent enemy. It gave to Christianity —
> her most valiant champion,
> her most ardent evangelist,
> her most brilliant leader,
> her most profound thinker, and one of
> her most attractive saints.
> It made possible the rich legacy of his writings for the counsel and encouragement of all later centuries. It defines, more clearly than any doctrine, the essential purpose and meaning of the Gospel, and it demonstrates with inescapable force the divine power that is at work in Christianity.

No finer *apologia* of Paul's conversion has been written than this from Dr. White's most gifted pen. Let us now try to examine, more particularly, what happened that day on the Damascus Road when the Lord dramatically intervened on behalf of His harried little flock. In many respects that was the most momentous day in the history of the Church — an event so crucial that God caused four full-length and complementary accounts of it to be recorded (Acts 9:3-19; 22:6-21; 26:12-18; Gal. 1:11-17). These accounts differ slightly in details respecting accompanying phenomena, but agree substantially as to what Paul saw, heard and said, and his subsequent relationship with Ananias in Damascus.

The circumstances were these: Paul was proceeding to Damascus with letters from the chief priests at Jerusalem to punish any followers of Jesus Christ whom he might find there. The roads over which he had to travel would only permit a journey on horseback —

a journey of about six days for Paul and his companions. Tradition tells us that they toiled along in the heat of the sun, by morn and eve, till within sight of Damascus. Saul was a little behind the rest, and alone, when suddenly something happened. At midday, when the sun was beating down, a still brighter light shone around him, and immediately he fell to the ground and heard a voice, clear and distinct, saying in the Hebrew tongue, "Saul, Saul, why persecutest thou me?" (Acts 9:3, 4; 26:13, 14).

Before we consider such a remarkable event itself, it may be profitable to discover some of the elements in the preparation of Saul of Tarsus for such a dramatic change of life and character. The glorious revelation of Christ to the persecutor, and his complete about-face, was sudden and instantaneous, and in the twinkling of an eye the miracle of transformation happened. But there were previous hammer-blows upon Saul's hard heart that helped to condition it for the final blow that broke it. When they were ultimately face to face, Jesus said to Saul, "It is hard for thee to kick against the pricks" (Acts 9:5).

Familiar with the Greek poets as the result of his education in the schools of Tarsus, Saul would understand the significance of our Lord's illustration. One of the poets had taught that "to resist a power altogether superior to our own is a profitless and perilous experiment." One Greek proverb ran, "With God we may not strive." Pindar had written:

> But to bow down the willing neck,
>   And bear the yoke is wise;
> To kick against the pricks will prove
>   A perilous enterprise.

What were the "pricks" against which Saul had been "kicking" — the promptings, warnings and evidences he had been guilty of resisting and defying?

The salvation of Barnabas, his friend and companion of his youth

The later close friendship between Paul and Barnabas seems to suggest that there had been some previous companionship (Acts 9:27; 11:25). Ellicott says that it may well have been that Barnabas went from Cyprus to be educated in the famous schools of Tarsus, and met Saul then or practiced with him in early life the craft of tent-making — an occupation in which they were afterward fellow-laborers (I Cor. 9:6). Among the reports Saul received of converts to the faith whom he set out to destroy, would be one about the conversion of Barnabas, and the way in which he disposed of all his possessions for the sake of the saints. Such a surrender must have "pricked" the conscience of Saul who was bent on destroying such noble men.

The speech and advice of Gamaliel (Acts 5:33-40)

Having been brought up in the school of this hero of rabbinic history, Saul must have been impressed as a member of the Sanhedrin, as he listened to his old instructor anticipating the teaching of the Sermon on the Mount in the advice he gave to the Council about doing nothing to others they would not wish done to themselves. Peter and the other apostles (5:29), were before the Council because of their witness to the death and resurrection of Christ, and the verdict had been reached to slay these fearless witnesses. From the tone of Gamaliel's defense of the apostles, it would seem as if he was in the company of the "many" of the chief rulers who secretly believed in Christ, but shrank from openly confessing Him (John 12:42, 43). Gamaliel may have had his one-time disciple in mind as he addressed the Council, intending that his words of warning were specially chosen to restrain the fiery and impetuous zeal of Saul. Here, then, was another "prick" he "kicked" against. Such was the effect of Gamaliel's plea that the apostles were beaten and released, and went out ceasing not to teach and preach Jesus Christ.

The defense and death of Stephen

That angel-face of Stephen as he stood before the Council accused of blasphemy must have disturbed the conscience of Saul. He could not forget it. That glory-face haunted the persecutor of the little flock. Illumined with the glow of an ardent zeal and the serenity of a higher wisdom, such a face radiating divine brightness was another "prick," which Saul tried hard to "kick" against. Then the heroic spirit of those who followed Stephen to his martyrdom was not lost on Saul. Watching the martyr being brutally stoned to death, and seeing how a saint could die, greatly disturbed Saul, and the very ferocity he manifested against the saints after that bloody scene was but a reaction against such a sacrificial faith and fidelity — an evidence that Saul's conscience was becoming more disturbed.

As a man does not persecute people of whom he knows nothing, we can be assured that Paul knew a great deal about the Nazarenes whose quality of life and conduct, and courage and possession of an inner peace in the face of trial, he secretly admired and which made him think more deeply than ever about the Master for whom they willingly suffered. A Spanish artist has painted Paul by the side of Stephen on the way to martyrdom, which was his attempt to show the close connection of these two figures in the development of church life. We read of the ancient Hebrews that "the more they were persecuted, the more they multiplied and grew," and Ste-

phen's spirit rose again in the heart of his enemy who had consented to his cruel death. God buried His brave workman, but He carried on His work. Paul may have tried to escape from the haunting memory of Stephen's terrible end, yet the prayer of the martyr was answered in the young persecutor's conversion who was commissioned to continue the life-work of Stephen, and become the apostle to the Gentiles.

The growing disillusionment of Judaism

Although Paul had been exceedingly sensitive to the requirements of the Law, which he himself had observed most meticulously, yet doubts arose that the Law was able to save a man accursed (Gal. 3:10; Phil. 3:6). Gradually he came to despair of ever fulfilling all the demands of the Law, and his intense, almost savage attempt to obliterate Christianity only reflected a sense of insecurity prompted by misgivings and doubts. He came to prove that external observance and inward fulfillment of the Law were not one and did not issue in victory and emancipation of the soul (Rom. 7:7). Thus, his condition prior to his conversion when, like a stubborn ox he persisted in kicking against the goads, hurting himself more than anyone else, is described with remarkable vividness in his epistle to the Romans (Acts 26:14; Rom. 7).

Added to his despair as to the Law's efficacy, was the growing awareness of the reality of the claims of the Man of Galilee. It is a somewhat debatable question as to whether Paul had ever seen the Jesus of history. He came to mention that he had known Christ "after the flesh," that is, from a human point of view (II Cor. 5:16), and various allusions in his epistles to the character of Jesus seem to suggest that he carried in his mind impressions gained through a personal contact with His earthly life. This much is evident, he learned much about Jesus while hunting down His followers. He could see how inseparable their character was from the claims of Him whom they declared to be the Messiah. John Knox in *A Life of Paul* says that, "Christ had begun to make Himself known to Paul — perhaps against the latter's will — as the Spirit of the persecuted *koinonia* before He made Himself known in the visual experience in what Paul's conversion culminated."

S. A. Deissman wrote in *The Religion of Jesus and the Faith of Paul,* that "the lightning of Damascus "struck no empty void," but found "plenty of inflammable material" in Paul's soul. Thus with reasonable certainty it may be affirmed that the tremendous radical transformation he experienced and which he came to describe as God being pleased to reveal His Son to him, was not without considerable preparation on the part of heaven (Gal. 1:16). Did he not declare that he was destined for apostolic ministry before he was born (Gal. 1:15)? We now come to think of the supernatural and sudden conversion forming, as it did, the last stage of a long preparatory process. What were some of the aspects of the vision resulting in a vocation?

Paul had a revelation of Jesus

He actually saw the crucified Jesus of Nazareth as the living Christ. One qualification of apostleship was the witness of Christ as the Risen One — "a witness with us of his resurrection" (Acts 1:22). And when he came to his *Magna Charta* of the resurrection and enumerated all who had actually seen the One who is alive for ever more, Paul concluded, "and last of all he was *seen of me also*" (I Cor. 9:1; 15:8). The inner voice Paul had

tried to silence now becomes audible and speaks, not reprovingly but tenderly, as it repeats the name of the one arrested, "Saul, Saul, why persecutest thou me?" The whisperings of that pleading voice he had heard in the past now rolls through the hollow chamber of his inmost being and demands a reason for his persistent animosity. What a dialogue this was between the risen and ascended Lord and a persecutor, acting ignorantly in unbelief!

It is clearly evident from the narrative that Paul saw the form of Jesus as well as heard His voice, and it was to this visible presence he afterward bore witness (I Cor. 9:1). Paul saw Him as Stephen had done when he said: "I see the heavens opened, and the Son of man standing at the right hand of God" (Acts 7:56). Paul, who had heard those words of the martyr, thought them to be blasphemous. Now he, too, saw Jesus in the glory of the Father stretching forth His delivering hand, not, as in the case of Stephen to receive His servant who had been faithful unto death, but in answer to that dying victim's prayer, to transform Saul, who had consented to his death, into the likeness of his victim (Acts 7:60). And this was the miracle that happened that day on the Damascus Road. In many respects, that sudden conversion was the greatest of the centuries. As we think of the iniquitous state of the world and the plight of the Church today we find ourselves praying, "O Lord, do it again!"

It is somewhat remarkable that it is only here, Acts 9:4, 17, that Jesus used the Hebrew form of the Benjamite name, *Shaul, Shaul!,* as if He suggested that seeing Saul gloried in being above all things, a Hebrew of the Hebrews, now hearing himself claimed as such from heaven, as Samuel had been of old (I Sam. 3:4-

18), he must decide whether he would continue kicking against the pricks or yield, saying with Samuel, "Speak, Lord, for thy servant heareth." It is because he immediately and deliberately responded to that heavenly voice, and was not disobedient to such a heavenly vision, that Paul came to enrich the Christian faith, as no other man has done, with its glorious evangelical message.

Paul recognized the lordship of Jesus

Calmly Paul answered the divine question, "Why persecutest thou me?" with one of his own, "Who art thou, Lord?" which at once was answered, "I am Jesus [the Nazarene] whom thou persecutest." Then after a short pause, a silence of soul, a touch of the Spirit within (for no man can call Jesus Lord but by the Spirit, I Cor. 12:3) Paul responded, "Lord, what wilt thou have me to do?" The first question was *Who?*, the second, *What?*, and in every true conversion the one follows the other. Having accepted the despised Nazarene as his Savior and Master, he had to go into Damascus to await his marching orders. Doubtless his repetition of the title *Lord*, was the natural response of respect and awe because of all he saw and heard. With the fuller revelation of the Spirit, Paul came to understand and proclaim the lordship of Christ as no other apostle. From that moment when Christ was formed in him (Gal. 1:16), he never faltered in his allegiance to his Lord.

It is in this awesome truth of the lordship of Christ that we can discern a difference between the apprehension of Paul and the rest of the apostles before him in Christ. The twelve who had companied with Him for almost three years grew slowly into the full revelation of Christ's prerogatives as *Lord*. It was not easy for them to discern in the One who had been a carpenter in Nazareth, the Lord of Glory. Because of the very familiarity existing between Christ and His own, there was a slowness to believe in His lordship. Their eyes were somehow holden, but gradually they were opened to grasp in the fullest sense all that their Master was, and of His mission as the vicarious Substitute for a world of sinners lost, and ruined by the fall.

With Paul it was totally different for he did not "grope his way through preconceptions and prejudice to a slowly maturing revelation. He learned with all the suddenness of a surprising and blinding vision what his fellow apostles had learned with dull, reluctant, and hesitating receptivity. The deity of the Lord came upon him almost as the dawning of a glorious summer morning after the deep darkness of the night, and he was able to grasp the larger, deeper meaning of the Saviour's death and resurrection with a quickness and breadth of apprehension which had not been given to the rest." Instantly Paul recognized Jesus as *Lord,* and it is to him, more than to any other New Testament writer, that we owe the fullest exposition of the facts and mysteries of Him who is Lord over all (Col. 1:15-19).

Paul learned of Christ's identity with his people

On the face of it there seems to be a contradiction between "Saul breathing out threatenings and slaughter against *the disciples of the Lord,*" and the question of the Lord to Saul, "Why persecutest thou me?" (Acts 9:1, 4). Jesus was not among the hounded disciples, and Saul had never confronted Jesus personally with threatenings and slaughter. Then how startled he must have been to hear the quiet voice through the blinding light say, "Why persecutest thou *me?*"

In a most forcible way Jesus impressed upon Saul His identification with His people, and that the wounds inflicted upon the saints were wounds He endured. It was not the disciples and brethren alone whom Saul was persecuting but also their Lord, for what was done to them He counted done as unto Himself.

Had He not said in the days of his flesh, "Inasmuch as ye did it unto one of the least of these my brethren, ye did it unto me"? That the true church is the body of Christ, and that any service rendered to, or suffering inflicted on it, is reckoned as done to its Head, was the first sublime truth that gripped the soul of Saul, and became one of the great themes of his writings. "The body is one, and hath many members . . . so also is Christ" (I Cor. 6:15; 12:12-31; Eph. 4:25; 5:30). All the saints are one in and with the Lord Jesus.

Oh, teach us, Lord, to know and own
    This wondrous mystery,
That Thou in Heaven with us art one,
    And we are one with Thee.

Paul's remarkable conversion was a pattern

In his first letter to the Corinthians Paul uses a peculiar phrase. He wrote of himself as "one born out of due time" (I Cor. 15:8,9). Phillips translates it, "one born abnormally late." The A.V. margin has it, "an abortive," that is, an untimely birth. The apostle distinctly states he is referring to what happened when Christ met him and saved him, and may have meant that he had not had the privilege of being among His first chosen apostles. He was as an "untimely born" one, and was therefore the least of the former apostles in this respect, and not meet to be called an apostle seeing he had persecuted the rest.

But somehow we feel there is a deeper significance in the phrase

about being born "out of due time." As C. I. Scofield puts it, "Paul thinks of himself here as an Israelite whose time to be born again had not come nationally (Matt. 23:39), so that his conversion by the appearing of the Lord in glory (Acts 9:3-6) was an illustration, or instance, before the time of the future national conversion of Israel" (See Ezek. 20:35-38; Hosea 2:14-17; Zech. 12:10-13:6; Rom. 11: 25-27). Paul's dynamic change remains as a type of the salvation of the nation he represented who, as they come to look upon Him whom they pierced, will mourn for Him.

A similar thought is found in his first letter to Timothy. "That in me *first* Jesus Christ might shew forth all longsuffering, for a *pattern* to them which should hereafter believe on him to life everlasting" (I Tim. 1:16). If, as "the chief of sinners," Paul had been graciously saved by the Redeemer, then there is hope for any other sinner willing to repent and believe. To all sinners, Paul was a pattern of the Lord's patient waiting to emancipate any sinner from the shackles of sin. In this age of grace, none need despair of finding mercy if God could save a man like Saul of Tarsus, the persecutor and blasphemer. But there is the wider significance of Paul's conversion as a type of Israel's restoration to divine favor and blessing.

All of us are familiar with the most exhaustive study of the epochal event of Paul's conversion by the parliamentarian, Lord Lyttleton, and his lawyer friend Gilbert West, both of whom were infidels persuaded that the Bible was an imposture. Lyttleton concentrated on Paul's Damascus experience, and West on the resurrection and as the result of their separate studies, they were both converted. In his published treatise Lyttleton wrote that, "The conversion and apostleship of Paul alone, duly considered, was of itself a demonstration sufficient to prove Christianity as a Divine Revelation." Countless thousands since Paul's remarkable conversion have experienced the same power to transform their lives instantaneously — this writer is one of them!

It needed a great, sudden crisis to affect a man like Saul of Tarsus who had "so clear a mind, so firm a will, so definite a purpose, so successful a part; a conscience which did not bear the burden of great sin upon it, but rather the satisfaction of duty done, and duty lived, and duty as before. Two things were needed in Saul. A total change of opinion as to Jesus of Nazareth was one; the other was a new revelation to God, not as an obedient servant, but as a forgiven sinner. The two things were to go together, the hated Nazarene was to be the way of approach to the Holy God."

4. An Apostle of God

As the circumstances following Paul's surrender to Christ are well-known there is little need to linger over them. What happened to his companions who were stricken dumb by the light and voice from heaven, we are not told. Paul rose from his knees smitten with blindness and had to be led by the hand to Damascus. But although he rose from the dust, blind and helpless and shattered, he was nevertheless a "new man in Christ Jesus." His entrance into Damascus, however, was totally different from what he had expected. It was his plan to enter the city as the zealous persecutor of the followers of Jesus of Nazareth, but he had met the Man Himself and, humbled and humiliated, spent the first three days in Damascus, sightless and foodless (Acts 9:9). What a reverse for the proud Pharisee bent on the imprisonment of the saints! He had come to make the Nazarenes tremble; he was now a Nazarene himself!

Ananias knew of Paul and was afraid of him, but divinely assured that the old Saul had been radically changed, he became his friend and counselor. As for the fearful saints, they took fresh courage, and magnified God as they saw a violent spiritual upheaval had produced so mighty a preacher of the Savior. With the return of his sight and the baptism with the Holy Spirit, he witnessed in the synagogue at Damascus to his new-found faith (Acts 9:20). That Paul had much to learn ere he could function as an apostle, is evidenced by the fact that in between his witness in Damascus, he went into Arabia. As writer after writer has dwelt upon Paul's visit to Arabia, affirming that as there were "silent years" in the life of Jesus, so there were "silent years" in the life of Paul, let us examine just what Paul himself said about this visit.

Surprisingly, he did *not* say that he was in Arabia for three years, nor did he record why he went there nor how long he stayed there. We can assume that his sojourn there was for reflection upon the great task before him, and for the shaping of the message God had called him to deliver. He returned to Damascus from Arabia, and some time later went up to Jerusalem. "Then after three years I went up to Jerusalem to see Peter" (Gal. 1:17, 18). This phrase simply means that after an absence of three years from Jerusalem, he returned to it. He had left the city with letters from the High Priest to arrest the Christians in Damascus, and now, after three years, he finds his way back to Jerusalem. The period mentioned, then, is to be reckoned from the time of the great turning-point in Paul's career — his conversion — and is not to be interpreted as the time he spent in Arabia.

Returning to Jerusalem, Paul spent fifteen days in fellowship with Peter and James (Gal. 1:18, 19), then unsuccessfully tried to win over the rabbis to his newly-found faith. What followed in the next few years is not too clear. Evidently Syria and Cilicia were evangelized (Gal. 1:21), and then there came the remarkable ministry at Antioch, where the disciples were first called *Christians,* and from this center Paul entered upon his glorious task as the apostle to the great Gentile world (Acts 11:25, 26; 13:1-4), becoming, as Dr. White describes him, *Apostle Extraordinary.*

As we recall the marvelous ministry of Paul who was pre-eminently designed and fitted by birth, education and earlier experience to fill a peculiar place in the establishment and extension and edification of the church, we cannot but assign him the foremost place in "the glorious company of the apostles." As to his apostleship, Paul never had any doubt about it, and was emphatic in his claim to such, and never allowed it to be challenged without solemnly and strenuously reasserting it. This apostolic title was bitterly contested, and he triumphantly defended it on the double ground that, though he had not companied with Jesus in the days of His flesh, he he seen Him after His glorification (I Cor. 9:1); and though he was not one of the original twelve, his apostleship had the Lord's own sanction (II Cor. 12:12). Nineteen times Paul calls himself an apostle, and argues his claims as such (I Cor. 9:1-6; II Cor. 12).

Humbled by the recollection of his former enmity to Christ and His disciples, Paul, in all modesty, confessed that he was the least of the apostles and not worthy to be called an apostle; but when any doubt was thrown upon his calling to apostleship there was always "the answer of a noble dignity and an assured confidence ready," as he affirmed that he was not a whit behind the chiefest of the apostles. Although chosen after all the rest, yet "in labours he was more abundant than they all." Paul was that one born out of due time to exercise a spiritual potency greater than others in the apostolate. The original apostles quarrelled as to "which of them should be the greatest." Such an honor was reserved for Paul, "called to be an apostle, separated unto the gospel of God" (Rom. 1:1, 5).

5. A *Missionary to the Gentiles*

The two dominant personalities in the Acts are Peter and Paul. In chapters 1 - 12, Peter is prominent as "The Apostle to the Jews." From Chapter 13 through the rest of the book, Paul is outstanding as "The Apostle to the Gentiles." Paul, as a Hebrew of the Hebrews, had a passion to win his own kinsmen for Christ, but they rejected his witness, and so the break came when he said to Barnabas, his co-missionary, "Lo, we turn to the Gentiles." And out he went to gather multitudes of non-Jews for the Savior who died for Jew and Gentile alike (Acts 13:46-52; 22:21; Gal. 2:8, 9). What a vast circuit he covered, and what an example to all soul-winners he is of self-denial and Christian devotion! We find Paul laboring in Seleucia, Cyprus, Pamphylia, Pisidia, and Lycaonia (Acts 13; 14). Then the call came from Macedonia, and so into Europe (Acts 16). Thessalonica, Berea, Athens, Corinth, Ephesus, Galatia and Rome were also covered, Paul knowing that at every step bonds and afflictions awaited him. What else can we do but appreciate the ardor of that love of Christ which thus constrained him to serve his Master so sacrificially!

The influence of Paul's three great missionary expeditions upon the history of mankind cannot be over-estimated. The time covered in these tours was about ten years, and the distance covered about 8,100 miles — insignificant in these days as jet planes unite continents, but remarkable in those days when they had no planes, cars, trains, or fast-going sea vessels. The apostle continued laboring thus for some thirty years, till, as is generally believed, he was beheaded by order of Nero at Rome, about A.D. 66. This world's greatest missionary was at home over all the then known Roman world. It has been said that —

> Even before his conversion Paul desired to be not only a Rabbi but a missionary, to devote his life to the propagation of true righteousness, and to the overthrow of everything which in any way interfered with its advance, and in which in any way hindered the people from giving themselves individually to the practice of the Law.

As a result of the miracle that happened that noon on the Damascus road, such missionary zeal was not quenched but changed in direction, sanctified and intensified. How apt at this point are the lines of John Keble in his poem on *The Conversion of St. Paul*:

As to Thy last Apostle's heart
Thy lightning glance did then impart
Zeal's never-dying fire,
So teach us on Thy shrine to lay
Our hearts, and let them day by day
Intenser blaze and higher.

Thereafter, by life, labor, teaching and example, he laid down for all time the principles of fruitful missionary service. As J. Oswald Sanders expresses it, "Paul approximated more nearly to the Divine pattern than any missionary the world has seen. In him Christ possessed an instrument of His Kingdom. Other missionaries have opened a continent to the Gospel. Paul opened a world." Paul firmly believed that he had a Gospel for the whole world, and made it the supreme purpose and passion of his life to make it known, whether to Jews or Gentiles. He was indeed a chosen vessel unto the Lord (Acts 9:15; 22:21).

Paul, like the God he served, had no respect of persons. All kinds of men had a claim upon his time and talents, and as a debtor to all, he faithfully discharged his obligation (Rom. 1:14-16). His whole nature rose up in the true enthusiasm of humanity, to embrace, and boast of, and preach continually a redemptive message for all. By all means, he would seek to save all men. For this end he would live, for this he would die. As Christ died for Paul, so Paul suffered and died daily that he might bring sinners to the cross. And to all of us who have any desire to serve the Savior, Paul points to his undying passion for souls and says, "Be ye followers of me, even as I also am of Christ" (I Cor. 11:1).

As you follow Paul from country to country (Rom. 15:19), mark how he suffered for Christ's sake in his missionary labors. Here is a list for you to ponder over with your open Bible—

Enduring every species of hardship, encountering every extreme danger (II Cor. 11:23-27). Assaulted by the populace, punished by magistrates (Acts 16:19-24; 21:27). Scourged, beaten, stoned, left for dead (Acts 14:19-20). Expecting wherever he went a renewal of the same treatment and the same dangers (Acts 20:23). Driven from one city, he preached in the next (Acts 13:50, 51; 14:5-7, 19-21). Spent his whole time in missionary work, sacrificing to it his pleasures, his ease, his safety (Acts 20:24; Rom. 1:14, 15; Phil. 1:20; 3:8). Persisted in this course to old age, unaltered by the experience of perverseness (Acts 28:17); ingratitude (Gal. 1:6; 4:14-20); prejudice (II Cor. 12:15); and deser-

tion (II Tim 4:10, 16). Unsubdued
by anxiety, want, labor, or persecution, unwearied by long confinement,
undismayed by the prospect of death
(Acts 21:13; II Cor. 12:10; Phil. 2:17;
4:18; II Tim. 4:17).

At his conversion, Paul was warned
of the many things he would have to
suffer for Christ's sake (Acts 9:16),
and as he came to suffer he never
sighed or moaned but gloried in his
tribulations and was prouder of his
scars in battle than a soldier of his
medals and decorations (Gal. 6:17).
What a warrior-missionary he was!
The world has never seen his like.

6. A Prisoner of the Lord

A particular aspect of Paul's sufferings for the Master was that of his
prison experiences. In his unconverted
days when he made havoc of the
church, and forced his way into the
homes of saints, he took men and
women and committed them to prison
(Acts 8:3; 26:10). But he came to
reap what he had sown — yet never
thought of himself as a prisoner of
any authority, always as a "prisoner
of Jesus Christ." Toward the close of
His ministry, the Master asked His
disciples: "Are ye able to drink of the
cup that I shall drink of, and to be
baptized with the baptism that I am
baptized with?" (Matt. 20:22). Paul
was not among the original apostles
who heard that question, yet he became the finest embodiment of that
discipleship of self-sacrifice which the
cup and the *baptism* symbolized. So
completely did he come to identify
himself with Christ and "share His sufferings" (Phil. 3:10), that from the moment of his conversion to the moment
of his death, thirty years later, he
found life and liberty only in being
"the slave of Christ," or "the prisoner
of the Lord," whose love controlled his
every activity and constrained him to
live no longer for himself but only for

Him who for his sake "died and was
raised" (II Cor. 5:14-15; Philemon 9).

Paul tells us that he was in "prisons
oft" (II Cor. 6:4, 5; 11:23-27), and
our modern prisons are palaces compared to the infested dens in which
he languished. Yet all was borne without a murmur. His experience of prisons was extensive, varying from the
mild form of restraint he encountered
in Rome (Acts 28:30), to the severity
of "the inner prison" at Philippi (Acts
16:24), and the final horrors of the
Mamertine dungeons. Yet the apostle
never looked upon his many imprisonments as misfortunes, but as opportunities the Lord permitted for the
extension of His cause. This is why
he refers to himself not as Nero's
prisoner in bonds, but as heaven's
"ambassador in bonds" (Eph. 6:20).
His bonds were "the bonds of the
gospel" (Philemon 13). Whenever
he speaks of his captivity the tone is
the same, an experience to glory in.

When Paul speaks of *bonds* he, of
course, means "chains," which describes the Roman method of fettering
prisoners (Acts 12:7). One end of a
chain, that was of commodious length,
was fixed about the right arm of the
prisoner, and the other end was fastened to the left arm of a soldier. Thus
soldier was coupled to prisoner, and
everywhere attended and guarded
him. It was thus that Paul was secured.

Fettered in this manner, he delivered his apology before Festus, Agrippa and Bernice. And it was this circumstance that occasioned one of the
most pathetic and affecting strokes of
true oratory that ever was displayed
either in the Grecian or Roman sen-
ate: "I would to God, that not only
thou, but also all that hear me this
day, were both almost, and altogether
such as I am, *except these bonds*"
(Acts 26:29). When the great earthquake shook the very foundations of

the prison in which Paul and Silas had been cast, what troubled the prison-keeper and led him to contemplate suicide, was the sight that all the prisoner's chains were loosed, and he thought that all had fled (Acts 16: 26, 27).

What a wonderful opportunity of soul-winning these chains gave Paul, and with his unceasing desire to win the lost he took full advantage of it! As there was the periodic changing of the guards to whom he was chained, think of the many soldiers who heard his testimony, and whom he must have led to the Savior. What a constant round of witness his bonds made possible — and what else could the soldiers do *but listen?*

Is there not something touching in the way Paul commences his letter to Philemon? He did not use his authoritative title of *apostle* in his appeal for the return of Onesimus, the run-away slave, but he used the name, *prisoner*. He did not command but for love's sake entreated Philemon to take back his unprofitable servant. While Paul usually dwelt upon his captivities as a ground of gratitude, here he uses his imprisonment as a cause of sympathy. Although he was only about sixty years of age at this time, he writes as "Paul the aged," meaning that he was prematurely old after a life of unexampled labor and suffering for Christ's sake. His was the weakness of an old age accentuated by suffering in chains (Eph. 3:1-13; 4:1; 6:20; Phil. 1:12-20; Col. 4:18).

Further, Paul did remain a witness or ambassador, although in bonds, as the conversion of Onesimus proves. Of him the apostle speaks as "My son, whom I have begotten in my bonds," and the one who, in turn, ministered unto Paul in the bonds of the Gospel (Philemon 10). Thus the hindrances and hardships of imprisonment did not prevent Paul from continuing his wonderful soul-saving ministry. With Richard Lovelace, 1618-1656, Paul experienced that —

> Stone walls do not a prison make
> Nor iron bars a cage;
> That for a hermitage;
> Minds innocent and quiet take
> If I have freedom in my love,
> And in my soul am free;
> Angels alone, that soar above,
> Enjoy such liberty.

Chained and ill-treated, Paul had a soul that was free, and he could thus pray and sing praises unto God, even though he had just been scourged, and it was the midnight hour and his feet were in stocks (Acts 16:23). No wonder the other prisoners were amazed at such indifference to suffering! Do you recall Lord Byron's *On the Castle of Chillon?* —

> Chillon! thy prison is a holy place,
>   And thy sad floor an altar — for 'twas trod,
> Until his very steps have left a trace
>   Worn, as if thy cold pavement were a sod,
> By Bonnivard! May none those marks efface!
>   For they appeal from tyranny to God.

Ever conscious that his precious Lord was with him while in bondage, Paul made his prison a holy place, knowing that the tyranny he endured was an appeal to God to vindicate "His prisoner." The last glimpse we have of the apostle is as a prisoner, "waiting on one of Nero's mad fits for his martyrdom." But Paul had an anchor within the veil. Aytoun, 1813-1865, in his poem on *The Execution of Montrose*, has the expressive verse which we can apply to Paul as he went from prison to paradise —

> He is coming! He is coming!
>   Like a bridegroom from his room,
> Came the hero from his prison
>   To the scaffold and the doom.

As it would seem that Paul's reference to the time of his departure from this life being at hand was written while imprisoned at Rome, awaiting martyrdom (II Tim. 4:6-8), there is something pathetic in his appeal to young Timothy to hurry to him with a thick cloak, which he had left at Troas, to keep him warm in the cold damp prison as he lingered there in frail, shattered health. Then he requested Timothy to fetch his books, probably a few choice works on Jewish history, and on poetry; also "especially the parchments." It is likely that these were his own precious papers containing notes he had made on the Scriptures. As these notes represented many years' reading and study, he wanted to go over them again as long as life remained to him. John Trapp says that these parchments made from "the skins of animals were notebooks of his own making and collecting." Erasmus, commenting on the prison request of Paul, said: "Behold the apostle's goods are movable: a poor cloke to keep him from the weather, and a few books."

Although Paul was facing death, body and soul must be cared for. Prisons could not deter him from spiritual and mental culture. A parallel can be found in the request of the martyr Tyndale who in his prison at Vilrorde asked for warm clothes, his Hebrew Bible, Grammar and Dictionary, "that I might spend my time with study." So, like Paul, Tyndale was a student to the last — engaged in the pursuit of knowledge on the very verge of heaven. Any preacher or student is a fool if he thinks that he has made so much progress that he does not have to persevere to the end.

Another feature of Paul's ability to turn a prison into a holy place is the way he could send out what are known as his "prison epistles" to the Ephesians, Colossians, Philippians, and to Timothy, Titus and Philemon. What a tremendous debt the Church owes the apostle for these marvelous letters, written under much suffering, but which greatly helped to shape Christianity, and still mold the lives of saints! John Bunyan could call his Bedford prison cell his *den* where he meditated and wrote his immortal *Pilgrim's Progress*, which even our modern TV and radio have serialized. It was in his prison on the Isle of Patmos that the apostle John received and gave to the world *The Revelation of Jesus Christ*.

> Masters have wrought in prisons,
>   At peace in cells of stone:
> From their thick walls I fashion
>   Windows to light my own.

7. A Prince of Preachers

Any preacher desiring to thrill his congregation with a series of messages on Paul, the mighty apostle and master church-builder, should saturate his mind with the sixteen chapters Alexander Whyte gives us in his incomparable *Bible Characters*, as a background to his private study. He will find himself lingering over the chapters on —

Paul as a Preacher,
Paul as a Pastor,
Paul's blamelessness as a Minister.

There are phrases in Whyte's chapter on "Paul as a Preacher" which arrest the reader and will not let him go.

> Paul rips open all the dark secrets of our consciences, and all the hidden rottenness of our hearts, till he is the one preacher of all preachers for us. . . .
> "He alone is a 'right divine' who can preach the faith of the Son of God properly," says Martin Luther. He is a "right preacher" who can distinguish, first to himself, and then to his people, faith from the Law, and Grace from works, says the Reformer.

Now Paul was a right divine and he was the first father and forerunner of all such. . . .

To preach the faith as I have never yet preached it: and then, you would perhaps take my epitaph out of Luther on the *Galatians,* and would write this sentence over me — "Come, and see, all ye that pass by, for here lies a right divine."

Why is it that this epitaph is so seldom to be read in any of our churchyards over our ministers? Why are there so few divines so right as to satisfy Paul and Luther?

The first glimpse we have of Paul after his startling conversion is as a *preacher* — "Straightway he preached Christ in the synagogues, that he is the Son of God" (Acts 9:20). The last glimpse Luke gives us is the same, for the last verse of the Acts reads, "Preaching the kingdom of God, and teaching those things which concern the Lord Jesus Christ, with all confidence, no man forbidding him" (28:31). There is no benediction to the Acts for by his life, labor, and literature Paul is still preaching.

As we know, Paul's epistles are saturated with the term "preach" and its cognates. "Preach the Word"; "Preach Christ and him crucified"; "Preach the Gospel"; "Preach the faith" are some of the apostle's keynotes for present day preachers. Love for Christ and for the souls of men became Paul's supreme passion and directed his whole being (II Cor. 5:14), so that he became a herald controlled by Christ, with one supreme passion to preach Him to the nations (I Cor. 9:16). Such was the power of his preaching that the exorcists at Ephesus used the revealing incantation, "I adjure you by the Jesus whom Paul preaches."

The elements making Paul's preaching so powerful were reproof, rebuke, and exhortation with all long-suffering and doctrine (II Tim. 4:2). He knew that he was not as eloquent as Apollos, and so laid no claim to oratory: "I came to you, not with excellency of speech" (I Cor. 2:1). Pride and self-confidence in preaching he abhorred: "I was with you (preaching) in weakness, and in fear, and in much trembling" (I Cor. 2:3); and his preaching was not in plausible words of wisdom, (I Cor. 2:4), but in demonstration of the Spirit and of power.

As a good student of *homiletics* Paul knew how to vary his preaching method. A word often used of his public utterances is "reasoning" (Acts 17:2; 18:4, 19; 24:25). He was no intellectual coward. He had clear convictions and he was ready with that remarkable mental acumen of his to meet any argument. Yet how persuasive his preaching was, overflowing with love and passion. He knew how to warn his hearers "with tears." Paul was one preacher who never suffered from "the curse of a dry-eyed Christianity." And that he observed the necessity of versatility in his preaching is seen in how he could adapt his message to his audience, without trimming his sails in any way. As J. Oswald Sanders puts it:

Paul was equally at home with Roman governors, Greek professors, Asiatic officials or Hebrew theologians. He readily adapted himself to Jewish congregations in the synagogues, Greek philosophers at the Acropolis, pagan crowds at Lystra or to a court assembly such as when he appeared before Festus.

It has been said that, "the true preacher can be known by this, that he deals out to people his life — life passed through the fire of thought." Such a preacher was Paul who lived to preach, and lived what he preached. What a marvelous revival of Christianity in our crazy world there would be if only all pulpits had a host of preachers like Paul the preacher whose eye was never lifted from the end he had in view.

8. *A Writer of Renown*

An impressive feature of the New Testament is that out of the twenty-seven Books composing it, fourteen — if we include *Hebrews* — came from the brilliant mind, and Spirit-inspired pen of the Apostle Paul. What a body of divinity, what treatises on Christian living his matchless epistles contain! They are unsurpassable in the realm of literature. Since Paul wrote these letters of his — sent to churches and persons — multitudes upon multitudes of commentaries, textbooks, and expositions have been written about them. It one could count up all the books published through the centuries on the literary labors of Paul, the total would prove to be colossal.

Without doubt, Paul's letters are a primary source of first magnitude, since they were written with a spontaneity, courage, and a frankness that disclose not only his own personality in all its depth and richness and variety, but also the first clearly formed, profound yet simple, theology of the Christian faith. G. A. Deissmann in his monumental work on *Paul, A Study in Social and Religious History,* says that, "Every letter is a picture of Paul, and therein lies the unique value of the letters as sources for a historical account of this author. There can be but few Christians of later days for whose inner lives we have such thoroughly undesigned sources of information."

An impressive feature of his letters is his influence as a spiritual and ethical teacher, for in Paul's thought, religion and ethics, or faith and works were the two sides of one coin. Thus he never divorced morality from its theological reference. The goal of his ethics was always the same, that Christ may be formed within (Rom.

8:29; Gal. 4:19). The pattern of his ethic was found in the will of God which he spoke of as "the law of God" and "the law of Christ" (Rom. 7:22; I Cor. 9:21). To Paul, "Christian living is always the result of true Christian doctrine; ethical fruits have theological roots."

What Christianity and the world owe to the letters of Paul will never be known, not only for their portrayal of his unique personality, and their account of, and influence upon, the Early Church, but for their abiding truths which continue to change the lives of men. The Christian faith and Christian practice, which they declare, have built churches and added countless numbers to the roll of saints. It was under God that Paul, in his writings, interpreted Christianity to the world. What must not be forgotten as we think of the inestimable value of the epistles the apostle was inspired to write, is the fact that it was Paul who began to write the New Testament. Years before any of the four gospels, or any other of its books, were in existence, Paul had sent out his epistles to the Thessalonians, to the Corinthians, to the Galatians, and to the Romans. These six were among his earliest, and formed the beginnings of our wonderful New Testament. They were written by Paul not when he had strength and vigor, but when he was broken, feeble, fevered, pained, probably handicapped by severe eye-trouble, watched over by his doctor, Luke.

As an interpreter of Christ and of Christian doctrine as found in his literary works, Paul stands, as he has always stood, unrivaled as the greatest expounder of the mystery of the incarnation and the facts of redemption. Next to our Savior's own words, his words have been and still are the dearest treasures of the Christian heart. Macknight, in his *Preliminary Essays*, points out that:

> While the inspired epistles of other apostles deserve to be read with the utmost attention, on account of the explication of particular doctrines and facts which they contain, and of the excellent precepts of piety and morality with which they abound, the epistles of Paul must be regarded as the grand repository in which the whole of the gospel doctrine is lodged, and from which the knowledge of it can be drawn with greatest advantage.

Because Paul was called of God to the apostolic office, claimed apostolic authority, vindicated his claims by miracles, imparted supernatural gifts, manifested the utmost disinterestedness, submitted to the severest sufferings, received acknowledgment from the other apostles, therefore when he spoke and wrote in Christ's name, his apostolic writings were composed by divine command. Thirteen of these epistles bear his name, other disciples being witnesses that Paul wrote them (I Thess. 1:1; II Thess. 1:1). Generally he wrote by an amanuensis, who testified to the genuineness of what Paul told him to write; and in these instances he added his signature and salutation (Col. 4:18; I Cor. 16:21). Usually he sent his epistles by private messengers (Rom. 16:1; Col. 4:7, 8; Eph. 6:21; Phil. 2: 25). He gave them the name of *Scripture* because they contained not his words, but words the Holy Spirit gave him. What he received from the Lord, he communicated to the church.

In his second letter to the Corinthians Paul says, "That I may not seem as if I would terrify you by letters. For his letters, say they, are weighty and powerful; but his bodily presence is weak and his speech contemptible" (II Cor. 10:9, 10). What he lacked in physique and eloquence he certainly made up for in his match-

less writings which are full of truth, and of inexhaustible spiritual teaching. We only wish we could take the epistles one by one, and beginning with *Romans*, outline their chief contents, but such is a task requiring a book to itself.

While Paul wrote principally for the Church and believers of his own time, he must have known that his epistles would carry an abiding value, and be the means of saving countless numbers and cheering and blessing millions of saints in succeeding generations. To Paul and his writings we owe so much, and by the divine grace he extolled, we would follow him even as he followed the Master he deeply loved and sacrificially served. We recognize the fearlessness of his position in the apostolic company, and how Christ magnified His grace and proved His perfect wisdom and divine foresight in making Paul the last and crowning addition to "the glorious company of the apostles."

How manifold are the lessons we can learn from the witness and writings of this intrepid, happy warrior who fought such a good fight for the Captain of his salvation!

The first characteristic of the apostle worthy of emulation is *the spirit of love* which he manifested even when bitterly persecuted by his countrymen. Wherever he went, his conduct testified to the sincerity of his declaration that he bore no animosity against the severest ill-treatment from the Jews. His conscience bore witness in the Holy Spirit that his heart was heavy with grief over their hatred, and that he wished himself accursed from Christ for their sake (Rom. 9: 1-3). On every occasion of the rejection of his testimony by his own kinsmen, he took the opportunity of overcoming their evil with good, by entering their synagogues to instruct them (Acts 13:4, 5; 14:1, 19; 17:1, 2, 10). In the old days as a fiery zealot for Phariseeism, he acted differently. Then the spirit of love was absent. What or *who* had wrought such a change in the spirit of this man? (Acts 9:1; 26:11; I Tim. 1:13).

This same *spirit of affection* pervades his two epistles to the Thessalonians in which he urges the truth of Christ's Second Coming as a ground of comfort under bereavement, as well as a motive to holiness. Trace the apostle's —

Joy at their stedfastness, his tenderness of affection (I Thess. 2:7).

Fervent prayer for them (I Thess. 1:2; 3:10, 13).

Earnest desire for their prayers (I Thess. 5:25).

The second epistle breathes the same spirit of earnest affection and prayer characterizing the first epistle, with the addition of various precepts as to how professed saints should walk and witness. Paul's precious brief Letter to Philemon also offers us a lesson in skilful approach to a matter requiring great delicacy. As Paley expresses it, "We have in *Philemon* the warm, affectionate, authoritative teacher interceding with an absent friend for a beloved convert; aged, and in prison, content to supplicate and entreat, yet so as not to lay aside the respect due to his character and office."

This subdued, loving feeling also appears in his epistles. For instance, in *Galatians* Paul sharply refutes, yet with the tenderest affection, the insinuations about him emanating from false teachers (Gal. 3:1; 4:15, 16). As for *Philippians* which he wrote "weeping," the tenderness, dignity, humility, and disinterestedness of the apostle, are very observable (3:12, 18; 4:11, 18).

The practical influences of the doctrines of grace he taught affords a pattern, not only for preachers to copy, but believers in every age.

Think of these fine illustrations in the character of Paul:

His awful sense of responsibility as a minister, and his jealousy over himself (I Cor. 2:3; 9:16, 17).

His entire dependence for success on the divine blessing, yet his diligent use of legitimate means (I Cor. 3:6-9; 15:10).

His prudence, fidelity and tenderness (I Cor. 3:2; 4:14; II Cor. 2:4).

His humility, even while asserting his apostolic authority; and his little regard for the gifts, by which he was so distinguished, as compared to Christian love (I Cor. 13).

Another trait of his character was *his most zealous care* not to *praise himself*, even when enumerating his labors and sufferings, and apostolic powers and successes. He gloried only in the Lord. What an insight Paul's second letter to the Corinthians gives us into the remarkable devotion and self-effacement of such a remarkable man! Here are a few of the virtues he exhibited:

His intense affection for those carnal Corinthians, as his spiritual children in Christ (I Cor. 4:14, 15; II Cor. 12:15).

His joy at their return to repentance, yet anxiety that it should be perfected among those who still inclined to the false teacher; the delicacy and address with which he exhorts them to a more liberal contribution (II Cor. 9).

His astonishing labors taken in connection with the deep sense he everywhere expresses of his insufficiency to think or to do anything as of himself (II Cor. 3:5).

His humility in noticing his thorn in the flesh, and in allowing fourteen years to elapse before he mentioned his most extraordinary supernatural experience (II Cor. 12).

His courage which knew no fear. By grace he had learned how to rise above and triumph over his trials (I Cor. 2:3; II Cor. 7:5).

Are we prepared to follow the example of Paul, and make our life an argument for the faith we profess? He "pressed toward the mark for the prize of the high calling of God in Christ Jesus," and would have us be thus likeminded. Are we (Phil. 3:14-16)? Does he not urge us to follow him, even as he lived and labored as a follower of Christ (I Cor. 11:1)? The word here for "followers" is *imitators* (Eph. 5:1). Although we shall never reach the eminence of this "apostle extraordinary" we can, by God's grace, serve God as faithfully as Paul did.

SILAS

THE APOSTLE WHO PLAYED SECOND FIDDLE

Our authority for including Silas, "the merry singer" as he has been called, among the wider circle of the apostolate, is Paul himself. When he wrote about being burdensome as "the apostles of Christ," he was referring to Timothy, Silas, and himself (I Thess. 1:1; 2:6; II Thess. 1:1) and what a wonderful trio they proved to be! The inclusion of Silas among Paul's companions is a further evidence of his genius for friendship. Many of the saints in church history had the greatness of isolation, but with the apostle it was different. He leaned heavily on his friends and if one forsook him, as Demas did, he was well-nigh heartbroken. His record shows that he was desperately lonely when isolated from his friends. His love for them was never fickle but deep and beneficial for those he had captured and who gave him intense loyalty, for in them he reproduced himself in Christian leadership.

As "Paul's friendship with Timothy is a model between an older and a younger man, and his friendship with Luke, the beloved physician, a fine example of the intimacy of men of similar age and tastes," so the bond binding Paul and Silas together illustrated how a self-effacing man became an indispensable companion of the most prominent of the apostles.

As Joseph of old, Silas was content to ride in the *second* chariot, or to change the metaphor, to play "second fiddle." In ancient times when the first line of battle was composed of archers, one of the first considerations was that of the broken string on the bow. Thus, in a phrase that became proverbial, the prudent soldier saw that he had two strings to his bow, and a man held in reserve came to be termed "a second string." Dr. C. Harrington Lees in his most refreshing volume on *St. Paul's Friends,* says that "when the cord of fellowship with Barnabas snapped, Silas was Paul's second string.... One glory of Christ's teaching has always been that it gives men a readiness for unobtrusive service, and makes them to contend for positions of secondary importance. If Christ, the Captain, places them there and He is pleased, that matters most."

It is never easy to be the subordinate of a person of conspicuous ability and dominating personality, and to retain the friendship and companionship of such an one. The sun always shines more brightly than a star. Often brilliant and richly endowed persons are lonely, because those of far lesser gifts cannot get along with them. But Paul, with all his outstanding abilities, had to have companions, and it is a testimony to divine grace that a lesser light like Silas and he became such loyal companions and maintained their companionship through many trials and dangers. A lesser man than Silas might easily have refused the position of armor-bearer through ambition to command, but he was content to follow, not lead. Deissmann in his study of *Paul* says that, "his first companion, Barnabas, was at least equal in authority, but the later associates are decidedly subordinate to him."

Sometimes mutual love was tested, as in the parting with Barnabas whom Paul always remembered kindly, and in the disagreement with Peter on a vital issue (Gal. 2:11), but Paul truly loved all of his friends "in the blameless family of God."

The *Silvanus* and *Silas* Paul mentions (Acts 16:19, 25, 29; II Cor. 1:19), were the same person, *Silas* being an abbreviation of *Silvanus*. Perhaps *Silas* was the real name of this comrade of Paul, and one of Semitic origin, while *Silvanus* was an adopted Roman name, and chosen because of the sound. Many such abbreviations of name are to be found in Scripture. *Priscilla* in Acts 18:26 is given as *Prisca* (II Tim. 4:19), and *Sosipater* (Rom. 16:21) as *Sopater* (Acts 20:4).

Where Silas was born and what kind of a background he had, or how he became a disciple of Christ, or how he ended his days, we are not told. Tradition tells us that he was one of the Seventy whom Jesus sent forth to witness two by two (Luke 10:1). If this is so, then having labored with, and for, the Master and witnessed His death and resurrection, he had the prescribed qualification for apostleship. His record is very brief, following his first appearance on the stage of church history at the Council of Jerusalem. God has the full facts of his life and labors written down in His book, but the scanty records we have are enough for us to read between the lines and describe some-

thing of the honor that belongs to Silas, Paul's second string, the companion who was always ready to follow.

1. *A Prominent Brother*

The first thing we learn about Silas is that Judas, surnamed Barsabbas, and he were *"chief* men among the brethren,"* with great authority in council matters in the Early Church (Acts 15:22 - 27). We may have thought Silas to be a somewhat colorless character — that he had a story but no history, a life but not a career. But Luke the historian would have us know that Silas was an important person in the Christian community. The word Luke uses for *chief* implies "a ruler of importance." Being held, then, in repute as a leader at the Church's headquarters would imply being an "early disciple," like Mnason. Years had elapsed since Calvary and Pentecost, and Silas had proved himself worthy and capable of shouldering responsibility.

The circumstances under which Silas makes his first appearance are given us by Luke in Acts 15. In the year A.D. 50 a Church Council was called to meet in Jerusalem for a final settlement of the vexing question whether Gentile converts must submit to the ceremonial law to become members of the Church. High churchmen of Jewish birth and training insisted that compliance with the Levitical law was necessary to salvation. But Paul maintained that Gentile converts were truly saved solely on the basis of personal faith in Christ. The controversy was somewhat heated and a serious breach in the Church was threatened, the crux of differences being as to the fundamental doctrine of justification by faith alone.

Peter rose up and in addressing the Council reminded his hearers of what had happened twenty years before when, on the day of Pentecost, the gospel door was opened to Jew and Gentile alike in the words, "The promise is unto you and to your children and to *all* that are afar off." Then Paul and Barnabas followed and, reporting on their first missionary journey, related the wonderful conversions wrought by the Holy Spirit "without respect of persons." These two apostles were followed by James, pastor of the mother church in Jerusalem, who addressed the assembly. Although he was naturally predisposed to the Jewish side of the thorny question on hand, he suggested that mutual concessions, without sacrifice of any principle, satisfactory to both parties and enabling them to work together in peace, be embodied in a resolution to be sent to all the churches. This was done, and the resolution is given *verbatim* in Acts 15:23-29.

Now Silas, or Silvanus, appears on the scene. The decree of the Council was regarded as of sufficient importance to warrant its immediate transmission to the churches scattered here and there. A committee consisting of Paul, Barnabas, Judas and Silas was appointed to carry out the decision of the Council. It was no light task to visit the churches in view of long distances and awkward means of communication, but out they went on their long and hazardous journeys. The presence of Silas on this committee charged with duties so delicate and far-reaching indicates that he was recognized as a tactful man of a peaceful and conciliatory disposition. Doubtless it was at this time that Paul became impressed with the character and efficiency of Silas as a fellow-servant of Christ, and when need arose for a companion and fellow-worker in his missionary work, the apostle chose such a valuable man to accompany him.

2. *A Christian Prophet*

The messengers reached Antioch with the epistle from the Council. The church there rejoiced over its content, and Judas and Silas being *prophets* exhorted the members of the church with many words and confirmed the saints in their faith (Acts 15:30-32). The term *prophet* implies one who, because of communion with God, is able to receive a divine message and proclaim it openly. "The prophesying of the New Testament prophets was both a preaching of the divine counsels of grace already accomplished and the fore-telling of the purposes of God in the future."

There is no doubt that Silas was an efficient and authoritative teacher of the Word. When he came to Berea he must have found himself at home among the Bible-loving believers there who "received the word with all readiness of mind, and searched the scriptures daily, whether those things were so." A remarkable feature, however, is that although we have frequent reference to the preaching of Silas, no one single sentence of any message he preached has been preserved for our edification. We can imagine what a forceful and spiritual preacher he must have been, ranking second only to his fellow-apostle; and likewise he had the position of an ecclesiastical equal of Barnabas, yet no word he uttered has been recorded. What treasure would be ours if only we possessed some of the peerless exhortations of Silas!

3. *A Roman Citizen*

This was an honor Silas shared with Paul for when the apostle protested at the beating received from the hands of the prison's officers, they were afraid when they heard that Paul and Silas were Romans (Acts 16:35-40). In this respect Silas was the social superior of Barnabas. Ro-

man citizenship was a valuable qualification for the itinerating work Paul
and Silas were doing, for both of them
could claim the privileges to which
being Romans entitled them. Both
Roman citizenship and spiritual insight made Silas sympathetic toward
the larger movement of welcoming
converts from heathenism ungrudg-
ingly. With the breadth of true vitality, he threw himself into this new
stream, and went out to win Jew and
Gentile for the living Christ.

Sir William Ramsay reminds us that
being a Roman citizen was a proof of
distinction and of moderate wealth,
and thus Silas would have a standing
among the aristocracy of any provincial town. Thus Paul and Silas were
able to meet with and lead to Christ
wealthy and influential people like
Lydia, and other women (and men)
of honorable estate (Acts 16:14; 17:
12). The Roman name, *Silvanus*, also
provided him with an *entrée* into high
circles. Harrington Lees observes,
"Following the affectionate familiarity
of Luke we usually call him Silas; but
Paul, more careful of his dignity, and
Peter, with equal deference, style him
in the official documents of the
Church by his Roman name *Silvanus*."

4. *A Missionary Companion*

Silas is conspicuous in the sacred
record as the apostle who took the
place of Barnabas on Paul's second
missionary journey, just as later on,
Timothy took the place of John Mark.
At Antioch, the four commissioners
sent out by the Jerusalem church remained for two years, preaching the
Gospel with such power and notable
results that Antioch supplanted Jerusalem as the center of operations for
the Christian Church. But Paul was
restless, for his was a passionate missionary zeal, and he had to be on the
move preaching the Gospel everywhere. It was thus that he resolved

to set out on another missionary journey, and said to his companion, Barnabas, "Let us go again and visit our
brethren in *every* city where we have
preached the word of the Lord, and
see how they do" (Acts 15:36).

Barnabas agreed to go but wanted
his nephew, John Mark, to accompany
them, but Paul objected because John
Mark had failed them on their first
missionary itinerary, turning back at
the foot of the Pamphylian hills (Acts
15:37, 38). Godly men though they
were, Paul and Barnabas parted after
a contention that was *sharp*. Paul
doubted the ability of Mark to stand
daily tests. It was not so much being
afraid of taking Mark, as of having
him continually with him in different
places. What a painful break of
friendship that must have been! It
would seem as if Paul was right, for
Barnabas does not appear in the Acts
again. Later on, John Mark made
good and is found with Paul just as
the apostle refers affectionately to
Barnabas (I Cor. 9:6).

Being the last man in the world to
travel and work alone, Paul must have
a yokefellow in the place of Barnabas, and so Silas was chosen as a companion for the second missionary journey. Heart-sore and grieved over the
break with his friend, Paul saw in Silas
one with whom he could work without
reserve, one who would be more reliable than Mark and more accom-
modating than Barnabas. Thus Silas
was the brother born for adversity,
and out Paul and he went from Antioch with their faces toward the northwest, pausing at Derbe, and then on
to Lystra, where they were joined by
young Timothy who had taken the
place of John Mark as a courier and
general helper. On they went to Iconium and Troas, where Paul had the
vision of the man of Macedonia calling, "Come over and help us"! This
brought the fearless heralds of the

cross to Europe — the invasion of a new continent for Christ.

Can you not envisage Silas ever at the side of Paul as brother, friend, and ministering comrade? How Paul must have been gratified to have such a loyal companion! Then how the churches they visited must have blessed the choice of Paul in Silas! It must have gladdened the apostle's heart to see how his fellow-delegate took his share in adjusting the decision of the Council to the constitution of the churches visited, and to watch Silas as he consolidated weak spots, reasoned with perplexed Bible students, and took his share in intercession for the churches (I Thess. 1:2). Luke joined the missionary trio, for from now on Luke, who wrote the Acts, uses the pronoun *we* instead of *they*. So the missionary quartette, Paul, Silas, Timothy and Luke, commence the journey to Philippi, all girded for service and suffering there.

One most interesting feature of the ministry of Silas is the way he functioned as a gleaner in the harvest work of Paul, who, when he left one city for another further on, is said to have left Silas behind "to gather up the loose grain of the harvest." For such follow-up activities he had all the necessary qualifications of binding together the converts, establishing them in their most holy faith, thus forming them into a local church where one did not previously exist. Too often in present-day evangelistic efforts much fruit is lost after crusades are over, because of the lack of nurturing the converts to grow in grace and in the knowledge of the Lord.

5. A Happy Prisoner

There is a proverb to the effect that wherever Paul went you could look for "a revival or a riot." Once the apostles reached Philippi and set about preaching the Gospel, they ex-perienced *both a revival and a riot,* as the record in Acts 16 proves. It would appear as if Luke and Timothy, who likewise entered Philippi with Paul and Silas, escaped the shameful treatment in the riot and lawless procedure there (I Thess. 2:2). But Silas, who had joined Paul for better or for worse, was ready to run the gauntlet with his brave and daring companion. The authorities at Philippi recognized the importance and prominence of Silas, who stood the test before him like a hero, and shared with Paul the commendation from an evil source, "These men are the servants of the most high God, which shew unto us the way of salvation" (Acts 16:17).

Several days after their entrance into Philippi Paul and Silas made their way to a riverside prayer-meeting to which many *women* had gathered, doubtless to intercede that the messengers of the Gospel would be blessed in their visit to the city. These praying women proved to be "the man of Macedonia" who had beckoned for help. Paul did the preaching, for one of them who came under its spell "attended unto the things which were spoken by Paul" (Acts 16:14). Evidently the witness of Paul and Silas was in the power of the Spirit for there were many trophies of grace, the first being Lydia, cultured and wealthy, the astute seller of purple who, once her heart was opened by, and to, the Lord, gave the apostles the hospitality of her home.

Then there was the transformation of the unnamed slave girl who had been used for divination, seeing she had a spirit of clairvoyance, and who brought the man who owned her a good deal of money by foretelling the future (Acts 16:16-24). Exercising his authority and power as an apostle, Paul commanded the evil spirit to come out of the degraded girl, and it did so immediately and she became a new woman in Christ Jesus. These two recorded conversions prove God's power to save all classes of sinners. Lydia was far removed from the slave-girl in refinement, morals, wealth and position. One was at the top of the social tree, the other at the bottom — the best and the bad — yet both were saved by the same matchless grace that Paul preached.

The owners of the wonderfully transformed spiritist-medium, seeing that their hope of further financial gain had vanished, stirred up a commotion that landed the two missionary-evangelists in court where they were tried and given a severe scourging, and then cast into the inner part of the city prison. Yet though the backs of Paul and Silas were bleeding because of the lashing received, and their feet were in uneasy stocks and their wrists chained, they triumphed over their adversities, for, at the midnight hour, Paul and Silas prayed and sang praises unto God, who alone can give His sore and weary saints "songs in the night." To pray and praise under such circumstances testified to the joyful defiance and unabated courage of these two sufferers. Do you think they were inspired by the example of the Master they were willing to die for, who went out to His brutal death singing a hymn?

Luke gives us a delightful touch in this prison episode. He says that "the prisoners heard them," praying, praising, and how impressed they must have been at such courage! As a young believer, I had the privilege of hearing General William Booth, founder of the *Salvation Army*, preach on "The Conversion of the Jailer," and although the bulk of the stirring message was gradually forgotten, one sentence gripped my mind and has remained with me for more than sixty years. Coming to the climax of his message Booth said, "God was so well-pleased with the prayers and praises of Paul and Silas that He cried *AMEN!* with a mighty earthquake." Well, God knows how to vary His method. It required no earthquake to open the heart of Lydia. It opened as silently to Jesus as a bud to the morning sun. But it took an earthquake to burst open the prison door, wrench the chains from the hands of the prisoners — and open the hard and brutal heart of the jailer.

What a night! Yet calm amid all the upheaval were Paul and Silas who kept the jailer from committing suicide. "Do thyself no harm: for we are all here." Completely broken by the display of divine power and the magnificent spirit of Paul and Silas, the jailer fell at their feet, crying "Sirs, what must I do to be saved?" It took an earthquake to change such a hard man, indifferent to human suffering, but so real was the change, that he took Paul and Silas at the same midnight hour and "washed their stripes" — stripes he himself had given them (Acts 16:23, 24, 33). Salvation was preached to all in the jailer's house, and all present believed and with the jailer were baptized. A joyful feast followed that most memorable day and night. After a short rest in the home of Lydia, Paul and Silas, freed by the authorities, went on their way to capture more territory for their King.

6. *A Faithful Friend*

Many years after the Philippian experience of Paul and Silas, Peter wrote his first epistle. He closed with this commendation, "By Silvanus, a faithful brother . . . I have written briefly, exhorting and testifying that this is the true grace of God" (I Pet. 5:12). From this reference to Silas it is evident that he was with Peter in his closing years, sharing his trials and persecution and as a faithful brother serving as Peter's amanuensis, and then as his postman to convey the great apostle's message to the saints scattered abroad. But the description, "A faithful brother," covers the whole life of Silas as a follower of the Lord. Although he never coveted the limelight, yet he ever shone as a faithful servant of his Master, and a faithful friend and companion of Paul, and then Peter.

Leaving Philippi, Paul and Silas traveled to Thessalonica, where again there was both a *revival* and a *riot*. For three weeks they taught and preached, and a mighty spiritual upheaval was experienced and a large church was formed there. But then there came the riot which resulted in Paul and Silas being hurriedly dispatched by night to Berea where for a time they rested, and had the opportunity of teaching the Word in which the Bereans rejoiced. The coming of a deputation of hostile Jews from Thessalonica, however, brought interruption to rest and ministry, and Paul was quickly removed from the scene, but Silas and Timothy remained behind.

Let us not forget the strenuous manual labor of the apostles while in Thessalonica. Paul, Silas, and Timothy were not afraid of working hard with their hands. At the time there was much distress all over Greece with well-nigh famine conditions, and these brave apostolic missionaries refused to be a load upon the impoverished Christians, and so earned their own bread as the humblest man in Thessalonica. It was thus that Paul wrote: "We did not loaf in your midst, we did not take free meals from any one. No, toiling at our own trade, we worked day and night so as not to be a burden" (See I Thess. 1:1; 2:9; II Thess. 3:10). Those rough times were not shirked. As good soldiers of Jesus Christ, Paul, Silas, and Timothy endured hardness. Such discipline and endurance must have drawn these apostles closer together.

After his speedy exit from Thessalonica, Paul reached Athens and was not long in sending for his courageous co-workers. It was at Corinth that Paul did his best work after Silas and Timothy rejoined him. The spell of confident, exultant preaching there is noted by both Luke and Paul, with its subject of Christ as God's eternal pledge of granted grace (Acts 18:5, r.v.; II Cor. 1:19). After this glorious season of blessing, Silas is not again mentioned by name in the Acts. He dropped suddenly out of history, for we do not read of Paul and Silas working together again. Yet we somehow believe that he continued to stand by Paul in his trials and triumphs for many days, and proved himself to be, in every way, "a faithful brother."

It is about ten years later that Silas again appears along with Marcus, or Mark, and as usual is found modestly occupying the place of a second string, writing a letter at Peter's dictation, and then acting as letter-carrier to the scattered Jews, many of whom he had previously come to know when he was Paul's traveling companion and faithful helper. "Two are better than one," said Solomon, "for if they fall the one will lift up his fellow." It was thus with Paul and Silas. In describing *Mr. Great-Heart*, John Bunyan had him say, "Hark to what the shepherd boy saith!" Then said the guide, "Do you hear him? I will dare to say this boy lives a merrier life, and wears more of that herb called heart's-ease in his bosom, than he did clad in silk and velvet."

Paul and Silas were a merry pair. There was the garment of praise for the spirit of heaviness while in prison because at all times they knew how to cheer each other in "psalms and hymns and spiritual songs."

As *Christian* and his comrade in John Bunyan's allegory passed through danger after danger, singing as they went, until they were welcomed by angels at the gates of *The Celestial City*, so was it with the two pilgrims, Paul and Silas, God's missionaries and minstrels for whom the trumpets sounded on the other side. Happy is the laborer in the Lord's vineyard who has a *Silas* as a yokefellow, one who is ever near when the shadows of Philippi appear, and whose presence through gloom and gladness is a benediction.

> Farewell, Silas, it has been an inspiration to tarry with you for a little, faithful brother and true comrade in the Gospel of the grace of God! What a thrill it would have been to have had some letter from you, or record of your sayings! Still, your witness speaks volumes, and although dead for so long now, you still have much to say by example. May I be enabled to manifest the same valued friendship toward others, as you did while with Paul and Peter!

TIMOTHY

The Apostle Who Was an Understudy

If Paul had a favorite companion among the whole circle of saints whom he mentions by name in his writings, it was surely Timothy, to whom he addressed two of his matchless epistles. Altogether Paul names Timothy in sixteen passages; in six of these he insists on the identity of thought and aim between them both; in another six, Paul associates Timothy with himself in the authority of an epistle; in the other four passages he addresses his young comrade as son or heir. Such prominence proves that Timothy was Paul's dearest friend and closest associate.

From the attention Paul gave to

Timothy's training he would appear as if he regarded him as his *understudy*, chosen and trained to fill a part when his principal was for any reason unable to undertake it. Occasionally this *understudy* of some twenty years of age had the chance of individual distinction. Said an English king of his hard-pressed son in a fierce battle, "Let the lad win his spurs." Paul sent Timothy back from Athens to the storm-center of Thessalonica, to complete the organization of the church there, which Paul was not able to realize because of his sudden ejection from the city (I Thess. 3:2). In time, Timothy rejoined Paul at Corinth and reported on the faith and suffering of the saints, bringing a welcome gift of money for pressing needs (Acts 18:1, 5; II Cor. 11:9). Thus Paul is his *understudy*. "He worketh the work

of the Lord, as I also do" (I Cor. 16:
10).

"Timothy was to be not merely an
evangelist," says Dr. Hort, "but Paul's
special associate in *his quite unique*
evangelistic work." Piecing all Paul's
references to Timothy together it
would appear as if the apostle
dreamed of Timothy as a kind of prodigy. While he must have possessed
some force of character for Paul to
take such pains over his training, Timothy's personality is elusive. The record of his movements is not very
startling. "It is possible to sum up the
twenty years in Timothy's New Testament story as simply a series of journeys and missions, with nothing very
striking about any of them."

What no one can gainsay is the exhibition of the beautiful friendship
between Paul and Timothy, which,
between an older and a younger man
is commonly helpful to both, and in
which each can be the real complement of the other. Each by his abundance can supply the other's wants,
whereas men of equal age would have
common wants and common supplies.
This is evident, is it not, in the friendship between these two? Paul had
the impulse and enthusiasm — Timothy, the reflectiveness and reserve. In
them, *constraint* and *restraint* were
wedded. Timothy met that intense
craving for sympathy which is felt in
Paul's writings, and must have called
himself, "the disciple Paul loved." It
was, of course, Paul's love which led
to Timothy's later advancement, and
not the young understudy's success
which kindled the apostle's love.

In touching upon the fact of Timothy's life being complementary to that
of Paul, Dr. A. Gurney in his most
helpful volume on, *The First Epistle
to Timothy,* aptly remarks:

> There is the deepest unity in its
> diversity. It is not like to like, but
> like in difference. God needed Timo-

thy to place side by side even with a
Paul. How weak he appears sometimes against the giant strength of
"such an one as Paul the aged." Yet
how confessed a source of strength
Timothy really was, how necessary,
how encouraging. The one, spiritual
father — the other, "beloved son."

Contrasts between the two are most
noticeable, as Dr. Gurney goes on to
indicate in the following ways:

> The one, born leader of men, chosen
> pioneer of a new and untried faith,
> burning with intensity of zeal for
> Christ, as once he had breathed out
> threatenings and slaughter against
> the Lord —
> The other, naturally wishful to be
> second, and not fully sure of himself,
> dependent by natural characteristic,
> fellow-labourer, not chief.
> The one, so strong, so fully per-
> suaded, more than conqueror through
> his mighty faith, sure that, though de-
> serted by men, he is helped by God,
> convinced that in authority lies "not
> one whit behind the chiefest of the
> apostles." The other, so modest in his
> use of spiritual authority, that he
> shrinks back from a self-assertion,
> justified by the duties of his position,
> till he is in danger of being despised,
> (I Cor. 16:10, 11), and needs a stif-
> fening up against too easy acquies-
> cence.

Timothy stands out as a "peace-loving
man of humble heart and true." Like
Silas, whom we have just considered,
he was a good second, the fervent and
constant friend, the man in whom you
see the mirror, not of the missionary
so much as the pastor and overseer.
Unequal as they were in gifts and
characteristics they were bound together by a common faith and a common devotion to Christ. Together,
Paul and Timothy seemed as two
strings of a lyre sounding forth the
praise of their Savior-God. Both
shared an undying love for the Mas-

ter, and sought to make Him known where His Gospel had never been heard before. Their two hearts were one in the fulfillment of God's redemptive purpose.

As Paul sketches a full portrait of his young son in the faith, let us now seek to enumerate the facts and features we have of Timothy in the apostle's writings.

1. *He Was an Apostle*

We feel it necessary to commence here, for the question has been raised as to Timothy's apostleship. Was he an apostle of the wider circle, or was his service that of deputy apostleship for Paul? If apostleship was extended to men of apostolic character like Andronicus and Junias (Rom. 16:7), why did Paul seem to withhold apostleship from Timothy in references to him? (II Cor. 1:1; Col. 1:1). What we said of Silas' inclusion in the apostolic band applies to Timothy, for in his first letter to the Thessalonians, Silas, or Silvanus, and Timothy are linked together, and Paul, when he speaks of "the apostles of Christ," is referring to himself and to his two companions in travel (I Thess. 1:1; 2:6). "Paul, Silvanus and Timotheus . . . the apostles of Christ." Although a minor apostle alongside of a major apostle like Paul, Timothy nevertheless exercised an apostolic ministry.

2. *He Had a Godly Heritage*

Paul testified to Timothy's Christian upbringing when he testified of him, "From a child thou hast known the holy Scriptures" (II Tim. 3:15). That the apostle must have often thought about the fragrance of the home in which Timothy was reared, is borne out in the apostolic greeting commencing the second letter he sent to his young *understudy*: "When I call to remembrance the unfeigned faith that is in thee, which dwelt *first* in thy

grandmother Lois, and thy mother Eunice, and I am persuaded that in thee also" (II Tim. 1:5). The two women, then, who greatly influenced Timothy from his childhood up, were his grandmother and mother. We know nothing of Timothy's unnamed father save that he was a Greek, or Gentile (Acts 16:1). Evidently he was a non-Christian, seeing that he is not named with those who shared in Timothy's Christian education. Seeing that Timothy, as a child, became familiar with the Old Testament, his father had no objections to his son learning the ancient Hebrew Scriptures, but he drew the line at circumcision, which his mother, as a Jewess, believed in. Therefore, the Jews in Lystra, Timothy's home town, would not take kindly to this uncircumcised son of a Jewish mother.

When Timothy came to join Paul in his great missionary work, he found that while Gentiles would listen to him, Jews turned from him because of his uncircumcised condition. Probably by this time, his unnamed father was dead, and Timothy, following the council of Paul, his spiritual father, submitted to the painful operation of circumcision for expediency's sake. It is to the credit of Timothy that he willingly complied. Thereafter he would become acceptable to both Jew and Gentile. What Timothy owed to his father we are not told, but as his mother and grandmother were united in his holy training, let us take a brief look at these two "mothers in Israel."

Lois — a relatively common Greek name — was the grandmother whose faith and godliness must have impressed Paul whenever he visited the home. A renowned Indian who deeply felt the lack of parental influence said that "India's crying need was a new grandmother." Timothy never labored under this disadvantage. A German proverb has it, "The grandmother's correction makes no impression." But of this we are confident, that the corrections of Timothy's godly grandmother made a great impression on his character. A devout Jewess by conviction, she instructed her family in Holy Scriptures, and must have been a tower of spiritual strength, in the home. Incidentally this is the only time the term *grandmother* is found in the Bible. *Grandfather* never appears.

Eunice, her daughter, is described by Paul as being "a Jewess who *believed,*" that is, believed in and accepted the Messiah as her Savior (Acts 16:1). The implication here is that her husband did not share her faith. He was an unbeliever. It would also appear as if Eunice had not always believed, which may explain why she was married to a Gentile husband. Although a Jewess at the time she met him, and perhaps not a very orthodox Jewess, she made the mistake of marrying a heathen. Once she believed, however, she set herself to retrieve the error against the Jewish code of marriage by surrounding the son of her marriage with holy influences. Some expositors think that possibly Eunice was converted to Christ during Paul's first missionary visit to Lystra, seeing that when he next came to the city she is spoken of as the Jewess who *believed.* How much the world owes to its godly mothers will never be known! How privileged is the child who has a saintly mother eager to bring up her offspring in the fear and admonition of the Lord!

An evidence of the faith and devotion of Eunice can be found in the name she gave her son — *Timothy,* which means, "Honor God," and true to his name he honored Him throughout his life (I Sam. 2:30). From a "babe," as the R.V. of Second Timothy 3:15 expresses it, Timothy had known the sacred Scriptures, and it was the careful training in them by Eunice his mother, and the shrewd comments on them by Lois his grandmother that gave Timothy a foundation which made him "thoroughly equipped for his good work" (II Tim. 3:17). How often does a mother's unfeigned faith give a Timothy, a David Livingstone, a Mary Slessor, a D. L. Moody, to the church! How often from remotest quarters, from simplest homes, from lowliest parentage God replenishes the exhausted treasures of His Church.

The responsibilities of those who have known the Scriptures from earliest days are greater than those bereft of such a privilege. It is an inestimable boon to have learned the Word in childhood from godly parents. The truths of God instilled in the minds of the young are seldom forgotten. To come to know Christ and His truth in later life without any previous knowledge of such, or without the influence of a Christian upbringing, is to start the Christian race somewhat handicapped. Yet by divine grace a handicap can win the race.

3. *He Was a Convert of Paul*

With all his knowledge of the Scriptures and Christian upbringing, Timothy was not a committed Christian himself until he came under the spiritual influence of the Apostle Paul. That Timothy was one of Paul's converts is proven by the way he speaks of him as his beloved and faithful son in the Lord (I Cor. 4:17); as "my own son in the faith" (I Tim. 1:2); and as "Timothy, my dearly beloved son" (II Tim. 1:2). Timothy ever maintained a deep affection for his mother whose influence over him had been heavenward, but the day came when, to use Paul's phrase, "Jesus Christ the crucified was placarded," before Timothy's eyes, and the work of grace was completed in his soul (Gal. 3:1 *Moffat*).

Through Paul's ministry the old knowledge of Scripture which Timothy had, was kindled into newness of life, and he became wise unto salvation, as many came to see in his transformed life.

Probably Timothy was converted during Paul's first visit to Iconium and Lystra, seeing that he refers to the persecutions heaped upon him there and which, because Timothy belonged to Lystra, he would know about (II Tim. 3:10, 11). On Paul's next visit to Lystra and Derbe, Timothy was already one of the believers there (Acts 16:1). In his enlightening commentary on the Acts, Dr. G. Campbell Morgan has this suggestive description of Timothy's conversion:

> At last Paul came to Lystra, the place of stones, the scars of which were still upon his body: the memories of the day when they beat fast and furiously upon him were still with him. At Lystra they found Timothy. How often God's servants return, after years of absence to some rough and rugged place of battle and of blood and of agony only to find the fruitage. When did Timothy become a disciple? The question cannot be answered dogmatically, but the probability is that he became a disciple in those days of Paul's previous visit. Paul had once been a young man, and had watched the stoning of a saint called Stephen, minding the clothes of such as stoned him. He had heard the dying prayer, and the vision of the face of Stephen had fastened like goads in his heart and life. At Lystra, he had gone through Stephen's experience: and, perchance another man had seen the stones hurled. Now he went back to find Timothy in the place of stones, and from that moment began that rare and beautiful friendship, the friendship of an old man for a young man.

It has been suggested that when Paul recovered consciousness after being mobbed and stoned, on his re-entry into the town it was in Timothy's home he found shelter. If this be true, then we can imagine how easily young Timothy would be impressed with the reality of Christ when His servant Paul was willing to suffer such hardship for Him. At the time, Timothy would be an earnest lad about fifteen years of age, and how he must have listened to Paul and Barnabas as they preached Christ which fitted in so marvelously with the Scripture lessons his godly mother had taught him.

If Paul left for dead and thrown outside the gates, was taken to the home of Timothy, we can visualize how his mother and grandmother would tenderly nurse and care for the injured missionary, and how the young son of the house now, perhaps fatherless, developed a filial love for Paul, and reverence for Paul's Master. Paul's heart, still sore over the absence of John Mark, yearned for youthful companionship, and found consolation in young Timothy who became his son in the faith.

Thereafter, Paul carried the memory of Timothy with him in his absence, and "recalled to him long years after how the day of his serious injuries was the time when their path interlaced (II Tim. 3:10, 11). The stones of the Lystrans were as shuttles weaving two hearts into one." It was, of course, on Paul's second visit, some five years after his previous visit, that he learned of Timothy, as a disciple well-reported on by the brethren at Lystra and Iconium and adopted him as his missionary assistant in the place of young John Mark. Luke marks the event in his own peculiar style, "*And behold*, a certain disciple named Timotheus" (Acts 16:1). As we have already remarked, Paul circumcised Timothy out of deference to the Jews so that his usefulness would not be prejudiced on account of his semi-

Greek extraction. Submitting to this rite, Timothy obtained free admission to the synagogue.

4. *He Became a Minister of the Gospel*

It was quite natural that Timothy, owing to his unique knowledge of the Scriptures, should be adopted as his spiritual father's fellow-worker, and his entrance into the ministry stands out because of its important features. A young man, about twenty at the time, Timothy was called and questioned by the elders, and with courage and clarity gave "a noble profession of faith before many witnesses." A solemn service of prayer and dedication was held, at which Paul and attendant elders laid their hands on Timothy's head, and the Holy Spirit filled him with power for the tasks ahead. Paul refers to the reception of the gift of God and the sealing of the Spirit (II Tim. 1:6,7); and the laying on of hands (I Tim. 4:14; II Tim. 1: 6).

Admitted thus to a sacred "charge" or "trust," Timothy could never surrender this in the days ahead, unless he proved unfaithful. His was a solemn, life-long charge without reservation and was to prove arduous and even perilous. Ordained thus for the service of the Lord, Timothy became the intimate companion of the mighty apostle. Willingly he left a loving mother and grandmother, and a pleasant home, to share the apostle's labors and sufferings. At once, there began a life of true human fellowship, for from the moment of his ordination, "as a son with the father," Timothy served Paul in the furtherance of the Gospel (Phil. 2:22), and they became one in their journeyings, their perils, and their sufferings for Christ's sake. In times of bodily separation, Paul yearned for the presence of his son in the faith.

The records show that Timothy, as the friend, came ever and again to gladden the heart of Paul in seasons of distress, solitude and conflict. He was the one nearest of all to the strong, tender heart of Paul, and most indispensable as a travel-companion (Acts 17:14-15; 18:5; 19:22; 20:4, etc.). Having no son of his own, possessing one of the warmest fatherly hearts, Paul must have watched the spiritual growth of his son in the Lord with gratitude, having perhaps, the idea of adopting him as his heir. Paul does seem to have performed a father's part at Timothy's admission into the Jewish church (Acts 16:3). For the years they were together, Timothy was Paul's other self in the work of the Gospel.

Reading between the lines of his various exhortations to the young minister, it would seem as if Paul had a dream of reproducing in this receptive youth the fruits which Christ had wrought in his own spiritual life. Thus, he sought to train him, not only to keep pace with his teaching and conduct, purpose and faith, and to learn to set before others all Paul's ways in Christian life and work, but also that he might become like a second Paul in the furtherance of the cause of Christ (I Cor. 4:17; II Tim. 3:10). So his whole care was centered upon the value of those heirlooms of the faith which Timothy was to "inherit in trust," when his own strong apostolic voice was stilled.

Paul himself must have had a strong constitution to endure all he did, not only on his missionary journeys, but in the constant beatings, stonings, and imprisonments he had to face. Many a thorn in the flesh was his, but his young friend was not blessed with the same iron frame as the apostle possessed. It would seem as if he was frail of health because of some deep-seated stomach trouble, hence Paul's reference to Timothy's health and his prescription for his physical infirmity. "I should advise you to drink wine in moderation, instead of water. It will do your stomach good and help you to get over your frequent spells of sickness" (I Tim. 5:23, *Phillips*). An interesting fact to observe is that although Paul had the power to heal the sick, he never relieved himself of his infirmities in any miraculous way, nor did he touch Timothy's body to cure him of his dyspepsia, but prescribed medicine as a means for his relief.

In spite of his lack of physical robustness, Timothy was a true child of an indomitable father in the Gospel who had "no other likeminded." Is it not somewhat singular that Paul adds the word "mercy" to the usual couplet of "grace and peace" in Timothy's call to service? Said Chrysostom, "Teachers stand more in need of mercy than others," and because Timothy was called to an office carrying high spiritual possibility and responsibility he was on that very account more liable to fall short of its ideals, hence the provision of *mercy*.

5. *He Was an Evangelist*

From Paul's explicit instructions, Timothy would make full proof of his ministry by doing the work of an *evangelist* (II Tim. 4:5), and in breaking new ground as a pioneer of the Gospel he would thus emulate the example of his spiritual father (Acts 17:14). Enjoying in the highest degree the apostle's confidence and affection, the young soul-winner had the benefit of Paul's constant instruction for such an all-important task (II Tim. 2:2; 3:14). It was in this way that he functioned in the province of Achaia during a season of great spiritual awakening (Acts 19:21, 22). There is no evidence that Timothy was a man of commanding skill or overwhelming eloquence. Unlike Paul, he

may not have been fitted for a position of first consequence in the church as the repeated and urgent exhortations to courage and vigilance addressed to him seem to suggest.

Timothy appears to have been, naturally, of a gentler and even somewhat irresolute disposition. Yet he had the qualities of piety and faithful affection and for fully sixteen years he possessed the love of, and deserved the confidence, shared the evangelistic labors, and alleviated the sorrows of the great apostle. Bishop Handley Moule says of him:

> His face full of thought and feeling and devotion is rather earnest than strong. But it has the strength of patience, of absolute sincerity, and of rest in Christ. Timothy repays the affection of Paul with unwavering fidelity. And he will be true to the end, to his Lord and Redeemer through whatever tears and agonies of sensibility.

Coupled with his evangelistic work, Timothy was also charged to act as an ambassador charged with difficult and delicate responsibility to correct a backsliding church (I Cor. 4:17). For such a task, both gift and grace were required. That he was able also to soothe the saints, as well as save sinners, is seen in his mission to comfort and establish believers in the midst of tribulation (I Thess. 3:2). His charge had a negative and positive aspect, namely, the repudiation of error and the declaration of revealed truth. Timothy's innate timidity made the work of an evangelist more difficult, but, conscious of the poverty of his own resources, Paul urged upon him to depend more fully upon divine enduement which meant "the power of hearing the divine voice and catching the divine inspiration."

6. *He Was a Type of the Church*

Half Jewish and half Gentile extraction made Timothy a good link between the two. Having a Gentile father and a Jewish mother, the blood of both was in his veins. Dr. Campbell Morgan made the observation, "The ideals of Hebraism and Hellenism were merged and fulfilled in the teaching of Christ. Here is a man in whose very blood the two fires mingled, in whose mental calibre the two ideas were found and the man by nature at once Hebrew and Greek: by grace well reported by the brethren."

Paul, the apostle to the Gentiles, came declaring that in the composition of the Church, regenerated Jews and Gentiles are merged into one, and here in his devoted companion was one who illustrated such a fusion in his own being. The great truth of Jew and Gentile as one body in Christ is fully dealt with by Paul in Ephesians (see chapter 2).

The composition of the Church is what Paul called "the revelation of the mystery, which was kept secret since the world began" (Rom. 16:25) — a mystery which he, more than any other apostle, understood and preached (Eph. 3:11-12). It was no mystery to Old Testament prophets that Jews should be saved, or Gentiles saved. The mystery hid from the past, but revealed through the coming of Christ, and which Paul so clearly proclaimed, was that of a new society — the Church — in which regenerated Jews and regenerated Gentiles are woven into such a mystic fabric as "the Church of the living God."

7. He Was the Recipient of Two Letters

Out of the fourteen epistles Paul wrote, two were addressed personally to Timothy, his son in grace. These two epistles along with the one to Titus are known as *the pastoral epistles* because they are largely composed of practical exhortations and advice concerning the life and work of those who are responsible for the edification and expansion of the Church. It is not our intention to outline and expound what Paul teaches in his letters to Timothy, but simply to indicate some of his personal references to his companion. Timothy, to whom Paul wrote, "Let no man despise thy youth," realized that he needed all the spiritual correction and spiritual reinforcement he could get, and in these two anxiously-worded letters, Paul pointed him back to the promise of the Comforter with great tenderness. As we read between the lines of these letters, we can sense some possible weak points in Timothy's character, and also something of Paul's fear of a break-down on the part of his understudy, on whom he had pinned his hopes. Dr. Harrington Lees says that "amid all the plaintiveness of the letters we keep catching echoes of disappointment. The cement of Timothy's character seems never to have really set." A German proverb has it, "The greatest favorites are in the most danger of falling."

Paul's anxiety cannot be entirely without cause. "You do not tell a man to be brave half a dozen times in the space of two letters unless you have doubts of his courage. One who is bidden to stand by his friend must be in danger of deserting him. Paul was not sure of Timothy, and that is the pathos of his eventide." The first epistle was written some thirty years after Paul's conversion which adds great weight to his declaration that he was the chief of sinners (I Tim. 1: 15). He cherished to the end of his life a deep sense of his sinfulness, and by such a confession he sought to stimulate Timothy into being the chief of saints. But somehow such an ideal was beyond the young evangelist, and the undertones of Paul's letters to him suggest the impression of inadequacy in his understudy. "There is no afterglow of Pauline splendor in Timothy's subsequent history."

A noticeable feature is the way Paul always mentions Timothy with the greatest affection, and joins his name with his own in six of his epistles. It is out of a heart of love that in his first letter to his beloved son in Christ, he shows him how to regulate his own conduct and ministy, both in the refutation of error and the establishment of truth. Both letters are pertinent in their appeal.

In the First Epistle, Timothy is enjoined to *preach a straight Gospel* and to *guard* the *doctrine* which is our message from God — *The Silver Trumpet.*

In the Second Epistle, Timothy is exhorted to *live a straight life* and to *guard* his *testimony* which was his life from God — *The Player behind the Silver Trumpet.*

The personal element in these letters is strongly marked, and contains the veteran worker's final advice and appeal to a younger fellow-laborer. In no other epistle of his does the true, loving, undaunted and trustful heart of the great apostle speak in more consolatory yet moving accents as here in First and Second Timothy. As the second epistle is the last one to leave the gifted pen of Paul, and is thus known as his *Swan Song,* it is a most precious document seeing it is the last will or testament of the writer addressed to his favorite disciple, and contains his final wishes, written under the shadow of approaching death and bears the stain of his blood.

This last letter was written in a cold, damp Roman dungeon about A.D. 67 toward the end of Nero's reign. Paul is shortly to appear before the Emperor and the immediate motive in writing to Timothy was the apostle's intense desire to see his dear friend — which urgent desire is several times expressed in the letter (1:4; 4:

9, 11, 21). The request for his spiritual son to come and be with him in his last hours shows how true and tender was the affection binding these two saints together. But whether Timothy reached Rome in time to comfort his devoted partner before the bitter end is not known. Not knowing whether he would be spared to give last instructions with his own lips, Paul fills his letter with fatherly exhortations applicable to Timothy's circumstances.

Paul had previously appeared before Nero but his case had been adjourned (4:16, 17). He expected to come before the Emperor again in the winter and wrote urging Timothy, whose liberty from prison (Heb. 13: 23), made it possible to come at once, to hasten to his prison with his only goods and chattels he had left elsewhere (4:9, 11, 13, 21). Expressing his longing to see Timothy again, and reaffirming his affectionate regard for him, Paul counsels him not to shrink from sharing his shame and suffering for Christ and His truth. By God's grace he must function as:

A faithful minister of the Word.

An opposer of false teachers.

A prophet in perilous times.

A sufferer in Christ's cause.

The character and conduct of Timothy occupies a third of this last epistle which Paul wrote.

Apparently Timothy was of a shrinking disposition. Paul urges him again and again to be bold (I Tim. 4:12, 16; II Tim. 1:3-8).

Dark days are coming, and many are to wax cold and apostatize, hence the stirring call all through the letter for Timothy to be firm and courageous (1:6-14; 2:1-12; 3:14; 4:1-5). The Lord would stand by him, even as He had stood by Paul in dark and difficult hours. But the letter has a sad note. Death is to free the apostle from his bonds, toil and anxiety, thus bringing him home to Christ; his approaching martyrdom is also to take him from the churches he had brought into being and who sorely needed him, and from a host of friends who loved him and had come to lean upon him. Nowhere in Paul's writings is there a loftier tone of Christian courage than that which pervades these dying words; nowhere a holier rapture than that which the reward and crown of faithful labor is contemplated as now exceeding nigh at hand. Can you not imagine how Timothy's heart was moved as he read his letter, and how his tears must have stained the parchment? Surely such a poignant letter must have led him to yield his life more unreservedly to the Savior whom his beloved father in Christ had so faithfully and sacrificially served?

Saintly Bishop Moule said of Paul's *last will and testament*, "I have often found it difficult deliberately to read these short chapters through without finding something like a mist gathering in my eyes. The writer's heart beats in the writing." May it be our determination to catch its heart-beats anew, so that at the end of the road we too can confess —

I have fought a good fight —
I have finished my course —
I have kept the faith (4:7).

Paul had no fear of death for he could say "To die is gain." With G. A. Studdert-Kennedy he could say —

> So I looked up to God
> And while I held my breath,
> I saw Him slowly nod,
> And knew — as I had never known
>   aught else,
> With certainty sublime and passionate,
> Shot through and through
> With sheer unutterable bliss.
> I knew
> There was no death but this,
> God's kiss.
> And then the waking to an everlasting Love.

TWO UNNAMED APOSTLES

With many of the apostles already considered, we have nothing more than their names, significant though they may be. But Paul refers to two apostles and does not pause to mention their names, even though they were conspicuous in their way for Christ. One of the two was a brother, "whose praise is in the gospel throughout all the churches" — a wonderful testimony to have! (II Cor. 8:18). The other one was the brother of whom Paul said, "Whom we have oftentimes proved diligent in many things" — another commendable record! (II Cor. 8:22). Then the apostle brings the two brethren together and says of them, "They are the messengers of the churches, and the glory of Christ" (II Cor. 8:23). *Messenger* is the same word as *apostle* in the Greek, hence the R.V. use of *apostle* in the margin. Rotherham translates it, "Our brethren, apostles of assemblies, and Christ's glory." Doubtless *apostles* is in the less strict sense of, e.g., Acts 14:14.

The epithet, "They are ... the glory of Christ," or "Christ's glory," is a most unusual one. Certainly these two apostles or delegates to the churches labored only for the glory of Christ, but we gain a deeper insight if we connect it with what Paul says previously about "Beholding as in a glass the glory of the Lord" and being "changed into the same image from glory to glory, even as by the Spirit of the Lord (II Cor. 3:18). In effect, Paul is saying of these two nameless saints — yet well-known among the churches—"These messengers, so apostolic in their ministry are like Christ in character: they reflect His glory. You may see that glory in them." Can we say that we are "Christ's glory"? Is He constantly glorified in, and through, us? Are we fulfilling the prayer of Christ? — "I am glorified in them" (John 17:10).

THE LORD JESUS CHRIST

THE APOSTLE OF THE APOSTLES

One of the most important books of the New Testament is the epistle to the Hebrews, which, if it was not Paul's *writing*, certainly contains his *thinking*. Theologians have created difficulties regarding its authorship. These are too involved to consider in this coverage of the apostles. Personally, I have no doubts about its Pauline atmosphere even though it comes to us as an anonymous work. What greatly impresses us about this epistle is the way it honors and magnifies the Lord Jesus Christ! It is supreme among the books of the Bible in this respect. Among the many titles used of Him which the writer

calls us to consider, is, "The Apostle and High Priest of our profession" (3:1), and it is from this verse that we have our warrant for including Jesus among the apostles mentioned in the New Testament.

This is the only occasion where He is given the title *apostle,* although the root meaning of the term is frequently used of Him. As we have previously indicated *apostle* implies "to go to a place appointed by the sender," and Jesus came to earth as the One *sent* by the Father (John 17:3, 18; 20:21). As the "Sent One" we have an allusion to His mission from God man-ward, as the Son of God. In many passages Jesus designates Himself as the Sent One of God, using the very word from which *apostle* is derived (John 3:17; 5:36, etc.). There is little difference between *apostle* and *prophet* — the former is the one who brings into relief the mission; the latter, the office and position. Each presents a thought complementary of that contained in the other title given in the verse, *High Priest.* As Bengel the renowned expositor expressed it, "As *Apostle* Jesus pleads the cause of God with us: as *High Priest* He pleads our cause with God." It may be that these two terms contain a reference to the special mission of Moses and the priesthood of Aaron; our Christian confession looks to one Mediator (Heb. 3:2; 8:6; 12:24; I Tim. 2:5).

Jesus, then, was *the Apostle* who chose the twelve apostles, and who brought all others known as such in the New Testament, into His service. It was because of all that He was in Himself as the Sent One from heaven, and all that He accomplished, that He was able to command the allegiance of the many He sent forth to preach the Gospel, which His death and resurrection made possible. The Greek poet wrote of his favorite hero, Achilles, "He alone is the living Man, and all the rest are shades," and all the apostles we have portrayed are but shades of Him who came as "The Apostle and High Priest." Delighting to do the will of the Father who sent Him into the world to die for its sin (John 3:16), Jesus looked upon His disciples as His *sent ones*. They were His Father's gifts to Him as the perfect Apostle, and He guarded them as the apple of His eye.

We have already considered how He sought to shape and train them as true apostles. Out of His love for them came the patience and forbearance which made the charm of His teaching and handling of them. How He prayed for them until His prayers had all the passion and urgency of tears and blood-drops! When one of the apostles, Judas, was lost, it was as if a string had broken in His heart. How He strove to gather His apostles under His wings for protection, and mother-like, forgive their mistakes, and encourage all their honest attempts. Often they grieved Him, but He did not tell them of the hurt, but answered it with the same unfailing, infinite kindness and perfect trust. Unwearyingly, He would repeat His lessons, until little by little, the tuition bore fruit.

Ultimately, the Sent One gained love's mastery over those He chose and sent forth, and they became as vessels made meet for the Master's use. The twelve apostles found in Christ not only a common center to which they all turned, but a point of union among themselves. The nearer a group tries to reach an object in the center of a circle, the nearer the people are to each other. It was so with Christ's first disciples who, for the main part, were strangers to each other till they were "charmed by His voice divine," and rose up and followed Him. And all down the ages heaven's Apostle has captured the admiration and adoration of countless numbers and bound them to Himself with bands of steel. While we have no evidence that Napoleon Bonaparte, the French Emperor and one of the greatest military geniuses of all time, was a born-again believer, the following reputed testimony of his is remarkable insight into the character and mission of Jesus, the Sent One:

I see in Lycurgus, Numa and Mohammed only legislators who, having the first rank in the state, sought the best solution of the social problem, but I see nothing there which reveals divinity. On the contrary, there are numerous resemblances between them and myself, foibles and errors which ally them to me and to humanity.

Everything in Christ astonishes me. His spirit overawes me, and His will confounds me. Between Him and others in the world there is no possible term of comparison. He is truly a Being by Himself. . . . The truths which He announced, His manner of convincing, are not explained either by human organization or by the nature of things.

His birth and the history of His life, the profundity of His doctrine, which grapples the mightiest difficulties, and which is, of these difficulties, the most admirable solution, His gospel . . . His empire, His march across the ages . . . is for me a prodigy, a mystery insoluble, which plunges me into a reverence which I cannot escape . . . a mystery which I can neither deny nor explain. Here I see nothing human.

His religion is a revelation from an intelligence which certainly is not that of man. There is a profound originality, which has created a series of words and maxims before unknown. Jesus borrowed nothing from our sciences. One can find nowhere, but in Him alone, such a life as His . . .

I know men; and I tell you that Jesus is not a man. Superficial minds see a resemblance between Christ and the founders of empires and the gods of other religions. That resemblance does not exist. There is between Christianity and whatever other religions the distance of infinity. . . . I search in vain in history to find the equal of Jesus Christ.

Several years ago *The New York Times* ran as a reprint the following remarkable observation made by Bishop Phillips Brooks, the renowned preacher of the eighteenth century. It is herewith repeated for reference:

Here is a man who was born in an obscure village, the child of a peasant woman. He grew up in an obscure village. He worked in a carpenter's shop until He was thirty, and then for three years He was an itinerant teacher. He never wrote a book. He never held an office. He never owned a home. He never had a family. He never went to college. He never travelled more than two hundred miles from the place where He was born. He never did one of the things that usually accompany greatness. He had no credentials but Himself. He had nothing to do with this world except the power of His divine manhood. While still a young man, the tide of popular opinion turned against Him. His friends ran away. One of them denied Him. He was turned over to His enemies. He went through the mockery of a trial. He was nailed upon a cross between two thieves. His executioners gambled for the only piece of property He had on earth while He was dying — His coat. When He was dead He was taken down and laid in a borrowed grave through the pity of a friend.

Nineteen wide centuries have come and gone. Today He is the centerpiece of the human race and the Leader of the column of progress.

I am far within the mark when I say that all the armies that ever marched, and all the navies that ever were built, and all the parliaments that ever sat, and all the kings that ever reigned, put together, have not affected the life of man upon this earth as powerfully as has *That One Solitary Life.*

Because "The Apostle and High Priest of our profession" is the same today and yesterday (Heb. 13:8), He is still calling many to follow Him. An oft-recurring key-word, suggesting an action of high significance, is the word *began.* Jesus "began to send them forth" (Mark 6:7). "All that Jesus *began* both to do and teach" (Acts 1:1). What He commenced He has not yet completed. "He began to send them forth," and He is calling and sending forth laborers into the vineyard, and will only end such a task when His Church is complete. "Jesus *began* both to do and teach," and, praise Him, He still continues this blessed ministry of expounding to loyal and loving hearts the things concerning Himself. Would that multitudes more would respond to His appeal, and be willing to be sent forth by Him into all the world to preach, teach, and *live* His Gospel! It was Whittier who taught us to sing:

In simple trust like theirs who heard,
　Beside the Syrian sea,
The gracious calling of the Lord,
Let us, like them, without a word
　Rise up and follow Thee.

Oh, Sabbath rest by Galilee;
　Oh, calm of hills above,
Where Jesus knelt to share with thee,
The silence of Eternity,
　Interpreted by Love.

IV

The Legendary Deeds and Deaths of the Apostles

We cannot but have a legitimate curiosity as to the doings and ends of many of the apostles who made such an impact upon the world in their own day and generation. What happened to the majority of them beyond their story in the sacred record is lost to us, apart from what we can gather about them from the somewhat vague and shadowy land of tradition and myth. Nothing solid can be built upon legends and romances, for the fact remains that we have no authentic evidence as to where or how long the majority of the apostles bore their witness and filled up their appointed service and died tragically, or naturally. From ecclesiastical history we gather that most of them sealed their testimony with their blood, nobly enduring their bitter trials and martyrdom.

It would be quite natural for the early Christian Church to know more of the subsequent labors and history of all the apostles than the New Testament tells us. Consequently quite a library developed containing a mass of apocryphal material which was marred by many self-contradictions and records of incredible and useless wonders. One of the first of these apocryphal books was written by Leucius. It appeared in the second century, and attempted to fill up the blank that inspired records had left. An effort was made by the writer to map out the different parts of the world in which, severally, the apostles carried on their labors and how they finished their earthly course. Johann Albert Fabricius of Hamburg made an effort to sift grains of truth from piles of legendary material, and in 1864 Alfred von Gutschmid; and later on Tischendorf and Lipsius went back to the oldest sources of apocryphal "acts" or "journeyings" or "preachings" of individual apostles. From these later writers came a compilation of general statements gathered from the work of recorders of the fifth and sixth centuries. Gutschmid sought to show that there were historical elements capable of verification from independent sources, thereby giving us a clue to the field of labor occupied by some apostles whose subsequent history is obscure. It has been pointed out that: "Tradition, however an unfaithful and uncertain preserver of character and events, is rarely an inventor," and so, although the mass of traditional documents purporting to the acts or gospels of the apostles were all written long after the first century, it is possible by exercising patience and intuition to glean from these old stories some mellow sunlit sense of original truth. Legends and descriptions of apostolic labors which lie smothered in sectarian tradition or which emerge in odd fragments, are interesting when used as a follow-up of the pure and simple authentic knowledge of the apostles as given in the New Testament.

Eusebius, the church historian around the third century, said that, "The apostles and disciples of the Savior scattered over the whole world, preached the Gospel everywhere," and the enumeration of the countries represented at the Day of Pentecost should be borne in mind in the traditional record of post-New Testament history. The countries mentioned cover broadly the region occupied by the Jewish Dispersion, and that therefore to which the apostles first directed their labors. Luke's specification is precise:

> Parthians, and Medes, and Elamites, and the dwellers in Mesopotamia, and in Judaea, and Cappadocia, in Pontus, and Asia, Phrygia, and Pamphylia, in Egypt, and in the parts of Libya about Cyrene, and strangers of Rome, Jews and proselytes (Acts 2:9, 10).

In writing on *What Became of the Apostles?* Robert Ellis Thompson observes that, "The omission of all Europe, except Rome, and of all Africa except Egypt and the Cyrenaica, is notable. We know, from the Acts, of Jews in the cities of Macedonia, Thessaly and Achaia (Greece); but these are passed over, probably because they held a much less important place in the Dispersion than did the Asiatic region, which was divided between the Parthian and Roman Empires." Peter also mentions Asiatic regions of the Dispersion, "Pontus, Galatia, Cappadocia, Asia and Bithynia" (I Pet. 1:1). The diffusion of Jews in the Asiatic direction greatly enlarged their historic consciousness and made them a mighty religious force.

ANDREW

Tradition tells of the indefatigable activities of Andrew as well as a long record of healings of disease, sin, and death, even to the raising of thirty-nine dead sailors washed ashore from a shipwreck. Miraculous acts portray him as a kind of a magician at whose simplest word mighty things happened. Early tradition says that he went to the land of cannibals, located on the southern coast of the Black Sea, inhabited by pirates. He also figures as a missionary to Russia, and as the Patron Saint of Scotland! The

Church at Byzantium, now Constantinople, claims Andrew as its founder. A fourth century account reports his death by crucifixion at Patras in Greece in the year 60 under the governor *Aegeates*.

Briefly, the story of his martyrdom runs like this: The wife of the governor was converted through the preaching of Andrew, and blind with rage and jealousy, after doing his utmost to tear his wife away from the new faith, the governor ordered the apostle to be cruelly crucified on a cross decussate in form, that is, in the shape of the letter 'X' — where he hung alive for two days exhorting the people all through his agony to be constant and faithful to the truth. Flamion calls this passage from Andrew's last discourse, the *Epitre Grecque*.

> Ye men that are here present, and women and children, old and young, bond and free, and all that will hear, that ye take no heed of the vain deceit of this present life, but heed us rather who hang here for the Lord's sake, and are about to depart out of this body; and renounce all the lusts of this world, and contemn the worship of the abominable idols, and run unto the true worshipping of our God that lieth not, and make yourselves a temple pure and ready to receive the Word. And hasten to overtake my soul as it hasteneth toward heavenly things, and in a word despise all temporal things and establish your minds as men believing in Christ.

Tradition goes on to say that the Consul, overawed and overpowered by the turbulence of the populace and the passion of the scene, sought to loose Andrew from the cross, but he would not permit him to take him down, crying out, "O Jesus Christ, let not thine adversary loose him that is hung upon Thy grace; O Father, let not this small one humble any more him that hath known Thy greatness." The martyr gave up the ghost and all present wept and lamented over his death.

Jerome records that the remains of Andrew were taken from Patras to Constantinople by command of the Emperor Constantius in A.D. 357. From this the body was taken to Amalfi, Italy in 1208, and in the fifteenth century the head of Andrew was taken to Rome, and was returned by Pope Paul VI in 1964 to the Greek Orthodox Church in Patras.

Then there is also the connection of Andrew with Scotland. Tradition says that some of his remains were brought over to that country in the eighth century, and the victory of the Picts in battle, and their conversion to Christianity were attributed to the relics of St. Andrew. The apostle became the Patron Saint of Scotland with his cross emblazoned on its national flag. Murillo, the renowned artist, made the scene of the martyrdom of Andrew the subject of one of his finest paintings. As representatives of the ancient Scythians, the early Russians also acknowledge Andrew as their Patron, and used the flag reversed in colors, namely, a blue cross on a white ground. Then there is a legend of the fifteenth century that the cross on which Andrew was crucified was brought to Marseilles in the first century by Estienne, King of Burgundy, who made it his ensign in battle. This Burgundian cross was red. But in spite of the various colors used to describe Andrew's cross, it is ever a symbol calling men to put their trust in a Power transcending earthly force.

As for Andrew himself, while not a very conspicuous figure in New Testament history, tradition and legend have made him a compelling figure indeed because of all the apostles, he had the honor of being the first preacher of the Gospel his Master came to proclaim. One of the ancients praises the character of Andrew in this glowing fashion:

> St. Andrew was the first-born of the apostolic choir, the main and prime pillar of the Church, a rock before the Rock, the foundation of that foundation, the first-fruits of the beginning, a caller of others before he was called himself: he preached the Gospel that was not yet believed or entertained; revealed and made known that life to his brother, which he had not yet perfectly learned himself. . . . How art thou become a prophet? whence thus divinely skilful? What is it that thou thus soundest in Peter's ears — *We have found Him?* . . . We have found Him, whom Adam lost, whom Eve injured, whom the clouds of sin have hidden from us, and whom our transgressions had hitherto made a stranger to us.

BARNABAS

Although Scripture references to Barnabas cease with his sad parting from Paul after their quarrel over John Mark, and his return to his native island of Cyprus, there are differing traditions as to his further labors and death. There is an apocryphal work called *The Journeys and Martyrdom of Barnabas,* which has been proved a forgery from the fifth century. A Cyprian monk by the name of Alexander also wrote a most glowing account of the apostle's great deeds. Subsequent church tradition finds Barnabas in Alexandria and ascribes to him *The Epistle of Barnabas* made up of twenty-one chapters. Its authenticity was defended by many early writers, but it is now believed to have been written in the second century. Some of the apostolic fathers pictured Barnabas in Rome where they assume he wrote *The Epistle to the Hebrews.* To stress its independence, the church of Cyprus, and later even that of Milan, claimed to have been founded by the apostle Barnabas who became its first Bishop. Some early legends affirm that he was stoned to death by Jews at Salonica. Yet other sources relate that Barnabas, the man of Cyprus, returning to his much-loved island, remained and found a grave there. Wherever he was buried we lay our ivy wreath with the hope that his memory in the Christian world will ever remain an inspiration.

BARTHOLOMEW

As already indicated in our coverage of this apostle, he is likewise the *Nathanael* Christ met under the fig-tree. Eusebius in his *Church History* relates that when Pantaenus of Alexandria, a philosopher renowned for his wisdom, visited India in the second century he found there a Hebrew copy of *The Gospel According to Matthew*, which had been left behind by Bartholomew who had preached the Gospel through the Asian Ethiopia. This apostle is also said to have ministered in Parthia, Lycaonia and Greater Armenia. He is traditionally said to have been crucified with his head downwards, or flayed to death at Albanopolis or Urbanopolis in Armenia at the command of King Astyages after the conversion of King Polymios. His remains are said to have been transferred ultimately to the Roman Church of St. Bartholomew on an island in the Tiber. A feast in his memory is celebrated in the Latin Church on August 24, and in the Greek Church on June 11. A most unworthy gospel was forged in his name by heretics who persecuted his memory after his death. Gelasius, Bishop of Rome, branded this work as apocryphal and most unworthy of the name and patronage of such an apostle as Bartholomew.

JAMES, SON OF ALPHAEUS

Ecclesiastical or traditional sources tell us little of an authentic nature about this particular James, after our Lord's ascension. His story is much obscured by Ebionite fables, some of which are reproduced by Hegesippus, A.D. 170. Myrtle Strode-Jackson refers to a very ancient, curious, Dutch map of the Mediterranean which she reproduces in her volume on *Lives and Legends of the Apostles*. The top right-hand corner reads, "See by this map how the voice of the apostles has been heard in every clime." On the left-hand corner is written, "This is a map of the climes according to the theologians who, in accordance with a natural and convenient method, have studied the region habitable by man." Then there are notations around this old map that Matthew was in Ethiopia, the old term for Arabia: that Thomas labored somewhere in the East of Asia where men are small and beasts are large."

Below the map it is stated that, "Compostella is a great city, where rests the body of St. James, distant fourteen miles from the land's end, seven hundred miles from Hambourg, and the same from Rome, at the extreme of the mild clime according to the map." The town was Santiago de Compostella, northwest Spain. Theodomis, Bishop of Iria in A.D. 865, claimed to be guided by a star to the spot where the body of James was buried. Ever since Santiago has honored the life-work of James. The Orthodox Church commemorates the Son of Alphaeus on October 9. Some ancient writers affirm that he did a great work in Spain, others in Britain and Ireland where he planted Christianity and appointed a few select disciples to perfect what he had begun, and then returned to Jerusalem, where he had a popedom over the whole Christian Church. A late legend of martyrdom in Persia has no authenticity.

JAMES, SON OF ZEBEDEE

The stirring and active zeal of James, his bold reproof of the Jews, and his vigorous defense of the Christian faith brought James under the wrath of Herod Agrippa, son of Aristobulus, who had the apostle arrested and cast into prison. Sentence of death was passed upon him and on the way to the place of martyrdom, the officer who had guarded James was so impressed by the mighty courage and constancy he displayed, that he repented of his sin and fell down at the apostle's feet, and begged pardon for the part he had played in the rough treatment he had accorded James. The apostle raised up the officer, embraced and kissed him, saying "Peace, my son, peace be to thee, and the pardon of thy faults." Immediately transformed, the officer publicly confessed his surrender to Christ, and was beheaded along with James.

James, the brother of John, was speedily to be baptized with that baptism of death of which Jesus had spoken, and which he had avowed his willingness to suffer. By the brutal hand of Herod (Acts 12:2), he was the first of the twelve to bear his bleeding witness and to be restored to the presence of the Lord he loved. Stephen and James were the first martyrs to give their lives for Christ. Unlike Stephen's end, however, the cloak of silence falls over the last hours of the apostle James, apart from the very old tradition quoted about the officer, conscience-stricken and converted on the spot, dying with the apostle.

JAMES, THE LORD'S BROTHER

Although this James was the brother of Jesus according to the flesh, we have already seen that he never fully surrendered all trust and allegiance to Him as Master until he was spiritually and literally convinced of His resurrection. Thereafter, he was untiring in his ministrations for nearly thirty years, until his martyrdom about A.D. 62. When we remember the long years of protection and preservation he experienced in the heart of Jerusalem during a period of seething Pharisaism, fanaticism and unrest, we wonder why he was not kept from such a terrible, violent death at the end.

According to a canonical tradition, James was surnamed *the Just,* and was a Nazarite from his mother's womb, abstaining from strong drink and animal food, and wearing linen. It is said that he was always kneeling in instruction for the people so that his knees were calloused like a camel's. He was cruelly martyred by the Scribes and Pharisees. Finding him at the southeast angle of the temple wall, where the pinnacle of the temple stood, his foes cast him down into the valley (See Matt. 4:5; Luke 4:9). He fell near the workshop of the fullers who carried on their trade there, and they, finding him there still alive, beat him to death with their clubs. Just opposite the corner of the temple area, across the valley of Jehoshaphat is a sepulchre called "The Tomb of St. James." Whether this is the actual last resting-place of the mortal remains of the first pastor of Christianity no one can affirm. From the dead dust of earth we can turn to James' noble *epistle* which ever remains a living monument to the faith, character and wisdom of the brother of our Lord.

JOHN

We are certain of the fact that John outlived all other apostles, that he was banished to Patmos because of his witness for Christ; that he spent his last years in Ephesus, laboring to promote love among Christians; that he died during the reign of Trajan, which began A.D. 98. But much of the apocryphal record of the apostle John can be rejected as being dubious. *The Muratorian Fragment,* A.D. 75, tells us that he wrote the gospel bearing his name at the persuasion of his brethren in the ministry. Church history confirms that he had as disciples in his old age, three men who became famous in the early church, namely Polycarp, Papias, and Ignatius, all of whom wrote affectionately of John, and testified that he was loving, lowly, patient and good to the end of his days.

The stories told of John are manifold, and it is well-nigh impossible to decide if any of them grew out of imagination or fact. One legend says that John was accustomed to wear on his forehead, like the High Priest of old, a golden plate, on which was inscribed, "Holiness to the Lord." Evidently this story is only a literal rendering of the virtue of holiness being written over the apostle's very face. Another tradition tells us that he was once condemned to drink a cup of poison, and that he did so, without suffering in any way. Yet a further story says that he was put to death and buried, but that next day he rose again from his grave, and lived on as before.

A legend widely circulated was the one stating that while in Rome, John was thrown into a caldron of boiling oil, which was one of the cruel deaths to which Christians of that time were subjected. This legend is known as *St. John before the Latin Gate,* that is, the outer gate leading to Latium, where he was cast, by order of Domitian, into the boiling oil. But God preserved his servant for he suffered no torture and found the burning oil a refreshing bath in which he seemed to renew his youth. Domitian seeing John come forth full of life and strength attributed his deliverance to magic, but nevertheless was so far restrained by fear of the faith which had

sustained his victim that he dared not inflict any further sufferings on the apostle, but banished him to Patmos, where he remained until the Emperor's death, when he returned to Ephesus. On the spot of his deliverance stood a church from the days of the first Christian emperors, named *S. Giovanni in Olio.* Since his death, John's name has been given to hundreds of churches. "St. John before the Latin Gate" was also honored in many places as their Patron Saint by printers, coopers, candle and lampmakers.

The most pleasing and plausible and probable tradition regarding the final days of John is that which affirms that he was carried to and from the Lord's Day services shortly before he died, being so feeble because of his 100 years that all he could do was to say the closing word to his disciples, "Little children, love one another." Thus he died, naturally, in the expectation of eternal blessedness, and was buried in Ephesus. The remarkable thing is that although the local traditions of Ephesus are so full of Paul, and Luke who was buried there, little is said of John as if to suggest that the old, quiet, and retiring spirit, which led him always to the last, and silent where possible, had continued there. Said John's Master, "Learn of me for I am meek and lowly in heart."

Because of his extreme old age, John the Beloved had lived long enough to feel that the world had become very lonely, with all those whom he had loved best gone, and he lived until he almost sighed for the change which would bring him face to face with the Master again, whom he so deeply loved. Hippolytus, Bishop of Porto, and scholar of Clemens of Alexandria, ranked John with Enoch and Elijah as never tasting death, but experiencing a sudden translation from earth to heaven. This erroneous theory that John never died was built upon a wrong understanding of our Lord's conversation with Peter concerning what his fate was to be, and then his question to Jesus regarding the end of John, seeing he was the disciple Jesus loved. The Master rebuked Peter's curiosity by saying, "If I will that he tarry till I come, what is that to thee?" The apostles misunderstood this reply and so the report went out amongst them, "that that disciple should not die." But John, who records this conversation (John 21:21-23), was careful to correct this misunderstanding, "Jesus did not say, he should not die" but only "What if I will that he tarry till I come?"

We accept the fact that John died at the close of the first century, and at the end of a serene life passed away serenely, but that his grave, like that of Moses, is known only to God. "He died like a summer's day, his heart expanding like the setting sun," says Daniel McLean. "The clouds spent of their thunder catching up the twilight glow of warm light as if the chariot that bore Elijah into heaven had returned in softened sweetness to bear aloft the beloved of the Lord. He crowned the apostolic age; he closed the Book of inspired revelation with a short echo of the promise at the ascension, 'Even so come, Lord Jesus,' and that coming ushered John into the full enjoyment of what he had formerly seen in thought. He now walks with Christ among the golden candlesticks."

JUDAS ISCARIOT

There is no need to linger over the sad ending of this disappointing apostle, seeing the Bible fully describes his terrible deed and tragic death. It is interesting to note that the phrase Peter used as to the manner of the betrayer's death, "All his bowels gushed out" (Acts 1:18) is the Hebra-

ic equivalent of our modern phrase, "broke his heart." His was the only suicide's grave among the apostles, and "The Tree of Judas" is still shown to travelers around Jerusalem — "the pathetic relic is a traditional thought of the death of the traitor which, though impossible in fact, is really suggestive of the curse that clings to the valley." Guides point to the traditional spot *Aceldama,* "the field of blood," which for centuries was "the place to bury strangers in."

Dr. J. Elder Cumming in his description of a visit to the Holy Land speaks of standing on the traditional site where Judas hung himself on a tree, on the day when the One he betrayed was condemned. "There, under that burning sun, the body hung, became discoloured and swollen, and being probably a stout, gross man, the rope having broken, the miserable carcase fell, and rolling down the hill-side, landed, a wretched mass at the far bottom of Gehenna." Then Dr. Cumming goes on to observe, "Alas! alas! for the broken hopes of a promising youth; the bitter disappointment of fervid, impetuous manhood; the ruin of selfish passions which had become an instrument of the enemy of men; the vivid and visual catastrophe of the man who had said to evil, Thou art my God! How far can a man fall, who had once been so near to salvation, and, in a sense, to Christ."

Does not the history of Ahithophel come to mind as we think of Judas who, in ecclesiastical legends and in sacred art is generally treated as the incarnation of treachery, ingratitude and impiety. The character, betrayal and suicide of Judas are described in numerous legends particularly in Coptic works. In Muslim polemic literature Judas is white-washed. He ceases to be a traitor and is said to have lied to the Jews in order to defend Jesus who, such sources say, was not crucified. Mba-al-Dimarki, a fourteenth century cosmographer, maintained that Judas assumed the likeness of Jesus and was crucified in His place. Papias went as far as to say that Judas was one of the earliest Christian authors of the New Testament. Dante, one of the greatest poets of the past, had no doubt as to the deserved end of Judas. He paired the traitor with Brutus and Cassius, Julius Caesar's murderers, in the deepest chasm of hell.

MATTHEW

It is generally supposed that for eight years after the ascension of Christ, Matthew preached the Gospel in Judaea. Beyond this we have no reliable evidence as to where he journeyed or how he died. Socrates, the ecclesiastical historian of the fourth century, speaks of Matthew preaching in Ethiopia and Arabia. From other sources it is said that he labored first in the Syrian colony established at Palmyra, or Tadmor, in the wilderness between Damacus and the Euphrates, and that he passed eastward to the Median people of Carenania. Yet another tradition takes him to labor with Andrew among the man-eaters on the coast of the Black Sea. The fact is that the truth of his travels for the advancement of the Christian faith are irrecoverably lost in a crowd of legendary tales.

Numerous miracles were said to have been performed by the apostle, like that of the wand he received from Christ who appeared to him in the form of a beautiful youth. Matthew pitched the wand into the ground, and immediately it grew up into a tree. As to his death, an ancient writer affirms that he suffered martyrdom in Ethiopia, being slain by the sword. Dorotheus recorded that Matthew was honorably buried at Hierapolis in Par-

thia, one of the first places in which he preached the Gospel. The resting place of his mortal remains matters little to us. The Church will ever remember the great transformation wrought in his life by Christ; and how he became the writer of the first book of the New Testament which even Renan, the brilliant French sceptic, said was "the most important book of Christendom — the most important book that has ever been written."

MATTHIAS

Of Matthias, appointed to take the place in the apostolate which Judas vacated, nothing authentic is known, apart from his brief and only appearance before Pentecost. Clement of Alexandria refers to some "Traditions" of Matthias, one of them being that he is identified with Zacchaeus, the publican. *The Acts of Andrew and Matthias* is a romance preserved in Greek and Syriac, and in part, Latin, but fragments of it are scanty and buried in questionable sources. In such, Matthew's remarkable adventures among the man-eaters are described. He is supposed to have worked first in Judaea and lastly in Cappadocia, where, amid a wild and barbarous community, he was stoned and then beheaded about A.D. 61 or 64. From legendary sources the general impression is gathered that Matthias remain faithful unto death. His body is said to have been kept a long time at Jerusalem, thence thought by Helen, the mother of the great Constantine, to have been translated to Rome, where some parts of it were showed with great veneration for a long time. Others say with as great eagerness that his remains were brought to and preserved at Triers in Germany. His memory is still celebrated in the Greek Church on August 9th. In the Western Church, St. Matthias' Feast Day is February 24th.

PAUL

Being "in deaths oft," Paul anticipated the end of his earthly sojourn. Sentences like, "I have finished my course"; "I am now ready to be offered"; "To die is gain"; "We that are in this tabernacle do groan," indicate that the apostle was under no delusion as to the nearness of his decease and possible martyrdom. The three missionary journeys of Paul and an account of cities and towns he visited and of his ministry therein are clearly indicated for us in the Acts and in the Pauline epistles, but as to a greater circuit in other parts of the world, tradition gives us more fancy than fact. Remembering that he was "The Apostle to the Gentiles," ancient writers gave Paul a far larger diocese than that found in the New Testament. Theodoret and others tell us that the apostle not only preached in Spain, but went to other nations and brought the Gospel into the isles of the sea, meaning Britain.

It was in A.D. 435 that Theodoret wrote:

> Paul, liberated from his first captivity at Rome, preached the Gospel to the Britons and others in the West. Our fishermen and publicans not only persuaded the Romans and their tributaries to acknowledge the Crucified and His laws, but the Britons also, and the Cimbri.

Venantus Fortunatus, in his *Christian Hymns*, A.D. 596, also speaks of Britain being evangelized by Paul. A still further startling assertion is made by the Venerable Bede, the renowned historian of Anglo-Saxon history, who declared that at the solicitation of King Oswry to Pope Vitalian, the remains of Peter and Paul and of four other martyrs were removed from Rome to England, and were deposited at Canterbury A.D. 656. Whether Paul actually visited Britain and his hon-ored dust is buried there is a matter of conjecture. What is certain is the way the Gospel that Paul preached transformed the lives of countless Roman soldiers who in turn brought his message to ancient Britain and persuaded Gauls and Britains to embrace the soul-saving truths Paul convincingly proclaimed.

Britain's greatest cathedral, in London, is rightly called St. Paul's, and the love which that name inspired is evidenced by the vast sums of money which have been raised to repair and restore it from time to time.

So long she has reigned by the river,
A sign of what cannot die,
Holding the Cross above her,
Stedfast against the sky.
So long within the city,
Wherever her deep voice calls,
Men know the soul of London
Is sounding in St. Paul's.

While we do not know the complete itinerary of Paul, we are certain that the apostle died in Rome about the summer of A.D. 68. Tradition has always been clear that he was beheaded in the reign of Nero, and that Nero himself met his end in June of the same year. Surely there was never in all history a more striking contrast to be found than that between Paul, the condemned criminal, and Nero, the judge whose character was stained with unspeakable crimes. Nero was clothed in imperial purple, and as king of the then known world with unlimited power, had incense offered to him on a thousand altars.

Condemned by Nero, Paul the aged would be fettered, dressed in rags, despised, and perhaps not considered important enough to be brought into the august presence of the Emperor, and finally led out of the city to a martyrdom of which no record has been kept. Yet this poor criminal was the man the Lord had honored more than any other. At his remarkable conversion he asked, "Lord, what wilt thou have me to do?" He was given the task to proclaim the whole Gospel to the whole world, and with remarkable devotion and a gaiety of heart he counted every loss a gain, as he "pressed toward the goal of his calling."

As to Paul's last days, tradition says that after waiting in the cold dungeon of the Mamertine for his second trial, the first trial dating about the close of the year A.D. 60, he was brought out at a time when Nero was breathing out fury against Christians. Paul was condemned to death, having only the privilege of dying as Roman citizens did, not by crucifixion, but by the sword of the executioner. This was toward the end of the year A.D. 66 when the apostle was about sixty-three years old.

In the neighborhood of Rome, some three miles to the southwest of the city, is a church, rebuilt after a fire, beauteous and spacious, called *St. Paul's Without the Walls*, and enclosed within a wall are three small chapels, one of them containing in its area three fountains of living water springing out of the ground. An old tradition says that it was on this very spot the execution of the great apostle took place, and that the three fountains mark three spots on which that revered head had touched the ground. What a dark moment of pain and shock Paul endured as the axe fell, but what a thrill of light and joy must have been his the very moment when, for the second time, he saw the radiant face and heard the gentle voice of Jesus of Nazareth! For him to live had been Christ; for him to die was gain, for death meant to be with Christ, and this was far better.

PETER

After being imprisoned by Herod and miraculously released we read that Peter "departed and went to another place" (Acts 12:17). Thereafter the only other mention of him in the Acts is at the Jerusalem Council (Acts 15:7-11). Peter may have visited the church at Corinth, where a party owed allegiance to him (I Cor. 1:12). While the sacred record names many of the places Peter visited and preached in (Acts 9:32, 36; I Pet. 1:1), tradition mentions other areas he covered, concluding with Rome where he became the first bishop of the church, and according to the Roman Catholic Church, its first Pope.

Legend has it that as soon as Peter reached Rome he encountered Simon Magus, the sorcerer and arch-magician mentioned in the Acts. After being exposed by Peter, this trickster fled to Rome, where, by means of his impositions, he curried much favor with the populace so that he soon became honored as a god. Justin Martyr tells us that a statue was erected to him bearing the inscription, "To Simon, The Holy God." Hegesippus, who wrote in the fourth century, describes the contest between Peter and Simon Magus over a kinsman of the Emperor raised from the dead, and then how the deceiver reached a tragic end. Because of this, the Emperor, who treated Simon Magus as a favorite, was so enraged that he had Peter cast into prison.

That Peter was martyred is strongly suggested by the words addressed to him by Christ: "When you are old, you will stretch out your hands, and another will gird you and carry you where you do not wish to go" (John 21:18 RSV). There may also be a hint at martyrdom in Peter's own exhortation to the elders, "I . . . am also an elder, and a witness of the sufferings of Christ, and also *a partaker of the glory* that shall be revealed" (I Pet. 5:1). Whether Peter was ever in Rome and died a martyr's death there, is a question over which much controversy has raged. Ignatius, in his letter to the Romans, affirmed that Peter held authority in the Roman Church; and the Roman episcopal lists make Peter the first Bishop of the city. Macarius of Magnesia said that Peter was crucified in Rome after shepherding the flock for a few months. It is highly probable that Peter did go to Rome and was martyred there during the Neronian persecution.

From various apocryphal documents dating from the second century, to which Peter's name is attached, we learn that a "Preaching" or *Kerygma,* a "Gospel," and an "Apocalypse" survived in fragments only. There is also *The Acts of Peter,* extant in fragments, save for the account of his martyrdom, which contains the detail that his bishopric lasted twenty-five years, and also the legend, which Origen also mentions that Peter was crucified head downward. When he was brought to the cross he made the request, "Not with my head up: My Master died that way! Crucify me head downward. I die for my Lord: but I am not worthy to die like Him." In this way he made amends for the memory of his fall and denial.

It is from this same source that we have the *Quo Vadis* story, relating how, in the time of persecution, Peter was persuaded to save his life by flight. Succeeding in escaping from prison the night before the day appointed for his death, he crept through the dark lanes, reached the city gates, and was out on the Great Appian Road — *free!* But as he stood there a stranger met him, and somehow Peter felt that he had seen His features before, and then he discerned it was the Master Himself. Falling on his knees he cried, *Domine, quo vadis? Domine, quo vadis?* — "Lord, Lord, whither art Thou going?" The answer came, "I had a disciple who

was imprisoned there, and was to be put to death. He is escaped, and is free. I go to die, a second time, for *him.*" Peter cried, "Lord, go not: I will return and die!" Back he went to die the next day, not like Paul by the sword of an executioner, but on a cross, bearing the punishment of a slave, seeing he was not a citizen of the Roman Empire. It is said that a presbyter named Marcellinus embalmed and buried his body in Mont Vaticanus, a hill on the western banks of the Tiber, near the *Triumphal Way.* Quite recently Rome claimed she had identified the bones of Peter interred in the vaults at the Vatican.

Another legend concerns Peter's wife who was said to have been the daughter of Aristobulus, and to have been martyred first. As she was led forth, Peter called to her by name and comforted her with the words, "Remember the Lord," and rejoiced exceedingly that his dear one was called to so great an honor and was now on her way to see the King in His beauty. Between husband and wife there had been agreement in those things that had been dearest to them; now their mutual devotion to Christ was seen in their death for His dear sake. It reveals how little woman's work was worth in those days that we know next to nothing about Peter's valiant wife.

Such, then, is the traditional story of Peter, *The Big Fisherman,* who became an unworthy apostle when he forsook his Lord. But Pentecost made him the courageous witness he became, and at the end he felt there was nothing too precious to render his Lord! "What shall I render to the Lord for all His benefits toward me? I will take the cup" — *of martyrdom, and will drink it for His sake!* How appealing are the lines of E. B. Browning —

"Today thou girdest up thy loins thyself
    And goest where thou wouldest: pres-
        ently
Others shall gird thee," said the Lord, "to
        go
Where thou wouldst not." He spoke to
        Peter thus
To signify the death which he should die
When crucified head downwards — If He
        spoke
To Peter then, He speaks to us the same;
The word suits many different martyrdoms
    For 'tis not in mere death that men die
        most;
And after our first girding of the loins
In youth's fine linen and fair broidery,
To run up hill and meet the rising sun, —
We are apt to sit tired, patient as a fool,
While others gird us with the violent
        hands
Of social figments, feints, and formalisms,—
Reversing our straight nature, — lifting up
Our base needs, — keeping down our lofty
        thoughts,
Head downward on the cross — sticks of
        the world.
Yet He can pluck us from that shameful
        cross.
    God! set our feet low and our forehead
        high,
And show us how a Man was made to
        walk.

While it is not within the province of our cameo of Peter to discuss the preposterous claims of the Roman Church as to the apostle's primacy, it must be said that the belief that Peter is continued in and confined to the bishop of Rome is nowhere stated in or implied by the New Testament. Christ never meant His true Church to have a visible center concentrated in one place and in one person. It is only in the imagination of an ambitious hierarchy that Peter was the bishop of Rome. Daniel McLean observes that, "as Michelangelo has been truly called the Architect of Italy, so we may call Peter the satirical saint of Rome, for he haunts its churches like a restless ghost, laughing at the mummery of its priests and the credulity of its ignorant devotees. The spirit of his life contradicts the worship of the saints and the primacy of the popes. Rome imitates the errors of Peter, but misses his excellencies." Origen rightly observed that only "he who has Peter's faith is the rock of the Church. He who has Peter's virtues keeps the keys of the Kingdom."

PHILIP

That the apostles undoubtedly journeyed far and wide often alone and seldom more than two or three in company, we can readily imagine, but what we cannot accept is the way their legendary service is embroidered with fantastic notions and grotesque imagery. Philip the apostle, in unison with all the other original apostles, was signally blessed at Pentecost, and went forth to share in the witness to Christ in various regions. Tradition tells us that he went to Phrygia with his old companion Bartholomew or Nathanael, and also accompanied by his devoted sister, Mariamne, who became conspicuous in the distribution of food to the needy. These three went on to Asia Minor, and then to Hierapolis, a city devoted to the idolatry of a gigantic serpent, possibly in memory of that infamous act of Jupiter who, in the shape of a dragon, was worshiped.

Legendary acts of Philip and of his companions are most numerous. One adventure concerns their encounter with a leopard and a kid both speaking with a human voice. They also met a dreadful dragon, over 100 cubits long, and other enormous reptiles. These the three travelers destroyed. Entering Hierapolis, the three missionaries were the means of the conversion of Nicanora, the wife of the Proconsul. Apocryphal records tell of their terrible persecutions and miraculous deliverances, and of the final martyrdom of Philip who because of his protest against the idolatry of the city holding the inhabitants in trembling bondage, was crucified in the city which was the most wickedly idolatrous one of the Near Eastern world, devoted to the worship of the goddess Cybele, whose rites were orgies of cruelty and sensualism. Four of the early fathers of the Church mention the Apostle Philip as laboring in Phrygia, of which Colosse was a city, and as dying, being hanged on a pillar, and being buried at Hierapolis.

As to the mode of his actual death, one tradition says that Philip died from natural causes; according to another tradition he was crucified. Yet another says that he was executed. When he rebuked the Phrygians for the solemn veneration accorded to such an odious creature as a serpent, many repented of their idolatry and became Christians. But the city magistrates seized the apostle, severely whipped and scourged him and cast him into prison. Later he was brought out, and hanged by the neck against a pillar. As Philip was being executed the earth suddenly quaked and when it seemed as if the people present were in danger of being swallowed up alive, they bewailed the evident act of divine vengeance upon their idolatry and repented, and immediately the earth closed. The tradition goes on to say that Bartholomew took down the bodies of Philip and Mariamne, Philip's sister, and he buried them, and exhorting the people to remain true to Christ, departed from the city.

As previously pointed out in our study of Philip the apostle, he must not be confounded with Philip the deacon-evangelist, who, with Stephen, was one of the original deacons chosen to care for assembling matters. It is well nigh impossible to trace the wanderings of the lesser known disciples with any degree of certainty after their appearance in New Testament history. But the certain thing is that, "the first Christian missionaries in remote countries fell in the midst of their enemies, and the obscurity of their death is the best guarantee of their heroic fidelity."

SIMON THE ZEALOT

There are one or two interesting legends concerning this apostle conspicuous for his zeal and burning enthusiasm, who came to learn of the purer, deeper, and stronger zeal of the Master he followed. One story says that he found his field of activity in the Parthian Empire which at that time was governed by two brothers, *Vardana* reigning at Babylon and *Nerseh* in Persia. Beginning his labors in the South at Babylon, Simon moved northward through the Empire, and met a violent death at Colchis in the far north.

Eusebius in his *Church History*, however, names Simon Zelotes as one of the apostolic missionaries who "passed beyond the Ocean to the isles called the Britannia Isles." After preaching in Egypt and Africa, Simon at last penetrated beyond the Mediterranean Sea, and landed upon the English shore, and his soul was filled with peace at the mission awaiting him among the tribes there. As to the end of Simon, according to the apocryphal *Passion of Simon and Jude*, after preaching the Gospel in Egypt, Simon joined Judas, or Thaddaeus, in Persia where both were martyred, Simon being sawn asunder, as some saints were (Heb. 11:37). October 28 is the Feast of Simon and Jude.

THADDAEUS

Previously we pointed out that this is the apostle of three names, Lebbaeus, Thaddaeus, and Judas (not Iscariot). Legend says that he found his field of service in the Syrian kingdom of Osroene, with its capital at Edessa, where its King Adgar was suffering from an incurable disease and sighed for relief. His reign extended from 15 B.C. - A.D. 50, and he was thus King of Edessa at the time of our Lord's ministry. Hearing of Him as the Savior and Benefactor of men, Adgar resolved to write and ask Him to visit him. Thaddaeus was sent who, in the name of Christ, healed the King of his disease, and also many other sufferers in the city of their various infirmities. As a result, the King became a convert, and a great many of his subjects also believed, and Edessa became the first Christian country.

After the death of Adgar, the kingdom of Armenia was divided between his son, Ananoun, and his nephew, Sanatrouk. The latter, who reigned in Armenia, was converted but apostated, through fear of the Armenian Satraps. Thaddaeus and his Christian companions were taken prisoners and martyred in the province of Schavarschar, and various relics and superstitions became attached to their memories.

THOMAS

Of this apostle there are fuller legendary accounts than of most of the apostles. Mixed with the miraculous to an extraordinary degree, there are yet easily discovered historical elements in the stories surrounding Thomas. He went out to labor in the Parthian Empire, on the frontiers between Parthia and India, at a time when the Buddhists of India were making inroads on the Zoroastrians of Eastern Parthia, and the Parthians were retaliating by conquests of the Indian province called White India and Arachosia. Tradition says that the Savior appeared to Thomas in a night vision and said unto him, "Fear not, Thomas, go thou unto India, and preach the Word there, for My grace is with thee." Thomas hired himself as a slave to an Indian merchant, and sailed with him and entered the service of the King of the Indians, Gondophares, whose image is found on ancient coins, and who is often mentioned in the Thomas-legends and in ancient sources.

From the traditional source we learn that Thomas was the means of converting "the three kings of the East" who came to bring their gifts and adoration to the infant Savior. As to his death, Thomas' career ended on the Indian coast near Bombay, where he was martyred by a lance thrust through his body while he was kneeling in prayer. A monument to his memory long continued to be shown at this spot. The Syrian Christians, settled on this coast centuries at least before European navigators reached India, claim Thomas as their founder. Don Emanuel Frea, governor of the coast of Coromandel, at great cost and care, removed the remains of Thomas along with the bones of King Sagamon whom he converted to the faith, and interred them in a memorial church. (See articles on *Thomas* and *Gospel of Thomas* in *The Zondervan Pictorial Bible Dictionary* or other Bible dictionary or encyclopedia.)

If it were not outside the province of apostleship, we would have liked to have mentioned other renowned followers of Christ like Mark, Luke, Titus, and others who at their end drank of Christ's cup of death, and entered, thereby, the fellowship of His sufferings. All of those who were most intimately associated with the Master became martyrs and remained, by His grace, faithful unto their cruel deaths.

Appendixes

Before we conclude our fascinating meditation on the lives and labors of the apostles, there are several interesting features to which attention can be drawn, and which we have classified for the benefit of readers.

APOSTOLIC SYMBOLS

Because of incidents in their lives or traditional records of their martyrdom, the apostles came to be identified by badges or symbols which are usually added to pictorial presentations of the apostles. For a lengthy catalog of the symbols of saints, the reader is directed to Brewers *Dictionary of Phrase and Fable*.

THE TWELVE

The original apostles came to be symbolized as a company as well as individually. For instance, in one early carving *twelve doves* are used to represent the twelve — an allusion to our Lord's word about sending them out as harmless doves. In yet another carving, the twelve are depicted each with a sheep, or as *twelve sheep* — another of His metaphors describing His disciples.

ANDREW

Tradition says that while Andrew was preaching in Greece he was put to death on *a transverse cross*, resembling our capital X, and so he is known in every school of art as an old man leaning on a cross of this type, with the Gospel in his right hand.

BARNABAS

Included in the wider circle of apostles, Barnabas, especially successful as a preacher of the Gospel, is symbolized by an open Bible, by which he lived and which he revered. Artists have portrayed him carrying *the Gospel in one hand*, and *a pilgrim's staff or a stone in the other*.

BARTHOLOMEW

Usually this apostle, otherwise known as Nathanael, is represented by *three flaying knives*, because he was flayed to death by a sharp knife.

JAMES THE GREAT

Renowned because of his labors at Compostella, this James is portrayed with three *scallop shells*, a pilgrim's staff, or a gourd bottle, because he came to be known as the Patron Saint of Pilgrims. *The scallop shell* was supposed to be the symbol of pilgrimage and represented the apostle's zeal and missionary spirit. Erasmus recorded that this emblem was adopted because the shore of the adjacent sea abounded in scallops. Pilgrims used the shells for cup, spoon and dish, and returning home, the pilgrim placed his scallop shell in his hat to command admiration, and adopted it as his coat of armor.

JAMES THE LESS

Two symbols are associated with this apostle. First, he is represented by a *saw* since it was held that his body was sawn asunder after a horrible martyrdom. Then he is shown with a *fuller's pole*, because he was killed by a blow on the head with a pole, dealt him by Simeon the Fuller.

JOHN

Early writers state that John once drank from a poisoned chalice and was unharmed, and so he is given the symbol of *a cup with a winged serpent flying out of it*, in allusion to the tradition about Aristodemos, Priest of Diana, who challenged John to drink the cup of poison. Roman Catholic tradition says that John made the sign of a cross on the cup, and Satan, in the form of a dragon, flew from it, and John then drank the cup without harm.

JUDAS

The Betrayer is identified by a *bag* because as the treasurer of the apostolate he carried the purse. "When he was in charge of the purse he used to help himself from the contents" (John 12:6, *Phillips*). What a witness the bag is to the avarice of Judas!

MATTHEW

Two symbols are attached to this most attractive apostle. He is symbolized by *three purses* referring to his original profession as a tax collector. Then, because legend has it that he was slain at Nabadar with a halberd, Matthew is given a *hatchet* or *halberd*.

MATTHIAS

Chosen by the eleven apostles to take the place of Judas who hanged himself, Matthias is symbolized by an *open Bible and a double bladed battle-ax across it,* an allusion to the tradition that he was first stoned and then beheaded with an ax because of his allegiance to Christ.

PAUL

The renowned apostle to the Gentiles is represented in a two-fold way. First, he is seen with *a sword,* because his head was cut off with one. The Convent of La Lisla, Spain, boasts of possessing this very instrument that sent Paul to heaven. Then, he is symbolized by *an open Bible* with the words across it, *Spiritus Gladius* — "Sword of the Spirit." Behind the open Bible is the figure of a sword.

PETER

Two symbols are given this apostle who denied yet finally died for his Lord. He is seen holding a *bunch of keys,* because it was to Peter that Jesus spoke about "the keys of the Kingdom." Then sometimes he is depicted with *a cock* near at hand, seeing that he wept bitterly as he heard the cock crow.

PHILIP

The apostle Philip is symbolized by *a basket with two loaves,* and *a long staff surmounted with a cross.* The first symbol suggests Philip's remark to Jesus about feeding the hungry multitude (John 6:7), and the second is associated with the death he suffered by being suspended by the neck from a tall pillar.

SIMON ZELOTES

First of all, this fiery witness is identified by *a book on which rests a fish,* indicating that it was through the power of the Gospel that Simon became a fisher of men. Then he is sometimes represented by *a saw* because of the tradition that he was sawn to death in a time of terrible persecution.

THADDAEUS

Because legend has it that this apostle was martyred with a heavy club, he is symbolized by *a club.* We cannot read of the horrible sufferings of the apostles without realizing what it cost them to be true to the Master they loved.

THOMAS

In his statue of Thomas, Thorwaldsen represents him as a thoughtful man with measuring rule in hand, the patron saint of architects and builders. Usually he is given *a carpenter's square and a spear* — the square, speaking of a church he built with his own hands in India; and the spear reminding us of his persecution there, and how a pagan priest pierced through his body, at Meliapore, with a lance or spear.

APOSTOLIC SAINTHOOD

Early in its existence, Roman Catholicism invented a saint-producing machine, for the purpose of elevating to sainthood, apostles, popes, priests and nuns who became renowned for saintliness and miraculous works. Such sainthood was only allocated a considerable time after death. All Rome's saints are dead ones, but all Christ's saints are living ones. Catholics are taught that those who have been canonized as saints may be prayed to and also worshiped. From *Explanation of Catholic Morals,* Rome says: "Of course the lives of all the Saints are not history in the strictest sense of the word. But what has that to do with the Communion of Saints? If simplicity and naivete have woven around some names an unlikely tale, a fable or a myth, it requires some effort to see how that could effect their standing with God, or *their disposition to help us in our needs.*" The A.V. New Testament gives sainthood to its writers, so the first book is The Gospel According to *Saint* Matthew, and so on. The R.V. does not use the term *Saint* before the writer's name. But the apostles themselves would be the first to deprecate the use of any such title save as they, and we, are all saints in Christ Jesus. We cannot imagine Paul agreeing to be called *Saint Paul* in the way Roman Catholicism employs the sacred term. He preferred being known as "the chief of sinners," or "less than the least of all saints." Every true believer is called to be a saint (1 Cor. 1:2). All born-again Christians are saints, but some are more saintly in character than others.

As we have reached the end of our coverage of all the apostles mentioned in the New Testament, it has been a most glorious experience to tarry in their company for awhile. Intimately associated with the Master as they were, they must have been conscious of His over-ruling care of those whom He called to serve Him. The majority of them sprang from lowly origins, and had few advantages as far as wealth, education and prestige go, but He who said, "*I will make you*," made them what they ultimately became, namely, messengers and martyrs for the faith. As heirs of their intrepid self-sacrifice, may we prove to be as true and faithful in our age, as they were in theirs. If we are not privileged to wear a martyr's crown, as all the apostles probably did, we can — and must — adorn the martyr's spirit. Many have found it comparatively easy to die for Christ. How hard it is to live as He would have us in the midst of a godless world!

As Christ is the same today as yesterday, all He accomplished in and through those He chose, He is able to do in your life and mine if only we are utterly yielded to Him. So as we take our leave of His first disciples we praise Him for making:

Andrew, the lover of souls,
Barnabas, the example of faithful stewardship,
Bartholomew, the conqueror of idolatry in far countries,
James, the first witness by death to the certainty of eternal life,
John, the sublime interpreter of God's love to man, and of man's love to God,

Matthew, the writer of the Gospel of the Kingdom,
Matthias, the faithful missionary in isolated outposts,
Paul, the good soldier of Jesus Christ,
Peter, the courageous evangelist of Christ to the Jews,
Philip, the fearless witness among serpent worshipers,
Simon, the sower of the Seed in far-off islands,
Thaddaeus, the practical missionary among savage kingdoms of the East,
Thomas, the prosaic witness, who worked — and lived — by the square.

Of His humble, faithful, sacrificial followers, Jesus could say: "Ye which have followed me, in the regeneration when the Son of Man shall sit in the throne of his glory, ye also shall sit upon twelve thrones, judging the twelve tribes of Israel" (Matt. 19:28). Having suffered for Him they are to reign for, and with Him. But such a position of royalty and reign is not for the apostles alone. Jesus told John to write: "To him that overcometh will I grant to sit with me in my throne, even as I also overcame, and am set down with my Father in his throne" (Rev. 3:21).

Apostle, as we have seen, means "one who is sent," and all whom the Savior saves, He sends out into the world to be the means of saving others. Alas! many who are saved, seem to forget the *sending* part; and consequently there are more godless souls in the world than there should be.

Men die in darkness at your side,
   Without a hope to cheer the tomb;
Take up the torch and wave it wide,
   The torch that lights time's thickest gloom.

APOSTOLIC SUCCESSION

Because of the false claim of the Roman hierarchy to be the exclusive administrators of the church and the dispensers of its gifts, offices, and sacraments (a claim likewise advanced by the High Church section of the Anglican communion so near to the Roman Catholic order of masses, rubrics, and vestments), we deem it necessary to examine the question of *Apostolic Succession*. Did the apostles have delegated power to appoint successors, and did they exercise such authority? Has there been, as Rome asserts, a long unbroken line of apostolic successors continued in the order of popes, archbishops, and bishops up to the present day? Is such affirmation at variance with New Testament teaching and with the commonly accepted evangelical beliefs?

Briefly expressed, the doctrine of apostolic succession is that popes and bishops represent a direct, uninterrupted line of descent from the apostles chosen by Christ, and that from the apostles they derive special powers, the chief of which is the authority to ordain priests and to teach and rule over the clergy and laity of their diocese. The contention is that the mission given to the apostles by Christ must extend to their successors in an unbroken line (Matt. 16:19; 28:19; John 20:23). Accordingly, this means in practice that only those clergy who have been ordained by Bishops who are themselves in the succession can administer the sacraments and perform other sacerdotal functions. Needless to say, there is absolutely no warrant whatsoever in Scripture for such teaching. When Jesus said to Peter, "I will give unto thee the keys of the kingdom," He was not giving peculiarly to Peter anything which was not likewise given to the rest of the apostles. Nor do these words of our Lord's to Peter impart anything of a successive infallibility that was to be derived from him with any distinction beyond the other apostles: unless it were a priority of order and dignity. There is not the least hint that any authority was to descend from him to any See or Succession of Bishops.

The apostles *did not* exercise any power of appointing successors. Matthias was a probable exception, when the eleven took it upon themselves to fill the vacancy in the apostolate caused by the death of Judas Iscariot. But such an unauthorized election was set aside by Christ's own choice of Paul, who did not ask or wait for the recognition of apostleship of the other apostles. Paul never wavered in the assertion that he was not in the service of Christ by their appointment, but by a commission received direct from the Lord of Glory. As the apostle *par excellence,* Paul never taught apostolic succession nor did he believe that one apostle or bishop could transmit the gift to another, nor that the sacred office could be confined to any channel or given or withheld by those who already enjoyed it.

The apostle believed in the priesthood of all believers, and that men were made priests not as human authority determined but by the Holy Spirit, who, as wind, blew where He listed. Paul held firmly to God's free election. As to the custom of the laying on of hands, this only signified a recognition of fitness, and not the conferring of spiritual gifts or the exclusive right to select and appoint men to the ministry of the Word. Neither Peter or Paul established a line of succession or attempt to transmit any of their powers to others. They had no *successors* as we understand the term. They were chosen by their Lord for a specific task and endowed with peculiar gifts for its accomplishment, and their office and their gifts terminated with the apostles when their work was finished. Our Lord never gave the least hint that the apostles He chose were empowered to elect others to apostleship or to any ministerial office. The first disciples had no part in their appointment. It was the Lord who chose them and sent them out to witness in His name (Luke 10:1).

The distinctive feature of Roman Catholicism is that its head, the pope, who sits in St. Peter's chair, by virtue of his succession to such a dignity claims to be the visible head of the Church, the spiritual ruler of Christendom, the vicar of Christ on earth, and the infallible authority on faith and morals. But such a pretentious, extravagant assumption is contrary to the whole tenor of Scripture. This papal pretension proceeds on the theory that Peter was the first bishop of Rome, and in that office claimed and established precedence and superiority over all other bishops. The known character and teaching of Peter disprove any claim on his part to be the first bishop of Rome. Was it not this apostle who wrote: "Be subject one to another, and be clothed with humility: for God resisteth the proud, and giveth grace to the humble"? These are words hardly suited for the lips of Rome's imaginary ecclesiastical Peter.

It is almost ludicrous to think of the disciple who denied his Lord as the first pope and the supreme arbiter with regard to the doctrines and practices of the church. Further, all about Peter suggests how thoroughly human he was in his fallibility. A great gulf is fixed between the Peter the Bible portrays, and the exalted Saint Peter of the Romish Church. Never at any time did he assume the position of a Primate. Rome has made of the lowly-minded Peter we know, a caricature and a figment of tradition. Calling himself a "fellow-elder," did not Peter warn the other elders about exercising lordship "over God's heritage" (1 Peter 5:1, 3)? The Greek word for "heritage" is *Klēros*. Coming from a root meaning "an object used to cast lots," it has given us the word "clergy"; but in the context, we are face to face with the local church *in its entire membership*. Is this not striking when viewed in the light of the exalted ecclesiasticism of our time? God's people are His clergy. The New Testament knows nothing about the separate classes we know as "priests" and "laity." In Scripture *Laoi*, or "laity" are the people beyond the pale of the church. They form the unresponsive masses from whom the *Ecclesia*, or The Church, is drawn.

The Head of the *Ecclesia*, is not a fallible Pope, but the infallible Christ who walks in the midst of the seven golden candlesticks, and whose prerogative it is to remove any one of them (Rev. 2:5). While, in the early days of the church, the apostles appointed elders, there were no instructions regarding the handing on of this to succeeding generations (Titus 1:5). Paul made it clear that the impartation of spiritual instruction, and not the conferring of office or of gift, is the mind of the Lord (2 Tim. 2:2); and through succeeding centuries of church history churches have practiced the principles taught and exemplified in the New Testament. What Paul envisaged was a true and spiritual apostolic succession, or a succession of faithful men perpetuating the apostolic teaching (Acts 20:32; 2 Tim. 2:2).

Alas! however, such a Pauline conception of succession was not long in being perverted or stereotyped into something formal and professional. Ignatius, one of the Early Fathers, anxious to maintain orthodoxy and debar heresy from the church, laid stress upon the function of the monarchical bishop — an office first appearing at the beginning of the second century. Ignatius insisted that the bishop or someone delegated by him was the only church official qualified to conduct a valid baptism or eucharist. Six of the seven letters Ignatius wrote are filled with exaggerated exaltation of the authority and importance of the bishop's office. In his letter to the Smyrnaeans he wrote, "Let that be held a valid Eucharist which is under the bishop or one to whom he shall have committed it. It is not lawful apart from the bishop to baptize or to hold a love-feast" — that is, conduct the Lord's Supper.

As Dr. B. H. Streeter in his *Primitive Church* expresses it: "To Ignatius the monarchical episcopate is an *ideé fixe* — that is, an obsession. While this renowned church father may have had no thought of any episcopal succession in mind, his pronouncement laid the foundation of it, and the end of the second century saw its emergence. It was not long, thereafter, when a bishop, tracing his connections back to the apostles, claimed apostolic validity for his acts, and gradually the emphasis was shifted from the actual maintenance of the apostles' teaching and fellowship to the external fact of historical continuity."

With the Reformation under Martin Luther the original emphasis was restored, and, as one writer expresses it, "It is by making Scripture the rule of faith that the Reformed Church stands in the true apostolic succession." The assumption of priestly power we abhor as being most contrary to the spirit of Christ and of His apostles. As J. G. Greenhough so clearly puts it, "The real successors of the apostles — if they may be said to have had any at all — are not the officials, clergy, bishops, and ministers of the Church, by virtue of their office, but these, and equally all non-official Christians, in so far as they have the mind of Christ and bear true witness for Him, and are thus sharers in the zeal, devotion, and elevated purpose of The Twelve."

APOSTOLIC FATHERS

This is the title of a group of Greek Christian writers who were born toward the end of the first century and exercised their ministry through the second century. Tradition associates Clement and Hermas with Peter: Ignatius, Polycarp and Papias with John. At first these writers were called *Apostolic Men*. The term *Apostolic Fathers* came into use about the sixth century, after the authority of the Fathers had been developed. Later the title was broadened to include other writers. A brief resumé of the earliest of these Fathers must suffice. For an exhaustive treatment of all the *Apostolic Men*, the reader is referred to such works as *The Apostolic Fathers* by E. J. Goodspeed, and R. M. Grant's volume, *The Appeal to the Early Fathers*. A satisfactory coverage can also be found in *The Encyclopaedia Britannica*.

Ignatius, A.D. 70 - 115, would have been a young man between twenty-five and thirty years of age when the apostle John ended his career. This second bishop of Syria was one of the earliest of the Apostolic Fathers, and wrote seven epistles of unique importance, some of which his contemporary Polycarp quoted. Tradition has it that Ignatius wrote these epistles while on his way to martyrdom in Rome. Traveling across Syria in chains he shouted, "I am made happy by these wild beasts." His yearning for martyrdom has led some scholars to regard him as being somewhat neurotic. When he reached Rome, and the Christians there tried to prevent his martyrdom, he said: "I am the wheat-corn of God; let me be ground to death by the teeth of wild beasts that I may become the pure bread of Christ."

Polycarp, A.D. 70-155, as Bishop of the much persecuted Church at Smyrna, was a conspicuous figure in the early church. Probably a disciple of John and a friend of other contemporaries of our Lord, Polycarp had much to do in the development of the church and also in the formation of the Canon of the New Testament. His writings mirror the sayings of Christ, and the teaching of Paul. As he was being prepared for burning, he was urged by his persecutors to save his life by reviling Christ, and made his famous reply: "Fourscore and six years have I been His servant, and He hath done me no wrong; how, then, can I blaspheme the King who saved me?"

Clement, A.D. 30 - 100, is the oldest of the Apostolic Fathers, who is said to have been the first bishop of Rome — a tradition the Romish Church does not accept. Toward the end of the first century Clement wrote his renowned Epistle to the Church at Corinth urging its dissident members to return to peace and apostolic order. Christians of the third and fourth centuries regarded his letters as Scripture. One of his Epistles began with the words: "Brothers, we must think of Jesus Christ as of God."

Papias, A.D. 60-150, is said to have been another disciple of the apostle John. Early in the second century he served as Bishop of Hierapolis in Phrygia. A work from his pen bore the title *Exegeses of the Dominical Oracles,* in which Papias drew much information from Peter's epistles, and testified to *Mark* as being the earliest of the four gospels. Papias was also the first one to affirm that Matthew wrote the discourses of our Lord in the Hebrew Tongue.

Irenaeus, A.D. 120 - 200, was a devoted pupil of Polycarp, and became Bishop of Lyons. He was the author of two important works, namely *Against All Heresies,* in which he bore witness to almost the whole of the New Testament, especially to the four gospels. Then *In Proof of the Apostolic Teaching,* Irenaeus gave the Church, "a sort of *vade mecum* (pocket manual, or handy reference book) for an intelligent Christian." In it, he explained his faith, or as he called it, "a remembrancer of the more essential things."

Hermas is the Early Father, born about the end of the second century, who produced a book known as the *Shepherd* — a title taken from the guise of the angel who appeared unto him, and which contains five visions he had, and also twelve moral "commandments" and ten "parables." He represented a kind of Jewish Christianity that seems to have flourished in Rome during his period.

In the latter decades of the second century and during the third century, many others appeared, and some of their writings reveal a significant decline from the Christianity of the apostolic age, especially in relation to Paul's doctrine of grace. The earlier apostolic fathers bore a clear testimony to the New Testament, and during their ministry the church was evidently a spiritual force in the new age. Justin Martyr, A.D. 100 - 165 was the Samaritan philosopher who embraced the Christian faith on the grounds of reason, and by observing the stedfastness of Christians in the face of martyrdom. A prolific writer, he addressed two *Apologies* to the Roman Emperor in defense of Christians and also wrote the *Dialogue With Trypho,* in which he justified Christianity for Jewish minds. He died a martyr's death.

Others grouped among the Fathers are *Tatian, Tertullian, Origen, Clement of Alexandria, Cyprian,* and several of the third and fourth centuries, whose careers can be followed in any reliable work like that of *The Apostolic Fathers,* by Bishop Lightfoot or Schaff's two volumes on *Church History.* The reader will find the study of these conspicuous figures of the earlier centuries a fascinating and rewarding task, especially in their treatment of the writings of those who composed the New Testament.

APOSTOLIC CREED

The regularly repeated creed known as *The Apostles' Creed* did not have its origin with the apostles but is so-called because it is generally supposed to be an epitome of some of the cardinal doctrines taught by the apostles. This particular creed is the oldest one, and is the basis for all others. There is a legend to the effect that the creed took shape at the dictation of the twelve apostles, each of whom supplied a phrase. Thus Peter, under the inspira-

tion of the Holy Spirit, commenced with —

"I believe in God the Father Almighty" Andrew, or John, it is alleged, followed with the line —

"And in Jesus Christ, His only Son, our Lord."

While the apostles certainly referred to Scripture as their rule of faith, the creed bearing their designation was not composed until the fifth or sixth century. It was received into the Latin Church in its present form around the twelfth century.

Around the second century a baptismal confession was made by converts, containing no more than the sentence, "I believe that Jesus is the Son of God." The word *creed* is from "credo," meaning, "I believe," and early in church history brief, precious and dogmatic definitions of the teachings of Christ and of His apostles began to appear. Although the term *creed* is used in a general sense now, and we speak of a political creed or scientific creed, etc., the word is peculiar to Christianity, as a summary of Christian truth believed, and a testimony to its unchanging substance.

Efforts have been made to abolish the use of creeds, but those of a positive Christian character ever remain, "the crystalline reflex of the thought of the Church, the expression of her vital faith, the pulse of her spiritual life. The death-like torpor of the Middle Ages was attended by controversies, *but it produced no creeds.* Creeds thus become significant features — milestones and finger-boards in the history, both of Christian doctrine and life." *The Apostles' Creed* as now used reads —

"I believe in God the Father, Almighty, Maker of Heaven and Earth;
And in Jesus Christ His only begotten Son our Lord;
Who was conceived of the Holy Ghost,
Born of the Virgin Mary;
Suffered under Pontius Pilate,
Was crucified, dead and buried;
He descended into hell: (term for grave)
The third day He rose from the dead;

He ascended into heaven, and
sitteth at the right hand of God
the Father Almighty,
From thence He shall come to judge
the quick (living) and the dead.
I believe in the Holy Ghost.
The Holy Catholic Church; (*Catholic*
does not mean "Roman Catholic."
The word means, "Universal."
German Lutherans changed "Ca-
tholic" to *Christian*).
The communion (fellowship) of
saints;
The forgiveness of sins;
The resurrection of the body;
The life everlasting. Amen."

What a remarkable compendium of
Christian truth *The Apostles' Creed* is!
For an enlightening exposition of each of
its clauses, the reader is referred to the
volume by Dr. Wm. Graham Scroggie.

Thinking of the *creed* as containing
truths taught by the apostles, mention can
be made of *The Didache,* or Teaching, the
longer title of which reads, "The Teaching of the Lord, by the Twelve Apostles,
to the Gentiles." Clement of Alexandria
referred to same as "Scripture." Atha-
nasius, another early father, however, denied its canonicity, but acknowledged its
utility. This work does not profess to
be written by the apostles, and its doctrinal standpoint follows James rather than
Paul, and it seemed to have a four-fold
purpose:

1. *Didactic* — teaching intended to prepare candidates for baptism
2. *Devotional* — covering worship and
   rites
3. *Ecclesiastical* — embracing instructions for church officers —
   extraordinary and ordinary
4. *Eschatological* — suggesting exhortations to watchfulness in
   view of the Second Advent

APOSTOLIC SPOONS

Around the fifteenth century there was
manufactured a matching set of twelve
spoons known as *Apostle Spoons* having
the figure of one of the apostles at the
top of the handle. There were also sets
of thirteen spoons when the figure of

Christ was used along with the twelve
apostles. There were also sets of four,
with the four evangelists represented, one
on the handle of each spoon. It was the
custom to present one of these spoons as
a gift to a child being christened. Sets
are now sold as souvenirs.

APOSTOLIC FRAUDS

It is interesting to note that *apostle* and
apostate have a common root. Denouncing
certain persons who had wormed their way
into the church, Paul described them as
"false apostles, deceitful workers, transforming themselves into the apostles of
Christ" (2 Cor. 11:13) The Greek term for
"false apostles" is *pseudapostoloi;* and that
for "apostles" is *apostoloi.* While the actual
English word "apostate" is not used in
the New Testament, its Greek form is
found in "the falling away" of which Paul
wrote (2 Thess. 2:3). Jesus predicted an
apostasy from the truth (Matt. 24:10-12).
The word "apostate" means, a standing
away from — a falling away — a with-
drawal; while "apostle" implies one who
follows and is sent forth. Julian, the
Roman Emperor, A.D. 331 - 363 is known
as *The Apostate.* He was brought up as
a Christian, although it is most probable
that he never vitally embraced the Christian faith. On his accession to the throne
in 361, he announced his conversion to
paganism and proclaimed the toleration of
all religions.

The defection of an apostate from Christianity may be *intellectual* as in the experience of Ernst H. Haeckel, the famous
biologist and philosopher, 1834-1919, who
because of his advanced materialistic philosophy, publicly and formally renounced
Christianity and the church; or it may
be *moral and spiritual,* as with Judas Iscariot, who for filthy lucre's sake basely
betrayed his Lord. Alas! we have reached
a time when there is a widespread deliberate defection or departure from "the
faith which was once delivered unto the
saints" (Jude 3). Church leaders openly
declare that they cannot subscribe any
longer to the fundamental truths of Christianity, and so patent historical records are
treated as myths or fables; whole sections
of the Bible are irrelevant and can be

discarded; God is dead, and Christ is no longer necessary as a Savior, for man with his scientific advancement is well able to save himself. As for any ancient creed, well, it is weekly repeated because church law demands its repetition, but its tenets are not believed by many who recite the creed.

The Hebrews of old, who were on Christian ground, were in danger of departing from the *living* God, and some from Christianity altogether, to return to the dead forms of Judaism (Heb. 3:12; 6:6). The tragedy is that we have teachers of theology and ministers of the church who have departed from the Biblical conception of the *living* God, and who openly proclaim a graveyard theology. Faith in the truths the apostles firmly held (and died for) is openly ridiculed, and yet such religious apostates are not treated as heretics, or even rebuked by the council of the denomination they represent for their blatant rejection of the foundational truths of Christianity. Many of them remain in high office in their church, receive its pay, go the round of a dead formalism, and continue to handle the law of the God whom they know not.

What dire need there is in our sick, sinful and impoverished world for the return of our many agnostic church leaders to the dynamic truths and soul-saving methods of the men of the Upper Room! What glorious conquests the church would experience if only those who represent it would cease doubting their beliefs, and believing their doubts! Those apostles we have considered would never have turned the world upside down had they not believed and lived all their Master had taught them. Luke could write of those things most *surely* believed among the apostles (Luke 1:1), and such a faith knew no frontiers. Because of their experience of the grace of the true and living God, they triumphed over geography, and went out into all the world preaching a positive Gospel. They refused to allow false teaching or the tide of secular affairs, to choke the main stream of their evangelistic mission.

Amid religious and imperial persecution, and pressure on all sides to divert their God-given channel of service, they resisted by saying, "We will give ourselves to prayer and to the ministry of the Word." In *prayer*, they touched their enthroned Lord; in the *preaching* of gospel certainties they touched multitudes to the finer issues of eternal life. So, as we take our final look at the apostles and seek to compare them with many of the blind leaders of the blind today, we earnestly pray for the emergence of a vast army who will follow in their train.

The men Christ chose for His service had hardly any exterior differences to distinguish them from ordinary men; they wore no official badge; they carried no insignia of office. Their very simplicity was their strength, and by the power of the Spirit they went forth offering a lost world a new deliverance, a new dynamic, and a new destiny through the cross and resurrection of their Lord who was their all in all. Ours is an apostate age, with its overthrow of "The Faith" becoming more marked with the passing days, as Jesus said it would (Luke 18:8, *margin*). The most pressing need of the church is another Pentecost, for it is only such a mighty effusion that can drive any phase of apostasy back into the hell that gave it birth.

APOSTOLIC LITERATURE *

The literature on *The Apostles* and *Apostolic Age* is as various as it is vast. For those pursuing such rewarding studies, there are hundreds of volumes of an explanatory, enlightening and expositional nature to choose from. A gifted bibliographer could fill a weighty book on all that has been written about the men Christ chose, the message they preached, the mission they undertook, and the permanent influence of their lives, labors, and literature.

In 1900, Dr. George T. Purves, who was then the Professor of New Testament Literature in Princeton Theological Seminary, published his most comprehensive study on *Christianity in the Apostolic Age*, in which he deals with the supernatural facts and forces behind the rise and course of apostolic Christianity. In a "Selected Biography," Dr. Purves quotes a long list of works representative of various schools of investigation, in which he distinguishes General Works of the Apostolic Age, Lives of the Apostles, Chronology of the Apostolic Age, and The Theology of the Apostles. While this most valuable treatise is now out of print, students eager to concentrate on all that is associated with the apostles, should search it out in some well-stocked theological library and try to secure the reference books Dr. Purves mentions.

As for biographical material on individual apostles, the reader is referred to the Bibliography in the writer's work on *All the Men of the Bible* (published by Zondervan). Specific books wholly taken up with facts and features of all the apostles, which I found most helpful in the preparation of this study include:

The Men Whom Jesus Made, by Dr. W. Mackintosh Mackay, 1920.
Lives of the Apostles and Evangelists, by George Peck, 1837.
Lives and Legends of Apostles and Evangelists, by Myrtle Strode-Jackson, 1928.
Studies on the Apostles, by Daniel McLean.

The Apostles of Our Lord, by J. G. Greenhough, 1904.
The Chosen Twelve, by Dr. J. Elder Cumming.
Lives of the Apostles, by Dr. William Cave, 1840.
Christ's First Missionaries, by M. V. Hughes.
The Apostles As Everyday Men, by Robert Ellis Thompson, 1910.
These Twelve, by Frederick Edwards, 1895.
The Glorious Company of the Apostles, by Dr. J. D. Jones.
The Training of the Twelve, by Dr. A. B. Bruce, 1898.

The section in all Bible Dictionaries and Encyclopaedias dealing with the Apostles should also be consulted. As for valuable exposition material on same, reliable Commentaries like Ellicott's and Matthew Henry's yield a rich harvest for the workman of God, who seeks to rightly divide the Word of Truth.

Bibliography

Preachers and students desiring a more extensive and exhaustive study of the twelve men Christ chose, will find themselves *embarras de richesses* as they search out material on each of the apostles, dealt with separately in biographical material. For instance, detached articles on any of these men in a great work like *The International Standard Bible Encyclopedia* afford much useful sermonic help. The same may be said for the incomparable volumes on *Bible Characters* by Dr. Alexander Whyte, and in the articles on those Christ called in Hastings' *Bible Dictionary* and in *The Zondervan Pictorial Bible Dictionary*. See also the author's volume on *All the Men of the Bible*. Literature on Early Church History likewise provides the searchers with added information.

Then there are multitudinous volumes dealing with Bible characters that may be consulted, such as Glover's *Matthew*, F. B. Meyer's *Peter*, Griffith Thomas' *John*, R. E. O. White's *Paul — Apostle Extraordinary*, etc. The following lists are books in which all twelve apostles are discussed.

The Master and His Men, by Dr. F. Townley Lord. The Carey Press, London, 1927.

The Representative Men of the New Testament, by Dr. George Matheson. Hodder & Stoughton, London, 1904.

Studies on the Apostles, by Rev. Daniel McLean. John Menzies, Co., Edinburgh.

The Apostles of Our Lord, by Rev. J. G. Greenhough. Hodder & Stoughton, London, 1904.

The Story of Christ's First Missioners, by M. M. Penthouse. National Society Depository, London.

The Apostles as Every Day Men, by Robert Ellis Thompson. Sunday School Times, Co., Philadelphia, Pa.

The Training of the Twelve, by Dr. A. B. Bruce. T & T Clark, Edinburgh, 1898.

These Twelve, by F. Edwards. Alexander and Shepheard, London, 1895.

The Glorious Company of the Apostles, by Dr. J. D. Jones. James Clark Co., London.

He Chose Twelve, by Dr. Elder Cumming. Drummonds Tract Depot, Stirling, Scotland. (Dr. Cumming quotes a study of A. M. Symington on *The Apostles of Our Lord*.)

Lives and Legends of the Apostles, by Myrtle Strode-Jackson. Religious Tract Society, London, 1928.

SCRIPTURE INDEX

274

276

277